CITYMAKERS

CITYMAKERS
The Culture and Craft of Practical Urbanism

Cassim Shepard
Foreword by Rosalie Genevro
Principal photography by Alex Fradkin

The Monacelli Press
In association with The Architectural League of New York

For my mother Samina Quraeshi who taught me about culture,
my father Richard Shepard who taught me about craft, and
my mentor Richard Sennett who taught me how they come together in the city.

CONTENTS

FOREWORD

Rosalie Genevro

Two attitudes, triumphalist and dystopic, seem to dominate current thinking about cities. Cities are our destiny and our salvation; the ineluctable dynamism of density and concentration will make us richer, happier, more contemporary and prepared for the future. Architects, planners, software designers and other top-down rule-makers will set cities in order for us, and creative class workers and other elites will propel us into an ever more comfortable tomorrow. Or, cities will descend quickly into chaos, as the chasm between winners and losers in the national and global economies becomes unbridgeable. The rich will increasingly remove themselves to redoubts of privilege and safety, while the poor battle over insufficient resources and ineffective systems, with the increasingly omniscient apparatus of the surveillance state sensing and tracking everything.

In *Citymakers: The Culture and Craft of Practical Urbanism,* Cassim Shepard offers a very different narrative: a perceptively observed, calmly hopeful way of understanding the contemporary city and its prospects as the collective, ongoing creation of engaged citizens. The citymakers of the title are landscape designers, city bureaucrats, housing campaigners, photographers, techies, architects, Forest Service personnel, Occupy activists, architectural historians, immigrant advocates, planners, and others, acting with enormous commitment and persistence to shape and change New York City. They are quotidian heroes, originating, testing, executing ideas; challenging inertia and power; nurturing and creating beauty. Their work affects the lived experience of millions of New Yorkers in manifold ways, and the city would not function without them.

This is not the abstracted city, the statistical city, or the speculative city: it is the observed city. One line of the methodological tradition of close observation of urban activity in which Cassim is operating runs back through the engaged observation of William Whyte and Jane Jacobs to John Dewey, Jane Addams, Robert Park, and the Chicago School of sociology; this strand observes, analyzes and reports in order to engender action for improvement. Another line traces back to the urban theorists Walter Benjamin and Georg Simmel, sensorial urbanists who seek to understand the experience of the city in order to synthesize their observations and characterize urban life. Both traditions consider economic factors as just one among many aspects of the context of urban reality; both continuously consider the mutual influence of social life and its physical setting, because the city is understood as a social organization with a physical form, not as either alone.

The intricate, ongoing, multivocal story that close observation makes it possible to tell, of why and how citymakers do the work they do, is the story of how a great city is made.

The springboard for this book is the work Cassim carried out for six years as the founding editor of *Urban Omnibus,* the online publication of The Architectural League of New York, of which I am executive director. The League launched *Urban Omnibus* in order to provide a view into a world of city-focused innovation, passion, and possibility, and to open up this world to a wide audience. My impetus to develop the project in 2007 came from my own deep love of the city in all of its variety, my eagerness to know more and to communicate about the exhilarating design and community initiatives that were taking place in many parts of the city, and my sense that we were at a significant moment of convergence of four developing trajectories. These were, first, the growth of a broad general interest in physical planning and architecture in a newly self-confident New York City; second, the rethinking of disciplinary objectives and boundaries, as well as the growth of new modes of practice, in architecture, landscape architecture, and other design fields; third, the evolving interests and work of The Architectural League to emphasize architecture in the world and to connect excellence in design to issues of social justice, environmental sustainability, and civic delight; and fourth, the rapidly intensifying pace and impact of change in the production and dissemination of journalism and other media. In 2007, the Rockefeller Foundation had just inaugurated a new program, the Cultural Innovation Fund, to support experimental projects by arts organizations in New York City. Winning one of the first round of grants made for an auspicious beginning for *Urban Omnibus,* and I hired Cassim as founding editor soon after being notified of the grant in the spring of 2008. With Varick Shute, who was already a League staff member and who joined the *Omnibus* team as founding managing editor, and advised by a diverse array of design, art, and community figures from around the city, we set to work. UrbanOmnibus.net launched in January 2009.

Why did we decide to focus *Urban Omnibus* on covering New York City, using the formulation "great ideas for cities everywhere, tried and tested in the five boroughs of New York?" I felt at the launch, and still believe, that the focus on New York gives *Urban Omnibus* a very important specificity, without detracting from its potential interest to readers in other places. New York is both an idiosyncratic and emblematic city. It is idiosyncratic, of course, in its specific geography and history, and because it is the largest city in the United States, the most influential city in the Western Hemisphere, and one of a handful of the most influential in the world. It is, in the first two decades of the twenty-first century, a prosperous, magnetic place. Yet it is nonetheless emblematic as well: New York faces the challenges that many metropolises face, including extreme income inequality, inadequate housing supply, a troubled criminal justice system, and growing impacts from climate change. The mechanisms that help achieve New York's successes and address its challenges can resonate everywhere.

New York's self-perception has swung widely over the last 50 years, from the dark moments of retrenchment and population decline in the 1970s to the money-worshipping swagger of the 1980s, the disorder and inchoate sense of immanent possibility of the 1990s, and the stricken but resilient New York of the early 2000s.

By 2007, when I began to conceive the project, New York had rediscovered its self-confident, capable, forward-looking self, and the city was enthusiastic about what it saw: openness and attractiveness to young people and to innovators; resurgent neighborhoods; an official embrace of immigrants and the energy they brought to the city. New York had regained its footing as an encouraging platform for entrepreneurialism and invention, with a dynamism that seemed to echo earlier periods of vitality and growth, such as the era following the 1898 consolidation of the city and the years following World War II. During the mayoral administration of Michael Bloomberg (2002–13), New York was demonstrating again that it could get things built, from new parks to reconfigured streets to a reclaimed waterfront, and that while doing so it could achieve a high level of design quality. Mayor Bloomberg had talented commissioners leading the agencies most directly responsible for the physical city — city planning, design and construction, transportation, parks, housing — and committed a great deal of money to capital projects. Certainly all was not rosy as residential neighborhoods in the city remained extremely segregated, and the city continued to struggle with housing shortages and unaffordability, as well as with high rates of poverty and a lack of good educational options and job opportunities in many communities. But in multiple ways, and particularly in comparison to other American cities, New York was in a very strong position to chart its way forward.

In the early years of the decade, as New York worked to figure out how to rebuild after 9/11, the Lower Manhattan Development Corporation and the press encouraged the engagement of the public in unprecedented ways, inviting citizens to think about, question, and react to ideas for what should be built to replace the World Trade Center and adjacent buildings. Large numbers of people attended public forums on the rebuilding, organized by the LMDC itself or by one of the many civic groups that asserted themselves in the process. In doing so, these engaged citizens learned not only about specific proposals for the Trade Center site, but about architecture and planning and their terminologies and concerns more generally. In the late 1990s and into the new millennium, a national and international rise in the celebrity of individual "starchitects" and a large number of high-profile new buildings around the world, particularly museums, also contributed to a growing awareness of and interest in architecture. In 2004, with the goal of building on this base to encourage a more complex understanding of how the city is built and go beyond a focus on famous individuals, the media producer Susan Morris and I proposed to the local television station NY1 an ongoing program, in partnership with The Architectural League, on architecture and planning in the city. The proposal did not move forward, but started the thinking that eventually led to *Urban Omnibus*.

While public curiosity about architecture was on the rise, architecture and its companion disciplines were in the midst of some very significant realignments in the late 1990s and 2000s. Digital computation and the sophisticated drawing, modeling, and coordination programs it made possible, which had preoccupied architects and design educators in the early 90s, had by the new millennium come to be understood as simply one particularly powerful tool among many. The formidable digital skills many designers acquired in school opened up new possibilities for data visualization, for example, which designers used to study and map complex bodies of information that made possible new understandings of the spatial implications of all kinds of phenomena. Many designers developed a strong interest in digitally driven fabrication and material experimentation, which created opportunities for new types of practice and entrepreneurship focused on production.

Simultaneous with the reconceptualization of the role of the digital, architectural theory moved away from absorption in the internal concerns of the discipline and towards a renewed engagement with the practicalities of program, structure and materials, and the organization of the design and construction process to produce built work. Young architects experimented with new structures for practice, including taking on the real estate developer's role as well as that of designer, in order to self-generate projects and control all decision-making in their production. Landscape architecture surged in influence, in part because of the articulation of positions by proponents and critics of landscape urbanism, who argued over the relative importance of the ground plane and architectural form in structuring the city and how to effectively incorporate ecological function into landscape and urban design. In both fields, a resurgent interest and new organizations in public interest design have created new avenues for designers to engage with communities and individuals who traditionally have not had access to design services.

Parallel to these changes that were reshaping the practice of architecture, particularly for younger architects and designers, The Architectural League was developing and pursuing projects that engaged with the city in new ways, and that substantially broadened its purview. Since its founding in 1881 by a group of ambitious young draftsmen as a venue for mutual education and encouragement, The Architectural League has been committed to supporting the creative, intellectual, and civic development of architects and designers. The League's charter and by-laws describe its purpose as "the encouragement and promotion of the art and science of architecture and related arts and crafts, and the bringing together of fellow practitioners of architecture and such related arts and crafts, to the end that ever-improving leadership may be developed for the nation's service." League lectures, conferences, competitions, exhibitions, and publications are all conceived to stimulate and educate the eyes and minds of architects and others toward more skillful, beautiful, powerful work.

Virtually from its earliest days, the League has also been engaged with issues and causes in its home city of New York. Even as its national and international influence grew through juried annual exhibitions in the first few decades of the twentieth century, The League weighed in on questions in New York City, from late nineteenth-century advocacy for longer hours at the Metropolitan Museum of Art, to surveying areas where government efforts in low-income housing should be targeted in the early years of the Great Depression. More recently, The League has organized a series of design studies that serve both to support the creative development of individual architects and designers, and to offer approaches to issues in the collective environment and experience of the city.

The first of these, Vacant Lots, was organized in 1987 to propose approaches to building affordable housing on the small scattered sites that increasingly made up the inventory of city-owned land. Vacant Lots gave the participating designers a chance to work on a socially engaged program, instigated new partnerships and new investigations of materials and construction technologies, and launched conversations about how to provide housing for neglected or newly emerging groups with special needs, such as individuals living with AIDS. Subsequent studies looked at design strategies and development mechanisms for small schools; ideas for simultaneously developing water supply and recreation infrastructure; overall planning strategies for the disinvested neighborhood of East New York; and approaches to developing housing in the ecologically fragile setting of the Rockaway Peninsula. The two most recent studies — Making Room, in 2011, and Re-envisioning Branch Libraries, in 2014, undertaken respectively with the Citizens Housing and Planning Council and the Center for an Urban Future — commissioned teams of architects to challenge outdated regulations governing multi-family housing, and to reimagine the physical expression of branch libraries to more effectively serve their burgeoning functional importance in the city's neighborhoods. With each of these studies, the League asserted the power of design as research methodology and mode of investigation to explore possibilities for change and improvement in the city's environment.

A third track of the League's work involves taking on broad themes and topics that have received too little attention in academia and the profession, such as the exhibitions Women in American Architecture (1977) and Ten Shades of Green (2000), on architecture that combines aesthetic and environmental ambition.[1] In 2006, to celebrate The League's 125th anniversary, we created the project Architecture And..., to solicit proposals for projects that would explore the intersection of architecture with other realms of inquiry and action. Through Architecture And... we were able to help support and develop two path-breaking projects. "Architecture and Justice" provided the first opportunity for the exhibition of Laura Kurgan and Eric Cadora's now widely known Million Dollar Blocks project, which radically reframed national understanding of the geographic concentration and social and economic impact of incarceration by mapping the home addresses (rather than addresses where crimes were committed) of incarcerated individuals and then by neighborhood aggregating expenditures related to their confinement. "Architecture and Situated Technologies," included a symposium, nine-part pamphlet series, commissioned installations, and book. Mark Shepard, Omar Khan, and Trebor Scholz who conceived the project, started questioning and theorizing the relationship of urban space to the explosion of processing power and data that has given rise to the "smart city" and the internet of things — now widely acknowledged features of our cities — at a

---

[1] Susana Torre, ed., Women in American Architecture: A Historic and Contemporary Perspective (New York: Whitney Library of Design/Watson-Guptill Publications, 1977), and Peter Buchanan, Ten Shades of Green: Architecture and the Natural World (New York: The Architectural League of New York, 2005).

very early stage. In addition to their substantial intrinsic significance, these projects and their demonstration of the broad civic importance of spatial perspectives helped pave the way for an expanded field of operations for The League's work that led to *Urban Omnibus.*

Even with increased general interest in design and architecture, and the flourishing of innovative projects and technologies with relevance to urbanists, media coverage of ideas and news related to the making of the city had always seemed inadequate in frequency and depth — there just wasn't enough of it and what there was often did not seem deeply informed. The advent of digital media had increased the number of people writing about design and neighborhood projects, but much of that was quickly produced and often promotional rather than critical or researched. Both traditional and digital media were searching for a viable economic model, since advertisers needed neither one to reach customers once the web made direct access possible. This situation created both a frustrating gap and an opportunity for a specialized non-profit organization such as The Architectural League to develop a strategy and vehicle to fill the gap. In a note called "Why Urban Omnibus?" written just after the site launched in January of 2009, I described the outpouring of ideas and work by designers and others that seemed to offer such appealing possibilities for the city, and how we hoped *Urban Omnibus* could encourage and support them:

> Much of this activity remains just out of sight, and we think it needs to be better known. With *Urban Omnibus,* The Architectural League wants to cultivate and hybridize the thousand flowers of digital media to engage a large audience in learning and thinking about design and New York City's physical environment. We want to provide a platform for the written word and for aural and visual information of all kinds; we want the immediacy of a blog and the carefully reasoned perspective of critical writing to stand side by side.
>
> Most of all, we want to connect people with ideas they can use.

The activity we aspired to make visible has been vividly communicated on *Urban Omnibus* in hundreds of features and shorter pieces published since the publication was launched. In Citymakers, Cassim Shepard has contextualized representative examples of this work in fascinating ways, drawing on the insights and theories of figures not often mentioned in discussions of urbanism, such as the ecologist Aldo Leopold, the economist Elinor Ostrom, and the legal scholar Brett Frischmann. By constructing the genealogies and projecting the implications of the ideas that propel the actors and the work discussed in the case studies, he has built an urban vision that suggests how technological innovation, public policy, activism, and design can work together to create an inclusive, generous, cosmopolitan, public-focused city. Such a city acts on a core belief in the importance of inclusiveness and public life, invests for the benefit of all, and operates on all time frames simultaneously, meeting short-term needs while also planning and building for the long term. It accommodates, celebrates, and profoundly benefits from the difference and the diversity, on every register, of its people.

Early 2017 is certainly not the moment of optimism that was so buoying in January of 2009, when we launched *Urban Omnibus* with such high expectations. Nativism, intolerance, racism, and a deep lack of belief in the value of government are casting a pall on public life, in the United States and internationally. Cities, though, as vessels for aspiration and inclusion, endure. Cities — and the intrepid, committed, passionate people who make them — offer the hope that we can build to a better day.

CHAPTER 1

THE CULTURE
OF CITYMAKING

Cities are huge right now.

Spatially. Statistically. Politically. As the scale of cities and their populations continue to grow, literally and figuratively, urbanism looms ever larger in public awareness.

Interest in cities and the processes of urban development has grown substantially over the last decade, and the number of books, Web sites, and publications now devoted to the subject has exploded. Yet, too much of the work in this increasingly crowded field elides the experience of citizens and, crucially, the work of practitioners. A quantitative language of statistics, demographics, and economics has subsumed urban discourse, rendering cities as abstract accumulations of capital flows, growth rates, consumption patterns, housing prices, and carbon footprints. Undoubtedly, contemporary urban thought has challenged modernist orthodoxies that treated architecture as somehow autonomous from lived experience. Now, at long last, we acknowledge use patterns and individual behavior as primary in assessing designed environments. This shift, now over fifty years in the making, has led to a facile opposition between an undifferentiated and rather nostalgic idea of "community" (often characterized as resistant to large-scale change) and a nefarious cabal of undemocratic "experts" (often characterized as conspirators in building projects that are insensitive to local impacts). The rise of participatory processes in urban development projects, while still imperfect, is welcome and overdue. But the binary of top-down versus bottom-up approaches is too simplistic to capture the full scope of intentionality that gives cities both meaning and form; it homogenizes the agency of lay citizens and undermines the influence of practitioners.[1] This books aims to interrupt this trend toward abstraction by focusing on accounts of individual people, projects, and perspectives that support an argument about how cities are made today. In so doing, I intend to offer a distinctive approach—blending journalistic, theoretical, and essayistic modes of writing—to make evident the connections between what are often considered to be unrelated ways of understanding and intervening in the city.

To do so, the chapters that follow build on seven years of thought, research, and writing created for *Urban Omnibus,* an online publication launched by The Architectural League of New York in January 2009[2] to define "the culture of citymaking." The central premise of *Urban Omnibus* is that "citymaking" involves more than design, politics, policy, and economics; it also includes articulated observation, artistic production, technological innovation, and civic activism. Throughout this book, projects and perspectives featured on *Urban Omnibus* serve as a springboard for analytical writing that refreshes generic categories of urban intervention and reinvents traditional approaches to public space, infrastructure, technology, and housing.

As such, the aim of this book is to advance a new, expansive vision of twenty-first century urbanism by investigating how the work of *Urban Omnibus* reflects the evolving ideas, preoccupations, and production of urban change-makers in the years since the economic crash of 2008. References to work showcased on *Urban Omnibus* are by no means intended to present the publication as a representative cross section of significant work done in the urban, public realm. On the contrary, it is a curated sample. Naming the biases that have given rise to that subjective slice is an important part of assessing which patterns of contemporary urbanism identified in this book are new and which signify the cyclical nature of intellectual attitudes and professional priorities. If some aspects of today's urban thought and practice are in fact new, do the broad challenges we face — namely: the volatility of the global climate and the widening of social inequality — demand disciplinary realignments? If so, how can design practice meaningfully absorb new priorities without undermining its embedded knowledge?

A core part of the *Urban Omnibus* approach has been the effort to connect the global, national, and local by presenting good ideas for cities worldwide that have been tried and tested in New York City, the most populous of US cities, home to both the richest and poorest neighborhoods in the nation.[3] This book incorporates both the place-based perspective of New York City, where The Architectural League is based, and broader interpretive lenses drawn from the best of international urban thinking, professional as well as scholarly.

Each chapter is based on transdisciplinary imperatives distilled from six years of analyzing and contextualizing exemplary urban projects and practices. First, incorporate long-term use and maintenance, along with the practice of citizenship, into any discussion of public space design and delivery. Second, reconceive infrastructure as a multifunction public good and a constituent element of landscape. Third, embrace technologies that support, rather than disrupt, effective democratic governance to make urban processes more legible rather than merely quantified. Fourth, reconfigure existing housing to meet shifting demographic needs. Implementing these imperatives will require everyone who cares about cities to foster and seek out greater intimacy with the choices that give form to the built environment through community input, informed observation, and creative expression.

---

[1] Throughout this book, when I use the word practitioner, I do not differentiate between professionals in the private, public, or nonprofit sectors; nor does my use of the word prioritize any particular discipline (a trained engineer working in an architecture firm and a trained engineer working in a management consultancy are both practitioners.) I use the word to refer to anyone whose mention in this book is attributable to his or her job.

[2] The initial concept for *Urban Omnibus* was developed by Rosalie Genevro. The project team, from 2008 through 2014 consisted of Genevro, Varick Shute, and myself. Initial planning meetings in 2008 and 2009 also included members of an advisory board consisting of Kadambari Baxi, Andrew Blum, Adam Greenfield, Olympia Kazi, Hoong Yee Lee Krakauer, Laura Kurgan, Deborah Marton, Ellen Pollan, Susan Morris, Daniel Seltzer, Mark Shepard, Beth Stryker, and Rosten Woo.

[3] Before redistricting, the 2010 census found that New York's Sixteenth Congressional District, in the South Bronx, had the highest percentage of constituents living at or below the federal poverty level, and New York's Fourteenth Congressional District, just across the Harlem River, has among the highest median incomes in the nation.

THE PLAN OF THE BOOK

This book revisits generic categories of urban analysis: public space, infrastructure, technology, and housing. Rather than critique the increasing staleness of these categories and suggest new buzzwords, my aim is to refresh and reactivate existing ones. These areas of focus are by nature interdisciplinary; none corresponds obviously with specific professional expertise or academic discipline. Yet certain subsets of urbanists have aligned their emphases with one another. Urban sociologists and landscape architects have fetishized public space as, respectively, the last vestige of the commons or the appropriate locus for nature to make urban density "livable." In so doing, they have narrowed the discussion of public space to parks and plazas to the exclusion of streets, sidewalks, and subway stations. Infrastructure, neglected by politicians, has become the preserve of engineers, other than those rare instances where it is politically palatable to make it architecturally iconic. Housing — that peculiarly urban term for shelter that is still redolent of outmoded codes for poverty such as "inner-city" — has arguably yielded more specialization within public policy than it has in architecture. Mainstream media has credited technology for productive disruptions in business and economics, but social theorists, policymakers, and designers have been slow to articulate a normative vision for how technological innovation might align with a post-financial agenda for politics or the environment. Meanwhile, those same media have absorbed the term communication to the extent that it has become coterminous with broadcasting, marketing, or social networking, such that its transformational, expressive potential (the means by which artists, activists, and organizers find or build common ground) has yet to be defined within urbanism.

Over the past six years, we have observed the reinvention of these spheres of activity by practitioners as well as interpreters of the craft of citymaking. In the Lower East Side of Manhattan, designers and housing advocates work together to make neglected open space perform urgent environmental functions while creating new and beautiful pathways (physical and emotional) to social cohesion.[4] Throughout Staten Island, public servants are turning the infrastructural liabilities of rapid land development into opportunities for an unprecedented experiment in managing water.[5] In Red Hook, Brooklyn, a community-owned wireless network provides internet resources and, more importantly, a platform for local communication in one of New York's most isolated and climate-vulnerable neighborhoods.[6] In Jackson Heights, Queens, an advocate's call for formalizing informal housing arrangements[7] is met with architectural solutions that can yield more housing

---

[4] Kerri Culhane, "Making Connections: Planning for Green Infrastructure in Two Bridges," *Urban Omnibus,* August 8, 2012.

[5] "The Staten Island Bluebelt: Storm Sewers, Wetlands, Waterways," *Urban Omnibus,* December 1, 2010.

[6] "Local Connections: The Red Hook WiFi Project," *Urban Omnibus,* September 25, 2013.

[7] Seema Agnani, "Bringing Basements to Code," *Urban Omnibus,* March 10, 2010.

In the summer of 2013, the artist Thomas Hirschhorn installed a temporary monument to Italian philosopher Antonio Gramsci in Forest Houses, a New York City Housing Authority (NYCHA) complex located in Morrisania, Bronx.

from existing housing stock without overburdening existing systems.[8] And in Morrisania,[9] on the Grand Concourse,[10] and along the Bronx River,[11] coalitions of artists and advocates from public housing, social services, and environmental justice sectors are empowering citizens by communicating a real sense of transformative possibility.

The Morrisania example merits a brief digression into intellectual history. In the summer of 2013, Swiss-born, Paris-based artist Thomas Hirschhorn installed a sprawling, interactive, and ephemeral environment intended to commemorate Italian philosopher Antonio Gramsci in the open spaces of Forest Houses, a New York City Housing Authority (NYCHA) public housing complex located in Morrisania, the Bronx. Gramsci's writings contributed to the development of Western Marxism by theorizing the role of culture (in addition to the means of production and administration) in maintaining the hegemony of the ruling class. In other words, taking over the factories and the state isn't enough to make the revolution stick, you also have to reinvent the aesthetics and social mores that pervade society's everyday consciousness.

Hirschhorn's means of memorializing and reactivating Gramsci's thought, however, went beyond the theoretical; it was a physical, inhabitable space made of accessible lo-fi materials installed in a public housing complex. Whatever you think of the artwork (and opinions were definitely mixed), the improbable insertion of Marxist philosophy into the urban landscape of the Bronx can't help but recall Gramsci's laying claim "to an expansive urbanity" in which the city operates as an attitude and an image, complicit in the cultural narratives of any given society. The other examples cited above do not relate to a single philosophical project like Gramsci's, but are no less instructive of how the established categories of urban thought and action can be productively reactivated on their own terms. In other words, from managing stormwater runoff in Staten Island to advocating for accessory dwelling units in Queens, these examples demonstrate that traditional categories of urban analysis are still useful, if viewed through the normative lens of principle: *what kind of city do we want?*

We know that unprecedented numbers of people want to live in dense, urban environments.[12] We see a range of professional, artistic, and academic disciplines expanding their scopes of expertise to address the environmental, financial, and intellectual implications of urbanization. And we have pretty good scholarship for what that shift means in economic, political, and cultural terms. But the analytics, poetics, and ethics of urbanism have yet to be fused with the craft of design and building, the art of policymaking, and the practice of citizenship. This book is an attempt to begin that process, to define what we are talking about when we talk about cities by asserting the agency of individual citymakers: among them photographers, tenant rights advocates, civil engineers, graphic designers, lawyers, historians, and many more. This classificatory impulse to enumerate lists of different roles that fall within our definition of *citymaking* is not just inclusivity for the sake of laying claim to and populating a new identity. Rather, it is a way to push forward the popular understanding of cities by telling the stories of some of the people who take it upon themselves to shape cities for the better.

In Latin, *omnibus* means "for all." This original meaning ramifies through the word's modern usage both as a vehicle for public transport—borrowed from the French and subsequently shortened to "bus"—and in reference to proposed laws that bundle several measures into a single legislative act.

Etymologists tend to attribute the initial, modern use of the term to the banker Jacques Laffite, a staunch liberal who personally stabilized the French economy after the fall of Napoleon only to be marginalized for his defense of press freedoms. But the transport historian Peter Gould disagrees and locates the origins of omnibus transport not in Paris but outside Nantes. In 1823, Stanislas Baudry opened a flourmill in Richebourg. Relentlessly entrepreneurial, Baudry was loath to waste the surplus heat from his steam-powered milling operation, and so he devised a system to use this excess capacity to heat water for a public bath. In order to drum up business, he introduced a free service to transport customers from Nantes Central Station to this remote amenity. Gould continues:

> The service started on the Place du Commerce, outside the hat shop of a M. Omnès, who displayed the motto Omnès Omnibus (Latin for "everything for everybody" or "all for all") on his shop front. When Baudry discovered that passengers were just as interested in getting off at intermediate points as in patronizing his baths, he changed the route's focus. As a result, in August 1826, he abandoned the public bath and started running two 16-seat covered vehicles on a route from Salorges to Richebourg via Nantes, purely as a transport service. His new voiture omnibus ("carriage for all"—presumably inspired by M. Omnès' slogan) combined the functions of the hired hackney carriage with a stagecoach that travelled a predetermined route from inn to inn, carrying passengers and mail.[13]

By 1830, the word omnibus was being used in New York City to market intracity transit routes. What distinguishes omnibus service from the older format of stagecoach travel is "that it plied for hire along the route, picking up and setting down passengers in the street," removing the need to book in advance or wait for long periods at various boarding points.

---

[8] For *Making Room,* a design study convened by the Citizens' Housing and Planning Council and The Architectural League, a team led by Deborah Gans worked on a proposal for joint-family housing in Ravenswood, Queens.

[9] Steven Thomson, "Thomas Hirschhorn's Precious and Precarious Bronx," *Urban Omnibus,* July 1, 2013.

[10] "The Andrew Freedman Home is No Longer Empty," *Urban Omnibus,* January 25, 2012.

[11] "We Want it Back: Reclaiming the Bronx River," *Urban Omnibus,* January 9, 2013.

[12] According to the US Census Bureau, the nation's urban population increased by 12.1 percent from 2000 to 2010, outpacing the nation's overall growth rate of 9.7 percent for the same period.

[13] Peter Gould, "Horsebus," *Local Transport History.* Accessed April 18, 2014. www.petergould.co.uk.

This anecdote offers more than interesting trivia. The invention of a new mode of public transit — widely accessible and affordable — emerged from an observation about excess capacity and evolved into a profitable business. It enabled new patterns of behavior, opened up new markets and job opportunities, and soon came to be expected as necessary infrastructure, eventually provided by government. Many innovations during the Industrial Revolution follow a similar model. This case is instructive in symbolic terms not only because of the almost accidental nomenclature but also because of the way the notion of "for all" infuses a story of individual entrepreneurship and innovation with public purpose.

Urban Omnibus began as a celebration of innovation. On the occasion of its founding in January of 2009, with the extent of the financial crisis becoming clear and the new Obama presidency inspiring optimism, Rosalie Genevro — who, as executive director of The Architectural League, conceptualized and initiated the online publication — offered this explanation:

> In New York City in January 2009, we live in an extraordinarily vibrant place that faces huge challenges. We are more aware than ever of how fragile the economic health of the city is, and of how many New Yorkers are already suffering, or on the edge of, economic hardship. Our neighborhoods are going to feel the economic straits of the city government and the city's households in the year ahead. Beyond our economic vitality — but inextricably connected to it — are the many demands New York faces over the next few decades specifically related to the physical city: how to adapt to climate change and minimize our environmental footprint, rebuild our infrastructure, and provide enough housing and open space to make a comfortable, civilized, just city.
>
> But for all the challenges we face, this is also a time for optimism about the future. From the creative initiatives of forward-looking city agencies, to the self-generated experimentation and investigations of architects and engineers and designers, to the inventive entrepreneurialism of community activists, there is a lot going on in New York that can make the city better. There is a ferment of ingenuity and invention at work that can lead to new ways of generating and distributing energy, of transporting people, of making more beautiful public spaces, of rethinking how we build schools or configure our workspaces or dispose of our garbage. Artists and designers and architects are creating visualizations of the processes and flows of the city that can radically enhance our understanding of how the city works, so that we can design it to work better.[14]

That sense of excitement about the range of good ideas for the future of cities that weren't quite managing to bubble up into a citywide conversation is what motivated *Urban Omnibus* in its early days. My colleagues and I shared a desire to accommodate, editorially, the full range of that "ferment of ingenuity and invention." The title *Omnibus* spoke to the desire for this experiment in online publishing to be inclusive, anthological, and diverse.

---

[14] Rosalie Genevro, "Why Urban Omnibus?" *Urban Omnibus,* January 22nd, 2009.

Much of that desire emerged in response to the increased specialization of professions that design and manage urban space (architecture, landscape architecture, civil engineering, urban design, urban planning, public policymaking, and real estate development); the growth of academic interest in urban social relations (in sociology, anthropology, economics, and political science); and the new emphases on urban subject matter from realms of inquiry not typically associated with cities (visual and performing arts, graphic design, natural sciences, and education). Meanwhile, the sectors that have always worked on behalf of the social and physical assets of cities and neighborhoods (local government and community-based advocacy organizations) have discovered new kinds of partners (designers, planners, researchers, educators, and artists) in a new field of urban experimentation.

This diversification of professional and intellectual attention reflects the growth of popular interest in cities as places to live in, visit, read about, or watch on TV. Lamentably, it also circumscribes the diffusion of new knowledge into limited silos of activity and communication, within which practitioners of a particular subset of urbanism share insights and innovations only among themselves. The *Omnibus* project sought to break down these silos and erect a big tent instead, inclusive enough to demonstrate the full range of contemporary urban practice.

We never saw our intended readership as primarily specialists. Neither did we aim to reach the widest audience possible. Instead, we defined our audience as "urban enthusiasts," which we joked internally was a nice way of saying "people who are

The original definition of an omnibus was a passenger-carrying vehicle that became one of the first forms of urban, public transit. Pictured is the Fifth Avenue omnibus in Manhattan.

nerdy about cities." We conceived of the urban enthusiast as the type of person irresistibly drawn to the peephole in a painted plywood construction fence, curious to catch a glimpse of how the city is made.[15] Our contention was that the young hipster architect in south Brooklyn in his twenties, the real estate attorney in midtown Manhattan in her forties, and the retired teacher and community board member in central Queens in her sixties had interests in common that weren't being met by either the mainstream or by specialized coverage. Among the specialists we did want to reach were people from outside of the New York area, curious to keep up to speed with the latest local projects and perspectives with worldwide implications for urban discourse and practice.

Our recognition of this overlap in media interest across these diverse constituencies coincided with a constriction of the traditional source for information on cities: the daily newspaper. As *Urban Omnibus* was gearing up to launch, *The New York Times* was winding down its City Section[16] and doubling down on foreign correspondents and style coverage. But even in earlier eras of more robust support for local reporting, a gap persisted between the two primary ways the urban environment made its way into newsprint: architecture criticism and urban affairs reporting.

As 2008 was drawing to a close — and with it the enthusiasm (and budget) for iconic architecture as placebranding strategy — architecture criticism continued to draw on art historical traditions that privilege form over context or condition and characterize the (st)architect as a lone auteur. The tendency was to avoid discussion of the political, economic, or social factors underlying a new building's appearance on the landscape. On the eve of President Barack Obama's inauguration, the *Times* published architecture critic Nicolai Ouroussoff's review of Jean Nouvel's Copenhagen Concert Hall. Writing in *Urban Omnibus,* Andrew Blum called this a "tone-deaf editorial stroke," especially on "the biggest of days for public space in America, not only because of the millions gathered in Washington, but because of the millions of smaller gatherings across the country."[17]

Meanwhile, traditional urban affairs reporting has treated the built environment merely as a backdrop to human interest stories. Individual residents and sometimes demographic or consumption trends serve to characterize entire neighborhoods with far less attention paid to the accretion of specific decisions on the part of policymakers, real estate developers, residents, and architects that give rise to their physical attributes and sense of place. The desire to integrate the art historical and the urban affairs modes of covering the city drove much of how we articulated the editorial sensibility of *Urban Omnibus*: we wanted to discuss the intentional choices that shape the form, and thereby the experience, of cities. And while this impulse emerged from identifying an absence, a gap in existing media offerings, the focus on intentionality also relates directly to a generative philosophical orientation, to what we mean when we say "the culture of citymaking." For us, this term refers to a conception of the urban environment as a product of the creative choices of individual designers, scholars, activists, policymakers, and engaged citizens. The word culture — broadly defined, poorly understood, and universally deployed — has always shared connotations with cities, from the courtly milieu of ancient civilizations to contemporary capitals that serve as the expected sites of cultural production, both artistic and popular, as well as inter-ethnic and cross-class interaction. But we were less interested in these connotations of "urban culture" as particular social relations, works of art, or opportunities for public assembly evident in cities. Rather, we found the term useful in reference to the constant formation of urban space and society through a series of overlapping creative acts. In *Keywords: A Vocabulary of Culture and Society* (1976), Raymond Williams, a leftist scholar who immersed himself in the analysis and definition of the word *culture,* reminds us that its etymology relates to the tending to crops or animals, but also, more broadly, to the fact that in most early meanings of this word in European languages, *culture* was a noun of process, of actions.

Williams pursued his philosophical agenda in the tradition of Gramsci and Herbert Marcuse, arguing against the traditional understanding that art was independent of its historical context and the structures of power therein. His agenda—to demonstrate how hegemonic forces inscribe their ideologies into cultural production— is less relevant to our understanding of citymaking than the etymologies he excavates: how the Latin *cultura* is derived from *colere,* which "had a range of meanings: inhabit, cultivate, protect, honor with worship" that have evolved into a diverse set of contemporary words: colony, cult, and couture. When culture passed into English from Old French in the fifteenth century, its primary meaning was "husbandry, the tending of natural growth." Within the following century, the meaning extended, by metaphor, to refer to human development and gradually to overlap in meaning with civilization. This evolution accounts for the complications of the word's modern meanings, associated variously with sophistication, rites and practices shared among a particular social group, or the sum of human intellectual achievement, art, entertainment, and media.

For all this definitional diversity, one of the word's least common contemporary usages is surprisingly relevant to what we mean by "the culture of citymaking." In the context of microbial biology, *culture* refers to the practice of selectively growing a specific kind of bacteria. This precise, nonmetaphorical usage recalls the original meaning of husbandry and cultivation and returns us to a conception of culture that is active, accretive, carefully considered, and sometimes boldly decisive: the stewardship of resources, the shaping of land, the balancing of conflicting priorities, and the blending of tradition, experimentation, and creativity.

These kinds of choices connect our concept of culture more closely to strategic thinking than to material craft, yet the latter is also important to the definition of this book's key terms. *Citymaking* is an invented word,[18] and the constituent elements

---

[15] Cassim Shepard, "Welcome to Urban Omnibus," *Urban Omnibus,* January 6, 2009.

[16] Jessica Pressler, "Times City Section to Close," *New York Magazine's* NYMag.com, March 30, 2009.

[17] Andrew Blum, "On Criticism: Is Architecture Criticism Still Architecture Criticism?" *Urban Omnibus,* March 9, 2009.

[18] I owe the use of this term to *City Making: Building Communities Without Building Walls* by Gerald Frug, a legal scholar whose work and insights are featured later in this volume.

of this compound coinage are less in need of etymological analysis than uncommon words like "omnibus" and overused words like "culture." The fact that "city" and "citizen" share the root of *civitas* does not contribute meaningfully to theoretical (and unhelpful) debates about whether geographic and physical attributes are more or less important than demographic and social conditions in determining the meaning of a particular place. The philosophical underpinnings of "making," however, do deserve further explanation.

Over the past forty years, Richard Sennett, a social analyst in the American pragmatist tradition, has dedicated his career to two distinct themes of modern life: the social possibilities of cities[19] and the changing nature of work in contemporary capitalism.[20] Over the past five, he has sought to combine these two objects of study into a philosophical trilogy he calls the *homo faber* project, "drawing on the ancient idea of Man as his or her own maker — a maker of life through concrete practices."[21] He is not the first thinker to engage the idea of Man as Maker. For early twentieth-century philosopher Henri Bergson, the idea became a means to harmonize instinct and intelligence in human thought and action.[22] *Intelligence* in this context is "the faculty of manufacturing artificial objects, especially tools to make tools."[23] Since instinct alone is insufficient to explain human consciousness nor to maintain human survival, the act of making becomes fundamental. *Homo faber,* or Man as Maker, is perhaps a more fitting label for the species than *homo sapiens,* or Knowing Man. For Hannah Arendt, the idea served to distinguish between the "worldliness" of work and the "life" of labor. The capacity to make and destroy the world is what separates *homo faber,* who seeks mastery over nature, from *animal laborans,* who labors exclusively to provide for bodily needs.[24] And for Sennett, the human capacity to make material objects is neither distinct from knowing nor superior to labor.

The first book of Sennett's *homo faber* project, *The Craftsman* (2008), concerns itself with the history and future of "doing a job well for its own sake." He takes issue with the intellectual hierarchy that Western thought has gradually, over centuries, applied to the distinction between Aristotle's three types of knowledge — *techne, phronesis,* and *episteme* — valorizing theory at the expense of craft or ethics.[25] The book begins the trilogy's project of recuperating the value of the wisdom immanent in the act of making things, from cabinetry to music. It posits making as a way for individuals and groups to make sense of material facts about where they live and the work they do. The second book, *Together* (2012), expands the scope of craftsmanship to its social dimension: its subtitle is *The Rituals, Pleasures, and Politics of Cooperation.* In it, Sennett announces that the final, forthcoming volume in the series will expand the scope of making even further: it will be "a book on making cities" that seeks to conclude his quest "to relate how people shape personal effort, social relations and the physical environment."[26]

Sennett's deep belief in making, in practical skill, as a means of recovering meaning and value in contemporary life, thus enabling people to become competent interpreters of their own experience, relates directly to one of *Urban Omnibus'* primary editorial ambitions: to expose how cities work and how they might work better by shining a light on the decision-making behind exemplary projects and perspectives.[27] Not all this decision-making is explicitly material, but all of it, in one way or another, influences the physical environment of cities. For us, *making,* like *culture,* refers to a series of overlapping creative acts with consequences for how we experience our surroundings.

This focus on intentionality — on encouraging greater intimacy with the choices that influence the form and experience of the urban environment — harkens back to another important origin story for *Urban Omnibus,* one that is institutional rather than etymological. The Architectural League of New York was founded in 1881. It began as a sketch club that evolved into a mutual education society and cultural institution. At a time when there were very few options for the professional study of architecture in the United States, a community of designers dedicated itself to further education by assigning one another sketch problems and critiquing the results. Over the years, it grew into one of the premier architectural forums in the country. Long before museums had design departments, the League held annual exhibitions that drew international attention to the best of contemporary American architecture. It also maintained its identity as a club, complete with a members' restaurant and bar, that encouraged fellowship among designers interested in advancing the art of architecture, as opposed to the technical, legal, or professional aspects of practice.

Over the last thirty years, The Architectural League has intensified the ways it advances the art of architecture by focusing on specific programs that recognize excellence in different stages in designers' careers. The institution is able to marshal that expertise for a wide variety of projects: exhibitions, publications, and design studies that explore pressing issues facing the design disciplines. These special

---

[19] See *Families Against the City* (Cambridge, Mass.: Harvard University Press, 1970), *The Uses of Disorder* (New York: W.W. Norton, 1972), *The Fall of Public Man* (New York: W.W. Norton, 1977), *The Conscience of the Eye* (New York: W.W. Norton, 1992), and *Flesh and Stone* (1994).

[20] See *The Hidden Injuries of Class,* co-authored with Jonathan Cobb (New York: W.W. Norton,1972), *Authority* (New York, W.W. Norton, 1980), *The Corrosion of Character* (New York, W.W. Norton, 1998), *Respect in a World of Inequality* (New York, W.W. Norton, 2003), and *The Culture of the New Capitalism* (Yale University Press, 2006).

[21] Richard Sennett, *Together: The Rituals, Pleasures, and Politics of Cooperation* (New Haven: Yale University Press 2012), page x.

[22] See Henri Bergson, *Creative Evolution* (New York: Cosimo Classics 2005). first published at *L'Évolution créatrice*, 1907.

[23] Bergson, *Creative Evolution,* 137

[24] See Hannah Arendt, *The Human Condition,* (Chicago: University of Chicago Press, 1958).

[25] In Nicomachean Ethics, Aristotle distinguished between *Episteme* as universal scientific knowledge, independent of context; *Techne* as practical craft, rational and instrumental; and *Phronesis* as ethics, or practical wisdom. Modern thought has valorized *Episteme* as "theory" and derogated *Techne* as "practice," while obscuring *Phronesis,* which has no modern equivalent in English.

[26] Sennett, *Together,* x.

[27] Richard Sennett himself was one of the first perspectives showcased on the site: *Urban Omnibus* inaugurated its Walks & Talks series with "A Walk with Richard Sennett," January 6, 2009.

projects seek to apply the embodied intelligence of the international community of designers that the League has fostered with a focus on issues of social and environmental justice in the community where it operates: New York City. Early examples of design studies include our projects with such institutions as the New York City Department of Housing Preservation and Development on a study and publication called *Vacant Lots* (1987); the Public Education Association on a study and publication called *New Schools for New York* (1992); and a group of community advocates in East Brooklyn for *Envisioning East New York* (1995), and several more recent collaborations.

Urban Omnibus springs directly from this legacy, and extends it outwards from the League's core constituency within the design community to a broader audience that includes concerned citizens involved in neighborhood groups, block associations, community-based organizations, local government agencies, real estate developers, construction and engineering industries, performing and visual arts, and unorganized expressions of urban enthusiasm.

Editorial projects like *Urban Omnibus,* of course, are not generating new ideas on their own to benefit communities in need so much as presenting good ideas developed in a wide variety of contexts. But while most journalism is the product of journalists—trained and skilled in the interpretive acts of reporting and writing — *Urban Omnibus* acts as a kind of oral history, an archive of first-person accounts of urban practice in New York since 2009. Recently, the publication has begun to engage professional writers to produce high-quality journalism, but the majority of features produced is either an interview with or an article by practitioners. Whether her work is an interpretation or an intervention, each is someone we consider a *citymaker.* These first-person accounts serve as the primary reference points for this book.

NEW YORK CITY IN THE EARLY TWENTY-FIRST CENTURY

New York City began the millennium with a trauma that changed the world. The terrorist strikes of September 11, 2001 cost many lives, almost 3,000 in the attacks, and it sparked wars that continue to cause suffering. Immediately prior, complacency had set in about the new world order — capitalist, neoliberal, globalized, and ideologically centered in the United States as a single world power — after the fall of the Berlin Wall and the dissolution of the Soviet Union a decade earlier. The attacks shook these beliefs to their core. The World Trade Center, a potent symbol of New York City's primacy as a global financial capital, was destroyed. Debates about what should replace it began before all the dead were identified.

Suddenly, architecture was front-page news. Of course, the subject of public discussion was not architecture in and of itself, but rather architecture's capacity to act as a container for public memory, to provide meaning. The debates about the proper uses and forms of what would emerge from the ashes of Ground Zero were about the prospective power of an imagined architectural future that might honorably replace and memorialize what had been lost. And while public debates and behind-the-scenes controversies forestalled decisions and construction for years at enormous cost, New York City was ready to build. As elsewhere in the country, a building boom was already underway. And part of what financed so much building was

The area south of the Brooklyn Bridge in Manhattan was once home to several waterfront, open-air, wholesale markets, including the Fulton Fish Market. 8 Spruce Street — a residential skyscraper designed by Gehry Partners and constructed in 2011 — is one of many new luxury developments in Lower Manhattan.

the cheap credit and irrational exuberance that would eventually lead to an economic disaster.

From June 2000 through June 2006, the price of residential housing in the New York City area doubled. The early 2000s saw a revolution in financial services regulation, fueling a real estate bubble that transformed the city. The ability of the wealthy to chase the higher prices was helped along by President Bush's tax cuts that lowered the tax rate on gains from investments. Across the globe between 2000 and 2015, "the poorest half of the world's population has received just 1 percent of the total increase in global wealth, while half of that increase has gone to the top 1 percent."[28]

At the lower end of the market, the United States Federal Reserve stimulus and the advent of "risk-based" pricing premiums on equity loans and mortgages (known as subprime) encouraged banks to lend widely and profitably to more customers, often with aggressive brokers and built-to-fail terms like exploding interest rates and balloon prepayment penalties. Higher prices boosted the construction industry: between June 2004 and June 2008, spending on new projects increased from $211 million to $1.5 billion.[29] The supply of residential housing increased by 14,358 units in New York City over the four-year period.

---

[28] Deborah Hardoon, Sophia Ayele and Ricardo Fuentes-Nieva, "An Economy for the 1%" Oxfam Briefing Paper: January 18, 2016.

[29] Rachel S. Friedman, "The Construction Boom and Bust in New York City," *Monthly Labor Review:* October 2011. Retrieved from http://www.bls.gov/opub/mlr/2011/10/art2full.pdf.

The Queens neighborhoods along the Rockaway Peninsula suffered some of the greatest damage during Superstorm Sandy in 2012. Pictured is an attempt to name the cause of the extreme weather on the Rockaways' famous boardwalk in the immediate aftermath of the event.

The stream of loans that fueled this housing boom weren't just made more accessible, they were also increasingly repackaged and made into complex asset-backed securities, offering the global investor class an investment vehicle that could be rated virtually risk-free by credit ratings agencies despite the unsustainable terms of the millions of underlying mortgages. In 1999, the repeal of the Glass-Steagall Act (Depression-era banking industry regulation intended to insulate the economy from massive shocks) enabled commercial banks, investment banks, securities firms, and insurance companies to consolidate. Many analysts have convincingly argued that this repeal amid the broader deregulation of the banking industry led to the economic crisis nine years later.

September 11, 2001 was also the day that New Yorkers were supposed to go to the polls in a nominating contest for their next mayor to succeed Rudy Giuliani. We elected Michael Bloomberg, a billionaire businessman who could wield private capital in unprecedented ways. Mayor Bloomberg also had more time for design than many who have held his office. He presided over a renaissance in many city agencies, notably those with authority over the built environment, such as the Department of Parks and Recreation, which, during Bloomberg's twelve years in office, was able to add more than 870 acres of parkland and more than 490 acres of new waterfront open space across the city.[30] Over this same period, the Department of City Planning initiated 124 rezonings, covering almost 40 percent of New York City's acreage. New York City has always been the home base of many of the country's most respected architecture offices, but many used to complain about the difficulty and rarity of designing high quality new buildings in New York. Not so in the Bloomberg years, when small and medium-sized "design-focused" firms competed for the chance to design new firehouses, schools, and public places, not to mention the new clients in the private real estate market in Manhattan and Brooklyn.

The frenzied pace of development pushed the frontiers of gentrification further and further into the outer boroughs, while many middle and working class home-owners overleveraged their homes in order to stay put or simply to stay afloat. The pace of neighborhood change undoubtedly raised the stakes for community-based organizations with missions ranging from social service delivery to environmental justice to economic and workforce development. Just like its high proportion of design firms, New York City has long been home to a magnificent diversity of non-profits and faith-based organizations working locally. Collaborations between these two clusters of creative and public-focused work were rare and exceptional in the boom years, but the economic shock of the Great Recession has inspired new kinds of coalitions.

When I moved to New York City in 2004, the neighborhoods I spent time in already gave off the palpable sense of being for rich people or for poor people, not for those in between. Between 2002 and 2010, while the United States suffered a 25 percent reduction in the number of manufacturing jobs, New York City experienced a 46 percent loss of approximately 64,000 manufacturing jobs.[31] Of course, blue-collar jobs weren't the only ones hit when the economy tanked in 2008. Even among those who did not become unemployed, incomes contracted sharply, and the rates of working New Yorkers living in poverty soared.

In 2005, another great coastal city was decimated by a toxic mix of a cataclysmic weather event, the cumulative effect of neglected infrastructure, and political and operational incompetence and corruption in the storm's aftermath. Hurricane Katrina laid bare the "bitterness of [America's] sharp racial divide, the abandonment of the dispossessed, the weakness of critical infrastructure. But the most astonishing and most shaming revelation has been of its government's failure to bring succour to its people at their time of greatest need."[32] From the seemingly safe distance of the Northeast, the storm and recovery seemed like a unique series of cascading failures. But a few years later, the Northeast didn't seem so safe after all.

Superstorm Sandy claimed only a fraction of the lives lost to or permanently displaced by Katrina. Nonetheless, it exposed similar and often harder to see inequalities: the concentration of public housing complexes in the low-lying, flood-prone areas of the city; the uneven reliance on outdated and brittle delivery systems for electricity, water, and gas; and the vulnerability of residents dependent on public transit or elevators. The scale of the devastation once again motivated creative problem-solvers who work on the physical form and the social dynamics of urban environments to think across boundaries and outside of boxes.

In the years since the Great Recession and the devastating storms of the past decade, both economic inequality and climate change have continually reasserted themselves as the defining challenges of our time. In different ways, they refract through a vast range of conflicts and calls for systemic change, from the enduring reality of racism to the resurgence of revanchist nationalism. They affect everyone, not just people in cities and certainly not just New Yorkers. The stories that follow are not about grand solutions to the existential threats facing our democracy and our environment. They are a diverse selection of local attempts to make cities and neighborhoods more sustainable, beautiful, and just. As such, they reveal the preoccupations, coalitions, and experimentation of change-makers in the early twenty-first century who care about the physical form and social experience of cities. Cities, for me and for many of the citymaking projects profiled in this book, are places where the social possibilities that arise from forced confrontation with people unlike oneself are greatest. Cities are also places where spatial inequalities are most explicit, where what we build most affects how we live and interact. That's why we have a responsibility to look closely at how they work and lift up what might make them work better, for everyone.

---

30 Office of the Mayor "Manhattan Progress," December 13, 2013. www1.nyc.gov/office-of-the-mayor/news/419-13/manhattan-progress/#/0.

31 Sarah Crean, "Did City's Industrial Policy Manufacture Defeat?" in *City Limits* Monday, Jan 3, 2011.

32 "The Shaming of America," *The Economist*, September 8, 2005.

CHAPTER 2

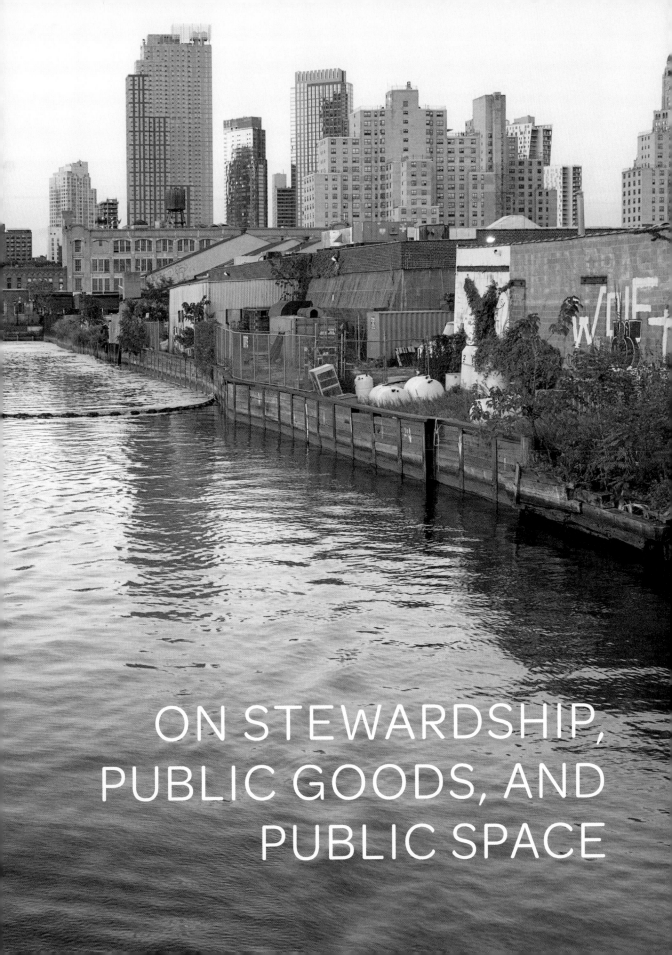

ON STEWARDSHIP,
PUBLIC GOODS, AND
PUBLIC SPACE

Johanna Willins has been growing fresh vegetables in a community garden near her home for the past twenty years. After retiring from a high-pressure job in TV news, she was able to devote more time to tending shrubs of hibiscus and bushes of green beans. In 1998, she began selling her produce at a small market stand on New Lots Avenue. "The average young person," according to Willens, "doesn't know that string beans don't come in a can." Yet through her efforts, along with those of dozens of urban farmers and community activists, local youth not only learn how string beans are actually cultivated but also get to spend time with each other outside of school, home, or work. "They just will hang out," she told me; "so instead of hanging out in bad places, they're hanging out here in the garden."[1]

Hanging out. Isn't that what public space is for? Throughout history, the concept of public space has been infused with all sorts of public benefits beyond leisure or recreation, from the health of citizens to the proper functioning of many types of government, democratic and otherwise. More recently, the economic advantages that well-functioning public spaces can confer to their surroundings have also come to be understood. Willens explains both types succinctly: "Community gardens are not just places to put food. Community gardens are places for people to gather, to sit. There's a lot more benefits than just fresh food . . . Everywhere you have community gardens, the values of the properties increase."

The passion with which she characterizes these benefits could apply to public space almost anywhere. But her perspective is inflected by the particular challenges her neighborhood has faced. East New York is on Brooklyn's eastern fringe, notorious for its high rates of vacancy and violence in the 1980s and '90s. From the very beginning of its development in the mid-nineteenth century, it has physically manifested some of the most potent effects of economic shocks and stresses, such as its current position as a red-hot property market at the crest of a borough-wide wave in real estate speculation. Home prices in many Brooklyn neighborhoods with histories of poverty have doubled since 2010, and the surge in property costs has nowhere to go but east. The intense speculation is helped along by the continued after-effects of the subprime mortgage crisis that was already underway when my colleagues and I began to explore East New York in the summer of 2008. At the time, while Washington was assuring the American public that credit markets were still healthy, most Americans were still a few months away from understanding the extent of the economic damage wrought by years of risky loans, inflated housing prices, and securitized debt. The signs of foreclosure were still emerging, only beginning to make themselves known in places like East New York.[2] Yet some of the vestiges of earlier cycles of disinvestment and abandonment — and the patterns of local ingenuity that emerged in response to them — were indeed visible.

When I first visited, I gazed out the window as the 3 train sped east above Livonia Avenue to see patches of green among smears of brick, vacant lots interspersed with the tire shops, garages, and the abruptly exposed, windowless sidewalls of rowhouses along the north-south streets. Look a little closer, and you can also see that what first appears to signal neglect testifies, in fact, to how the community has managed to turn historical liabilities into assets. Many of these "vacant" lots are anything but empty or abandoned. They are community gardens, like Willins farms — places where residents actively participate in the creation and stewardship of accessible open spaces that grow fresh food and engage both at-risk youth and isolated senior citizens. They also contribute to increasing property values, improving public health, and enhancing neighborhood security, stability, and vitality. East New York has the highest proportion of community gardens citywide,[3] and these emerged primarily through individual initiative, supported by a coalition of advocates in nonprofits and City agencies. How? Their story complicates the traditional notions of public space that prioritize particular typologies, such as traditional parks or plazas; particular categories of use, such as passive recreation; and particular modes of implementation, such as capital investment by government (often with private sector support) and design and construction by professional firms. The community gardens of East New York offer a vivid case study of a kind of citymaking in which community members co-create spaces to meet community needs, practicing an active and generative form of citizenship in which the participation of a few improves public life for all.

Of course, questions of citizenship and democracy have inscribed themselves onto histories of urban public space for millennia. Urban Studies 101 still invokes the *pnyx* and the *agora* of ancient Athens. The former, a political space where the legislative assembly *(ekklesia)* would meet, looked down from its higher perch onto the latter, an economic space in which all citizens (landowning males, that is) could assemble, shop, gossip, attend performances or athletic contests, and sometimes be corralled and marched up the hill to vote on new legislation. Plato, famously, believed the two types of spaces (and people) must be kept separate, lest the greed of the market, the petty lusts and transactions of the everyday citizen, weaken the republic's sense of

[1] Johanna Willins, interview, recorded for "East New York: Local Farmers," *Urban Omnibus*, January 6, 2009. All of the *Urban Omnibus* features cited in this book can be found at www.urbanomnibus.net/. Citations for other *Urban Omnibus* features will not include URLs. The permalink can be found according to the following example format of title and date: http://urbanomnibus.net/2009/01/eastnewyorklocalfarmers/.

[2] In 2008, East New York ranked third on a list of New York City neighborhoods with the highest rates of foreclosed homes, with 183 foreclosures. In 2009, it ranked sixth, with 1,195. In 2010, it ranked first, with 1,139. Data from RealtyTrac/OSC analysis, as quoted in New York State Comptroller's Report, "Foreclosures in New York City," March 2011. Accessed January 29, 2015. www.osc.state.ny.us/osdc/rpt13-2011.pdf.

[3] Lenny Librizzi, email message to author, January 21, 2015. See also www.oasisnyc.net/map.aspx.

what is good and just, ideals best safeguarded by a learned few. But the actions of citizens — a classification that has too slowly grown in the modern era to include women, the landless, descendants of enslaved peoples, immigrants, the poor, etc. — continuously re-assert the presence of the political, including but not limited to the possibility of revolution, into those urban places that everyone can access.

In recent years, the politics of public space have been heady, with multiple movements for broad political change coalescing in downtowns around the world. Much of the history of public space as a stage for political action relies on the symbolic or literal meaning of the protests' location[4]: the centrality of Tahrir Square to contemporary Cairo, or the proximity of Zuccotti Park to the beating heart of the American banking industry. Therefore, using these examples to insist on the democratic dimensions of public spaces risks attributing their political potential to the visibility of central urban locations, near the power bases of government and finance. But the history of protest bears an important relationship to those practices of citizenship that are largely hidden from view, such as the stewardship and cultivation of vacant lots into community gardens. This chapter begins by charting a role for the stewardship of public space as a component of citymaking. If citymaking is to be understood as the active and accretive layering of intentional acts in constant pursuit of a more equitable, sustainable, and emancipatory urban life, then we need to broaden our conception of *who* is performing those acts.

Of course, the answer to this question includes designers, planners, builders, and elected officials: the technocrats and politicians who comprise the "top" in "top-down." And, of course, it also includes urban dwellers everywhere, as political subjects as well as users of the built environment: the undifferentiated masses who populate the "bottom" in "bottom-up." But there is a category in between: the engaged citizens, community advocates, and public servants, as well as their professional allies, whose actions manifest an ethic and practice of stewardship, often sustained over years. For these citymakers, active, prolonged, and custodial engagement with particular public places reveals the politics and unleashes the power of such spaces just as much as, if not more than, dissent and protest.

PUBLIC SPACE AND CONTEMPORARY POLITICS

In January of 2011, Cairo's Tahrir Square became the media's focal point and exemplar for a range of citizen uprisings across the Middle East, with demonstrations in the grand plazas of older cities, like Tunis, Tunisia, or the traffic circles of newer ones, like Manama, Bahrain. As a public space, Tahrir Square reflects a multitude of ideas about the architecture of urban citizenship, with origins in Arab cultural histories, Islamic architectural theories, the policies of Ottoman, French, and British colonial administrators, and postcolonial Egyptian political attitudes. It has accommodated a distinct but related example of democratic practice to what took place in New York City nine months later. Starting in September of 2011, in order to voice brewing fury

[4] John R. Parkinson, *Democracy and Public Space* (Oxford: Oxford University Press, 2012).

The protest movement Occupy Wall Street encamped in Zuccotti Park, a "privately owned public space" near the center of New York City's financial district, beginning in September of 2011.

about wealth disparity in the United States, Occupy Wall Street protesters camped out in Zuccotti Park, near the downtown Manhattan headquarters of many of the banks and financial firms to which the protesters directed their rage. Both examples illuminate and obscure some of the political dimensions of public space.

Tahrir Square was also the result of an intentional insertion of urban design ideas into government policy. Khedive Ismail, who presided over the Ottoman territories of Egypt and Sudan from 1863 to 1879, initiated a series of ambitious plans that included a significant expansion of Cairo. Some historians have characterized his sweeping vision as an attempt to create a "Paris on the Nile." Ismail's modernization regime was not the wholesale clearance favored by Baron Haussmann,[5] but rather a series of surgical interventions into medieval Cairo, respecting the contextually sensitive urban expansion guidelines of Tanzimat reforms begun decades earlier.[6] Throughout the twentieth century, Tahrir Square, originally named Ismailia Square in honor of the Khedive, has manifested serial tensions between the zones associated with various political eras: a buffer zone between the British army barracks and the neighborhoods of Cairo's elite; the site of numerous unrealized plans in the late 1940s to transform vestiges of successive colonial regimes into an administrative and cultural center of the postcolonial state; and, since 1954, the locus of commemorating the 1952 revolution that sought to topple the monarchy, end British occupation, and establish a republic. This last incarnation is what led to its renaming as Midan al-Tahrir, or Liberation Square, which would become central to the popular revolts of 2011 and 2013.

Even though Tahrir Square was not an ancient site of public assembly and ritual, like the courtyard of Al-Azhar Mosque or the Maidan Bein al-Qasreen,[7] images of the thousands of protestors encamped there immediately brought to mind one of the ideals of public space in many Islamic civilizations, in which the faithful gather in the *sahn,* or open courtyard, of the mosque to offer their prayers while the *maidan,* or city square, visually frames the majesty of public buildings and operates as a circulatory conduit between spaces of worship and the secular spaces of markets and streets. The *maidan* is not the Greek *agora.* Yet it, too, is a mediating space, made and remade by the actions of citizens. The word *maidan* derives from the Arabic word for city, *medina,* and thus also embodies the name of Medina, the original city of Islam to which Mohammed's followers, adherents of a nascent religion, fled to avoid persecution in Mecca, instantly linking notions of migration, pilgrimage, refuge, and revolution to the Islamic concept of what a city is for, what a city means. *Maidan* is a powerful word, even if its meaning is not mystical. Via Persian, it has entered into the urban design lexicons of languages and cities from India to Ukraine, where another protest movement, named Euromaidan, reasserted the relationship between the urban public square and the revolutionary ambitions of popular protest.

The ambitions of Occupy Wall Street may have been less concrete than the protestors of Cairo's Midan al-Tahrir or Kiev's Maidan Nezalezhnosti (Independence Square). Nonetheless, Zucotti Park became a flashpoint beyond the growing debate about the sequestration of profit away from the 99 percent. The United States Steel Corporation, a private company, created this "privately-owned public space" in 1968 in exchange for government dispensation to build an adjacent building (now known as One Liberty Plaza) taller than existing height regulations would otherwise allow. Somewhat inadvertently, the protests made "privately-owned public space" a commonly understood term. In addition to its broader protest of corporate power and income and wealth inequality, the primary location of Occupy Wall Street served to critique the financial and regulatory mechanisms used to create public amenities for citizens. Local government reliance on the private sector to subsidize public goods is not new, but the site of the protests' command center served to underscore the codependence of public and private sectors in the delivery of those goods, buttressing the movement's grievances about the influence that corporations wield over government, especially in the financial services industry.

John E. Zuccotti, for whom the park was renamed after extensive renovations in 2006, was a public servant as well as a corporate executive (he passed away in 2015). A former special assistant in the United States Department of Housing and Urban Development (HUD), Zuccotti became a member of New York City's planning commission in 1971 and its chair in 1973, and he joined the administration of Mayor Abe Beame as First Deputy Mayor in 1975. These years marked the nadir of New York City's government, at least in fiscal terms. While the park honors his more recent role as a chairman of Brookfield Properties, a powerful real estate development firm, Zuccotti's service on the planning commission in the '70s coincided with one of the first dedicated efforts to codify urban design considerations within real estate development through specific public policies.

Between 1967 and 1980, the Urban Design Group, an influential body of architects and designers initiated by Mayor John Lindsay, worked within the Department of City Planning to create policies to further design goals; many of its policy recommendations relied on incentivizing the real estate market to provide public goods. Raquel Ramati, an architect and member of the Urban Design Group in its early years whom I interviewed for *Urban Omnibus* a few months before Occupy, characterized the objective as determining "how we could affect the city, not necessarily by dictating architecture or attracting a brand-name architect, but by creating *rules and objectives* with a cohesive vision. The Urban Design Group started with the approach that unless you involve the real estate developers, the city will continue to be built without any thought towards urban design whatsoever."[8] Hence the

---

[5] Baron Haussmann, was chosen by Emperor Napoleon III to carry out a massive program of urban renewal, resulting in new boulevards, parks and public works, commonly called Haussmann's renovation of Paris. Critics forced his resignation for extravagance, but his vision of the city still dominates central Paris.

[6] Nezar AlSayyad, Irene A. Bierman, and Nasser O. Rabbat, eds., *Making Cairo Medieval: Transnational Perspectives on Space and Place* (Lanham, Mass.: Lexington Books, 2005).

[7] Heba Farouk Ahmed and Basil Kamel, "Cairo: Three Cities, Three Periods, Three Maidans," *Built Environment* (1978–) 22, no. 2 (1996). 104–123.

[8] "A Conversation with Raquel Ramati," *Urban Omnibus,* March 30, 2011.

Occupy Wall Street began nine months after a series of pro-democracy protests swept the Middle East and North Africa. The media's focal point for these events, dubbed the Arab Spring, was the demonstrations in Tahrir Square that began in January of 2011.

desire to create more specific guidelines mandating the quality of the public spaces that private businesses create in exchange for permission to build beyond the bulk and height limits of zoning regulations.

Obviously, this approach to the provision of public space only works in parts of the city where the real estate economics make it viable, where there is enough demand for additional square feet to justify the additional costs of creating open space "for free." The open spaces of other neighborhoods, such as the neighborhood of East New York, owe their provenance to an opposite force: the negative demand of abandonment.

The term abandonment, however, erroneously connotes that owners desert property innocent of forces and policies beyond their control. East New York is a perfect example of what Walter Thabit, the city planner who chronicled the neighborhood's historical challenges in *How East New York Became a Ghetto,* calls the "machinations of the real estate fraternity, the racism and greed of the banking industry and the indifference of government officials." All of these forces "contribute to the creation of ghettos, which can be described as the destroyed remains of once viable communities."[9]

East New York is not destroyed. But its mention still more readily conjures images of entrenched poverty rather than of generative urban interventions. Certainly, the way the community gardens of East New York figure into the discourse of public space was not forefront in our minds as my colleagues and I went about identifying pilot subject matter to inaugurate *Urban Omnibus* as a new online space for the dissemination of innovative urban projects in New York City. We knew we wanted to launch with a suite of content that represented a range of neighborhoods, design disciplines, and media formats. We discussed and tested a number of ideas, and East New York emerged as a locale worth investigating after brainstorming a list of interesting, rapidly changing neighborhoods. Beyond its high incidence of violent crime, all I knew about it was that it had one of the biggest concentrations of City-owned land left in New York, a piece of trivia I had somehow retained from working a desk job in City government a few years prior and a fact that would prove central to its urban agriculture renaissance. My colleagues at The Architectural League were more intimately familiar with it, having produced a design study years earlier[10] that exposed them to the neighborhood's rich tradition of public debate and impassioned activism evident in community meetings and a wealth of local advocacy efforts. In the years since then, a slow and steady transformation of the neighborhood's vacant lots into agriculturally productive gardens paralleled other efforts at neighborhood

---

[9] Walter Thabit, *How East New York Became a Ghetto* (New York: NYU Press, 2003). In addition to Thabit's authoritative book on the subject, see also Vincent Cannato *The Ungovernable City: John Lindsay and His Struggle to Save New York,* (New York: Basic Books, 2009).

[10] *Envisioning East New York* was a 1995 design study conducted by The Architectural League of New York that called on architects, planners, and landscape architects to broaden the range of development possibilities for the City-owned vacant lots in the neighborhood.

stabilization, including new housing production, new retail developments, and renewed ecological interest in the northern shore of Jamaica Bay. As we sifted through multiple options for testing out our budding editorial strategy and production workflow, the neighborhood called to us as worthy of closer inspection.

URBAN AGRICULTURE IN EAST NEW YORK

By the 1830s, the intersection of several rail lines connecting the City of Brooklyn to Long Island yielded a growing settlement at nearby New Lots. Here, Connecticut financier John Pitkin, who had already found local success in developing Woodhaven in Queens, imagined a new city that would take advantage of this rail infrastructure to the north and the waters of Jamaica Bay to the south and grow rapidly to rival New York City and Brooklyn as an economic center. According to Thabit, Pitkin "bought 135 acres of land from farmers in the area, built a shoe factory on one parcel, and divided the rest into lots that sold for ten to twenty-five dollars each." Naming the new neighborhood East New York signaled the scope of his ambition for the new development, and he christened the first new thoroughfare Broadway, since renamed Pitkin Avenue in his honor. His vision would not be realized: "the financial panic of 1837 ended Pitkin's dream of metropolitan grandeur, reducing him to serving as the auctioneer of his own assets." This "panic" bore some resemblance to more recent financial crises in that its causes included a collapsing land bubble and speculative lending practices.[11] Its result was that East New York would not be a centrally planned settlement but rather a loose agglomeration of land parcels that gradually, between the 1850s and 1930s, would provide residential overflow for immigrant families from more congested precincts of Brooklyn. Much of East New York's building stock was constructed by real estate speculators in the 1910s and '20s, spurred by the extension of rapid transit lines. According to the WPA Guide of 1939, East New York's residents were chiefly Italians, Jewish, Germans, and Russians who moved in from Brownsville, Bushwick, and other nearby crowded localities."[12]

The gradual replacement of these ethnic, white immigrant families with black and Latino families was the result of a framework of policies and strategies that effectively meant that East New York was one of the only places people of color could move. Thabit's study shows how redlining (the denial of mortgages to particular communities, often along racial lines) was followed by blockbusting (a tactic used by speculators to scare white families into selling their homes cheaply before reselling them at much higher rates to families of color with few options). The manufacturing

---

[11] Other factors included rapid increases in the supply of silver from China and Mexico, as well as interbank transfers of government balances and the demand for coin rather than paper currency in the western states that drained the largest New York City banks of their specie reserves. See Peter L. Rousseau, "Jacksonian Monetary Policy, Specie Flows, and The Panic of 1837" in *The Journal of Economic History* 62, no. 2 (June 2002): 457–488.

[12] *The WPA Guide to New York City: The Federal Writers' Project Guide to 1930s New York* (New York: Pantheon Books, 1939).

East New York has one of the highest proportions of urban farms citywide. **Top:** The United Community Centers Youth Farm on Schenck Ave between Livonia and New Lots Ave. **Above:** Beverly, from the Temple of David Community Garden at the corner of Dumont Ave. and Bradford St.

jobs that had provided career opportunities for so many immigrants and people of color began to disappear as the United States, especially in Northern cities, began to deindustrialize in the 1970s. The resulting widespread unemployment exacerbated the high costs of being poor. Attempts by local and federal government to redress the concomitant increases in neglect, vacancy, and crime resulted in a net loss of habitable housing units. East New York's fabric includes built examples of every single urban renewal strategy attempted in the last forty years. Some families fled while others crowded themselves into fewer and fewer available housing units. With the costs of maintaining these units rising rapidly, many landlords strategically neglected their properties and their tax bills while continuing to collect rent. The City took over ownership of many tax-delinquent properties through a process called *in rem* foreclosure,[13] which in many cases led to fenced-in vacant lots adjacent to houses designed for one to three families but accommodating several more. Buildings burned.

These sustained challenges were not unique to East New York. Among others, Brooklyn's Bedford-Stuyvesant, the Lower East Side of Manhattan, Harlem, and, most famously, larges areas of the South Bronx suffered significantly from this combination of shortsighted policy and entrenched poverty. In fact, "Seven different census tracts in The Bronx lost more than 97 percent of their buildings to fire and abandonment between 1970 and 1980; forty-four tracts (out of 289 in the borough) lost more than 50 percent."[14] According to a 2006 working paper by the Furman Center for Real Estate and Urban Policy, "By 1979, New York City had taken ownership through tax foreclosure of over 60,000 units in vacant buildings and another 40,000 units in occupied and semi-occupied buildings. . . [which] continued to deteriorate under city ownership."[15]

Once again, Johanna Willins' description of the era is concise: "This used to be a not nice area: the bad stuff."[16] She briefly bristled at the memory before shaking it off, narrowing her focus on a rose. I got the impression that she prefers to look on the bright side: the positive trajectory of the neighborhood since those dark days and the role urban farming has played in that shift. She estimates that between two and four houses once stood on the lot where she farms. And even though the lot was probably vacant for over a decade, the garden and others like it were under serious threat of being redeveloped as housing in the 1990s.

Soon after meeting Johanna Willins, I went to see Holly Leicht, a lawyer whose career has included work on both affordable housing and open space advocacy. In East New York, she and her colleagues found a way to support the balancing of these two crucial social justice priorities. Now Regional Administrator for New York and New Jersey at the Department of Housing and Urban Development (HUD), at the time, Leicht was the Deputy Commissioner for Development at the City's Department of Housing Preservation and Development (HPD), the agency that found itself in the unintended and uncomfortable position of being the city's second largest landlord by the beginning of the 1980s.[17] As such, the agency's mission, to "make strategic investments that will improve and strengthen neighborhoods while preserving the stability and affordability of [New York City's] existing housing stock," could avail itself of an unprecedented amount of property.[18] The second clause of that mission statement is less open to interpretation than the first, and the role that open space might play in strengthening neighborhoods is neither statutory nor clear-cut.

In her office in Lower Manhattan, Leicht told me that "a lot of housing people are pretty myopic about housing. There's definitely a point of view that land that's in HPD's inventory should be all for housing." But Leicht brought to her job a strong interest in the other public goods that make housing work, especially open space. Of course, she concedes, housing is a "fundamental need that everyone has, but you can't build housing without creating neighborhoods."[19]

One of the more robust government interventions in the production of affordable housing in the last thirty years, the Koch Ten-Year-Plan, started as the crises of the 1970s were ending. From 1978 to 1989, the mayoral administration of Ed Koch coincided with a massive shift in the local economy from nearly bankrupt to booming. Over the course of the 1970s, the average sale price was $45 per square foot and average rent was $335 per month.[20] Over the course of the 1980s, those figures increased to $250 per square foot and $1,700 per month. These figures represent the largest percent change for both statistics (455.56 percent and 407.46 percent, respectively) for the century between 1910 and 2010.[21] The rapid change precipitated a housing crisis, and in 1985, Mayor Koch initiated what would come to

---

13 *In rem* (literally, "against the thing itself") foreclosure refers to the legal concept of taking action against property without regard for its owner; *in rem* foreclosure was the process by which the City took ownership of tax delinquent properties.

14 Joe Flood, "Why the Bronx Burned," *The New York Post,* May 16, 2010.

15 Furman Center for Real Estate and Urban Policy "Housing Policy in New York City: A Brief History," April 2006.

16 Willins, interview, 2009.

17 In 1980, only the New York City Housing Authority, the country's largest public housing authority, had a larger inventory. See Furman Center, 2006.

18 New York City Department of Housing Preservation and Development, "About HPD." Accessed March 2, 2015. http://www1.nyc.gov/site/hpd/about/about-us.page.

19 Holly Leicht, interview, recorded for "East New York: Land Transfers," *Urban Omnibus,* January 6, 2009.

20 Jonathan Miller, "Change is the Constant in a Century of New York City Real Estate," Miller Samuels, October 2012. Accessed March 2, 2015. www.millersamuel.com/files/2012/10/DE100yearsNYC.pdf.

21 Miller, "Change is the Constant…" 2012.

	1910s	1920s	1930s	1940s	1950s	1960s	1970s	1980s	1990s	2000s
sale price $/sq. ft.	8	15	5	8	12	25	45	250	590	1200
rental price $/month	40	60	45	50	60	200	335	1700	3200	3800
sale % change		87.50%	-66.67%	60.00%	50.00%	108.33%	80.00%	455.56%	136.00%	103.39%
rental % change		50.00%	-25.00%	11.11%	20.00%	233.33%	67.50%	407.46%	88.24%	18.75%

be known as the city's Ten Year Plan for Housing, with an eventual financial commitment of $5.1 billion in City funds in order to "renovate 82,000 units in occupied *in rem* buildings, rebuild 47,000 units in vacant *in rem* buildings, build 37,000 new units and upgrade 87,000 apartments in privately owned buildings."[22] While the plan did not focus on open space explicitly, HPD made clear its intention to create "more than just apartments — we're re-creating neighborhoods. We're revitalizing parts of the city that over the past two decades have been decimated by disinvestment, abandonment, and arson."[23]

The plan continued into the Dinkins and Giuliani administrations. But the Giuliani administration sought to accelerate the disposition of City-owned land, initiating an auction process that Miranda J. Martinez has called "absolutely unilateral and radically free market in its approach."[24] In her book *Power at the Roots: Gentrification, Community Gardens, and the Puerto Ricans of the Lower East Side,* Martinez blames the auction plan for a citywide crisis in community gardens in the late 1990s: "It denied recognition of a neighborhood right to comment on what local land could be sold, to whom, and for what purpose. Gardeners found their spaces would not be distinguished from non-garden parcels, and their prior claims to the land were denied." While the real estate dynamics were different in East New York than they were in the Lower East Side communities that Martinez has studied, the threat of alienating a type of shared space that residents had come to cherish was just as real. At the time, Holly Leicht was in-house counsel at the Municipal Art Society, a preservation advocacy nonprofit, where she worked with a wide coalition of partners to draft a "lawsuit that created a review system, so that essentially any time a garden was being considered for development, there would be a process where it wasn't automatically assumed that it would get developed. There would actually be a balancing of priorities." (The battle, finally settled in 2002,[25] included high profile figures like then-Attorney General Eliot Spitzer and entertainer Bette Midler, founder of the New York Restoration Project, which offers organizational and financial support to green spaces in underserved neighborhoods.)

Leicht brought this in-depth knowledge of the benefit these gardens provide to her work at HPD. In a political climate that did not distinguish between lots actively used for community benefit and those seen exclusively as a property development opportunity, this kind of legal advocacy is a necessary step. But once the threat of destruction is removed, jurisdictional questions remain, especially for a government wary of poorly maintained open spaces once again becoming their responsibility. Typically, the Parks Department only works with sites of one acre or more. The department responsible for community gardens, GreenThumb, rarely works with lots greater than half an acre. (GreenThumb is another legacy of the era of abandonment and disinvestment: founded in 1978, and funded largely by community block grants from the federal Housing and Urban Development program, the office coordinates leases for city-owned vacant land in order to outsource their maintenance "to energetic community groups willing to tend to them and wanting to encourage grassroots neighborhood revitalization efforts."[26]) Leicht discovered that HPD's inventory included a number of arable vacant lots in Central and Eastern

Brooklyn that were in between, 25,000 to 35,000 square feet. Some of these had already been designated as open space during the era of urban renewal,[27] but sat fallow and inaccessible as fenced-off lots for decades. So Leicht worked with local groups interested in scaling up their gardening operations. If these groups would commit to finding residents to farm these sites in the long term, then GreenThumb would put these larger sites in their jurisdiction. The relevant City agencies worked out an elegant series of swaps that made possible Leicht's goal of a "balancing of priorities." She described what made it possible as a "confluence of interest" between different government agencies and City Hall. In particular, she cited HPD's incipient receptiveness to the idea as crucial, despite a history of "tensions between housing and any other uses in communities." Of course, the constrained supply of public land presents increasing challenges for the creation of government-supported affordable housing, but Leicht explained that the housing agency is also aware that "the city is almost built out and our land is almost all gone but that also means that there's a lot of density in housing and you have to balance that with open space and other amenities for people to make a community livable." Other elements of these converging priorities include the "renaissance" of New York City parks during the Bloomberg administration, the commitment to sustainability under PlaNYC[28] and to healthy foods, all of which, Leicht concluded, "coalesced to make this a great moment for urban agriculture."

Other factors — and the hard work of various individuals — also coalesced. In addition to dedicated local farmers like Johanna Willins and dedicated public servants like Holly Leicht, several nonprofits with wide-ranging areas of focus, service, and catchment were instrumental. My next visit was to Perry Winston, who sadly passed

---

[22] Furman Center, "Housing Policy in New York City," 2006.

[23] New York City, Department of Housing Preservation and Development, 1989 as quoted in Furman Center, 2006.

[24] Miranda J. Martinez, *Power at the Roots: Gentrification, Community Gardens, and the Puerto Ricans of the Lower East Side* (Lanham, Mass.: Lexington Books, 2010).

[25] Jennifer Steinhauer, "Ending a Long Battle, New York Lets Housing and Gardens Grow," *The New York Times,* September 19, 2002.

[26] New York City Department of Parks and Recreation, "History of the Community Garden Movement." Accessed March 3, 2015. www.nycgovparks.org/about/history/community-gardens/movement.

[27] Urban Renewal was the comprehensive suite of policies enacted from the late 1930s to the 1970s that emphasized slum clearance as a strategy to redevelop low-income neighborhoods. See Samuel Zipp, *Manhattan Projects: Rise & Fall of Urban Renewal in Cold War New York* (Oxford: Oxford University Press, 2010).

[28] PlaNYC is the coming together of twenty-five city agencies and outside partners to address New York City's long-term planning challenges. First released under the Bloomberg administration in 2007, the successful implementation of plaNYC's initiatives is now the shared responsibility of the Mayor's Office of Long-term Planning and Sustainability and the Office of Recovery and Resilience.

away in 2015. An architect who devoted his career to planning for communities in need, Winston worked at the Pratt Center for Community Development in Brooklyn for 18 years. The oldest university-based community planning organization in the US, the Pratt Center works with neighborhood-based organizations to develop affordable housing and community facilities, in addition to working on manufacturing, transportation, and community planning efforts. Winston had already been working with community groups in East New York for five years when he began, in 1995, to participate in community-wide visioning sessions.

In a conference room above Union Square in Manhattan, a world away from eastern Brooklyn, Winston unrolled before me a series of maps. In many community-based planning contexts, "asset mapping" refers metaphorically to a collaborative process to identify locally specific opportunities for realizing a shared vision. But these were literal, physical maps, color-coded by official zoning categories: commercial, residential, and industrial.

"GIS was just coming into play," Winston explained, using the acronym for Geographic Information Systems software. He told me the story of the direction these community visioning sessions started to take, pointing out yellow and brown areas on the map to indicate recent housing developments and blue areas to indicate community facilities. "And then we started coming up with a lot of these little green spots all over the neighborhood . . . We knew that there were a lot of gardens in the area but we had no idea there were that many . . . We started isolating just the GreenThumb gardens and came up with 106 gardens."[29] Out of a citywide total of 582,[30] East New York had the largest neighborhood total in New York City. The Pratt Center and its partners[31] started thinking about how this special resource could be used to address what the community visioning sessions had identified as the neighborhood's top priorities: employment, security, health, and recreation. They engaged local youth "to work in the gardens and increase production to the degree where we would have enough to sell at these markets and therefore provide more of a rationale for preserving these community gardens [as] part of the food supply system." With visible pride betraying an otherwise reticent and composed demeanor, Winston described the day in late autumn of 1998 when Johanna Willins and David Crutchfield from the East New York Urban Youth Corps set up tables on New Lots Avenue, and for the first time, sold fresh produce grown in East New York.

The coordinated efforts Winston described helped to set the groundwork for East New York Farms!, a nonprofit organization established in 1995 specifically to deepen the relationship between youth development and urban agriculture in the neighborhood. Deborah Greig, who was coordinating the project at the time, met with me in the fecund half-acre garden tended primarily by youth in East New York Farms! programs. She echoed what I'd heard from the others — redlining, arson, and *in rem* foreclosure contributing to the prevalence of vacant lots, which local residents took upon themselves to clean and start gardening — but she also highlighted to other important assets that help fill out the story of why urban agriculture took hold in East New York. One was the large proportion of the population under eighteen, which explains why so many of the community visioning sessions prioritized youth programs and job training. The other was the cultural backgrounds of residents moving into East New York: many of the African-American and Latino families who made their homes in the neighborhood came from rural areas with farming experience. As well, more recent immigrant groups, particularly those from the Caribbean, West Africa, and Bangladesh, arrived already knowing how to grow their own food. The lack of access to fresh fruits and vegetables in local grocery stores also motivated residents to take matters into their own hands. Since that first November when Willins started selling vegetables on New Lots Avenue, the market has since grown to include dozens of vendors, including professional farmers from upstate New York and cooks selling prepared foods. In 2001, federal government food assistance transitioned from paper coupons (food stamps) to electronic benefit transfer (EBT) debit cards, which limited the ability of families dependent on such assistance to purchase fresh food at farmers markets, since they lacked access to the electricity and phone lines required to process EBT payments. But since 2005, partnerships initiated by GrowNYC, a citywide environmental nonprofit, have worked to close this gap, and in 2014, EBT payments were accepted at fifty-three greenmarkets.[32]

The benefits of urban agriculture are easy to overstate. Its potential is especially appealing to environmentally conscious citizens eager to reduce the distance between food production and consumption, which is of immense importance from a climate change mitigation standpoint. Other factors, not exclusively environmental, also add to its appeal: the recent vogue for "authentic" consumable goods — bespoke or vintage furniture, microbreweries, artisanal cocktails served in mason jars — that reflect, at root, some public desire to resist the increasing homogenization of many forms of production. But the fresh food grown in community gardens within city limits will never come close to providing for the population; and food localism might not remain quite so fashionable. But then again, in the words of Johanna Willins: "There's a lot more benefits than just fresh food." Perry Winston found the youth programs' continuing success to be especially rewarding, providing young people with "very basic work experience; it teaches them responsibility, how to relate to older people, teaches them a lot about growing." He also cited the momentum that urban agriculture has provided to neighborhood organizations working toward community economic development, as well as the significant income,

[29] Perry Winston, interview, recorded for "East New York: Asset Mapping," *Urban Omnibus,* January 6, 2009.

[30] Librizzi, email, 2015.

[31] Including the Cornell Cooperative Extension, United Community Centers, Local Development Corporation of East New York, Genesis Homes/HELP USA.

[32] GrowNYC, "Healthy Exchange." Accessed March 9, 2015. www.grownyc.org/greenmarket/ebt.

rising every year, that community gardeners earn from selling their produce. For Deborah Greig, the gardens' greatest strength is their diversity of uses: "a lot of them are community centers, a lot of them grow food, a lot of them are hangout spots." And for Holly Leicht, "The community gardens and the urban farms in East New York and other neighborhoods have been places of community gathering, [where] people came, had a sense of community and togetherness, and created something beautiful and good for their community; they've been the root of neighborhood revival all throughout the city." For me, the most significant potential of this type of project is the strategic introduction of an active and shared purpose among diverse stakeholders, a practical camaraderie that is one of the most basic components of community resilience.

My colleagues and I told this story as one of the inaugural features published on *Urban Omnibus* when we launched in January 2009. At the time, we were just beginning to test out what topics and formats made sense for our experimental project in online media highlighting good ideas for cities worldwide, tried and tested in New York City. We knew the story demonstrated the kind of interdisciplinary innovation we wanted to showcase. What we didn't yet know was how this story would resonate with a diverse range of public-space-related activities that would eventually teach us some valuable lessons about the importance of stewardship, especially when sustained over long periods, and would enlarge our conception of public goods, a crucial component to an emerging definition of *citymaking*.

THE ETHIC OF STEWARDSHIP:
FROM CONSERVATION TO CONSERVANCIES

The story of urban agriculture in East New York is a story of citymaking, of turning liabilities into opportunities, of finding points of intersection between distinct areas of urban intervention: in this case environmental remediation, housing policy, land use litigation, community organizing, asset mapping, youth development, and food justice. It also makes a strong case for how spaces such as these gardens insert a kind of politics into public space that is different from the more traditional reading of public-space politics, such as the spectacle of protest movements in places like Tahrir Square or Zuccotti Park. None of the four people I spoke with would describe their actions in terms of political theory or even the saturated discourse of public space. No one ever mentioned keywords like citizenship or democracy. Importantly, no one ever mentioned the word "design." Yet the way they told me this story opens up some crucial questions about citymaking. It points out how a phenomenon of urban change that began as uncoordinated, ad hoc responses to local conditions had to contend with external threats that emerged from the fierce competition for resources (in this case land) as well as shifting attitudes of local government about how best to deploy those resources. The solutions generated an unlikely coalition of local residents, public servants, and community-based organizations (some longstanding and some, like East New York Farms!, created especially for this effort), united by a shared vision. Most importantly, this kind of public space requires constant and consistent upkeep, exactly the type of active stewardship that so often disappears from how we talk about and finance urban parks and plazas.

As a field of study, urbanism sometimes suffers from the legacies of the visual language of design and planning that incubated it. As professionals, we tend to conceptualize the city in plan view, a static map of land use designations like the ones Perry Winston showed me in his office. But even with the advent of digital technologies that can introduce elements of interactivity to urban strategies, we still lack an adequate conception of the role of time, of the long-term layering of actions, in public space. Highlighting the importance of stewardship is a critical first step toward redressing the limitations of two-dimensional thinking, in which every space in the city has a singular and exclusive category of use and type of ownership and responsibility. It's vital to expanding and enriching our understanding of the city, who makes it, and how.

In the case of East New York, the primary act of stewardship is the literal cultivation of the land, but the term's applicability goes much further. To me, stewardship includes the ongoing programming of East New York Farms! And the public review process that is now required before developing a community garden on a City-owned lot. It includes long-term maintenance and, in some cases, everyday use. Like gardening or running a nonprofit, stewardship can be an active and concrete activity. Like establishing forward-thinking rules or operational finance arrangements, it can seem bureaucratic and downright dull. As a constituent element of a working definition for citymaking, the word is perhaps most meaningfully understood as an ethic.

This usage owes its provenance to conservation biology and the visionary American forester Aldo Leopold (1887–1948). Any reckoning with the promise of stewardship as a constituent element of practical urbanism requires revisiting his seminal work.

In 2006, The Cornell University Cooperative Extension, one of the institutional partners on the project that led to the creation of East New York Farms!, published a fact sheet for forest landowners entitled "The Stewardship Ethic." It begins:

> Aldo Leopold, the naturalist and author, once wrote, "We abuse land because we regard it as a commodity belonging to us. When we see land as a community to which we belong, we may begin to use it with love and respect." With these words, Leopold began a philosophy now known as the stewardship ethic [...] : the use and care of your land so that it remains fruitful and healthy for future generations.[33]

Leopold wrote *A Sand County Almanac,* his masterwork of nature writing and conservation theory, in the midst of the massive road-building and housing development

---

[33] Cornell University Cooperative Extension and New York State Department of Environmental Conservation "The Stewardship Ethic: A Guide for Using Your Land," 2006. Accessed March 9, 2015. www2.dnr.cornell. edu/ext/info/pubs/FC%20factsheets/FCFSstewardshipethic.pdf.

regime immediately following World War II. In it, he offers a subtle distinction between ethics in ecology and in philosophy: "An ethic, ecologically, is a limitation on freedom of action in the struggle for existence. An ethic, philosophically, is a differentiation of social from anti-social conduct." Both define the same tendency, for "interdependent individuals or groups to evolve modes of co-operation." In ecology, these co-operative modes are called "symbioses," and the political and economic systems we have developed are really just "advanced symbioses in which the original free-for-all competition has been replaced, in part, by co-operative mechanisms with an ethical content." Yet, Leopold laments, while those ethics concerned with how individuals relate to one another have multiplied and become more complex as populations have grown and societies evolved, we have no ethic dealing with man's relationship with the land, plants, and animals. "The land-relation," he writes, "is still strictly economic, entailing privileges but not obligations."

The obligations toward the land that Leopold hoped future generations would internalize included recognizing and caring for natural environments as living ecosystems, as "a biotic community" that includes humans. Much of mainstream ecology and environmentalism embodies aspects of this philosophical legacy, including the tendency of these disciplines, in their formative decades into mid-twentieth century, to prioritize wilderness preservation over serious inquiry into urban contexts and the natural processes taking place within them. As his analysis of the politics of cooperation suggests, the theoretical emphasis on the interdependency of multiple elements within a system is relevant to urban social theory as well as to conservation biology. This interdependency, this balance, includes elements that might seem harmful if viewed in the moment rather than in the generation cycle: Leopold was among the first to criticize the widespread policy of exterminating predator mammals, a practice considered "environmentally friendly" at the time, though no such term existed then. Killing all the wolves so the deer herd will grow is no different from the disastrous agricultural practices that led to the Dust Bowl, an analogy he subtly and elegantly invokes in describing what it means to "think like a mountain":

> I have lived to see state after state extirpate its wolves. I have watched the face of many a newly wolfless mountain . . . In the end the starved bones of the hoped-for deer herd, dead of its own too-much, bleach with the bones of the dead sage, or molder under the high-lined junipers . . . So also with cows. The cowman who cleans his range of wolves does not realize that he is taking over the wolf's job of trimming the herd to fit the change. He has not learned to think like a mountain. Hence we have dustbowls, and rivers washing the future into the sea.[34]

In his lifetime, Leopold might not have been able to predict the scale of anthropogenic climate change and the storm surges that would come to wreak havoc sixty years later, literally washing the future into the sea. But he knew all too well that humans' reluctance to be responsible stewards of their communities — our inability to find the proper equilibrium of cooperative mechanisms in an environment of competing priorities and diminishing natural resources — would have dire consequences.

Leopold was not writing for those unmoved by nature. On the contrary, he saw his audience as people, like him, who loved it. Where the attitudes of the nature-lovers of his day departed from his own was the fact that in all of their diversity — the duck shooter, the fern collector, the kid who "writes bad verse on birch-bark," the "unspecialized motorist whose recreation is mileage," and even Teddy Roosevelt, champion of national parks — each was primarily a hunter. Each sought a trophy of some kind: "To enjoy he must possess, invade, appropriate." Leopold's analysis of the idiosyncratic policies around outdoor recreation supported his belief that the ways people experience nature was primarily aesthetic and consumptive. An ethic of stewardship would encourage a deeper and more meaningful relationship with nature. Recuperating this line of thinking might enable urbanism to move beyond the idea of public space primarily as an amenity, a space for leisure, and allow us to reconnect with the political potential of public space as grounds for performing the active, intentional practice of citizenship. Such a practice is necessarily cooperative rather than individualistic. Through collaborative activities, stewardship fosters a sense of community shared among diverse participants.

Leopold's critique, of course, was directed at the leisure classes. He wanted nature-lovers (the ones who could afford to go on vacation, that is) to become stewards rather than consumers, to feel responsible for the wilderness rather than simply to look at its scenic beauty. The picturesque, however, was not always considered superficial; nor was it thought to be the exclusive preserve of the rich. The prevailing reasoning behind bringing nature into the city in the previous century held the natural world as completely distinct from the man-made world of (urban) culture, a realm apart whose scenery and "wildness" had salutary effects on individuals' physical and spiritual health. This line of thinking, with roots in Transcendental philosophy and European and American Romanticism in the arts,[35] supplied the rationale for one of the most significant investments in urban public space in American history: the creation of Central Park, starting in 1853, more than ten years before Abraham Lincoln signed the first National Park act into law.

According to Central Park's official history, "Advocates of creating the park — primarily wealthy merchants and landowners — admired the public grounds of London and Paris and urged that New York needed a comparable facility to establish its international reputation. A public park, they argued, would offer their own families an attractive setting for carriage rides and provide working-class New Yorkers with a healthy alternative to the saloon."[36] To realize this plan would require major government intervention: eminent domain to expropriate private property[37] and the conscription of some 20,000 workers to move the earth and lay the pathways to construct this heavily engineered version of a pastoral landscape

---

[34] Aldo Leopold, *Sand County Almanac* (Oxford: Oxford University Press, 1949).

[35] Anne Chapman, "Nineteenth Century Trends in American Conservation," National Parks Service. Accessed March 9, 2015. www.nps.gov/nr/travel/massachusetts_conservation/Nineteenth_Century_Trends_in_%20American_Conservation.html.

with its naturalistic scenery, circulation systems, bridges, and fountains The Central Park Commission (1857–1870) became the first official planning agency in New York City and oversaw the layout of uptown Manhattan as well as the management of the park. (The commission was a state agency, and the question of whether the State or the City would manage the park was contentious throughout the nineteenth century, prefiguring later debates). Frederic Law Olmsted and Calvert Vaux's design for the park continue to influence landscape architecture to this day.

As immigration boomed and overcrowding became rampant in the early twentieth century, park usage peaked. And, of course, one of the people with the most lasting influence on New York City was a Parks Commissioner named Robert Moses, appointed by Mayor LaGuardia in 1934 to oversee the newly centralized, citywide parks system.

Decades later, the same financial crises that laid waste to East New York in the 1970s also brought about such massive cutbacks in City services, at a time of rising crime citywide, that Central Park fell into disrepair. The sea change in park management that eventually brought Central Park to its current state as a clean, beautiful, and well-maintained New York City treasure did not originate with local government initiatives. In 1980, the Central Park Conservancy, a private fundraising body comprised of concerned residents who lived near the park, took responsibility for restoring various sites within it. Within a decade, under the impressive leadership of Elizabeth Barlow Rogers, the Conservancy eventually contributed "more than half the public park's budget and exercised substantial influence on decisions about its future."[38]

In some ways, the initiative of private citizens taking matters into their own hands and turning a derelict public space into a flourishing one, while creating lasting coalitions with local government in the process, resembles the story of urban agriculture in East New York. Certainly, the Conservancy and its staff were heeding Leopold's implied directive to practice "the use and care of your land so that it remains fruitful and healthy for future generations." On one hand, such stewardship efforts are praiseworthy. On the other, they herald a problematic precedent. In the years since, including the recent "renaissance era" in city parks that Holly Leicht invoked, an ambitious program of park construction has come to rely on private financing to pay for ongoing maintenance, effectively placing the funding of parks at the mercy of the real estate values and socio-economic demographics of surrounding neighborhoods. This shift is indicative of a much broader trend in the neoliberal era of public-private partnerships, such as the rules that begat Zuccotti Park and other privately owned public spaces, wherein local government merely creates incentives for the private market to provide public goods.

Many urbanists have researched and shown how this shift has corresponded with rising inequality in cities, not only measured in income or wealth but also in terms of the uneven delivery and distribution of public services.[39] The case study of urban agriculture in East New York, while illustrative of public space stewardship, should not be taken as a romantic call for city-dwellers everywhere to roll up their sleeves and provide for themselves what government used to provide. On the contrary, the notion of citymaking urges us to expect more from local authorities yet simultaneously encourages us to recognize the enormous effort and limited resources public servants bring to the management of urban life. To be sure, many public policies have had disastrous effects on the lives of citizens. The complicity of government in the redlining and blockbusting practices in neighborhoods like East New York is only one example. But the same democratic ideal that Plato questioned when he argued for the separation of the *agora* and the *pnyx* is still a work in progress. One person, one vote; it's still a radical idea. And while citizens have come to expect a growing number of services from government (especially in New York City, which provides many services that other city governments in the nation do not) has grown, the notion that those are "public" services has declined in the neoliberal era. Remember, the era of Mayor Koch was also the era of Reagan and Thatcher.

STEWARDSHIP AND THE URBAN COMMONS

Stewardship is not a word one hears every day. A steward is neither a professional identity nor a recognizable hobby. It sounds a little stiff and old fashioned, more readily suggesting the uncle who manages the finances of a Dickensian orphan or a 1950s flight attendant than an exercise of citizenship. Nonetheless, with Aldo Leopold in mind, stewardship strikes me as the best word to encompass a diverse range of practices at the intersection of volunteerism, environmentalism, civic engagement, neighborhood activism, and leisure. The first time I heard it applied in the context of academic urbanism was in the context of research being conducted in the New York City field station of the United States Forest Service (USFS). To be honest, I was surprised to learn that the Forest Service, the division of the United States Department of Agriculture that manages and protects 154 national forests and twenty grasslands across the country, even had an office in the city. I was

---

[36] Elizabeth Blackmar and Roy Rosenzweig, "Central Park," *The Encyclopedia of New York City*, Kenneth T. Jackson, ed. (New Haven: Yale University Press, 1995). Reproduced on centralpark.org/history.

[37] One of the communities that was destroyed through eminent domain was Seneca Village, a vibrant and self-contained community of African-American and Irish immigrant landowners.

[38] Blackmar and Rosenszweig, "Central Park," 1995.

[39] See, for example, Neil Brenner and Nik Theodore, "Cities and the Geographies of 'Actually Existing Neoliberalism,'" in *Antipode* 34, no. 3. (July 2002): 349–79.
See also:
- Neil Smith, *The New Urban Frontier:: Gentrification and the Revanchist City* (London: Routledge, 1996).
- David H. Koehler and Margaret T. Wrightson, "Inequality in the Delivery of Urban Services: A Reconsideration of the Chicago Parks" in *The Journal of Politics* 49, no. 1 (February 1987): 80–99.
- Daphne T. Greenwood and Richard P. F. Holt, "Growth, Inequality and Negative Trickle Down" in *Journal of Economic Issues* 44, no. 2 (June 2010): 403–410.

even more intrigued to learn that the field station's focus isn't limited to plant biology or soil toxicology. For years, social scientists at the USFS have investigated the stewardship of urban natural resources, documenting the who, how, where, and why of individuals and groups that take care of shared, green spaces, from watering street trees to maintaining dog runs. They have published impressive amounts of scholarship, touching on governance, organizational structure, comparisons between different urban contexts, and more. When I visited, they were exploring ways to map their findings on a publicly available interactive tool called the Stewardship Mapping and Assessment Project. "Stew-MAP" is an empirical study showing not only the locations where stewardship groups operate, but exposing their interactions with government agencies, NGOs, funding sources, and each other. The question that continues to guide the project is: "What are the social and spatial interactions among civic groups who conserve, manage, monitor, advocate for, and educate the public about their local environments (including water, land, air, waste, toxics, and energy issues)?"[40]

I visited Erika Svendsen and Lindsay Campbell, two of the researchers behind Stew-MAP, at the field station, tucked away inside the EPA's regional offices in the Foley Square Federal Office Building. This part of Lower Manhattan, with its high concentration of skyscrapers and government buildings is probably one of the least forest-like places in a city often called a concrete jungle. But forestry, I was to learn, is happening everywhere; the trailblazers that Svendsen and Campbell count as mentors and inspiration believed that "The city is the most complex forest, the most complex ecosystem." For Svendsen, who studied forestry before completing a PhD in urban planning, "forestry means land management, land stewardship." She defines land stewardship as a practice that "embodies a set of rights, responsibilities, learned skills, and adaptive science" applied in a particular place, which might just as well be a schoolyard, a beach, or a plaza.[41]

In other parts of the country where the Forest Service manages large swathes of land, the agency's responsibility for land management drives its approach to studying and deploying a wide range of ecosystem services. But in the New York field station, which is structured as an academic faculty, the researchers set the agenda. "As researchers, we try to understand aspects of an economic landscape, a social landscape, a biophysical landscape," Svendsen told me. "With the point being, the landscape is constantly evolving, whether you're harvesting for timber or trying to accommodate recreational uses or planning for new home development."

In an effort to understand local stewardship initiatives, Svendsen, Campbell, and their colleagues sent out a detailed survey to 2,500 groups within the five boroughs of New York. Rigorous analysis of the resulting data showed the diversity of motivations behind stewardship activities, some of which were not primarily environmental: "We found historic preservation groups that started out because what they cared about was building facades, but . . . ended up taking care of the trees on their block too. Maybe they started with youth: 'I want something for the kids to do in the neighborhood, well what can we do? We can clean up the park.'"

Other examples include groups whose primary focus area is senior citizens, animal care, arts and culture, transportation, or civil rights. No matter what the initial impulse, the survey results demonstrated a profound "converging of people coming from different places, and the nestedness of environmental concerns within other concerns."

By using a public mapping platform that shows the zones where each respondent is active, Stew-MAP is able to demonstrate clearly and immediately where there are overlaps and where there are gaps. The database lists who works with whom, how many staff or volunteers in each group, its budget information, the types of sites it works with, and so on. It's a powerful resource, useful to the groups who might want to join forces or refine their turf, to funders and allies who want to support these efforts, and to anyone who wants to learn how to get involved in his or her community. The Forest Service has since expanded Stew-MAP to five other cities around the country.

What distinguishes this type of activity from the potent American tradition of working with the land — the iconic cattle rancher, the residential gardener, or even the enterprising teenage mower of suburban lawns — is that the benefits of the stewardship practice are available to the general public. You don't have to be a member of the group, tending planters on telephone poles, to delight in their beauty any more than you have to be an active urban farmer to be able to purchase and enjoy fresh vegetables grown in your own neighborhood. Yet most of our national folklore surrounding environmental stewardship is about privately owned lands, whether a ranch, a homestead, or a backyard.

In a public conversation about American cultural attitudes toward land use,[42] I once asked Rebecca Solnit — a writer and activist whose work explores the interstices and interdependencies of American culture, climate change, art, place, and community — whether she thought there was something specific within American identity that could explain our societal choices about how much space we take up as individuals and families, and how readily we accept that most land should be private property. In her response, she invoked the legacy of "rugged individualism"[43] reminding the audience that the serial homesteader Pa Ingalls in the *Little House on the Prairie* books wanted to move "when he could see the smoke of someone else's chimney." She talked about the historic desire for autonomous territory, the resistance to allowing other people in your space, and the desire to create a myth of self-sufficiency within private houses that attempts to deny such homes' connection to infrastructural networks like water or energy. But she also talked about the rising tide of latent yearning to feel connected to the place you live

---

[40] United States Forestry Service, "Stewardship Mapping and Assessment Project." Accessed January 20, 2015. www.stewmap.net.

[41] "Who Takes Care of New York?" *Urban Omnibus,* March 4, 2009.

[42] Rebecca Solnit, "5KL: Land," remarks, The Architectural League of New York, September 26, 2014, www.archleague.org/2014/10/5kl-land/.

through stewardship activities. She mentioned community gardening in particular as one of a number of related recent trends in how people spend their free time, indicative of an impulse toward connecting through the collaborative maintenance of shared resources. Many of the diverse stewardship activities that the STEW-Map project has documented and analyzed reflect this same desire.

In Solnit's diagnosis, it is a reaction against various forms of privatization. "Before you can have economic privatization," she said, "you have to have psychological privatization." She explained the latter by referencing Margaret Thatcher, who was famously quoted as saying that there is no so such thing as society. Solnit then paraphrased the implications of this dictum: "I owe you nothing, I need nothing from you, you need nothing from me" before linking this "atomized philosophy" of individualism and privatization to the denial of the connections between public policies and societal outcomes. On the political right, this denial manifests as "sex education is not connected to lowered teen pregnancy, education is not connected to lowered poverty," while on the political left, it manifests as "vaccines are not connected to lowered disease rates." She offered these examples in the context of arguing that "climate denialism says that what seven billion people do has nothing to do with the health of the planet," yet the implications of her philosophical diagnosis bear upon issues at the community scale just as much as the global. It is at the community scale that people are taking the initiative to cooperate. And the research scientists at the Forest Service are not only interested in where and how, but also why. Their ongoing research uses surveys and other social science methodologies to collect data on the demographics, motivations, political leanings, and social networks of people who volunteer to participate in environmental stewardship activities, such as The MillionTreesNYC tree planting events,[44] at which they surveyed volunteers for a white paper entitled "Digging Together: Why People Volunteer to Help Plant One Million Trees in New York."[45]

Their thorough examination of the data, including regression analysis and other statistical methods, supports the observation that environmental stewardship activities are correlated with other forms of civic engagement: "volunteer stewards reported being engaged in all types of civic and political activities, from voting in an election to signing a petition" at rates higher than the general American population.[45]

---

[43] Ironically, *rugged individualism,* while often associated with the nineteenth-century American West, is a phrase that Herbert Hoover coined during the Great Depression, arguing that massive government intervention would erode Americans' cultural disposition to pull themselves up by the bootstraps when times are hard.

[44] MillionTreesNYC, one of the 132 PlaNYC initiatives, is a citywide, public-private program wherein The City of New York plants 70 percent of trees in parks and other public spaces, the other 30 percent coming from private organizations, homeowners, and community organizations. The goal to plant and care for one million new trees across the city's five boroughs over the course of a decade was achieved in 2015, two years earlier than expected.

[45] See also Dana Fisher, Erika Svendsen, and James Connolly *Urban Environmental Stewardship and Civic Engagement: How Planting Trees strengthens the Roots of Democracy* London: Routledge, 2015.

Top to bottom:

A youth volunteer plants one of a million trees for the MillionTreesNYC campaign in Queens.

The Gowanus Canal Conservancy takes care of flower and street tree beds in Brooklyn.

A resident tends to a nascent flower garden in the Vladeck Houses public housing complex in Manhattan's Lower East Side.

As such, the Forest Service's findings demonstrate a "countertrend" to political scientist Robert Putnam's famous argument about declining social capital in the US. His 2000 bestseller, *Bowling Alone: The Collapse and Revival of American Community,* shows how America's strong tradition of civil society, first systematically observed by Alexis de Tocqueville in the 1830s, declined as fewer and fewer Americans turned out to vote, showed up to community meetings, or joined hobby groups or sporting clubs. I believe this countertrend correlates with Solnit's observation about the desire to connect with our surroundings and our communities, to push back against the atomized philosophy that is so evident in our economic paradigm, our climate crisis, and our gradual retreat from civic engagement over the past few decades. I also believe these desires must be understood and incorporated into how we think about the design, planning, delivery, and maintenance of urban public goods of all kinds. If we can achieve that goal, we will have manifested a lasting culture of citymaking based on values of fellowship as well as stewardship.

An emergent culture of citymaking certainly aligns with and draws strength from contemporary leanings toward collective and participatory forms of civic engagement. But the rise of voluntary environmental stewardship cannot be explained exclusively as a salve for social alienation. While many of the activities documented in the Forest Service's research are self-organized, others come about in response to policy decisions. For example, the Bloomberg mayoral administration's MillionTreesNYC campaign provided an opportunity for informal and formal stewardship groups to recruit volunteers to attend official planting days, such as the ones where the data collection described above took place. Moreover, growing awareness about anthropogenic climate change — and the creeping feeling of individual impotence to counteract it — might provide partial motivation for citizens to take care of their environments. The data does not yet prove this contention scientifically, but it stands to reason. Other drivers are more locally specific, such as those that inspired Johanna Willins to start planting in the vacant lots near her home.

Across the spectrum of motivations, these activities exemplify what Marxist historian Peter Linebaugh has called *commoning.* He defines this somewhat awkward new verb as an activity "conducted *through* labor *with* other resources; it does not make a division between 'labor' and 'natural resources.' On the contrary, it is labor which creates something as a resource."[46] As such, *commoning* can be understood as the actions underlying solidarity, a zone of encounter where cooperation and the connection between the individual and her community / environment are what ground voluntary efforts to take care of something shared. Such concepts are crucially important to the project of embedding, in a meaningful and permanent way, social justice and environmental sustainability concerns in urban design, urban planning, and urban policymaking.

Linebaugh mentions Solnit's work explicitly when he offers a working definition of *commoning,* referring to her reportage on the self-organized, cooperative, and caring ways humans behave in the wake of disasters.[47] He is interested in classifying the communitarian ethos behind such activities in order to demonstrate their effectiveness in undermining global capitalism, or at least resisting its relentless privatization and commodification of everything. The commons, for Linebaugh, is antithetical to capital. And the privatization of formerly shared resources that he decries is intricately related to the phenomena of declining social capital or the philosophy of atomized individualism: his commoners don't bowl alone; they dig together.

Yet Linebaugh's analysis extends much further back than the neoliberal turn that began in the 1970s, the shift toward market fundamentalism otherwise described as the Age of Inequality or of economic globalization. He links privatization, as certain scholars have done for centuries, to what happened to traditional English commons in feudal times. Excavating this history helps to explain why urban public space remains such a precious resource for communities, suffused with a symbolic power that is not yet matched by the political will for significant and ongoing public investment in both construction and upkeep.

In medieval England, common land meant privately owned land to which other people had certain rights, such as to graze livestock, draw water, or gather firewood. The commons underwent a gradual but often violent process of privatization, called Enclosure, first authorized in the thirteenth century and intensifying rapidly during the Tudor period in the fifteenth century. In the final push, between 1760 and 1845, acts of Parliament converted seven million acres (one-sixth of England) from common to enclosed land.[48] A new physical and legal geography of fences, hedges, deeds, and titles deprived commoners of their traditional (subsistence level) self-sufficiency. This shift had enormous consequences: a new class of landless peasants forced to work for wages; greater efficiency and larger yields in English farming and textile production; and the enrichment of the aristocracy. Karl Marx described the process in the final section of *Das Kapital, Volume I,* and successive generations of leftist historians have turned to the episode to explain the roots of class struggle in the dawning age of capitalism. Some attribute the emergence of a language of individual rights to anti-Enclosure resistance[49] — wherein peasants rioted, tore down fences, and appealed to kings and barons for the reinstitution of common land — thus paving the way for the Enlightenment and modern democracy. Other historians highlight the grinding misery of subsistence farming prior to the era of Enclosure and the relative improvement of rural living standards and enormous

---

[45] Dana R. Fisher, James J. Connolly, Erika S. Svendsen, and Lindsay K. Campbell, "Digging Together: Why people volunteer to help plant one million trees in New York City," Environmental Stewardship Project at the Center for Society and Environment of the University of Maryland White Paper #1. Accessed April 1, 2015. www.nrs.fs.fed.us/nyc/local-resources/downloads/digging_together_white_paper.pdf.

[46] Peter Linebaugh, *Stop, Thief! The Commons, Enclosures and Resistance* (Oakland: PM Press, 2014), 13.

[47] Rebecca Solnit, *A Paradise Built in Hell: The Extraordinary Communities That Arise in Disaster* (New York: Penguin, 2009).

[48] Gilbert Slater, "Historical Outline of Land Ownership in England," in *The Land, The Report of the Land Enquiry Committee,* (London: Hodder and Stoughton, 1913) as quoted in "A Short History of Enclosure in Britain" by Simon Fairlie in *The Land,* Issue 7, Summer 2009.

innovations in agriculture as more and more property became private. Interpretation of this history is voluminous yet so contentious that non-ideological accounts are hard to come by.

One of the most famous and influential invocations is Garrett Hardin's 1968 essay "The Tragedy of the Commons." Hardin was an ecologist concerned about overpopulation and the depletion of the earth's finite resources. His article uses the example of overgrazing on the traditional English commons as a metaphor to argue that the welfare state will bring about a mass-starvation catastrophe of Malthusian[50] proportions. In Hardin's analysis, the self-interest of each rational herder motivates him to allow more and more animals to graze because the short-term benefit of each additional animal is greater and more immediate than the long-term costs of overgrazing, costs that are shared among all the herders. Therefore, "Ruin is the destination toward which all men rush, each pursuing his own best interest in a society that believes in freedom of the commons."[51]

Like Thomas Malthus a century and a half prior,[52] Hardin failed to account for or chose to ignore some demonstrable historical facts, including that overgrazed commons were relatively few and were often deliberately manufactured by wealthy

---

[49] E.P. Thompson, *Moral Economy of the English Crowd in the Eighteenth Centure* (Oxford: Oxford University Press, 1971).

[50] In 1798, Thomas Malthus predicted that population growth would inevitably overwhelm the Earth's capacity to provide food, a claim that was disproven by the subsequent century of agricultural innovation and decreasing birth rates. Nonetheless, his work continues to be debated, and includes among its adherents certain advocates of aggressive responses to mitigate the causes of climate change as well as proponents of eugenics, family planning, sexual abstinence, and refusing food aid to famine-stricken countries, and several other contrasting, controversial theories.

[51] Garrett Hardin, "The Tragedy of the Commons," *Science* 162, no. 3859 (December 1968): 1243–48.

[52] While Malthus' work was instrumental to introducing population growth as a concern of public policy, it immediately found harsh critics across the political spectrum who objected to its avoidance of questions of technological progress as a mitigating factor as well as its perceived insensitive endorsement of epidemics and other fatal phenomena that limited population growth. Interestingly, none other than Garrett Hardin is among those who have recently sought to reclaim the virtue of Malthus' predictions by selectively pointing out inaccuracies in his critics' characterizations, going so far as to dismiss blithely the intellectual competence of Percy Bysshe Shelley, Karl Marx, and Henry George for daring to question some of Malthus' assumptions in "The Feast of Malthus," *Social Contract Journal* 8, no. 3, (Spring 1998).

[53] Fairlie, "A Short History of Enclosure in Britain," 2009.

[54] Fairlie cites E.P. Thomson's *Customs in Common: Studies in Traditional Popular Culture* (New York: New Press, 1993) and Arthur McEvoy "Towards an Interactive Theory of Nature and Culture" in *Environmental Review,* 11, 1987, among other anthropological and historical critiques of Hardin's conclusions.

[55] Garrett Hardin, "The Tragedy of the 'Unmanaged' Commons," in R.V. Andelson, *Commons Without Tragedy* (London: Shepheard Walwyn, 1991).

[56] Elinor Ostrom, *Governing the Commons: The Evolution of Institutions for Collective Action* (Cambridge, UK: Cambridge University Press, 1990), 5.

landowners seeking to justify Enclosure.[53] Most commons, even in the medieval period but especially in the eighteenth-century examples that Hardin references, were well organized and regulated and only rarely suffered from resource exhaustion.[54] Hardin eventually admitted that he'd gotten it wrong when he publicly conceded, "The title of my 1968 paper should have been 'The Tragedy of the Unmanaged Commons.'"[55] Despite the inaccuracies, Hardin's essay and its titular catchphrase have become neoliberal dogma used to support market-based solutions to everything from greenhouse gas emissions (such as cap and trade) to poverty in the Global South (such as the conditional IMF and World Bank loans of structural adjustment programs). It became "one of the most cited academic papers ever . . . framed the debate about common property for the last 30 years, and has exerted a baleful influence upon international development and environmental policy." So writes Simon Fairlie, a British writer and farmer, who rigorously researched the history of Enclosure specifically to refute Hardin's thesis and the market fundamentalists who continue to use it to claim that private property rights are sacrosanct. Since free markets are "rational," so the thinking goes, then strong property rights and market mechanisms will leverage the profit motive to develop more innovative and efficient solutions to economic and environmental challenges than those devised by governments. Hardin, for his part, thought there were two possible alternatives to the commons dilemma: a private enterprise system with strong property rights or a totalitarian, centralized government that controls natural resource systems. And given the political context of the time — the paper was published at the height of the Cold War, just months after the Soviet-led invasion of Czechoslovakia and the formal announcement of the Brezhnev Doctrine — he and the majority of his readers found the latter unconscionable.

Hardin's tragedy narrative is a version of the prisoner's dilemma game. This economic model has fascinated scholars for decades because of the paradox it presents: "individually rational strategies lead to collectively irrational outcomes,"[56] according to the political economist Elinor Ostrom, who dedicated her career to analyzing institutional arrangements for the long-term, cooperative management of shared natural resources, work that was recognized with a Nobel Prize in 2009. Common ownership structures are as varied as the resources over which they preside, whether it's a pasture, a fishery, or an apartment building, and Ostrom's research explored all sorts of contexts around the world. In the introduction to her famous 1990 book, *Governing the Commons,* she outlines her scholarly agenda in light of three related models: the tragedy of the commons, the prisoner's dilemma, and the logic of collective action.

> What makes these models so interesting and so powerful is that they capture important aspects of many different problems that occur in diverse settings in all parts of the world. What makes these models so dangerous — when they are used metaphorically as the foundation for policy — is that the constraints that are assumed to be fixed for the purpose of analysis are taken on faith as being fixed in empirical settings, unless external authorities change them. The prisoners in the famous dilemma cannot change

the constraints imposed on them by the district attorney; they are in jail. Not all users of natural resources are similarly incapable of changing their constraints. As long as individuals are viewed as prisoners, policy prescriptions will address this metaphor. I would rather address the question of *how to enhance the capabilities of those involved to change the constraining rules* to lead to outcomes other than remorseless tragedies.[57]

The empirical settings Ostrom investigates include irrigation communities in the Philippines and Spain, fisheries in Turkey and Sri Lanka, and meadows and forests in Japan and Switzerland. She looks at the successes as well as the failures. Over many subsequent books and articles, she establishes a series of "design principles" for common pool resource management that include clearly defined boundaries, site-specific rules, sustained participation in decision-making, effective monitoring, sanctions for rule violators, easily accessible conflict resolution mechanisms, and recognition of the community by higher-level authorities and governments. Ostrom's work makes plain that entirely market-based and entirely state-run approaches to resource management are not the only two options. Moreover, the institutional arrangements that can lead to sustainably long-term management practices evolve over time. Inasmuch as her work refutes the inevitability of the tragedy of the commons thesis, both she and Simon Fairlie do credit Hardin for diagnosing the looming destruction of precious natural resources on a global scale, for "steering the environmental debate towards the crucial question of who owns the global resources that are, undeniably, 'a common treasury for all.'"[58]

This more expansive category of natural resources — the atmosphere, the oceans, Earth itself — are supposedly held in common by humankind yet are increasingly bought and sold. The conceptual reclaiming of the idea of the commons aims to resist the seemingly unyielding tendency toward commodification. Meanwhile, over the second half of the twentieth century, the term migrated out of ecology and political philosophy and into everyday life, and gained mainstream prevalence alongside the digital revolution and the environmental crisis. For example, the notion of a digital commons has demanded that information be added to the list of resources to be shared (and modifiable) by all. Creative Commons licenses have complicated traditional views of intellectual property. And the idea of the tragedy of the commons continues to provide an explanation for global climate change cited by activists who don't necessarily equate Hardin's catchphrase with the strain of free market dogma that co-opted it. The reason our addiction to extraction, pollution, emissions, and carbon puts us on a crash course with environmental calamity is not because too many resources are shared. Rather, it is because our capacity to cooperate has weakened at the hands of the modern-day versions of the barons who purposely overstocked common pastures to sow distrust and argue for Enclosure.

---

[57] Ostrom, *Governing the Commons,* 1990, 5.

[58] Fairlie, "A Short History of Enclosure in Britain," 2009, 6–17.

The citymakers chronicled on the pages of *Urban Omnibus* are not necessarily trying to dismantle global capitalism, and they might not even see themselves as climate activists. But for many of them, like the community gardeners of East New York or the volunteers researched by the Forest Service, active stewardship operates as a form of commoning that resonates deeply with the kind of cooperative practices that will be required for more overtly radical changes to patterns of human settlement and consumption. But it's not just about urban farmers and planting trees. There are countless other ways that citizens are volunteering their time to take care of a shared resource, to act as stewards of the landscape they live in. Understanding a little better how such activities operate can deepen our definition of the myriad ways people interact with urban environments, and thus help designers and policymakers to identify the public service gaps citizens are filling, to appreciate the evolving desires of citizens to feel connected to a place through cooperative effort, and to find clues for how we might scale up local examples of commoning in order to confront existential environmental and economic challenges. The stewardship of urban, public space is a good place to start.

This diagram of a typical medieval manor shows the complex interplay between productive, private agricultural lands and lands in which commoners were allowed to graze their livestock. William R. Shepherd, *Historical Atlas* (New York: Henry Holt and Company, 1923)

In an *Urban Omnibus* interview, I once asked the legal scholar Gerald Frug, an expert in local government law, what the word *public* means to him:

> I think of public as referring to the process of a democratically elected official allocating tax money to priorities. These priorities are for the elected officials' constituents, but not exclusively. Parks, for example, are open to more than just the residents of the city that builds and maintains the park. Maintaining a public park isn't free, but the costs are not borne by the park's users, they are borne by the public at large. Such an expenditure used to be widely understood as a good thing for a city to do, along with sanitation, health, education, and countless other things. These days, people don't seem to understand that, and instead are asking "What's in it for me?"[59]

Frug's argument harkens back to the microeconomic concept of a public good, which has two definitional components: non-excludability, meaning the goods in question are not exclusively available to those who paid for them; and non-rivalrous consumption, meaning that one person's use of the good does not detract from other people's ability to use or benefit from it. Public goods are not only places, of course: public education, fireworks displays, national defense, and clean air count, too.[60] And the resource classification scheme employed by economists does not articulate any particular role for governments or markets,[61] though many thinkers have added their views on these roles to some of the most important discussions (both within and outside of academic economics) about public goods.

One classic example is the lighthouse, invoked by such thinkers as John Stuart Mill, one of the most influential exponents of liberal individualism and utilitarianism; Arthur Cecil Pigou, the founder of the field of welfare economics who gave us the concept of externalities; and Paul Samuelson, a Nobel prize winner often referred to as the "father of modern economics."[62] Each uses the lighthouse to illustrate a rationale for government providing a necessary service that the private market could not profit from and therefore would not volunteer to provide.[63] This rationale goes beyond non-excludability and non-rivalrous consumption. It relies on the practical implausibility, presumed by Mill and Pigou, of charging the users of a lighthouse's services — passing ships — for the costs of those services. Thus the lighthouse represents "a proper office of the government" for these theorists. Samuelson takes this idea even further. He argues that even if lighthouse operators *were* able to extract some sort of fee from lighthouse users (which contemporary technology could certainly facilitate), "that fact would not necessarily make it socially optimal for this service to be provided like a private good at a market-determined individual price . . . Because it costs society *zero extra cost* to let one extra ship use the service; hence any ships discouraged from those waters by the requirement to pay a positive price will represent a social economic loss."[64] All of these usages are summarized by another Nobel prize-winning economist, Ronald Coase, in a 1974 paper that delves into the actual institutional and financial arrangements of lighthouse operations in England from the fifteenth through the nineteenth centuries in order to debunk the notion that collecting fees from users was impossible. On the contrary, collecting fees from ship captains was indeed the basis of much of the British lighthouse system in this period. Coase was a leading proponent of the study of real as opposed to hypothetical markets in economic research. His historical findings demonstrate that the lighthouse should not be used as an example of a service that can only be provided by government, but he stops short of arguing for privatization. His agenda is merely to point out the unsuitability of the example to economic writing, not to propose an operational alternative for lighthouses. Nonetheless, his fervent belief is clear: the proper role of government is to adjudicate disputes — especially through well-defined property rights[65] — not to provide services.

---

59 "The Underlying Structure: a Conversation on Law with Gerald Frug," in *Urban Omnibus,* August 27, 2013.

60 Roads, lakes, parks, and broadband are technically "impure" or "partial" public goods because the nonrivalry and nonexcludability depend on the number of users and available capacity at a given time. Philosophically, the concept of public goods is not altogether distinct from the concept of public assets. While the former is more often considered within classical and neoclassical economics, the latter has given rise to a subspecialization of policy planning known as "public asset management," which theoretically "incorporates the management of all things that are of value to a jurisdiction, its mission and purpose, and citizen's expectations" but is most often associated with accounting and business practices in those municipal utilities that charge ratepayers based on usage. See Gregory M. Baird, "Defining Public Asset Management for Municipal Water Utilities" in *Journal of the American Water Works Association,* May 2011.

61 Brett M. Frischmann, *Infrastructure: the Social Value of Shared Resources* (Oxford: Oxford University Press, 2012).

62 See, for example, John Stuart Mill "Principles of Political Economy," *The Collected Works of John Stuart Mill,* edited by V. W. Bladen and John M. Robson (Toronto: University of Toronto Press, 1965) 968; Henry Sidgwick, *The Principles of Political Economy* (London: Macmillan and Company, 1887) 406; A. C. Pigou, *Economics of Welfare* (London: Macmillan and Company, 1932) 183-84; Paul A Samuelson, *Economics: an Introductory Analysis* (New York: McGraw Hill, 1955), 45. All of the above are quoted in R.H. Coase's literature review of the topic, "The Lighthouse in Economics" in *Journal of Law and Economics* 17, no. 2 (October, 1974): 357–376.

63 Frischmann puts this another way: "Nonrival, nonexcludable goods present a well-known supply-side problem: The inability to cheaply identify and exclude nonpaying users (sometimes called "free riders"), coupled, with the high fixed costs of initial production and low marginal costs of reproduction, presents risks for investors, which may lead to undersupply by markets." (loc 738).

64 Samuelson, *Economics,* 1955, 151, as quoted in Coase "The Lighthouse in Economics," 1974, 359.

65 Frischmann (2012) writes that "Coase was skeptical of rote confidence in government institutions, and . . . challenged economists to evaluate critically any claims that relied on the expertise, competence, and benevolence/public-mindedness of government officials." See also Frischmann, (2012) footnote 38, who cites Harold Demsetz, "Toward a Theory of Property Rights" in *The American Economic Review* 57, no. 2, Papers and Proceedings of the Seventy-ninth Annual Meeting of the American Economic Association (May 1967): 347–359.

The lighthouse paper is not the only time Coase took aim at what he perceived as weaknesses in Pigou's thinking. Pigou's seminal explorations of externalities and social costs have made his name "synonymous with the idea of taxing activities that have social costs not reflected in their prices."[66] As examples, a Pigovian tax on gasoline would correct for negative externalities such as pollution and traffic congestion; the growing chorus calling for a carbon tax now includes an informal group of contemporary thought-leaders — including the likes of Michael Bloomberg, Al Gore, Alan Greenspan, and Thomas Friedman — that calls itself the Pigou Club.

Coase found Pigou's work on social costs to misunderstand the reciprocity of harm in situations with negative externalities: taxing the firm or individual whose business negatively affects another does not account for his revenue loss after being so taxed. The case study Coase offers is of a confectionary whose machinery disturbed the medical practice of the doctor who moved next door; creating a nuisance tax on the confectioner might solve the doctor's problem, but would unfairly burden the candymaker.[67] This argument, published in a highly influential 1960 paper "The Problem of Social Costs," has been applied to support the systematic deregulation of industries including transportation, energy, telecommunications, finance, and others. In the United States, this laissez-faire turn switched into high gear in 1971 with the deregulation of the railroad industry, which President Nixon signed into law right after he unilaterally ended the convertibility of the US dollar into gold, thus effectively ending the Bretton Woods monetary system. Both of these moves significantly hastened the advance of economic globalization. Instead of learning to think like a mountain, we doubled down on thinking like a market.

The calculative logic of cost and benefit arguments — the return-on-investment principle of market fundamentalism — does not encompass the full spirit of what the concept of public goods offers to the conversation about public space and city-making. Surveying the range of public space work covered by *Urban Omnibus* has led me to believe that we need to recalibrate our understanding of individual effort and government expenditure (in the long-term) in how we discuss open spaces like parks, plazas, and streets. I am referring to the individual efforts of citizens like Johanna Willins and local government agencies like HPD and GreenThumb. I am also considering subtler instances of individual stewardship and municipal planning that I will discuss in due course, such as cultural programming in a plaza in Corona, Queens, or the construction of birdhouses along the Gowanus Canal in Brooklyn, or even the activities of self-organized hobbyist groups in Floyd Bennett Field. Perhaps, public goods can be conceived as shared assets for which individuals and governments, in coalition, bear long-term responsibility but whose users are not limited to the individuals who participate in their upkeep nor to those who pay taxes to that local authority. Perhaps public goods can be considered as a nexus between the authority of government and the practice of citizenship. In this formulation, the practice of citizenship includes various kinds of engagement, including but not limited to stewardship, as well as the citizen's cultivated awareness of the ways government is (incompletely) empowered to operate on behalf of community interests and priorities.

To my mind, a *public good* is not only non-excludable, non-rivalrous, and difficult to finance through user fees. It shouldn't be defined only in terms of the nature of its consumption and the purchasing power of its users, nor should those terms serve as the means test for government involvement in their provision. Instead, the definition of a *public good* and the political will for public spending should emphasize the benefits, the multiple and overlapping gains a community derives from well-maintained and unalienable assets that are shared among the members of a community but are also accessible to outsiders. The same logic extends beyond public parks and applies to less obvious locales for communitarian enthusiasm. Government investment in public infrastructure, public housing, public art, etc. must reclaim the sense of common benefit that Gerald Frug believes we have lost. Conceiving of an ethic of stewardship can help with this philosophical recovery.

As a component of citizenship, such an ethic can empower residents by engaging them in the active practice of achieving collective goals. As a component of citymaking, it can provide an object lesson that might demystify some of the complexity of urban processes, whether we're talking about maintaining a public park or financing civic infrastructure. If the role of government is conceived as the allocation of resources to achieve public benefits, then greater public understanding about the systems and processes involved in identifying and realizing those benefits is an urgent priority.

Yet taxes, Frug argues, have come to be seen as a fee-for-service instead of a contribution to a commonwealth. The outsourcing of park management to private conservancies largely financed by nearby residents with disposable income is part of the same trend. If we are to include an ethic of stewardship as a constituent element of our working definition of citymaking, it must be an expansive ethic that is not just about the activities of lay residents but also the ways that public policy-makers fund maintenance and operations in addition to capital investments. In New York City as in many local governments, State law prohibits any mixture whatsoever of the capital budget (funded by debt, municipal bonds, and State and federal grants) and the expense budget (funded by taxes and other revenues). This legal requirement is no excuse for investing huge amounts of capital dollars in public parks without planning for how their upkeep will be financed. Relying on private fundraising won't close the gap, at least not in a way that is evenly distributed across the city. Nor will the increasingly creative ways new parks have leveraged real estate economics. Take, for example, one of the most celebrated new public spaces in New York, the High Line.

---

[66] Dylan Matthews, "Ronald Coase is Dead. Here are Five of his Papers You Need to Read," *Washington Post*, September 3, 2013. Accessed March 11, 2015. www.washingtonpost.com/blogs/wonkblog/wp/2013/09/03 ronald-coase-is-dead-here-are-five-of-his-papers-you-need-to-read/.

[67] The actual lawsuit, from 1879, is a landmark case in nuisance law, establishing the precedent that the fact the plaintiff "came to the nuisance" (i.e., moved to a house where the nuisance had been occurring without harming anyone or incurring complaints for twenty years) is not a viable defense.

The summer of 2009 felt a lot different in New York City than the previous one. The recession was in full force. Many recently constructed high-rise condominium buildings could not find buyers; ambitious plans were abandoned. But one of the most anticipated additions to the public realm, more than ten years in the making, was unveiled: the first section of the High Line, from Gansevoort Street to West 20th Street in Manhattan's Chelsea neighborhood. The success of this project — a disused freight rail line transformed into a beautifully designed and landscaped linear park — has prompted efforts in a variety of cities to follow suit. Philadelphia's Reading Viaduct, Chicago's Bloomingdale Trail, and the West Toronto Railpath are just a few of the proposals to repurpose infrastructural relics into public greenways. Within New York City, projects like the QueensWay, a 3.5-mile stretch of abandoned railway in Central Queens, and the Lowline, an underground trolley terminal in the Lower East Side of Manhattan, also seek to replicate the High Line's almost magical combination of effective grass roots organizing, savvy real estate economics, and high-quality design. All of these projects adopt the High Line's appealing rhetoric of historic preservation: turning a reminder of a city's industrial past into a pedestrian pathway to its green future. But the comparisons only go so far. None of these projects run through as desirable or expensive a neighborhood as Chelsea. Neither do they enjoy celebrity neighbors as allies, nor benefit from as favorable an economic and political climate as mid-2000s, pre-recession New York.

As we have seen, former Mayor Bloomberg presided over an impressive and significant investment in public space, committing an unprecedented five billion dollars to capital investment in parks over twelve years[69] and leveraging the frenzied pace of real estate development (in his first two terms) to subsidize new parks. Yet, somehow, the new open spaces built in the past decade — free and accessible to all — have come to symbolize, for some, just the opposite: elitism and the inequality of opportunity. Bloomberg's equally notable investment in cultural institutions, such as major capital projects at the Museum of Modern Art, Lincoln Center, and the new Culture Shed, came to be seen as strategic plays to attract talent in a global marketplace for highly skilled professionals or to maintain the tourist economy rather than attempts to distribute the benefits of New York City's rich traditions of cultural production to new local audiences. Mayor Bill de Blasio, Bloomberg's successor, staked his campaign on a vision of a more equitable New York, one in which his City Hall would demand many more concessions from real estate developers, and the glitzy growth that characterized his predecessor's tenure would give way to more affordable housing and early education.

Some of this shift in perception has to do with the fact that many of the new, grand parks delivered in the last decade, such as Brooklyn Bridge Park as well as the High Line, are managed and financed through public-private partnerships and big-money transactions reliant on high-end residential development.[70] New parks aren't the only element of public space policy that seems out of step with current political priorities. The Bloomberg era strategy for improving New York's streetscape — the building of bike lanes and the creation of pedestrian plazas out of vehicular lanes — has begun to take a backseat to the de Blasio administration's plans to eliminate traffic fatalities. A decade of innovative strategies seem to have made recent public space projects seem somehow less public and less palatable.

The capital and operating costs of these transformations are significant, the financing complex, and the timelines slow. The Lowline project is estimated to cost $50 million and its best hope for success makes it seem a whole lot more like an underground shopping center than a public park.[71] While the QueensWay project continues to estimate costs and consider implementation strategies, several counterproposals argue that reactivating the rail line to add much-needed public transit capacity would create more public benefits for this part of Queens than a park.[72]

As park planning projects in other cities come up against financial challenges as well as a changed political landscape in which access to jobs and housing are considered more urgent than access to recreational space, they might look to another example from New York City. Corona Plaza offers a model of creating public space that shares the High Line's ethos of bottom-up transformation, but just might be more feasible and less vulnerable to the cycles of the real estate market and shifting political priorities.

Corona Plaza used to be a triangular parking lot wedged between the shops of Roosevelt Avenue and the elevated tracks of the 7 train, in a dense and bustling Queens neighborhood known for its ethnic diversity. What began as a few local businesses putting up Christmas lights each year eventually grew into a broad coalition of community groups, cultural institutions, and City agencies dedicated to creating a vibrant, open space that accommodates both informal gatherings and planned festivals of food and dance celebrating the South American roots of many local residents. The City Department of Transportation (DOT) pedestrianized an access road and provided planters and seating, part of a low-cost, kit-of-parts strategy for pop-up open spaces that the DOT has deployed throughout New York. But what sets this plaza apart from others is the continued involvement of local stakeholders and cultural groups, fostered by the nearby Queens Museum, that keep the transformation process active and ongoing.

---

[68] See also Cassim Shepard, "From Chelsea to Corona," *Huffington Post,* August 28, 2014. www.huffingtonpost.com/cassim-shepard/from-chelsea-to-corona-pu_b_5731700.html

[69] Office of the Mayor "Manhattan Progress," December 13, 2013. Accessed March 12, 2015. www1.nyc.gov/office-of-the-mayor/news/419-13/manhattan-progress/#/0

[70] The High Line made innovative use of a city planning mechanism called the Transfer of Development Rights (TDR), in which owners of lots that are not built to the maximum area as allowed by the zoning code are allowed to transfer this excess area of developable space to a different lot, even lots that were already built to their maximum legal floor to area ratio (FAR). TDR around the High Line allowed for the property owners not to feel they were giving away lucrative property and enabled the development of some larger scale and incredibly valuable real estate adjacent to the new park.

[71] Henry Melcher, "Bottom-up Urbanism," *The Architects' Newspaper,* July 29, 2014.

[72] Michael Gannon, "Assemblymen Call for New Rail Service," *Queens Chronicle,* February 16, 2012.

Reporting on Corona Plaza's evolution for *Urban Omnibus,* Caitlin Blanchfield explains that "The ongoing transformation of this public space reflects the evolving nature of community needs, a dynamic that the Queens Museum aims to elucidate and communicate through workshops planned for this spring assessing how various players — from commuter, to stroller, to demonstrator — will use the space." In another powerful example of prolonged stewardship, these engagement efforts consistently evaluate community needs as well as the plaza's ability to respond to them in incremental steps. Performances, demonstrations, informal gatherings, and a variety of art interventions make this space feel truly public.

The kinds of activities possible in Corona Plaza differ greatly from what's possible on the High Line. Neither is a park in a traditional sense: no ball fields, no meadows. Yet both turned hard infrastructure into open space, and both required sustained community effort and creative partnership with local government. As cities continue to grow, we'll need more of both models. But the low-cost, flexible strategies evident in Corona Plaza just might be more replicable. Plenty of cities have industrial relics, elevated or underground, that could be repurposed with tens of millions of dollars, both public and private. Every single city on the planet has underperforming, street-level spaces that can be activated with much less.

And what about streets themselves? Parks like Central Park, community gardens like those of East New York, plazas like Corona Plaza are all a certain kind of public space: exterior open spaces anyone can walk through, eat lunch in, possibly attend an organized event. But such places are certainly not the only examples of public space.[73] In fact, the kind of gatherings and activities possible in a mixed-use street context like Corona Plaza distinguish it from nearby Flushing Meadows Corona Park — a large and well-used formal open space originally constructed as fairgrounds for the Worlds Fair of 1939 — in productive and illuminating ways. Unlike the plaza, which straddles well-worn pathways of transit and commerce and is thus a public space that extends the social possibilities of street life, "the park is a destination, not a node of informal congregation; a place for planned events, not chance encounters . . . On a cold winter day, the park isn't bustling with the spontaneous, if fleeting, encounters apparent in the streetscape." The plaza, however, is vibrantly alive.

As a term, *public space* suffers from the elasticity of its abstraction and the imprecision of its application. We know it when we see it — or think we do — but the shades of what we label "public" resist a firm correspondence between this classification of space and any particular built form. The street, the plaza, the park;

---

[73] Many urbanists argue that New York City's streets are its greatest public space. And, like parks, streets enjoyed a transformational amount of attention in the past few years, with the introduction of new modes of transit like bike lanes and dedicated bus lanes and the restriction of vehicular traffic in targeted areas, including Times Square. The media noted the irony that one of New York's most notorious road builders, Robert Moses, was at one point a Parks Commissioner, while the public official who oversaw the creation of new pedestrianized open space in congested Manhattan, Janette Sadik-Khan, was the Commissioner of the DOT, responsible for the city's streets.

Top: Corona Plaza is a a vibrant, open space for both informal gatherings and planned festivals of food and dance celebrating the ethnic diversity of its surrounding Queens neighborhoods.

Above: The High Line is a former industrial railway running from Manhattan's West Village to 34th Street transformed into a landscaped linear park.

these are easy. The market, the temple, the bus; these are a little more tricky. The contemporary spaces we hold in common with our fellow citizens are not innocent of questions such as who pays for them, who benefits, who is excluded, who determines their use. The human's capacity to be a part of a crowd elevates the categorical at the expense of the individual. Yet, when Giambattista Nolli made his famous map of Rome in 1748, distilling all urban space into the black and white of public and private, the distinction was not, as many think, between open-to-the-sky or closed-in-by-ceiling, volumes versus voids, figure and ground. Rather, the defining difference was between what a commoner could walk *through* and what he could not. Thus, the interior space of the duomo becomes as public as the street; the Pantheon is rendered a piazza. The possibility of public assembly takes the same forms as the capacity for private reflection in the company of strangers.

More recently, the encroachment of private capital into the commons — such as with the park conservancies or the High Line — further complicates any simple binary. The political potential of making the multitudes visible brooks neither dissent nor nuance. Mass protest has a way of assigning a particular meaning to where it takes place. Therefore, Tlatelolco, Tiananmen, and Tahrir become metonyms for massacres or rebellions. The symbolism of the horde is broadcast as unitary and monolithic. The quantity of people gathered serves to amplify the single voice. Public space, fetishized by urbanists and revolutionaries alike, begins to lose its most powerful attribute: the collective container for being alone together, or for doing different things in the same space, or for working cooperatively with strangers toward a common goal.

WORK AS RECREATION:
NOTES FROM GOWANUS AND FLOYD BENNETT FIELD

For the first year of *Urban Omnibus,* my colleagues and I worked from a small room in a former factory, now occupied by a mix of artists, artisans, and nonprofits[75] on the Gowanus Canal, which snakes northward almost two miles from the New York Harbor in Red Hook and Sunset Park toward the heart of Downtown Brooklyn. To our team, the Gowanus Canal and the eponymous neighborhood surrounding it became something of a microcosm of the issues and the kind of work we wanted to highlight on *Urban Omnibus:* environmental remediation, the adaptive reuse of outmoded buildings and derelict infrastructure, real estate development, community-initiated design proposals, artists' responses to urban challenges. We covered various projects related to the canal, from visual art projects to the public debate about whether to designate the canal as a Superfund site, which gives the federal government the responsibility for an extremely complicated cleanup of one of the most polluted bodies of water in the United States.[76]

The canal was once a brackish, tidal creek that nurtured an especially fertile crop of oysters. After it was canalized in 1869 (the same year that the Suez Canal opened, incidentally), it quickly became a major industrial thoroughfare, lined with mills, tanneries, and plants for manufactured gas and chemicals. At its peak after World War I, it trafficked six million tons of cargo annually. The Environmental

Protection Agency (which designated Superfund status in 2010) credits decades of "discharges, storm water runoff, sewer outflows and industrial pollutants" for its extremely high levels of "PCBs, coal tar wastes, heavy metals and volatile organics."[77] Despite its putrid toxicity, the canal has attracted intrepid kayakers to navigate it as well as developers eager to capitalize on its prime location between desirable Brooklyn neighborhoods and its glut of underutilized industrial building stock. And while development paused for a couple years during the recession, colorful renderings continued to circulate that imagined a transformed Gowanus — lined with new, loft-inspired apartment buildings — as a charming waterway-cum-public-space complete with jogging and cycling trails along its banks. Such a vision has yet to come to pass, despite numerous new residential developments. Nonetheless, the canal offers a small, unusual, and instructive example of public space steward-ship as an act of citymaking.

In November of 2008, The Architectural League helped to facilitate a brief, intensive exercise in public interest design led by Bryan Bell, a North Carolina architect at the forefront of architecture as community service.[78] The event, called "Make a Difference in Two Days," invited teams to create a small-scale project in the public interest and build it from found materials. Projects included a plywood corral for shopping carts at a Jersey City parking lot, a set of plastic bag dispensers to help curb dogs, and a series of birdhouses on either side of the Gowanus Canal.[79]

I live a couple blocks from the canal, and in subsequent months and years, I would often wander by the birdhouses on walks through the neighborhood. After *Urban Omnibus* documented the event and released our coverage as a weekly feature in 2009, I didn't give the birdhouses much thought beyond feeling pleased that they were still standing. But for Brian Davis, a young landscape architect beginning

---

[74] See also Taiye Selasi and Cassim Shepard, "The Gwangju River Reading Room" in *Gwangju Folly II*, edited by David Adjaye, Rem Koolhaas, and Do Ho Suh (Berlin: Hatje Cantz, 2015).

[75] The Old American Can Factory is an historic 130,000-square-foot, six-building complex built between 1865 and 1901. Today it is operated by XO Projects Inc., whose principal, Nathan Elbogen curates a wide range of tenants that include visual and performing artists as well as local manufacturing businesses.

[76] Superfund is the name given to a program established by the Environmental Protection Agency in 1980 to address hazardous toxic waste sites. The program allows the EPA, a federal agency, to clean up such sites and to compel responsible parties to perform cleanups or reimburse the government for EPA-lead cleanups.

[77] United States Environmental Protection Agency, "EPA Superfund Program: Gowanus Canal, Brooklyn, NY." Accessed April 6, 2015. www.epa.gov/region2/superfund/npl/gowanus/ and since archived at cumulis.epa.gov/supercpad/cursites/csitinfo.cfm?id=0206222.

[78] See, among others, Bryan Bell and Katie Wakeford, eds., *Expanding Architecture, Design as Activism* (New York: Metropolis Books, 2009) and Bryan Bell, ed., *Good Deeds Good Design, Community Service through Architecture* (New York: Princeton Architectural Press, 2003).

[79] "Make a Difference in Two Days," *Urban Omnibus,* April 8, 2009.

his career at the time, these birdhouses represented a powerful example of what he considers an important and under-recognized trend in what people do in public space. So he set out to understand exactly how this mode of active engagement in public space was actually operating. He published his findings in a series of detailed reports on his own blog and in an original article for *Urban Omnibus*.[80]

Davis learned that the four young designers responsible for the birdhouses[81] decided to continue building these birdhouses in the months following the "Make a Difference in Two Days" event. The group of friends would spend weekends "cutting up pieces of scrap wood, painting them and making them into little yellow birdhouses." In both aesthetic and pragmatic terms, Davis praises the birdhouses' design: "made of scraps from local cabinet makers and fastened atop an old reject piece of scaffolding which is cast in a five-gallon bucket, partially filled with concrete. The cost per birdhouse is a couple of dollars, and each house is a mobile little unit which can be inserted into almost any crevice along the Gowanus . . . the bucket-footing allow[s] for the houses to migrate season to season, slowly finding their way to the micro-habitats along the Canal that best suited bird species." What seems to impress Davis the most, however, is the way these inexpensive insertions into the landscape marry ecosystem awareness and leisure: "Bird species can be an indicator of ecosystem biodiversity in urban areas, and indicators of environmental health in a neighborhood. And people like birds. It's fun to see them hunt and fly and build; many have different colors and behaviors, and many of them migrate, marking the changing of seasons and passage of time."

The way these modest birdhouses evince Davis' larger observation about leisure is not exclusively ecological, however; it is also an incentive to broaden community participation. The Gowanus Canal Conservancy, a community-based nonprofit whose mission is to serve as the environmental steward for the canal's watershed, soon began to take note of the birdhouses. In addition to instigating design proposals for park space and stormwater control studies, one of the conservancy's primary activities is to coordinate volunteers to weed and collect trash. When the organization approached and started working with the team behind birdhouses, they were able to help source materials and workspace for construction while also to use "their birdhouse initiative as an organizing mechanism for the community volunteer days. Suddenly, volunteers had a wider variety of activities to engage in — bolting, painting, digging, hammering, and pouring concrete — and volunteer days ended not only with a cleaned patch of ground along the Canal, but also with the construction of something interesting."

---

[80] See Brian Davis (writing as FASLANYC) "Canal Nest Colony" on his personal blog (http://faslanyc.blogspot.de/search/label/canal%20nest%20colony) and "Canal Nest Colony," *Urban Omnibus,* September 15, 2010.

[81] The team, which called itself "Team NC State" during the Make a Difference in Two Days event, originally consisted of Hans Hesselein, David Moses, Andrew Nicolas, and Thomas Ryan.

Top: Installing a birdhouse along the Gowanus Canal in Brooklyn.

Above and following page: Hobbyists in Floyd Bennett Field showcase the model airplanes they regularly fly in the former airstrip that is now part of Gateway National Recreation Area, managed by the National Park Service.

The number of volunteers started to grow, and by the middle of the winter of 2009, the project, by now rebranded as Canal Nest Colony, had produced 25 birdhouses. Other institutions also joined the effort, including the Audubon Society, which advised on optimizing birdhouse design for particular species, the MillionTreesNYC initiative, a City government program, and Fiskars, a multinational supplier of gardening tools. Canal Nest Colony became a way to organize volunteers not only to build birdhouses but also to create plantings, a mini-park, and a composting operation at very little cost.

Davis interprets this project as a testament to how the Gowanus Canal "can operate simultaneously as an open sewer, ecological laboratory, and hipster playpen" and, more generally, "to the enduring ability of post-industrial wastelands to captivate the contemporary urban imagination, at least of those fortunate enough to have a bit of leisure time." A place to spend leisure time, of course, is at the root of most rationales for public space, even if the rhetorics of health, aesthetics, or civics continue to loom largest in the discourse. Yet the legacy of the grand parks designed by the likes of Frederic Law Olmsted continues to assume a primarily passive form of leisure: picnics and strolls, informal athletics. According to Davis, "while the consumption of public spaces and experiences — spectacle — is still the dominant mode of recreation, the efforts along the Gowanus Canal offer evidence that there is a desire for other types of recreation, ones that involve work, especially working with your hands." In contrast to the assumptions of mainstream landscape design, he characterizes these types of activities as "the ability to work on a small scale in ways that regular people can understand and contribute to" and asserts that they represent "a fertile field in the profession of landscape/architecture. It's a demystification of the professions that shape cities, in turn encouraging democratic compliance, not merely tacit approval, among both professionals and the public."[82]

As such, the kinds of activities Davis is reporting fit into a broad category that has been gaining ground within the architectural, urban, and landscape design fields for some time, that of "tactical urbanism," or small-scale, low-cost, often temporary interventions with tangible, salutary, and often immediate impacts on the urban environment. While he distinguishes between this approach and that of traditional design practice, many design firms have been working in this mode for a generation or more.[83] Indeed, the integration of ecological, infrastructural, and social considerations in landscape and urban design emerges in parallel to a growing subset of designers whose work overtly incorporates the need for improvisational, provisional, participatory, and inexpensive strategies. Just as with the community gardens of East New York or the cultural programming at Corona Plaza, the incremental and ad-hoc activities that produced Canal Nest Colony can never scale up to produce a large park. Nonetheless, what this example offers is not the ability of such efforts to replace traditional modes of delivering quality public space. Instead, it illustrates the growing appeal of proactive stewardship as a leisure activity. The ethos of do-it-yourself isn't just for home furnishings. Applying that desire to work with your hands — to create something new and beautiful and useful — to exterior, shared spaces just might help us arrive more completely at an ethos of do-it-together. Understanding shifts in how citizens want to engage with shared spaces in their neighborhoods should complement and inform, not replace, the constant progression of how professionals design the public realm.

A very different case, from the other end of Brooklyn, demonstrates that the shift toward work-as-leisure is not limited to contexts of environmental remediation, as in Gowanus, or social reinvestment in a distressed neighborhood like East New York. Floyd Bennett Field is a disused airport on Brooklyn's southeastern edge that has been administered by the national park service since 1972. In another article for *Urban Omnibus*, Davis surveys the range of activities taking place at this former military facility and posits their significance to the future of city park use.[84]

His analysis refers to both Olmsted and Moses, associating the former with the model of park as "pleasure ground" and the latter with the model of park as "recreational facility."[85] Floyd Bennett Field is neither, with its overgrown runways and seemingly abandoned hangars. Yet it does accommodate, in its own way, the kinds of recreation inherent to both models. Like the historical pleasure ground, "It is

---

82 Brian Davis, "Tactics V. Strategies: What would Juvenile Do?" on his personal blog, November 15, 2009 (faslanyc.blogspot.de/2009/11/tactics-v-strategies-what-would.html).

83 In 2012, *Spontaneous Interventions,* the exhibition of the American Pavilion at the Venice Biennale of Architecture organized by the Institute for Urban Design, was dedicated to cataloguing recent examples of tactical urbanism. See also: www.spontaneousinterventions.org/interventions.

84 Brian Davis, "Floyd Bennett Field: Recreation in the Wasteland," *Urban Omnibus,* May 26, 2010.

85 Davis owes this categorization scheme to an influential book by the sociologist Galen Cranz, *The Politics of Park Design: A History of Urban Parks in America* (Cambridge, Mass.: MIT Press, 1982). In the book, Cranz articulates these as two of four models, which she analyzes more or less chronologically: the pleasure ground, the reform park, the recreational facility, and finally, the open-space system.

expansive and primarily open green space," even though it looks more dystopian than traditionally scenic. Like the recreation facility, it "provides areas for organized sports and parking." You can "enjoy the activities envisioned by Olmsted and Moses — strolling, cycling, and picnicking as well as organized sports." But you can also fly radio-controlled model aircraft, construct exterior furniture (using power tools!) for the city's largest community garden, learn how to drive a car, camp over-night, even restore historic airplanes. Hangar B, for example, is stocked with "drill presses, metal routers and welding stations" accessible to volunteers with the Historic Aircraft Recreation Project. Davis sums up what distinguishes it from other parks:

> While including traditional forms of active and passive recreation, the Field also allows for the pursuit of recreational work through the provision of facilities including storage, power, water, materials, equipment, and programmable space. *Recreation, instead of relying exclusively on the consumption of images and experiences in a commoditized environment, becomes process:* the cultivation of a garden plot, the construction of new birdhouses or fencing for a garden, or the restoration of an historic airplane. This layering of work-recreation and traditional forms of recreation is a diversification in the possible, accepted programmatic activities in parks. And it offers a tantalizing glimpse at how our future parks might better serve the urban public. (emphasis added)

This mode of recreation — active, tactile, creative, gradual — is, of course, less overtly custodial than other kinds of stewardship discussed in this chapter. None-theless, these activities testify to an obvious yet elusive input in spatial design. Put simply: use matters. Form can't simply follow function, for the sequence is not that straightforward. Form must respond to shifting patterns of behavior, over time. Not only must activity and use inform the design of environments of all kinds, it must also influence how we conceptualize the social benefits we assume from public goods. Just as we should reorient our understanding of public goods, philosophically, toward demand-side questions, we should also learn to think about spaces, architec-turally, as modified by the people who use or inhabit them.

This reframing of use and time in the discussion of public space has policy implications as well; it's not just about philosophies of citizenship and strategies of park design. From a policy standpoint, we have to think about maintenance as a dynamic and ongoing design challenge, not an afterthought for future budget cycles to deal with long after capital funds for design and construction have been allocated. Even in the rare but increasing instances of citizens deciding themselves how to spend public dollars — in certain New York City Council districts, constituents can vote on how to spend a portion of their representative's discretionary budget — the funds earmarked for this experiment in direct democracy are limited to capital-eligible projects.[86] The ways in which governments account for capital and expense budgets creates a structural barrier to integrating plans for long-term public investments and annual operational expenses. In addition to integrating an ethic of stewardship into public space discourse, I am arguing for a renewed emphasis on maintenance in the conversations about public space and its provision. How a public good like a park will be maintained and how that maintenance will be financed should be part of the design brief. Yet in cases where it is, local governments too often resort to addressing this challenge by leaving it up to the market. While public-private partnerships can introduce a measure of efficiency to complex and expensive urban projects, they also perpetuate the uneven delivery of public goods by relying on valuable real estate (or the voluntary contributions of people with disposable income) to subsidize gaps in the operating budget. An expansive concept of stewardship can help bring equity to the fore, insisting on long-term even-handedness in the provision and upkeep of public goods.

PARK AS PROCESS AND THE MARKET FOR MAINTENANCE

The contemporary examples of public space cited thus far, with the exception of the High Line, have not been the products of a traditional design process. The citizens who co-create community gardens, build birdhouses, or program a pedestrianized plaza are not necessarily designers though they certainly are, to my mind, citymakers. Again, this book does not seek to undermine the authority of professional design services in the creation and adaptation of the urban environment. On the contrary, one of my primary goals is to re-affirm and strengthen the power and promise of design by identifying how designers have begun — and must continue — to forge new kinds of coalitions with other actors, including individual citizens, government agencies, and civil society organizations. The emergence, proliferation, and potential benefits of these new kinds of coalitions are my primary takeaway from close observation of urban practice in New York between 2008 and 2015. One of these benefits may be a deeper regard for the role of time within what we expect from traditional design practice, the self-evident yet under-considered notion that designed environments change. Some deteriorate. Others literally grow. Managing both of these transformation processes — through environmental stewardship, building conservation, operational financing, active programming, and community engagement — is as essential to successful citymaking as inspired design.

   "One of the amazing things about landscape architecture," according to landscape architect Michael Van Valkenburgh, "is that you've made something that's alive. It's the essence of what a landscape is about."[87] He was referring to Brooklyn Bridge Park, designed by the firm he founded and leads, Michael Van Valkenburgh Associates (MVVA), a nationally recognized leader in the landscape architecture of urban parks. The 85-acre site stretches 1.3 miles along the East River waterfront, from the Brooklyn Bridge to Atlantic Avenue. When I spoke with him, construction was underway but the park was far from complete. It was a cold day in early December and the hum of hydraulic excavators and tractors evoked the site's industrial past more than its recreational future. Nonetheless, with the undulating topography of

---

[86] John Surico, "The Right to Budget," *Urban Omnibus*, April 18, 2015.

[87] "Park as Process: Brooklyn Bridge Park," *Urban Omnibus*, September 29, 2010.

Pier 1 in place and almost ready to open to the public, Van Valkenburgh conjured an image of just how much use he expected the park to see in its first summer. The park was completed in stages, and as each new pier opened to the public, its popularity has borne out Van Valkenburgh's prediction that Brooklyn Bridge Park will give "Brooklyners a park that they desperately need."

Like any new urban park, particularly in a place like New York, where the supply of available land is so constricted, this park is about more than open space. It's about infrastructure, industry, environment, government and (of course) real estate. According to Gullivar Shepard, an architect at MVVA who worked on the project from its initial planning stages through design and construction, the site is "a bundle of amazing complexity: years and years of leftover rights-of-way, infrastructure claims on the site, pieces of actual working infrastructure that have to be maintained. So we can't just change the program of the land to accommodate park users, [the park] has to . . . hold up the functioning of the city."[88] In *The New York Times,* critic Nicolai Ourousoff's review appeared a couple weeks after the first section of the park opened to the public in 2010: "Much as Central Park embodied Frederick Law Olmsted's vision of American democracy on the eve of the Civil War, Brooklyn

Brooklyn Bridge Park, designed by Michael Van Valkenburgh Associates and opened in phases starting in 2010, occupies an 85-acre site that stretches over 1.3 miles of the East River waterfront, from the Brooklyn Bridge to Atlantic Avenue. Pictured is a site diagram produced during the design process that describes the scale of the park to come.

Bridge Park . . . is an attempt to come to terms with the best and worst of our era: on the one hand, concern for the environment and an appreciation for the beauty of urban life and infrastructure; on the other, the relentless encroachment of private interests on the public realm."[89]

As for the former — the mutual reinforcing of environmentalism and urbanism — the design of Brooklyn Bridge Park demonstrates what writer Andrew Blum has described as a "a concern for ecological processes that is not merely illustrative, treating nature as if it were a museum exhibit, but rather that is necessarily rooted in a holistic understanding of site ecology." For Blum, this approach "suggest[s] that nature could be legible as an integrated part of urban experience — a perspective crucial to reimagining cities as the keystone of a more sustainable way of life."[90] Sustainability, it seems, encompasses more than materials or environmental performance, it becomes a way to reorient the public perception of the city and how it works. That said, plenty in this park takes a literal understanding of sustainability to a new level: the park benches are made from wood salvaged from demolished shipping terminal buildings on the site; the "Granite Prospect" is made of stones recycled from the Roosevelt Island Bridge; stormwater-based micro-environments support diverse ecosystems. And it's also notably resilient to devastating weather. As compared with the hard edges and bulkheads that characterize other waterfront landscapes around the city, Brooklyn Bridge Park, with its salt marsh shoreline operating as wave attenuators, held up remarkably well to the damage wrought by Hurricane Irene and Superstorm Sandy. According to Eric Rothstein, a hydrologist who worked on the design and water systems planning for the park, there are many additional reasons to soften this formerly hard edge with a salt marsh: "it's about stewardship; it's filtering the water; it attracts wading birds; it's an educational moment in a signature park in New York City; it's beautiful. There are so many reasons to soften edges and put in habitat that we don't need to exaggerate them to justify the practice."[91]

As for the latter — the increasing reliance on private monies to provide public goods — the planning of Brooklyn Bridge Park explicitly acknowledges that the maintenance costs over time will far outweigh the construction costs. The proposed solution — up to 20 percent of the park's land can be developed to generate revenue — led to fierce debate and a court case that argued a violation of the Public Trust Doctrine.[92] In 2002, four years after the masterplanning process began, Mayor Bloomberg and Governor Pataki signed an agreement to provide the land and to create the Brooklyn Bridge Park Development Corporation (BBPDC) as a subsidiary of

---

[88] Gullivar Shepard, author interview, December 12, 2009.

[89] Nicolai Ouroussoff, "The Greening of the Waterfront," *The New York Times,* April 1, 2010.

[90] Andrew Blum, "Metaphor Remediation: A New Ecology for the City," *Places,* September 2009. Accessed April 21, 2015. (www.placesjournal.org/article/metaphor-remediation-a-new-ecology-for-the-city/).

[91] "Mitigate, Design, Restore: A Conversation on Hydrology and Habitat," *Urban Omnibus* January 21, 2015.

Empire State Development Corporation (ESDC). As the park's developer (and MVVA's client) the BBPDC would also develop commercial properties to fund maintenance and operational needs. Twelve days before Pier 1 opened, the nature of this city-state partnership changed dramatically. Governor Paterson relinquished the State's stake in the project, effectively handing control of the process to the City. The announcement of the new deal re-affirmed the need for the park to be financially self-sustaining and required it to look for alternative revenue sources beyond the site's residential developments.

The design for Brooklyn Bridge Park softens the edge between land and water; instead of the hard bulkhead found in many waterfront parks, the park benefits from a graduated shoreline, wave attenuators, boat ramps and salt marshes.

Parks are designed to evolve, to change and grow over time. In this case, that evolution will be marked by the growth of trees and plants, by the increase in New Yorkers' awareness of their relationship to the water and our city's industrial past, and, perhaps, by the shifting demands of the market. Most commentators, including Blum and Ourousoff, invoke Frederic Law Olmsted and Central Park when they talk about Brooklyn Bridge Park. We've had a century and a half to watch that park evolve and respond to the changing circumstances of the city that has alternately celebrated and neglected it. Yet when it comes to new parks, public discourse still tends to focus on opening day, the moment a ribbon is cut and a new public space is made available.

The slow accumulation of everyday acts, whether at work or in leisure time — turning the soil in a community garden, negotiating the purchase of a marshy parcel of land for public use, building a birdhouse with your friends — is a more useful indicator of public space performance than how it looks when first unveiled. This is why we must incorporate long-term use, custodial as well as financial maintenance, and the idea of stewardship as a practice of active citizenship into any discussion of public space. An ethic of stewardship, in the spirit of cooperative engagement advanced by Aldo Leopold, must become manifest and embedded within the way we talk about, design, pay for, and evaluate public spaces of all kinds.

As we have seen, over the history of public space advocacy, various different rationales have been employed to prove the public benefits of these public goods: opportunities to relieve the congestion and pollution of urban life; to communicate civic grandeur; to enable the practice of democracy, whether in protest or support; to promote leisure, recreation, and physical fitness; to provide chances for encounters and connection with people unlike oneself.

All of these are crucial attributes of well-functioning public places and well-functioning cities, and none has an exclusive claim on the importance of public space. Incorporating an ethic and a practice of stewardship into the discussions of its design and delivery is not an end in itself; it complements and enhances these objectives. It brings the element of time to an architectural discourse that continues to represent itself as somehow resistant to deterioration or obsolescence or even the dynamic, shifting needs of the population. It brings the element of equity to a policy discourse that increasingly relies on private monies to provide public goods. And it brings the element of cooperation and the active building of solidarity to a civic discourse that urgently needs both.

---

92 The Public Trust Doctrine is related to the concept of public goods; the principle holds that certain resources — often maritime resources such as navigable waters, fishery stocks, or subaquatic oil reserves — are reserved for public use, and that the government is required to maintain them on the public's behalf and forbid private encroachment. In the 2008 ruling which struck down the lawsuit, the judges found that "Contrary to the petitioners' contentions, the Public Trust Doctrine does not prohibit residential uses that are merely adjacent to public parkland."

CHAPTER 3

MULTITASKING INFRASTRUCTURES
MEANS TO MANY ENDS

On a chilly Saturday morning in the fall of 2012, my colleague and co-editor, Varick Shute, boarded a boat for a tour of New York Harbor. The sites on this tour weren't the familiar ones; no one was pointing out the Statue of Liberty or Ellis Island. Instead, along with 125 keen urban enthusiasts, she was there to witness how much the landscape of New York City owes its shape to the process of dredging, or the mechanized transport of subaquatic sand and sediment. In case you have been holding onto any lingering doubt that an era of deep urban nerdiness is upon us, the fact that over a hundred people would voluntarily gather, in the cold, to check out the techniques of managing sediment should put your mind to rest. Infrastructure is having a moment. However, growing popular and academic interest in the subject is, unfortunately, not translating into forward-thinking political will or public investment. We have more work to do to harness this enthusiasm in order to advance urbanism as a field of action that responds to the urgent crises of the day. The stories that follow point out some possible ways how.

The stakes are high: at the same time as we find ourselves in a moment of political and financial neglect of crucial infrastructure, we are also in a moment when our infrastructural systems — from the public spaces described in the previous chapter to the technology and housing projects described later on in this book — must perform more and more urgent functions in multiple dimensions and across multiple scales. Parks must offer more than fitness and recreation. Streets must become more than transportation networks. Shorelines must be more than the sites of transforming postindustrial landscapes into waterfront views. All of these spaces and systems must continue to carry out their basic functions, but they must also produce environmental benefits. Therefore, responsive citymaking requires an expanded notion of public infrastructure and its underappreciated role in addressing the causes and impacts of climate change. Urbanists of all stripes must expand our understanding of what it takes to create and maintain the public goods, large and small, that we hold in common. These range from the street tree, which sequesters carbon dioxide and can slow stormwater runoff, to the subway system, the biggest piece of a public transit network responsible, in part, for New Yorkers having some of the nation's smallest individual carbon footprints in the country. Consider the harbor, too. It is responsible for New York City's economic ascendancy and growth in the nineteenth century. While many of its original advantages were naturally occurring; its competitiveness has long been a function of heavy engineering that comes with a serious cost to the resilience of our coastlines — such as the removal of natural breakwaters to increase navigable routes — in a contemporary reality of strong and frequent storms.

The boat tour was part of DredgeFest, an event organized by the Dredge Research Collective, a group of young scholars and designers committed to the exploration

New York City's waterfront is composed of miles of in-fill shore and deepened channels, produced by moving thousands of tons of silt, sand, and clay. While much of the city's maritime industry has declined in the wake of advances in shipping technology, investment in New York's waterways and marine infrastructure remains critically important to the city's economy, transportation, and resilience to stronger storms.

"of human sediment handling practices through publications, an event series, and various other projects."[1] Many of the founding participants teach in architecture schools around the country and have used the Collective's shared research agenda to inform design studios they have led. The group includes people like Brian Davis, who investigated the Gowanus birdhouses and Floyd Bennett Field for *Urban Omnibus;* Rob Holmes, whose research exposes how the expansion of the Panama Canal has surprising aftereffects in New York (and elsewhere); and Tim Maly, a writer who focuses on material networks and infrastructural landscapes. In an article for *Urban Omnibus,* Maly summarizes some of the Dredge Research Collective's findings with respect to New York, characterizing dredging practices as "the greatest unrecognized landscape architecture project in the world."[2] The word "greatest," in this case, refers to scale: the extent to which the manipulation of underwater earth literally transforms the physical form of the city. The volume of earth involved is the most obvious indication of such greatness. Another way to reveal its scale is to unpack the complexities of how this process impacts global economies, regional ecologies, and local real estate, as Maly does in his article. For example, the freight rail line that became the High Line fell into disuse because the port facilities of Manhattan began to lose their competitive advantage over Port Newark-Elizabeth,

[1] The mission and projects of the Dredge Research Collaborative can be found on the group's website: www.dredgeresearchcollaborative.org/.

[2] Tim Maly, "A City Built on Dredge," *Urban Omnibus,* December 12, 2012.

when the latter began its ambitious dredging operation in 1956. The infill that forms the ground beneath Battery Park City comes from similar excavations.[3] Dredging influences more than the depth of the harbor floor.

The impact of logistical choices about ports and cargo on the city's shape is, therefore, a monumental and perhaps extreme example of the convergence between how we conceive the distinct concepts of infrastructure and landscape. The ways that a diverse range of landscape architects and urban designers are incorporating sophisticated understanding of infrastructure into their practices represents a significant shift in the philosophy of design, and hopefully will herald closer collaboration between designers and engineers in macroprojects to come — whether it's deepening a port or planning for the post-storm resilience of coastal communities. This shift should not be understood as the design community discovering anew this important driver of city form. A significant minority of design firms have conceived of infrastructure as fundamental to their practices for many years.[4]

Nonetheless, our current moment is one of hazardous neglect, wherein "shovel-ready" is code for shortsighted, and too many vital systems — water, roads, rail — are in precarious states of disrepair. Moreover, mainstream urban thinking is at risk of losing sight of the ambition to use infrastructure as the organizing principle of long-term development. Yet, if we look further back, designers are reclaiming and transforming earlier ideas, some from more than a century ago, about the design of urban systems.

DREDGING UP THE CITY BEAUTIFUL

Today, urban historians tend to characterize the City Beautiful movement — a coordinated effort to bring monumental grandeur to urban design — and its forebears in Beaux-Arts architecture of the late nineteenth and early twentieth centuries primarily on aesthetic grounds. We remember first the insistence on the civic virtues of visual iconicity: theatrical and symmetrical monuments, cardinal avenues and vistas, uniform heights. The emphasis on style has fueled critiques that visual order is tantamount to social control (an argument further supported by the demolition of neighborhoods and displacement of poor people to build, for example, the national capitol in Washington DC among other violent disruptions commanded by City Beautiful schemes.) Jane Jacobs goes so far as to lump City Beautiful in with Le Corbusier's *Ville Radieuse,* claiming both were "primarily architectural design cults, rather than cults of social reform."[5] Such criticism is legitimate, but what we often forget is that City Beautiful ideas went beyond superficially aesthetic considerations. The movement offered a productively holistic vision of the city as a system in which landscape, architecture, and infrastructure were distinct elements to be carefully orchestrated toward the greater civic good. Of course we can and should question the condescending, racist, and classist ways that many purveyors of this philosophy defined the civic good, how and by whom it should be realized, and who would benefit. In so doing, however, we should not lose faith in the once powerful belief that the built environment can be a source of virtue; it can foster communitarian fellowship across lines of race and class; it can serve as the infrastructure of solidarity. The movement's emphasis on the visual did not foreclose an understanding of the systemic.

A classic progenitor of City Beautiful planning in New York City is Grand Army Plaza,[6] the historical center of Brooklyn and the main entrance to Prospect Park. It is arranged as a pair of concentric ellipses. Landscaped berms between the two ring roads insulate the apartment buildings surrounding the plaza from the noise of the traffic crossing the inner ring, which encircles a paved oval with a fountain at its center. Soon after the completion of Central Park in 1858, civic leaders across the East River began to advocate for an analogous park in the independent City of Brooklyn, by that time the third largest city in the country. As with Central Park, the arguments for this public space were couched in terms of social cohesion and public health, as the park was certain to "become a favorite resort for all classes of our community, enabling thousands to enjoy pure air, with healthful exercise, at all seasons of the year."[7] Frederick Law Olmsted and Calvert Vaux collaborated again on the design. Some consider that they improved upon their earlier model, as they were allowed this time around to create an undulating landscape uninterrupted by the occasional flow of traffic.[8] This bucolic woodland refuge, then, demanded a grand architectonic gesture to separate it from the urban density and traffic beyond its borders, to mark the threshold between city and park. Olmsted and Vaux determined the appropriate form for such a gesture should be "in the spirit of Paris's Etoile (now the Place Charles de Gaulle), that circular twelve-spoked traffic rond point that bears in its central island the Arc de Triomphe."[9] The plaza's iconic statuary and arch were not added until some years later, but its monumentality was designed into the scheme from the beginning. Thus, Grand Army Plaza could provide a majestic node in the axial network of Brooklyn's major roads, in keeping

---

[3] The made land in the northern portion of Battery Park City relied on fill from harbor dredging operations, while the made land in the southern portion relied on fill from excavations to build the World Trade Center.

[4] Including Weiss/Manfredi (New York City), dLand studio (New York City), Urban Lab (Chicago), MAde Studio (Detroit), Stoss Landscape Urbanism (Boston), and more.

[5] Jane Jacobs, *The Death and Life of Great American Cities* (New York: Random House, 2002 {1961}), 375.

[6] Grand Army Plaza was known as Prospect Park Plaza until its rededication in 1926.

[7] Prospect Park Alliance, "Park History". Accessed March 12, 2015.
www.prospectpark.org/learn-more/park-history-slideshow.

[8] The original masterplan for Prospect Park, by Egbert Viele, suggested a site that spanned both sides of Flatbush Avenue, incorporating areas that are now part of the grounds of the Brooklyn Museum and the Brooklyn Botanical Gardens. After this plan was put on hold during the Civil War, Vaux found the idea of a park flanking the thoroughfare to be problematic, and suggested a reworking of the site such that the majority of the park's acreage would be continuous, to one side of Flatbush Avenue and that it would instead extend southwards beyond Brooklyn's borders into the independent town of Flatbush.

[9] Norval White, Elliot Wilensky, and Fran Leadon, *AIA Guide to New York City,* 5th ed. (Oxford: Oxford University Press, 2010), 68.

Top: Frederick Law Olmsted and Calvert Vaux's plan for Prospect Park, completed in 1873, shows the park's distinct regions — meadow, a wooded ravine, and a lake — as well as the oval plaza to the park's north that would become Grand Army Plaza.

Above: In 1915, five years after the Manhattan Bridge was completed, the architectural firm Carrère and Hastings designed an elaborate entry and forecourt to the bridge in what is now Manhattan's Chinatown.

with the Beaux-Arts and City Beautiful principles of formal visual connections between important sites.

The rationale for the plaza's design was not exclusively symbolic, however. It also performs an important and complicated infrastructural function. It connects eight radial roads on its outer ring, five of which penetrate its inner ring. One of these roads is also of Olmsted and Vaux's design: Eastern Parkway, the first boulevard in the country created expressly for "pleasure-riding" along its scenic, tree-lined route. Grand Army Plaza can be called "a masterstroke of city planning" precisely because of the way "this nexus joins their great Eastern Parkway, and Prospect Park, with the avenues that preceded it on other geometries."[10]

These avenues, of course, were built for horse-drawn carriages. Renovations to the traffic lanes encircling the plaza to accommodate cars led to an altogether different infrastructural challenge. Via the Manhattan Bridge, Flatbush Avenue is the primary connection between Lower Manhattan, Downtown Brooklyn, and the vast, residential neighborhoods to the borough's southeast. Soon, the flow of traffic made the plaza's central open space almost entirely inaccessible. Navigating it became extremely hazardous for pedestrians and cyclists (and pretty nerve-wracking for drivers, too). Car traffic was supposed to be just one of several infrastructural functions, yet it eclipsed all others, especially the plaza's role as a grand public space. It became, in effect, a dangerous, single-use, and not particularly convenient roadway. The shortsightedness of car-centric urban planning in the twentieth century is a well-worn topic in contemporary urbanism that we need not belabor here. Grand Army Plaza's relevance to the discussion at hand comes from the idea that infrastructure and public space used to be considered as integrated components of landscape design, a holism that we must recapture if we are to meet contemporary challenges.

By 2008, efforts were underway to reduce the number of traffic lanes and find other means of improving the experience of Grand Army Plaza. The Design Trust for Public Space, a nonprofit that matches City agencies and advocacy groups with design talent, organized an international design competition to "reinvent" it.[11] One of the jurors was Ken Smith, a prominent landscape architect known for his inventive approach to the adaptive reuse of existing urban fabric. While I was interviewing him for an *Urban Omnibus* feature about the competition, we discussed the growing interest in infrastructure among landscape architecture firms. In recent years, he told me, "Landscape architects have become more interested . . . to see how we can actually embed landscape into the body of infrastructure." He invoked the era of the Beaux-Arts and City Beautiful "when infrastructure and public space

---

[10] Ibid, 68.

[11] For the Reinventing Grand Army Plaza project, the Design Trust for Public Space's project partner was the Grand Army Plaza Coalition, a network of nonprofit organizations, business improvement districts, and cultural organizations.

were . . . conceived together," citing a different example of Beaux-Arts planning at one terminus of Flatbush Avenue.[12]

Talking with his hands, his eyes gleaming enthusiastically behind Corbusier-style, round and thick-rimmed glasses, he conjured a picture of the end of the Manhattan Bridge as it empties into Chinatown, pointing out "that's all public space *and* infrastructure." These days, any commuter can be forgiven for not taking full notice of Carrère and Hastings' arch, inspired by the Porte Saint-Denis in Paris, and colonnade, inspired by the Gian Lorenzo Bernini Colonnade at St. Peter's in the Vatican. These triumphal structures frame the entry to the bridge and spatially define what was once an elegant plaza. The tangle of traffic as Canal Street and the Bowery branch off from the bridge's mouth overwhelm any sense that this was once a walkable forecourt to a major piece of infrastructure, a grand yet contemplative space that used to invite pedestrians into walkways across the bridge, moving through additional Doric colonnades stacked atop the massive masonry anchorages. (After years of neglect, the plaza and the walkways were restored in 2001.)

Ken Smith doesn't place the blame exclusively on the rise of the automobile and modernist ideas about urban planning that prioritized efficiency and mobility above all else. The segregation of the various arts of city building also played a part. "By the middle of the twentieth century, things had gotten divided by profession, and infrastructure became much more single purpose. It's really the last twenty or thirty years that push back to see how we start to make infrastructure serve more than one function, to provide public [and] social places." Landscape architects — who practice a field of design that Smith defines as engaging with horizontality and the ground plane[13] — have been central to this reintegration. Alongside this shift, the field of ecology has also evolved from classical determinism and a valorization of stability and order toward an appreciation of dynamic systemic change and the related phenomena of adaptability, resilience, and flexibility.[14]

The landscape architects who organized DredgeFest (a generation or two younger than Smith and his contemporaries) take the expanding intellectual territory of their profession a step further. They have published papers[15] and friendly, critical ripostes[16] to each other's work that reveal how "slowly" and "fitfully" "landscape architecture is remaking itself." This evolution, they argue, may call for major realignments, and perhaps even a renaming, of the discipline. The pioneers of this shift, according to Brian Davis and Thomas Oles, "are venturing from the confines of garden, park, and plaza into strange and difficult territory, where they face challenges of a greater order. How will our cities adapt to rising seas? How do we respond to the mass extinction of our fellow species? How can we build places that are more just? Such questions mock the very notion of disciplinary boundaries."[17] The prominent architect Thom Mayne agrees. In the introduction to *Combinatory Urbanism,* a monograph of recent work by his firm Morphosis, Mayne declares that "The complex interplay of human and natural forces shaping cities today and into the future demands that architecture give form to urban forces active beyond traditional building and property lines, and also that large-scale planning assume more flexible and adaptive spatial structures that are capable of accommodating the unpredictable . . . If we are to adapt to these historically unprecedented changes in thinking and practice, new design methods must be created."[18]

Indeed. Across the spectrum of what I consider citymaking, designers, thinkers, and citizens are grappling with questions of increasing urgency and expanding scale. Some indicative projects fit squarely within traditional definitions of what particular design disciplines are expected to produce, such as the renovation of car-centric landscapes like Grand Army Plaza to accommodate walking, biking, and public transit as less carbon-intensive transportation modes. Others bring in strategies from ecological and biological sciences, such as the engineering of an oyster reef as a means to attenuate storm surges and improve water quality.[19] Still others grapple with economic development, such as the inclusion of workforce development and project-based learning as integral components of such efforts. Meanwhile, other types of activities with enormous effects on the physical shape of the city — such as using the sand dredged for port expansion to shore up eroding marshland in Jamaica Bay — don't read as design projects at all.

The drivers of such shifts reveal just how high the stakes are. Academic definitions and pedagogical and disciplinary evolutions, while instructive, are not the issue here. What matters are existential threats to society (the widening of inequality) and to the planet (the warming climate and its stronger storms). Much more work needs to be done, is being done, and will be done in the coming years to expose just how intertwined these two threats are and thus how integrated our responses must be. This work will obviously require the efforts of actors with fields of action much broader than cities and with power much greater than designers and other city-makers. Such actors include figures from national government, intergovernmental and nongovernmental organizations, global finance and commerce, the law, and the

12 "Reinventing Grand Army Plaza," *Urban Omnibus,* January 6, 2009.

13 See also James Corner's definitional account of Landscape Urbanism in "Terra Fluxus," in Charles Waldheim, ed., *The Landscape Urbanism Reader* (Princeton: Princeton University Press, 2006), 23.

14 See Chris Reed and Nina-Marie Lister, eds. *Projective Ecologies,* (Barcelona: ACTAR and Harvard Graduate School of Design, 2014).

15 Brian Davis and Thomas Oles, "From Architecture to Landscape: The Case for a New Landscape Science," *Places,* October 2014. Accessed April 18, 2015. www.placesjournal.org/article/from-architecture-to-landscape/.

16 Rob Holmes, "On Landscape Science," *Mammoth.* Accessed April 22, 2015, m.ammoth.us/blog/2014/10/on-landscape-science/.

17 Davis and Oles, "From Architecture to Landscape," 2014.

18 Thom Mayne, *Combinatory Urbanism: The Complex Behavior of Collective Form* (Culver City, Calif.: Stray Dog Cafe, 2011).

19 Oyster-tecture by Scape Studio for the *Rising Currents* exhibition at the Museum of Modern Art (MoMA) was a self-described "back to the future" project inspired by New York Harbor's historic claim as "oyster capital of the world." Scape led one of five teams selected by MoMA to develop innovative responses to coastal resilience in New York in the wake of Superstorm Sandy.

academy, in coordination with local efforts. The projects my colleagues and I have observed through *Urban Omnibus* over the past few years represent neither the global vanguard nor its followers in responding to the urgent tasks at hand. They do, however, reflect and embody an ascendant mode of practice motivated by the understanding that adequate response to these existential threats requires thinking big, working across disciplines and theories of knowledge, and recovering the belief that the built environment can foster social solidarity. One idea that will strengthen, accelerate, and diversify this promising mode of practice is an active reconception of infrastructure as a constituent and inextricable component of our shared urban landscape, a multifunction public good currently undervalued in both economics and politics, misunderstood and exploited by the market to our collective peril.

PUBLIC GOODS REVISITED: SHARED MEANS, MANY ENDS

Several of the examples cited in the previous chapter — the High Line, Corona Plaza, and Brooklyn Bridge Park — are open spaces repurposed from disused infrastructure: a freight rail line, a street intersection, and a shipping facility. While their primary purpose is no longer to convey vehicles or cargo, they are still infrastructure. To various degrees, all of the topics of this book — public space, technology, housing, and communication — can be considered forms of infrastructure, and there are many more besides: health care facilities, schools, prisons, the internet.

The term *infrastructure* is relatively new in English; the earliest appearance cited by the *Oxford English Dictionary* is not until 1927. Even in French, from which it is borrowed, the first recorded instance, in the *Dictionairre Robert,* is from 1875. ("Landscape architecture," by the way, was coined in 1840.) Infrastructure refers to an aspect of contemporary society so omnipresent that slippage between the metaphorical and literal uses of the term are constant. Infrastructure is everywhere. "Hard infrastructure" can dominate the landscape, like roads and bridges, or be hidden from view, like fiberoptic cables. "Soft infrastructure," like education or healthcare, is both. But whether visible or invisible, literal or metaphorical, what undergirds the full scope of what we label infrastructure is the belief in its necessity and the indeterminacy of its use. Infrastructure, too, is a public good, most often considered "a proper office of government," even if the political will to fund projects has declined precipitously in the neoliberal era. Its very ubiquity — and the resulting difficulty of isolating or measuring its demand and its benefits — is why infrastructure is so perilously undervalued.

The dangers of this neglect have been well documented. The American Society of Civil Engineers rates one in nine bridges in the nation as structurally deficient, and we take 260 million trips over these 70,000 at-risk bridges every day. One-third of major roads in the US are in poor condition. US air travel is the world's most congested, due to insufficient investment in airport runways and air traffic control systems.[20] In New York City, according to the Center for an Urban Future, a think tank, more than 30 percent of roads are in suboptimal condition; 2.7 million cars drive daily over forty-seven "fracture critical" and "structurally deficient" bridges; 403 water main breaks were reported in 2013.[21]

As *Urban Omnibus* was getting off the ground in early 2009, infrastructure was national news less for its embarrassing state of disrepair than for its purported ability to get the economy back on track. The American Recovery and Reinvestment Act (ARRA, otherwise known as the stimulus package), signed into law by President Obama less than two months into his first term in office, had an explicit primary objective of saving and creating jobs. Secondary goals included investment in infrastructure, education, health, and renewable energy. The idea of responding to the Great Recession with a Keynesian macroeconomic strategy, grounded in the belief that the government should increase public spending to offset the decrease in private spending, prompted comparisons between the stimulus package and the New Deal.[22] In the run-up to the bill's signing, many of the new president's supporters, especially architects and urbanists, felt positive that the era of hope and change ushered in by the Obama presidency would include a thorough transformation of how the federal government made policy with respect to the built environment, and that generations of direct and indirect subsidies of private cars and highways would give way to needed investments in high-speed trains and renewable energy projects. The optimism deflated almost instantaneously upon hearing the announcement that construction projects to receive immediate funding were required to be "shovel-ready." In other words, the stipulation that projects must have complete planning, engineering, and funding already in place, such that laborers can begin work immediately, effectively ensured that the stimulus would reinforce the status quo ante. Writing on *Urban Omnibus* weeks after the stimulus was passed, architect, planner, and real estate executive Vishaan Chakrabarti opined that the bill "feeds rather than fixes our ill-conceived land-use patterns, resulting in new "infrastructure" that runs the risk of being little more than a grab bag of roadway construction."[23]

In the years since, the condition of America's infrastructure did not improved much. The 2013 stats are a little better than those of 2009, but far from encouraging. Major infrastructure investment is not a significant part of the platform of either Democrats or Republicans. Locally, while Mayor Bloomberg committed unprecedented amounts of public dollars to capital infrastructure projects, his administration neglected to plan for funding the upkeep and maintenance of both new and existing infrastructural assets (not unlike the neglect of operational funds for the maintenance of parks mentioned in the previous chapter).[24] His successor, Mayor de Blasio, has also increased spending for infrastructure in the City's capital budget, but he's made clear that keeping citizens' household costs low is a higher priority: he postponed

---

[20] The American Society of Civil Engineers, "2013 Report Card for America's Infrastructure." Accessed April 15, 2015. www.infrastructurereportcard.org.

[21] Adam Forman, "Caution Ahead: Overdue Investments for New York's Aging Infrastructure" Center for an Urban Future (March 2014).

[22] See, among others, Michael Grunwald, *The New New Deal* (New York: Simon & Schuster, 2013).

[23] Vishann Chakrabarti, "A Country of Cities," *Urban Omnibus,* July 2009.

the urgent and long-planned project to complete Water Tunnel No. 3, without which the five million residents of Brooklyn and Queens must rely on an eighty-year-old water delivery system in danger of collapse. If one of the two existing water tunnels were to fail, half of New York's businesses and residences would instantly become uninhabitable.[25] Elected officials' avoidance of the issue points to a fundamental intellectual challenge surrounding the way we understand what infrastructure is and what it does.

One way to describe this challenge is through economics. Legal scholar Brett Frischmann, an expert on intellectual property and internet law (and a mentee of Elinor Ostrom), offers a cogent economic analysis of and promising alternatives to prevailing understandings in his book *Infrastructure: the Social Value of Shared Resources*. He asks, "how and to what extent infrastructure resources generate value for society" in an effort to call out the ways that "conventional economic analysis of many infrastructure resources fails to fully account for how society uses these resources to create social benefits, and as a result . . . fails to fully account for the social demand for these resources."[26] He explains that the discipline has traditionally evaluated infrastructure (to the limited extent that it has) in terms of ensuring adequate supply. What drives demand has received considerably less attention, and his overarching goal is to redress this disparity in order to argue for "managing and sustaining infrastructure resources as commons." Frischmann's work employs the theoretical language of economics precisely because the social thinkers who share his support for open access to infrastructural assets tend to "oppose propertization, privatization, deregulation, and commercialization [and thus] view the field of economics with sincere suspicion and doubt."[27] Therefore, the arguments emerging from such thinkers have not had significant impacts on economic thought nor, consequentially, policy-making. Supply-side thinking has prevailed.

Emphasis on the demand side of the equation is useful for a number of reasons beyond righting the balance of scholarly attention to both vectors of the curve. One of his key insights concerns the nonrivalry continuum. Again, a *nonrival good* is one for which there is no additional cost to providing it to an additional individual, up to a certain capacity. Because "infrastructural resources can be accessed and used concurrently by multiple users for multiple uses," writes Frischmann, "Nonrivalry can be leveraged."[28] It can be leveraged to expose the ways that public goods can beget other public goods. The fact that "Users determine what to do with the capabilities that infrastructure provides"[29] supports individuals' ability to create other public goods down the line. Infrastructures of telecommunication, like the fiber-optic cables on which the internet relies, don't merely enable each household's individual internet connection. They also enable the web developer who just might create an application in his dorm room that becomes a ubiquitous and indispensable information service on which certain forms of commerce depend and nearly everyone with an internet connection relies. The inability of traditional economics to take account of the value that might result from the use of infrastructure is a "'demand-manifestation' problem" that negatively affects "infrastructure allocation, design, investment, and management, as well as other supply-side decisions . . . To society's detriment, demand-manifestation problems can lead to the undersupply of infrastructure essential to various producers of public and social goods, and this undersupply can lead to an optimization of infrastructure design or prioritization of access and use of the infrastructure for a narrower range of uses than would be socially optimal."[30] This "narrower range of uses" echoes Ken Smith's concerns about the predominance of single-purpose infrastructure throughout the twentieth century. Furthermore, our societal failure to appreciate the social value that infrastructures provide helps to explain why public investment has declined, decade after decade, since 1960.[31]

Frischmann goes on to argue for commons management strategies for infrastructure, wherein "a resource is shared among members of a community on non-discriminatory terms . . . that do not depend on the users identity or intended use."[32] In other words, infrastructure managed as commons wouldn't have different rates for business class and coach, wouldn't assess licensing fees or require official permission for use, and wouldn't allow surge pricing or markdowns for buying in bulk. While most of the management proposals he offers basically amount to pricing rationales, his work has more far-reaching implications for citymaking. While Frischmann articulates his argument entirely within the discursive limits of economics, the thinking that undergirds it offers both a philosophical connection between the provision and management of a shared resource and the indeterminacy and immeasurability of potential benefits to its community of users. The social demand for infrastructure is more than a curve on a graph to determine price. The fact that it is impossible to quantify is evidence of its profound importance to society, not an excuse to discount it.

---

[24] To his credit, during and after he was mayor, Michael Bloomberg has been vocal about the need to invest in infrastructure nationwide; he is one of the cofounders (with former governor of California Arnold Schwarzenegger and former governor of Pennsylvania Ed Rendell) of the Building America's Future Education Fund, a bipartisan coalition dedicated to bringing about a new era of US investment in infrastructure that enhances our nation's prosperity and quality of life.

[25] Jim Dwyer, "De Blasio Postpones Work on Crucial Water Tunnel," *The New York Times,* April 5, 2016.

[26] Brett M. Frischmann, *Infrastructure: The Social Value of Shared Resources* (Oxford: Oxford University Press, 2012) location 566.

[27] Brett M. Frischmann, "An Economic Theory of Infrastructure and Commons Management," *Minnesota Law Review,* 89 (April 2005): 917–1030.

[28] Ibid, location 1398.

[29] Ibid, location 1398.

[30] Ibid, location 1422.

[31] Congressional Budget Office, "Public Spending on Transportation and Water Infrastructure" (November 2010). Accessed April 29, 2015., www.cbo.gov/sites/default/files/cbofiles/ftpdocs/119xx/doc11940/11-17-infrastructure.pdf. See also Chakrabarti, *A Country of Cities: A Manifesto for an Urban America* (New York: Metropolis Books, 2013) 180–181.

[32] Frischmann, *Infrastructure,* 2012, location 1895.

Historians of economics attribute the popularization of supply and demand curves to Alfred Marshall and his 1890 tome, *Principles of Economics*. In that canonical text, Marshall lays out the most basic argument for the economic benefits of infrastructure provision, describing how an efficient transportation network enables firms and people to locate near one another, so that they can benefit from shared access to inputs of production.[33] The *social* benefits of infrastructure, then, might be understood in terms of how a bridge — one that simultaneously and non-hierarchically accommodates cars, a subway line, bicycle and pedestrian paths, and well-designed and welcoming public spaces on either end — enables people to commute to work, exercise, hang out with each other, go for a leisurely drive, transport cargo, look at the East River, escape Manhattan in the wake of a disaster, eat lunch, and so on. The call to recognize and appreciate the indeterminacy of social demand relates directly to the need to design and manage infrastructural resources in a way that fosters their ability to perform simultaneously in structural, social, aesthetic, civic, and environmental terms. According to the National Research Council, "Infrastructure is a means to other ends, and the effectiveness, efficiency and reliability of its contribution to these other ends must ultimately be the measure of infrastructure performance."[34] I would tweak this formulation somewhat. I would posit that infrastructure is a means to many ends, and the necessity, indeterminacy, and immeasurability of its contribution to these many ends must ultimately be the indicator of its contribution to social welfare and its inextricability from the various systems, inputs, and outputs that enable it and that it enables.

Most of the traditional categories of infrastructure, like roads, bridges, and sewers, are also a part of our physical, urban landscape, contributing to how it looks and feels and instrumental to how it performs. Inasmuch as I think we need to conceive of infrastructure in an expansive and holistic way, we should also be mindful of the way infrastructure — especially the nontraditional forms it is increasingly absorbing, from cell phone signals to global manufacturing standards — is implicated in the consolidation of power outside of democratic institutions or the rule of law. The same flows that connect the Panama Canal to the dredging of New York Harbor contribute to the ways that, according to Saskia Sassen, a sociologist and preeminent scholar of globalization, "economic globalization has brought with it a new formalization of the private sphere, including a strengthening of its representation as neutral and technical, and of the market as a superior ordering from that of governments." I believe that a qualitative account of the public benefits and social demand for infrastructure is central to the intellectual and disciplinary realignments necessary to conceive of infrastructure as a multifunction public good integral to our urban landscape. At the same time, we must remember that "Much of what circulates through the public domain today is geared towards setting up the infrastructure for global operations of markets and firms, as well as for shedding the responsibilities of the social wage that are part of the preceding era."[35] Besides the social wage, other responsibilities once commonly understood to be "proper offices of government" have also been shed. Governments now devise incentives for private industry to provide infrastructure rather than providing it themselves.

The result is a weakening of the social contract between communities and government, and the rise of the idea that taxes are a fee for service. Just when the interdependencies that define the contemporary world are making themselves most clear, a self-concealing process of enclosure is upon us. And the commons management practices that Frischmann advocates, for all their merit, will not on their own return us to the Commons.

As Keller Easterling, an architect and theorist, reminds us in her excellent book *Extrastatecraft: the Power of Infrastructure Space,* the built environment of the world is fast becoming a series of "reproducible products set within similar urban arrangements." Because these "repeatable phenomena [are] engineered around logistics and the bottom line they constitute an infrastructural technology with elaborate routines and schedules for organizing consumption." In this light, this chapter's opening example of dredging cuts both ways. From one perspective, it serves to raise the stakes of the design of the landscape: it illustrates the connection between landscape formation and urban economies, jobs, and trade and thus might help to argue for greater collaboration between designers and engineers in macroprojects of this sort. From another, the example insists upon the ways that a city's literal, littoral shape confers competitive advantage to certain cities in a networked global supply chain whose mechanisms are often "far removed from familiar legislative processes."[36]

Easterling's analysis focuses on the reproducible "code" of infrastructure and identifies opportunities to "hack" it, as an architect or activist. Intervening in the mass-produced homogeneity of built environments the world over requires an awareness of operations that are often hidden from view. She reveals a global set of arrangements to be a "software" that is reproducing similar formats for "the parking places, skyscrapers, turning radii, garages, street lights, driveways, airport lounges, highway exits, big boxes, strip malls, shopping malls, small boxes, free zones, casinos, retail outlets, fast food restaurants, hotels, cash machines, tract housing, container ports, industrial parks, call centers, golf courses, suburbs, office buildings, business parks, resorts." She argues that the omnipresence of these forms is bringing infrastructure out of some unseen underground and into the light, such that it becomes "far from hidden." In fact, "infrastructure is now the overt point of contact and access between us all."[37]

Perhaps. However, the very ubiquity of this new infrastructure can make it just as invisible as the subways and sewers concealed beneath the experience of the

---

[33] Alfred Marshall, *Principles of Economics* (London: Macmillan and Co., 1890).

[34] National Research Council, *Measuring and Improving Infrastructure Performance* (Washington DC: National Academies Press, 1996).

[35] Saskia Sassen, *Territory, Authority, Rights: From Medieval to Global Assemblages* (Princeton: Princeton University Press, 2006).

[36] Keller Easterling, *Extrastatecraft: the Power of Infrastructure Space* (New York: Verso, 2014), location 129.

[37] Ibid, location 78.

Steve Duncan is an urban historian and a photographer who has been photographing subterranean water infrastructure for years.

Top to bottom:

Croton Aqueduct Self-Portrait, New York, 2006

Sunswick Creek Outfall, Queens, NY, 2007

Wallabout outfall, Combined Sewer Overflow #NC B5, Brooklyn, New York, 2011 street. Before we can hack infrastructure space, before we can insert a higher order of design intelligence into engineering macroprojects, before we can recover the sense that a traffic island or bridge plaza can simultaneously express civic grandeur and encourage social solidarity, we must learn to *see* it.

In different ways, the three citymakers whose stories come next — an explorer, an historian, and a planner — epitomize the kinds of transformational change that can result from learning to see infrastructure as an integral part of our social, environmental, and spatial experience of the city, with multiple and overlapping functions and benefits. The first example is an act of interpretation, the second an unbuilt proposal, and the third an ongoing project under active construction since the early 1990s. Discussing them together is an attempt to underscore the mutual relevance of various types of urban analysis and intervention, the necessary synthesis of theoretical, creative, historical, and practical attempts to influence the form and experience of the city.

SEEING GREEN:
INFRASTRUCTURAL VISIBILITY AND PERMEABILITY

Steve Duncan calls himself an urban explorer, historian, geographer, photographer, and occasional tour guide of the urban underground. Some might oversimplify and call him a sewer diver. I first heard about him from a cinematographer friend who knew him as a location scout for an independent film to be shot in subterranean New York. By the time I interviewed him for *Urban Omnibus*,[38] in the summer of 2012, I had become aware of his singular and inspiring brand of urbanism, which links infrastructural awareness with visual art, hydrography, history, and cartography. He's turned a youthful passion for sneaking into places he's not supposed to be into a unique career as an interpreter of urban systems. "Most people grow out of that kind of thing," he told me. "I didn't. I've kept on exploring layers of cities we don't normally visit."

I met up with Duncan in one of the most overt manifestations of globally homogenous urban form imaginable: a midtown Starbucks on 34th Street. But our conversation quickly turned to the specificities of how local infrastructural networks respond to New York City's natural landscape. He has the affect of a surfer, with sandy blonde hair always getting in his eyes and a conspicuous absence of cynicism. Like a surfer revealing his command of the tides, or a mountain-climber the geology of which rocks make the best holds, Duncan's laid-back demeanor belies a deep and fervent knowledge of the terrain he explores. He told me that his curiosity about subterranean cities matured into a fascination that motivated serious historical investigation once he "began to understand how this underground layer of wastewater infrastructure is a carryover from the original topography of the land: cities are engaged in processes of natural flow and natural resource utilization."

---

[38] "Undercity: The Infrastructural Explorations of Steve Duncan," *Urban Omnibus,* August, 2012.

He told me about how the sewer shed of Manhattan corresponds almost exactly to the pre-urban watershed, leveraging the contours of the island so gravity and groundwater would help drain the system. He explained that the shameful current state of New York's Victorian-era combined sewer overflow (CSO) system — in which rainfall and surface runoff combine with raw sewage and industrial wastewater to flow directly into the city's waterways during storm conditions — was an innovative solution at the time, rightly acclaimed as a triumph of engineering that saved countless lives from waterborne diseases. He referenced the widespread awareness and appreciation afforded to such solutions in the late nineteenth century, with sewer engineers publishing well-received books on the topic for the general public. His work does more than merely uncover these forgotten histories of urban development. Its true benefit is to show such histories as immanent within contemporary infrustructure. "What's made me into an historian is the realization that the past didn't go anywhere," he told me. "It's been integrated into the present."

To that end, Duncan is continuously testing ways to foster greater public awareness and appreciation of infrastructure. He takes sumptuous, long-exposure photos of what he has found underneath cities around the world. He collaborates with cartographers to overlay historical maps and surveys of pre-urban natural terrain with contemporary digital imaging techniques. He has a dream to create what he calls a "sewer viewer," which he describes as "a periscope on the sidewalk the size of a water fountain, kind of like those viewing platform binoculars you put a quarter into and are able to see some part of the environment that you might not focus on otherwise. The periscope would let you see into a tunnel and its flowing mass of water. I think opening that stuff to visibility would be very beneficial."

When I asked him why and how, he invoked two distinct benefits of visibility, which sound obvious but are nonetheless profound. Public awareness can inspire personal behavior change, which is crucially necessary given our environmental crisis. It can also instigate democratic political action:

By seeing, people would be better equipped to understand how stuff works as well as how previous generations dealt with these issues. In the 1860s, everybody could see that the ferry boats between Manhattan and Brooklyn were full, the long lines waiting to get on the boat, the amount of time to get to work in the morning. So when the Brooklyn Bridge was proposed, citizens could see how that would apply to their lives.

We don't see the processes going on underground, so we aren't aware of them until there's a problem. If the problems of CSOs were more visible, maybe people would be more conservative with their water usage when it's raining. Or if people could see how awesome some of these old tunnels are, then the next time there's a bond for infrastructure investment on the ballot, maybe people would remember that incredible tunnel from 1880 and vote for long-term infrastructure planning. I do think we have the power to make the city what we want it to be … we have the power to shape it in the future just as we shaped it in the past.

Our outdated sewers may not be the readiest example of a public good that begets unforeseen public benefits or the kind of infrastructural asset that can be conceived as multifunctional or multitasking. They are, however, a part of a dangerously antiquated water management system responsible for everything from drinking water to flooding streets. A first step toward updating that infrastructure is to encourage greater public familiarity with the system, which may indeed lead to greater public support for smart and long-range government investment. Awareness will also help to make the case for the manifold ways that the necessary renovations are realized in coordination with other priorities, including public space, but also public health, disaster preparedness and resilience, housing density, and much more.

A very important practice area for this coordination is a set of approaches referred to collectively as "green infrastructure," a growing field that offers an illuminating example of the increasing convergence between the organizing principles of infrastructure and urban / landscape design. As a buzzword of contemporary urbanism, the term is vague and expansive and encompasses a wide range of approaches to engineered structures that mimic natural processes or are otherwise environmentally "friendly." It can refer to anything from rooftops covered with vegetation to urban forests. One of the primary challenges green infrastructure addresses is stormwater runoff, which the United States Environmental Protection Agency (EPA) labels as one of the major causes of water pollution: "When rain falls in undeveloped areas, the water is absorbed and filtered by soil and plants. When rain falls on our roofs, streets, and parking lots, however, the water cannot soak into the ground. In most urban areas, stormwater is drained through engineered collection systems and discharged into nearby water bodies. The stormwater carries trash, bacteria, heavy metals, and other pollutants from the urban landscape, degrading the quality of the receiving waters. Higher flows can also cause erosion and flooding in urban streams, damaging habitat, property, and infrastructure."[39] In a city with a Victorian era stormwater management system like New York, the problem is exacerbated by the combination of stormwater, raw sewage, and industrial wastewater whenever it rains.

The sewers and combined outfalls that Steve Duncan explores are the conduit of this polluted discharge, but the real culprit is the imperviousness of urban ground built of concrete and asphalt. In some cases, even grass lawns are not as absorptive as we might think. A range of design solutions is at hand. Some are new kinds of building materials, like permeable pavers. Some are reengineered versions of familiar features like street trees that double as water-retaining bio-swales. These strategies allow designers and engineers to retrofit the urban fabric at the scale of the site, hacking the city's hard shell to allow rainwater to infiltrate. Since 2010, significant public policy initiatives have sought to incentivize property owners to

---

[39] Environmental Protection Agency, "Green Infrastructure," Environmental Protection Agency website. Accessed May 7, 2015. www.water.epa.gov/infrastructure/greeninfrastructure/gi_policy.cfm.

make this kind of site-scale hack: the NYC Department of Buildings offered a green roof tax credit; the EPA counseled municipalities to offer density bonuses to developers who incorporated green infrastructure projects into new buildings. Two particular projects in this vein stand out for me, both of which encompass a broader and more ambitious scope than an individual building or street but are nonetheless tailored to the specific nuances of their locales. That attunement, I think, is a product of the long-term commitment as well as the interdisciplinary approaches and uncommon perspectives of the individuals behind each project. The first is an historian who works at a neighborhood advocacy organization in the Lower East Side of Manhattan. The second is an urban planner who's dedicated more than two decades to one of the most comprehensive green infrastructure projects in the country, the Staten Island Bluebelt. Their projects are very different, but share an ecumenical, contextually informed approach to citymaking.

The first time I met Kerri Culhane, she was giving a presentation in the community room of Two Bridges Tower, a building overlooking the East River that houses formerly homeless and low-income working families. It was built in 1997, but the ethos behind the development harkens back to the Settlement House movement of the Progressive Era, with an onsite after-school program just one among a number of community programs run in the building's shared spaces. At the time, Culhane was the associate director at Two Bridges Neighborhood Council, which co-developed the building along with the Settlement House Fund. The organization got its start in the 1950s as a place to promote racial healing in a fraught, working class area that was historically a point of entry for various incoming immigrant groups to New

The open space in many tower-in-the-park public housing developments features large amounts of hardscaped pathways and fenced lawns that provide "light and air" as intended but do little to reduce flooding.

York and became one of New York City's first racially integrated neighborhoods.[40] This work grew to incorporate community organizing and planning during the 1960s, in response to industrial development plans that would have displaced hundreds of families. In the 1970s, Two Bridges' core mission — to promote a stable and harmonious neighborhood of opportunity for its residents — pushed the organization to develop affordable housing, and in the twenty-five years leading up to the unveiling of Two Bridges Tower, Two Bridges created almost 1,500 units of low- and moderate-income housing, many of which will remain permanently affordable.

When Culhane stood to address a crowd of invited community advocates, residents, and staffers for local elected officials, she unveiled an ambitious plan that was not primarily about housing inter-ethnic harmony, or even poverty. It was about infrastructure. The genius of the plan, however, is the way it illuminates so clearly the interconnections between urban history, infrastructural systems, social and environmental challenges, and the potential of design to generate a diverse set of opportunities for vulnerable populations.

She outed herself as an historian immediately upon reaching the lectern, modestly announcing that she feels more comfortable researching in a library than addressing an audience. A remark that was probably intended as a self-deprecating disclaimer for an imperceptibly nervous public speaker served instead to prepare the audience for the laying out of a green infrastructure plan of surprising historical nuance and narrative sweep.

All design proposals begin with a de rigueur nod to context, to existing conditions. Often these conditions receive cursory mention as challenges the design will overcome, like a sloping site or an inconveniently placed water main or load-bearing wall. Culhane's presentation marshaled her deep understanding of the multiple dimensions of this community's history — natural, geographic, social, political, and architectural — to outline why the Two Bridges neighborhood is uniquely suited to a holistic approach to green infrastructure, one that will address its extreme vulnerability to flooding and simultaneously help to knit the heretofore isolated neighborhood into both upland systems and waterfront amenities.

The presentation was in March of 2012, when the devastation of Superstorm Sandy was still months in the future but the damage wrought by Hurricane Irene was still fresh in people's minds. Two Bridges, low-lying and flood prone, was one of the most affected areas in both storms. The historical overview she provided (later refashioned into an *Urban Omnibus* article she authored[41]) touched on the neighborhood's eponymous position between the Brooklyn and Manhattan Bridges, as

---

[40] The service area of Two Bridges Neighborhood Council currently encompasses many neighborhoods across the Lower East Side, including Two Bridges, Chinatown, Little Italy, Nolita, the East Village, and the Bowery Corridor.

[41] Kerri Culhane, "Making Connections: Planning for Green Infrastructure in Two Bridges," *Urban Omnibus,* August 8, 2012. (Quotes in this section come from the article, not the speech).

well as the fact that the majority of its land is publicly owned, zoned for residential use, and human-made: "formed of centuries of landfilling and bulkheading that have transformed a natural shoreline of tidal marshes and stream mouths into an industrial waterfront of denticulated slips and piers in the shadow of the elevated FDR Drive."

This waterfront transitioned away from industrial activities earlier than the harbors on the West Side of Manhattan and Brooklyn. As early as the late 1930s, the City began to transform the adjacent area into a primarily residential community with a mix of "subsidized housing on the towers-in-the-park model . . . alongside densely-built city blocks of mid-eighteenth century artisans' houses, nineteenth century rowhouses and tenements, as well as nineteenth- and twentieth-century civic buildings and light industrial lofts." The (well-understood) challenges and (often overlooked) opportunities of towers-in-the-park will be discussed in greater detail in Chapter 5, but the term merits a brief explanation here. It refers to an architectural and urban design typology of multifamily, high-rise housing, located on a dedicated "superblock" of open space that is disconnected from the street system. In the mid-twentieth century, it became the de facto model of subsidized and public housing in the United States, replacing a "congested and unhealthy tenement district [with] the superblocks' swaths of green space providing ample 'light and air.'" In neighborhoods like Two Bridges, with histories of entrenched poverty and an abundance of City-owned land, the typology came to dominate the landscape. Today, superblocks cover much of this part of Manhattan, lining the East River for the two-and-a-half-mile stretch from the Brooklyn Bridge to 14th Street. As stark as this landscape looks to contemporary eyes, all of these buildings were "set within formally conceived park-like green spaces . . . [which] now form a mature canopy shading seating areas, play grounds and acres of grass. These planned, green features contend with the more recent, unplanned addition of infill parking lots and dumpster corrals. Open spaces are dominated by hardscape, and more area is dedicated to parking lots than to green space." This state of affairs has led some, Culhane among them, to deride the typology's current reality as "towers-in-the-parking-lot."

An upscaling of transportation and sanitation infrastructure coincided with this transformation. The FDR highway was elevated, turning the formerly vibrant, riverside South Street into the shadowy backside of the neighborhood: with one exception, all buildings along this street face away from the water. "When the public housing was built," Culhane writes, "proximity to the river was not conceived as a value-adding amenity." She continues:

> The city's rivers were its commercial and industrial center, points of entry for the majority of immigrants, and the fastest and easiest means of traveling throughout what would become the greater New York region. They also served as the most convenient dumps, and received millions of tons of raw sewage, chemical and slaughterhouse waste, solid waste, and the more-than-occasional dead body. While today the East River's toxicity is less than the peak it reached in the 1970s, it still receives regular "contributions" from the many combined sewer overflow outfalls (CSOs) and contaminated upstream watersheds that continue to empty to the East River.

Baruch Houses, in the Lower East Side, is the largest New York City Housing Authority development in Manhattan, occupying a site of almost 28 acres of which buildings cover 13.4 percent of the lot area. Pictured this page and previous are some of the development's open spaces which typify the ground conditions of many tower-in-the-park developments.

Yet, as we have seen with Brooklyn Bridge Park, the adaptive reuse of derelict industrial waterfronts into recreational zones has become a major urban planning priority in recent years. Multiple plans for rethinking the East River waterfront have resulted in significant development of piers into a combination of public space and privately owned and operated retail and athletic facilities. However, the possibility that Two Bridges residents would finally be able to access recreational amenities has given way to profound concern that the waterfront's government-subsidized transformation and beautification portends gentrification. As Culhane puts it, "In a neighborhood where 85 percent of residents rely on rent controls or subsidies, and whose location is much more desirable today than at any earlier point in its history, the general feeling is that the improvements were not intended to benefit the current residents." And while the danger of displacement by gentrification is real, "an equally inexorable threat is that of displacement by climate change. Every resident — in affordable or market rate housing — should be concerned with managing stormwater runoff to the CSOs that pollute their waterfront and storm surges that threaten the future of the neighborhood."

For Culhane and her colleagues at Two Bridges Neighborhood Council, this concentration of liabilities is precisely what provides such unique opportunities for conceiving of green infrastructure as a multipurpose, multibenefit public good. First, while physical geography is what makes it flood-prone, the fact of its position "at the lowest point in the Lower East Side's extensive, hardscaped East River watershed" means that Two Bridges is the "the last point on land to slow, capture and infiltrate the overland flow of stormwater before it reaches the river." Second, while the neighborhood's "acres of mown turf grass, concrete sidewalk and asphalt streets . . . still speed runoff to storm drains and to the river" the considerable open spaces of towers-in-the-park complexes could be retrofitted with "porously-paved paths and parking lots." Their lawns, "currently fenced off from resident use, could be returned to functionality as rain gardens and meadow, providing environmental benefits while preserving the integrity of the mature, forested landscape," with a tree canopy which offers "the dual benefit of localized cooling and mitigation of some stormwater runoff." And third, while the neighborhoods urban design and architecture has cut it off from both the street life of upland communities as well as from the riverfront, "embedding these types of green infrastructure features into walkways, streets and open space can create physical, visible and conceptual connections between upland areas (and their residents) and the East River Waterfront Esplanade and the future parks at Piers 35 and 42."

Culhane enumerates other benefits of this approach beyond managing stormwater runoff. The construction and stewardship of these spaces and bio-swales could serve as a kind of green-collar workforce development. Environmentally performative raingardens could double as public spaces that are more accessible to residents than the commercial recreation facilities currently being developed. In other words, thinking big about infrastructure as a multifunction public good and as an organizing principle of our shared urban landscape can mean scaling up individual environmental retrofits into a coordinated and ambitious vision that addresses a broad range of local challenges. The idea of turning constraints into opportunities is core to the philosophy of design. But the combination of contextually informed, locally specific solutions and ambitious, neighborhood-scale visions that synthesize historical, infrastructural, environmental, sociological, and architectural sensibilities is still relatively rare. That said, if the kinds of projects my colleagues and I have presented on *Urban Omnibus* are any indication, this type of big vision is on the rise.

Sometimes you find it hidden in plain sight, embedded in low-profile projects that have been going on for years without much notice from the press, the academy, or the professional literature of the various urbanist professions. Such is the case with the Staten Island Bluebelt, a massive green infrastructure project that got underway decades before anyone uttered the words green and infrastructure in the same sentence. In fact, the project's origins date back to the mid-1970s, when a group of civil servants at the Department of City Planning (DCP) observed the rapid growth of Staten Island far outpaced the provision of infrastructure. Staten Island became part of New York at the same time as Brooklyn and Queens, in the 1898 Consolidation, but much of the borough remained effectively rural until the completion of the Verrazano-Narrows Bridge in 1964, which immediately opened it up to speculative real estate development. The population rose 30 percent between 1960 and 1970, and had the highest growth rate of any county in New York State until 2015 (when it was overtaken by the Bronx). By the 1980s, the lack of underground pipes for sanitary and stormwater sewers had led to failing septic systems, degraded water quality, erosion, and flooding.

Dana Gumb has been working on the Staten Island Bluebelt since 1988.[42] He started first with the DCP and then went on to lead the Bluebelt project at the Department of Environmental Protection (NYC DEP), the agency responsible for the City's water supply: one billion gallons a day, 7,000 miles of water mains, and 7,400 miles of sewer lines. I went to see him in the agency's headquarters, a drab municipal building in Elmhurst, Queens, abutting the elevated interstate of the Long Island Expressway. I was greeted and led around the maze of lazily partitioned cubicles by a man from DEP's press office. City agencies are notoriously wary of "the press," and my gruff, muscular escort looked like he might prefer to be scaring local TV news crews away from a 2 a.m. water main break than chaperoning an in-office interview. Navigating the monotone, chipboard labyrinth, I felt a sudden

[42] "The Staten Island Bluebelt: Storm Sewers, Wetlands, Waterways" *Urban Omnibus,* December 1, 2010. See also:

- Dana Gumb, "Staten Island History and Bluebelt Land Acquisitions" in *Clear Waters* 39, no. 4 (Winter 2009): 22–26. See also:
- James Garin, Dana Gumb et al, "Bluebelt Beginnings" in *Clear Waters* 39, no. 4 (Winter 2009): 10-21.
- Robert Brauman, Dana Gumb, and Chris Duerkes, "Designing for Wildlife in the Bluebelt," *Clear Waters* 39, no. 4 (Winter 2009): 41–43.
- David Hsu, "Sustainable New York City," a project of the Design Trust for Public Space and the New York City Office of Environmental Coordination, 2006.

and immediate surge of respect for the hardworking public servants who spend their days in windowless rooms, far removed from the public benefits they enable. For Gumb, this work has meant dedication to one specific project for almost thirty years.

The ecology of the southern end of Staten Island (otherwise known as South Richmond) is unique in New York: a ridge of rocky hills slopes to a vast network of kettlehole ponds, streams, and creeks that drain into the Atlantic Ocean. It is New York City's last clutch of sizeable, freshwater wetlands: areas that are inundated frequently enough that their soil and vegetation can thrive under water. DCP officials reasoned that this natural resource might be put to productive infrastructural use.

Once again, neither the advent of green infrastructure in the last decade nor the visionary 1970s decision to capitalize on natural hydrology invented this idea out of whole cloth. And once again, Fredrick Law Olmsted bears referencing. Gumb mentioned Olmsted's plan for the Emerald Necklace in Boston. That green chain of open spaces designed in the 1880s, linked by parkways and waterways, utilized the idea of "stream valley parks" to provide open space amenities that doubled as a drainage system for the flood-prone areas of that city. The fusing of ecological and social benefits in multipurpose has a longer history than contemporary innovators often realize.

Besides, a fully conventional storm sewer system would have been very costly. A hard, constructed sewer system makes sense in a high-rise, urban context, but the economics are trickier in low-density suburban areas like Staten Island. So, DEP started acquiring property for the Bluebelt in the early 1990s and since 1995 has worked with a team of consultants including environmental planners, hydrological engineers, archaeologists, and architects.[43] The goal is to replicate the predevelopment hydrology of these wetland systems such that stormwater is held in detention ponds and slowly released, instead of rushing off rooftops and roadways all at once, thus flooding, contaminating, and ultimately destroying the stream system. The basic underlying principle is not so different from the raingardens proposed in Two Bridges, but in Staten Island the preexisting asset is not a constructed lawn but a natural ecosystem. Like the Two Bridges green infrastructure plan, the Staten Island Bluebelt has benefits that combine, in Gumb's words, "stormwater management with natural area restoration so we get a bunch of benefits in one go: flood control, water quality improvement, and a new natural area for birds, aquatic life, and . . . park access for citizens." The means are as multifaceted as the ends, probing the intersections between land-use planning, environmental engineering, improving public health, providing open space and sustaining biodiversity. Gumb gives a concise overview of the complex process, emphasizing the role of the engineered drainage solutions that are designed into the reconstructed wetland, called best management practices or BMPs:

---

43 The primary consultant on this project was the environmental engineering firm of Hazen and Sawyer.

The Staten Island Bluebelt is a complex stormwater management system that preserves natural drainage corridors, such as streams, ponds, and other wetland areas, in order to convey, store, and filter stormwater in a part of New York where rapid residential development rapidly outpaced investment in sewage infrastructure.

Top to bottom:

Prior to development, Staten Island was home to a unique variety of freshwater wetlands, kettlehole ponds, streams, and creeks that drain into the Atlantic Ocean. While some of this stream system remains, re-engineering the landscape to manage the flow of stormwater has required decades of work from dedicated civil servants.

Frequent cracks in Staten Island's hardscaped streets and parking lots reveal the poor drainage capacity of the borough's sewage infrastructure.

Prior to the development of the Bluebelt, Staten Island suffered from contaminants washing off street pavements and rooftops and making their way into the stream system.

To put it in a few words, we've based everything on watershed level planning. A watershed is a geographic area that contributes water to a particular stream or water body. South Richmond has about 15 or 16 watersheds, and for each one the first step is to look at zoning to determine the ultimate development pattern within that watershed. Next, we build a mathematical, hydrological model that will predict what the flows are going to be in the stream system. We then acquire the land around the stream system so that we can maintain the streams as a way to convey the stormwater to the ultimate receiving waters. In a conventional suburban sewer system, when the water gets to the end of the street it is simply dumped into the stream. The cutting-edge aspect of the Bluebelt is that at each and every storm sewer discharge point, at each point where the gray infrastructure transitions into green infrastructure, we have these special facilities — the BMPs — that address the issues of urban stormwater discharge in wetland conditions. Sometimes it's as simple as a series of sumps — or holes in the ground — that slow the storm water down and allow for sediments to settle, accumulate and eventually get removed by our maintenance forces. Once contaminants have flowed into the natural receiving water body, you can never get them out.

The land-use planning and property acquisition aspect is especially interesting from a public goods standpoint. While the most intensive development dates to the years after the Verrazano opened, Gumb explained that what made the Bluebelt possible "goes back to the boom times of the 1920s. Old farms were subdivided, streets were laid out on paper, and many little lots were sold sight unseen. Many people in Brooklyn and elsewhere were persuaded by the possibility of owning a little piece of New York — but little did they know that in certain cases the lot they bought was in the middle of a swamp. And then, when the Depression hit, people could not pay their property taxes and a huge amount of land went into City ownership." Additionally, the DEP had to target "the missing links," acquiring private property and accumulating "whatever public property we can: parkland, highway rights of way, land owned by the State's Department of Environmental Conservation." The watershed-level planning and implementation of this project would never have been possible without significant City ownership of land alongside a commitment to public investment that outlasts electoral cycles. As such, the story is a valuable example of what can happen when long-range planning is applied to public assets, a precedent that we should keep in mind in light of other pressing issues cities face, especially the challenge of housing affordability (to be discussed in Chapter 5). It also applies to a conception of infrastructure as the organizing principle of long-term urban development — a notion once commonplace and now perilously disregarded — even when the exact shape and the precise public benefits of that development cannot be completely anticipated.

INCREMENTAL INFRASTRUCTURES OF OPPORTUNITY

Vishaan Chakrabarti, mentioned earlier for his critique of stimulus spending, is an outspoken exponent of urban density. His quote above comes from the first in a series of ten opinion pieces he authored for *Urban Omnibus* that cast current

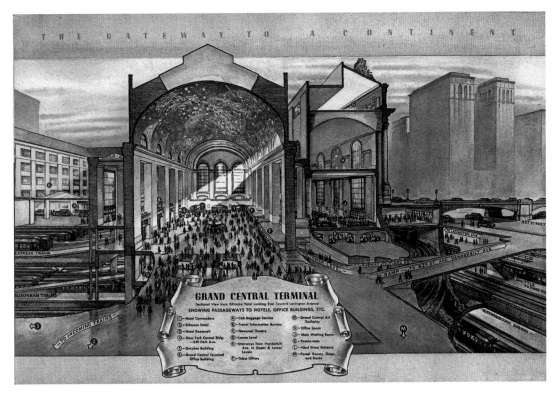

Grand Central Terminal benefits from numerous pedestrian access passageways connecting throughout the surrounding neighborhood. Many pass through private office buildings, making clear the coordination between private and public interests that enabled this iconic piece of transit infrastructure.

events — the climate talks in Denmark, the Gulf Oil Spill, the canceling of a major tunnel project between New Jersey and New York, the protests of the Arab Spring — as rallying cries in his passionate argument for urban density, for a country of cities. He contends that using design, policy, and finance to create cities dense enough to support high-speed mass transit (which he defines as 30 units per acre) is the silver bullet needed to combat America's intertwined challenges of "economic decline, energy dependence, oil wars, terrorism, xenophobia, protectionism, mounting debt, and spiraling health care costs." He went on to develop these arguments further in a 2013 book, titled, like the column, *A Country of Cities*. The book unpacks the history of postwar US public policy choices that have subsidized suburban sprawl and artificially increased the costs of urban living in ways that are not well understood or even acknowledged by the public. Media and politicians never hesitate to broadcast the dollar costs and subsidies of planned government investments in infrastructure projects like rail, bridges, and tunnels. The subsidies of gasoline, the auto and airline industries, highway construction, and single-family home ownership, however, go unnoticed. And when we factor in the negative externalities that this infrastructure of sprawl has enabled — the grotesquely enlarged carbon footprint of low-density living — the hidden costs are even higher. Chakrabarti has some specific recommendations for policymakers (eliminate the mortgage interest tax deduction), for real estate financiers (scale up and diversify the market for transferable development rights[44]), and for designers (create inviting mixed-use towers that people want to live in). But whether or not you find his hyperdense vision appealing — a sustainable future America of "trains, towers, and trees" instead of our gluttonous contemporary reality of "highways, houses, and hedges" — one of the underlying premises of his manifesto is relevant to citymaking at all densities. The benefits of forward-thinking infrastructure investment outweigh their financial costs in the short-term and amortize them in the long-term.

To recast this idea in the economistic terms of Frischmann, the user activities and the resulting outputs that infrastructure enables are the ultimate indicator of its value, therefore the demand for these downstream outputs is what determines the societal demand for infrastructure. For these reasons, infrastructure must be reclaimed as the organizing principle of urban development, not an afterthought financed in piecemeal ways that respond to market-driven population growth after the fact, too little, too late.

Just as Chakrabarti was beginning to author his series of opinion pieces, he and I took a walk through Grand Central Terminal, one of the most beloved pieces of civic or transportation infrastructure anywhere. Its architectural majesty is breathtaking. It makes possible tens of thousands of car-free commutes into Manhattan from the metro-region each day. It hosts unusually elegant (for a train station) non-chain retail offerings, including a fresh food market and world-famous dining options like the Oyster Bar. Best of all, it has survived against the odds, galvanizing a ground-swell of public support for historic preservation when it faced almost certain demolition in 1968.

A series of bankruptcies and mergers in the declining railroad industry since the mid-1940s, hastened by the rise of heavily government-subsidized highway construction, led the terminal's owners, Penn Central Railroad, to seek to replace the building with a more lucrative development, as they had done a few years earlier when they destroyed the original Penn Station to build Madison Square Garden. According to the owners, the historic designation that saved Grand Central, legislated soon after and largely in response to the outcry after Penn Station's demolition, amounted to eminent domain abuse. The lawsuit ended up in the Supreme Court, which ruled that the landmark designation did not constitute the City of New York violating Penn Central's property rights.

At the time that Chakrabarti and I met up by the iconic four-faced clock in the center of the main concourse, he was overseeing plans to develop Moynihan Station as a new intercity train station, an attempt to restore some of the architectural grandeur and infrastructural efficacy lost when the original Penn Station was replaced with an unsafe, unattractive, underground version. So he was especially sensitive to "why Grand Central works." (Though I suspect that this self-proclaimed, lifelong train nerd would be equally attuned under any circumstances.) As he led me around, he pointed out the graceful and innovative ways that the building organizes its vast network of tracks, ramps, and platforms, design choices that have influenced the design of train stations and airports for generations to come. He explained how Grand Central pioneered the new technologies of electrification, like the third rail. And, crucially, he showed me how the station was coordinated with a broad and incremental development agenda for the surrounding area of Midtown. The building is only one part of a larger exercise in citymaking. Grand Central catalyzed the development of some of the most commercially valuable real estate in the world.

Elsewhere in this book, I sound notes of caution about public-private partnership in the delivery of public goods. My skepticism about the prevalence of market-based urban development does not mean that I think private initiative has no role to play however. I share Chakrabarti's dismay that neither side of the American political spectrum embraces long-range infrastructure investment. "You have a political right that thinks all of this is about spending public money making unwise investment," he explains. "And you have a political left that thinks that anything corporate is bad and gives too much control to the private sector." Or, as Adam Gopnik puts it in *The New Yorker,* writing in response to a deadly Amtrak derailment in 2015, "What we have, uniquely in America, is a political class, and an entire political party, devoted to the idea that any money spent on public goods is money misplaced, not because the state goods might not be good but because they would distract us from the larger principle that no ultimate good can be found in the state."[45]

The development of Grand Central and its surrounds, over a hundred years ago and very much a collaboration between private and public interests, between the political class and the state, attests to a very different political and investment climate. One impetus to build the station and electrify its tracks was growing concern about the dangers of steam locomotives, especially after a fatal crash in 1902. The decision to bury a newly electrified railyard below ground not only eliminated noise and pollution on this stretch of Park Avenue, it also freed the land for development. Chakrabarti referenced some historic photographs from 1903, when station construction began, that show Park Avenue "as a series of development parcels." He loves the fact that real estate marketing of the era referred to the area as "Terminal City," acknowledging and even promoting the idea that proximity to transportation infrastructure — which at the time connoted the dirty, smoky, and noisy business of coal-powered steam engines — would become a desirable amenity.

---

[44] Transferable Development Rights (TDR) or "air rights" are real estate development tools that turn the municipal land use controls restricting the height and bulk of buildings into an opportunity to buy and sell finite units of undeveloped space above a building. Therefore, TDR provide local governments with an effective and flexible tool to ensure that the municipality can achieve the right mix of building density and open space without causing a financial burden to individual landowners or constricting desired development.

[45] Adam Gopnik, "The Plot Against Trains," *The New Yorker,* May 15, 2015. Accessed May 2, 2015. www.newyorker.com/news/daily-comment/the-plot-against-trains.

Another aspect of the coordination between infrastructure and real estate development, and another reason Grand Central works so well, is that, like "all great train stations, it [has] tentacles that reach out into the city. There's not just a front door." Wandering through the less than glamorous network of pedestrian access passageways that extend, in many cases, through private office buildings makes clear the level of coordination, staged in phases over many years, between different stakeholders. As we finally stepped out into the sun via a passageway that leads through the Chrysler Building, Chakrabarti foreshadowed many of the arguments that he elaborates in *A Country of Cities:* "People talk about infrastructure as being impossible: too expensive, too much investment. I think people lose track of how much has already been done and how much was done by our predecessors and how successful it's been as an *investment,* not just a spending program."

Stately, iconic, hard, and heavy, Grand Central Terminal is hardly the type of project evoked in the budding vanguard of multipurpose, soft, and "smart" infrastructure. The word *smart,* deployed so widely as to have become meaningless, often refers to the embedding of devices and environments — from watches to running shoes to apartments — with computing power, collecting and transmitting user data to improve performance. I discuss some of the possibilities and pitfalls of this technological revolution in urbanism in the next chapter. Before exploring that terrain, we should first ask: are there more productive ways to conceptualize urban infrastructure as a responsive and generative force for cities that include but are not limited to digital instrumentation?

My colleagues and I have posed variants of this question to a number of creative citymakers over the years, including a pair of architects, a regional planner, a transportation entrepreneur, and an urban sociologist. While their perspectives and work products are distinct, the common themes among them support the call to recognize and accelerate the emergent shift towards reconceiving infrastructure as a multi-use public good and an environmentally performative and flexible element of our shared urban landscape.

MULTITASKING, FLEXIBLE, AND SOCIAL INFRASTRUCTURE

Sheila Kennedy and Veit Kugel are two of four partners in the Boston-based architecture firm of Kennedy Violich Architects (KVA). In addition to traditional architecture projects for residential as well as cultural and educational institutions, KVA is experienced in a practice area dedicated to infrastructure and also operates an interdisciplinary research lab called MATx, which "explores material culture across scales." When I sat down with Kennedy and Kugel in the former bottling plant that they converted into their firm's office and laboratory space on the southern fringe of Boston's South End, the evidence of the lab's experimentation in optoelectronics and prototypes of photovoltaic fabric was all around us. The multiplicity of scales in KVA's work raises an important point about the vanguard infrastructural logic girding the projects and perspectives described in this chapter. While the embrace of infrastructure as an urban design challenge suggests a spatial expansion of architectural and landscape architectural practice beyond the individual building

Kennedy Violich Architecture's design for the 34th Street Ferry Terminal on the East River features many responsive elements, including optical sensors to track entry and exit, on-demand bench warming and drop-down rainscreen systems, and interactive LED lighting.

or garden, the attention to flexible systems and materials also has an object-scale focus. Kugel characterizes the firm's approach in transdisciplinary terms: the work "requires the mental facility of branching between different disciplines, to be able to approach a problem like an engineer or to think like a mason."

One of the projects to emerge from MATx research is called Portable Light, which provides adaptable textile kits to enable people to sew and weave bags, clothing, and blankets that harvest solar energy to be used as light sources or to charge cell phones and connect to the internet. Portable Light, now run as an independent nonprofit, is currently operating in Nicaragua, Mexico, Brazil, and South Africa, working with local NGOs to distribute the textile kits to vulnerable populations. Another innovative MATx project is the Soft House, developed for the building exhibition Internationale Bauausstellung (IBA) Hamburg. This housing prototype achieves carbon-negativity (not carbon-neutral, carbon-*negative*) through its use of solid-wood construction, an exterior membrane-like photovoltaic canopy, and a set of interior curtains that double as LED lights, arranged along a reconfigurable set of tracks that distribute the clean energy from the exterior solar canopy to the interior low-voltage grid. Kennedy described these innovative moves as "flipp[ing] the traditional roles of architecture and infrastructure . . . such that the structure is more permanent and the infrastructure is more like furniture: movable, networked, adjustable, and upgradable."

These groundbreaking projects would be reason enough to include the voices of KVA's leadership on *Urban Omnibus*. But the primary motivation for the interview was the opening, in 2012, of a new ferry terminal on the East River that the firm designed.[46] The project embodies exactly what smart or intelligent infrastructure should mean.

Like all of the citymakers cited in this chapter, Kennedy and Kugel referenced the overdue attention designers are beginning to pay to infrastructure and its role in cities, lamenting the intense specialization of architectural practice in the second half of the twentieth century. According to Kugel, "Many people use the word 'intelligent' in the sense of digital intelligence. But I think it's more productive to think about it as moving away from an exclusive focus on any single functionality. It's about integration, about situating systems to react to and function with natural as well as manmade environments." He cited San Francisco's iconic Golden Gate Bridge as an example of infrastructure that was responsive or "intelligent" long before the digital revolution, because the median barrier is moveable such that lanes can be allocated to northbound or southbound traffic based on demand. Kennedy would prefer we label this responsive turn as "resilient infrastructure," which she characterizes as "a new alliance between natural systems, architectural artifacts, and digital networks. The challenge of resilient infrastructure is to design these elements to work together in synergy."

Synergy is the watchword of KVA's approach. Kennedy continues: "If modern infrastructure is considered machine-like or mechanical, then the contemporary generation of infrastructure is more about the coordination and integration of parts. It's more biological, if you think of biology in terms of different elements working together in ways that aren't entirely mechanical or predictable." The design of the 34th Street Ferry Terminal is a perfect example, deftly integrating a nuanced understanding of natural systems, transit infrastructure, and information technology.

The project came about during the Bloomberg administration's efforts to scale up water-based public transit in New York, a lower carbon transportation alternative that can help alleviate congestion on city streets while providing a vital link in the emergency response chain, especially in light of the marine evacuation of half a million people on 9/11. Its primary purpose is transit infrastructure, of course, but the designers note it only serves as a transportation facility during peak commuting hours. "For this to be intelligent infrastructure," said Kugel, "it should never be idle. Whether it's used for fishing or just to hang out, it's a multitasking civic space."

In people, the word *multitasking* connotes an error-prone state of distraction at odds with the deep focus that masterful craftsmanship demands. In infrastructure, however, the word just might help us meaningfully to consolidate the social, environmental, urbanistic, technological, and aesthetic drivers of public architecture. Importantly, when Kennedy and Kugel talk about multitasking infrastructures, they are not only talking about simultaneous but also sequential functions. Their approach incorporates the dimension of time: daily and seasonal patterns of light, the flows of tides, the rhythms of commuters. The design "harvest[s] reflected light all along the underside of the terminal's canopy and use[s] is to inform where the openings to the river's reflecting pool would be. Optical sensors track people's entry and exit, information that is displayed in light along with real time data and announcements about the ferry schedule. Other interactive or responsive components include "a heat-on-demand bench warming system, adapted from the automotive industry; a rainscreen that drops down when there's a lot of horizontal rain; daylighting along with interactive LED lighting." When the client, a group of City agencies, asked the designers to show them examples of some of these responsive systems and original approaches to form and structure, KVA had to let them know that the work would be, literally, unprecedented. "The entire thing — the triangulated tripod structure, the detailing on the facade system, the double-wrapped tensile roof — is an innovation." One hopes that the terminal will become a precedent for future infrastructure design projects because of the elegant ways that it offers "lessons about how to create building services that interact with each other, how to reduce steel and create structures that can be fabricated largely off-site, how to harvest some of the effects of the sun besides solar power, [and] how to integrate environmental sensing in public space."

Tracking usage to identify efficiencies and priorities in infrastructure management is, of course, one of the advantages of embedding computing power into the built environment. But, as Kugel's Golden Gate Bridge example makes clear, flexibility is not a new idea. It's just one that needs to be reintroduced on a grand scale. We need to infuse it into the philosophy of design. We also need to use it as a

---

46 "Multi-tasking Infrastructures: A Conversation with Sheila Kennedy and Veit Kugel," *Urban Omnibus,* March 6, 2013.

A 1928 diagram of "New York City and its Environs," produced by the Regional Plan Association, shows the extent of the metropolitan area, traversing multiple government jurisdictions and state lines.

guiding principle in the structural reform of the governmental institutions that deliver and manage public goods.

One of the local organizations that has been leading the charge on planning for innovative infrastructure investment — and advocating for the institutional restructuring needed to make it possible — is the Regional Plan Association (RPA), which has been in the business of coming up with new ideas to make the New York metropolitan region work better since 1922. A few months before the Wall Street Crash of 1929, RPA released a plan for the region that helped to pave the way for the systems that supported New York's recovery from the Great Depression and subsequent growth. Their two subsequent long-range plans, in 1968 and 1996, have argued persuasively for coordinated planning across municipal and state boundaries that integrates community design, open space, transportation, housing, and economic and workforce development. I first interviewed Tom Wright, RPA's executive director in 2010, just as preliminary thinking about the Fourth Regional Plan (expected to be complete around 2020) was underway. Wright told me about the history of the organization's arguments for "creating infrastructure and building big systems to protect landscapes and water supplies, to provide more mass-transit, to plan for the region's growth." The nature of that advocacy has reflected the times. The 1929 plan emphasized preparing for expected population growth by constructing highways, mass-transit, airports, housing. Over the next thirty years, most of the recommendations were realized, with the important exception of the mass transit connections, thus hastening the suburbanization of the region. In the 1960s, when the ethos of urbanism had shifted to the more grassroots, community-focused approach typified by the work of Jane Jacobs, the RPA didn't "feel it was appropriate to dictate, in a top-down way, what the region's priorities should be. So instead, rather than publish a definitive Second Regional Plan, we put out a 'Draft for Discussion' in 1968." These recommendations also had results, such as the creation of the MTA and NJ Transit. In the 1990s, thinking big had once again become appealing and urgent. The Third Regional Plan, published in 1996, argued for building the 2nd Ave subway, connecting the Long Island Railroad to Grand Central, creating a new commuter rail tunnel under the Hudson River, and charging drivers coming into Manhattan to pay for it. The first two initiatives, long overdue, are fitfully underway, albeit with chronic underfunding, ballooning cost estimates, and repeated extensions of the completion date. The second two failed spectacularly due, respectively, to the partisan politics of austerity[47] and the dysfunctionally fractured state of local government.[48]

Jerry Frug, the local government law expert mentioned earlier, has written extensively about this dysfunction.[49] In an article published on *Urban Omnibus,* he applauds the work of the RPA in particular, but reminds us that "there's no one they can talk to — the government authority in this region is so fractured that it's hard to get any of the pieces to begin to fit together. Their problem is our problem. When we discuss ideas of transportation, labor, public space, and housing, we should keep in mind a fundamental question: who could possibly implement any of our ideas?"[50]

Nonetheless, the forthcoming Fourth Regional Plan promises to be ambitious. And it will not shy away from Frug's rhetorical question. At the RPA's 2015 Regional Assembly event, an annual convening of influential planners and policymakers,

---

[47] In October of 2010, Governor Christie, Republican of New Jersey, killed a major tunnel project called ARC or Access to the Region's Core. Writing on *Urban Omnibus*, Chakrabarti decried the decision to abandon a project "planned for two decades and considered vital to the lifeline of the northeast corridor . . . . Citing costs, the rebellious Republican ruled out increasing gas taxes or surcharges in order to plug the budget gap, instead rejecting billions in Federal and Port Authority funds. Unlike the manner in which we funded the extension of the #7 subway, which was constructed through debt that will be paid off by the future assessed values on the West Side of Manhattan, no such innovation was sought in New Jersey despite reports that clearly showed increased property values in the towns that would be connected to ARC."

[48] Polling indicated that New York City voters supported Mayor Bloomberg's 2008 proposal to charge cars entering central Manhattan, but it did not win the support of powerful state legislators representing the outer boroughs and suburban towns.

[49] Frug has published dozens of articles on local government law and is the author, among other works, of *City Making: Building Communities without Building Walls* (Princeton: Princeton University Press,1999); and *City Bound: How States Stifle Urban Innovation,* with David Barron (Ithaca: Cornell University Press, 2008).

[50] Gerald Frug, "Empowering the City: London / New York," *Urban Omnibus,* February 2010, adapted from a 2005 speech delivered at the Urban Age, London conference,

[51] Tom Wright, "Update on the Fourth Regional Plan," remarks delivered at the 2015 Regional Assembly of the Regional Plan Association, April 24, 2015.

Wright posed a provocative question of his own: "Are our public institutions, as currently structured, capable of tackling the challenges that face us? When do your major regional institutions need tweaks, and when do they need radical overhaul?" He then went on to relate how London, New York City's "primary competitor and analogue on the global stage," fundamentally restructured its government in the late 1990s, resulting in a metropolitan transportation authority under the direct supervision of the Mayor of London, an office established in 2000 as the first directly elected mayoralty in the UK. Since then, London has implemented congestion pricing and invested in a major and comprehensive upgrading of its transportation infrastructure.[51]

Frug has also explored the structural contrasts between London and New York City, and while his analysis touches on everything from health care to policing, it is particularly relevant to understanding the obstacles that impede the kind of visionary infrastructure that conveys people, goods, waste, and energy while simultaneously performing urgent environmental and civic functions. The societal disinclination to demand or design multipurpose, shared resources is real: taxes understood as a fee-for-service, mistrust of government spending, and so on. So too is New York City's lacking "the capacity to plan for, let alone determine, its own future" caused by New York State's splintering of government authority among a number of state-controlled public authorities.[52] "There is no document such as the London Plan for the City of New York — and no organization now exists with the authority to write one. There is also no government agency that is thinking about the future of the City of New York in terms of its connection even with the narrowest definition of its region — one that would include the parts of New Jersey right across the Hudson River." Even the infrastructure within city limits falls under multiple jurisdictions. To close the bridges and tunnels to Manhattan during Superstorm Sandy required the sign-off of three separate agencies: the Port Authority of New York and New Jersey, the New York State-led Metropolitan Transportation Authority, and the New York City Department of Transportation.

Infrastructure suffers not only from a demand-manifestation problem, but also from what might be called a demand-scale problem, wherein the catchment area of demand is so mismatched with the legal geography of governance that the competition between different local authorities undermines the appetites and arguments for sound investment. As many have pointed out, including experts at the RPA as well as commentators like Bruce Katz and Benjamin Barber, if over 70 percent of the national population now lives in metropolitan regions, then we need a governance structure that mirrors our new demographics.[53]

That said, a radical restructuring of New York City's government is not the only hope. Back in 2010, Wright told me that "the Fourth Regional Plan might end up being less about creating new systems and more about getting more efficiency and productivity out of the energy supply, the water supply, community development networks. The bad news is that we're doing a poor job of managing and operating these nineteenth- and early twentieth-century systems; the good news is there's a lot more capacity in them if we start to manage the systems better."

The identification and utilization of excess capacity has emerged as an important theme among a range of citymakers chronicled by *Urban Omnibus*. Examples include a pair of young architects converting the human energy of pushing revolving doors into electricity, a communication designer developing a system for tenants in the same building to share office equipment, and an artist brokering underutilized commercial real estate for use as art studios and performance spaces.[54] For me, the person who most clearly articulated the importance of excess capacity is an entrepreneur named Robin Chase, cofounder of the seminal car-sharing service ZipCar, which launched in 2000.

Almost a decade later and still a couple years before the "sharing economy" was a popular buzzword, I spoke with Chase on the phone about the implications of her work for urbanism.[55] She described the company's founding as "a perfect moment of confluence" between the emergence of wireless internet access, car-sharing precedents in Europe, and the irrational exuberance of the late '90s dot-com boom. But unlike the rash of overvalued start-ups that took the internet largely as a place to shop without having to leave your home, Chase remembers thinking, "Wow, this is what the internet was made for: sharing a scarce resource among many people!"

In her case, the resource in question was access to a car. Her family of five owned one car that her husband drove to an office "where it sits, unused, for eight hours a day" yet the costs of owning a second vehicle far outweighed the benefits. Thus began her efforts to decouple the use of a good from the need to own it exclusively, a quest that opens up big, important questions about the fixity of assets and the elasticity of sharing them. At the same time Chase, a serial entrepreneur, uses a clear language of consumer choice, balance sheets, and business plans that usefully summarizes the long-term costs when infrastructure is rigid, proprietary, and single-purpose and the long-term benefits when it is open-access, shared, and versatile. "Infrastructure is destiny," she said, because "when our infrastructure

---

[52] In his UO article "Empowering the City: London / New York," Frug explains, "Much of the important development in the city is controlled not by the City but by the Empire State Development Corporation — an agency, appointed by the Governor not the Mayor, that, directly or through subsidiaries, dominates major projects ranging from Ground Zero to Battery Park City to Times Square. The two most important actors on transportation issues are the Metropolitan Transportation Authority and the Port Authority of New York and New Jersey. The Metropolitan Transportation Authority is appointed by New York State's Governor, with only four of its seventeen members recommended by the City; the Port Authority is appointed by two Governors, without any City input. Public space is divided up into more than fifty business improvement districts governed by property owners and not city residents."

[53] See Bruce Katz and Jennifer Bradley, *The Metropolitan Revolution: How Cities and Metros Are Fixing Our Broken Politics and Fragile Economy* (Washington, DC: Brookings Institution Press, 2014); and Benjamin Barber *If Mayors Ruled the World: Dysfunctional Nations, Rising Cities* (New Haven: Yale University Press, 2013).

[54] See *Urban Omnibus* articles including "Fluxxlab: Making Ideas Happen" by Jenny Broutin and Carmen Trudell, (April 22, 2009); "Stackd" by Sidney Blank (August 19, 2009); and "chashama: Space to Create" (June 6, 2012).

[55] "A Conversation with Robin Chase," *Urban Omnibus,* June 10, 2009.

makes things easy and convenient, we do more of those things. When things are made difficult, we do less of them. We have set up our infrastructure to make getting in your car, going door to door really easy, as the cheapest, fastest way."

"I believe in a heartfelt way that energy efficiency has to do with behavior," Chase told me. "And behavior is driven by price and ease of use. By simplicity. For cars, the only way we will change our driving habits is when we're paying the real cost of driving: including the cost of carbon, the cost of congestion, the cost of building and maintaining the roads." She went on to list a number of technologies that could facilitate more accurate pricing of car, gas, and road use, including ubiquitous data grids, use sensors, and mesh networks. Fundamentally, however, she thinks "the most successful solution is to produce things that can be adaptable, highly adaptable. Infrastructure is destiny yet infrastructure, typically, is not adaptable. That's why it often plays out in bad ways. We need to make flexible infrastructure." As such, Chase's work illuminates the conceptual link between designed flexibility, infrastructural determinism, and the subject of the next chapter: digital information technology.

Flexibility is more readily applied to the agile world of technology, in which people hold powerful computing devices in their pockets and more and more services are automated and dematerialized, than to the durability we tend to expect from urban infrastructure like trains, bridges, or sewers. We expect our infrastructure to stand the test of time. Yet public investment in infrastructure is insufficient, and late-twentieth-century design and planning has prioritized single-function efficiency over the indeterminacy of overlapping functions. Furthermore, in the context of ever-stronger storms, we must demand infrastructure that can perform urgent environmental functions, such as streets, sidewalks, and waterfronts that enable stormwater to infiltrate the ground plane and therefore lessen the impacts of flooding, or train systems and stations that actually make it easy, comfortable, and quick to use mass transit to commute to work.

Our reality of frequent disasters also requires that our infrastructure perform socially as well as environmentally. One way to be ready for an emergency is to have contingencies and logistics in place for extraordinary circumstances, to make sure the power, transit, and communications networks stay operational as crucial lifelines of support in the aftermath of a crisis. A less recognized but perhaps equally important way is to invest in what the sociologist Eric Klinenberg calls "social infrastructure." Klinenberg got his start as a sociologist studying the devastating effects of the Chicago heat wave of 1995, analyzing why the death tolls varied so much between different neighborhoods.[56] His analysis led him to expand his conception of the kinds of infrastructures that can keep us safe in times of disaster, an analysis he applied to his investigations into the devastation wrought by Superstorm Sandy in 2012.[57] When I interviewed him about his work, Klinenberg explained the concept in terms of the manifold utility of robust public life:

We need to think about the social infrastructure as much as we do about the hard infrastructure of power lines and transit systems and communications networks. We need to think about the quality of our sidewalks and streets. We need to think about whether neighborhoods have open, accessible, and welcoming public places where residents can congregate and provide social support during times of need but also every day.[58]

In other words, one of the most important ways in which we need all public amenities — from streets and stations to public libraries and community gardens — to be multitasking infrastructures is to conceive of them as places woven into the fabric of everyday life that are also understood as places to go for support in times of crisis.

The weather is only going to become more extreme. After Superstorm Sandy, New Yorkers heard many calls to build more hard infrastructure, like flood barriers in the harbor, to protect us from future storm surges. Citymakers need to expand the conception of infrastructure at all scales in order to move us away from the notion of infrastructure as an after-the-fact, fit-to-purpose response to extreme conditions, and instead move toward the notion of infrastructure as an intrinsic, organizing principle of a dynamic urban landscape. That landscape is a layered combination of physical, social, and natural environments that have exigencies we can neither fully anticipate nor control.

---

[56] Klinenberg's study showed that the death tolls were greatest in neighborhoods with high degrees of abandonment and lower population density. In particular, adjacent neighborhoods with similar rates of violence, unemployment, and elderly residents, both poor and predominantly African-American, had drastically different mortality rates because the more densely populated neighborhoods possessed a street life — gardens, sidewalks, libraries, and shops — that drew people out of their homes and saved their lives; in the more abandoned neighborhoods, greater numbers of poor, elderly people stayed indoors and died from heat wave–related causes. Eric Klinenberg, *Heat Wave: A Social Autopsy of Disaster in Chicago,* (Chicago: University of Chicago Press, 2002).

[57] Eric Klinenberg "Adaptation: How can cities be 'climate-proofed'?" *The New Yorker,* January 7, 2013.

[58] "Towards a Stronger Social Infrastructure: a Conversation with Eric Klinenberg," *Urban Omnibus,* October 16, 2013.

CHAPTER 4

TECHNOLOGY
AND THE
LEGIBLE CITY

The story of Zipcar is a story of decoupling goods and services. These two building blocks of economic output — the former physical, the latter intangible — have long been considered as two dimensions of the same thing: to use something, you must possess it. Widespread internet usage and ubiquitous computing offer a challenge to this orthodoxy. You can use something that you do not own for the exact period of time when you need it; you can hire someone to perform a task without shouldering any of the responsibilities of employing him. This shift is variously described as sounding nice and neighborly — "the sharing economy" — or as fundamentally unstable and insecure, if not predatory — "the gig economy."

For Robin Chase, decoupling goods and services serves a moral purpose: lowering the demand for individual cars on the road will bring about environmental sustainability via greater efficiency. For legions of contemporary technological innovators in almost every sector of the economy, this increase in efficiency serves a different kind of purpose: greater profitability. In the words of one tech sector executive in the spring of 2015: "Uber, the world's largest taxi company, owns no vehicles. Facebook, the world's most popular media owner, creates no content. Alibaba, the most valuable retailer, has no inventory. And Airbnb, the world's largest accommodation provider, owns no real estate. Something interesting is happening."[1] Zipcar's market share has long been overtaken by more successfully distributed forms of on-demand access to cars: car2go, currently the world's largest car-sharing service, allows its users to rent whichever vehicle is parked on the street nearby, drive it from point A to point B, and leave it there. Uber's competitors, like Lyft, seek to capitalize on Uber's off-putting callousness about regulation or worker benefits or the application of its surge pricing during periods of high demand due to inclement weather, and even, notoriously, natural disasters and terrorist attacks. Airbnb's impact on distorting the rental housing market and raising home prices is starting to be protested, regulated, and restricted in desirable markets from Berlin to San Francisco.

The potential benefits to environmental sustainability and income-generation must be balanced against the negative impacts to livelihoods, worker benefits, household costs, and tax revenue that come with destabilizing the economic status quo. The so-called sharing economy and so many other manifestations of information technology's impact on contemporary lives holds up disruption and value-neutrality as unquestionably positive and progressive attributes. The prevailing thinking is not only about separating ownership and access through a dubious interpretation of what "sharing" means. It's also about quantifying and measuring our movements and behaviors to streamline decision-making in ways that fail to account for the messy dynamism of the real world. The "smart city" is a vision of urban development in which multiple information and communication technologies are woven into the urban built environment to manage or optimize public service delivery, from transportation to law enforcement to power and water supply. The smart city, the connected city, the digital city, the sharing economy: these tropes commandeer the rhetoric of democracy, participation, and efficiency by supposedly turning everyone and every place into an input. However, most often such visions consolidate the control of extremely complex systems in the hands of fewer and fewer people.

I believe we need to conceptualize and embrace a new urban ethics that is responsive to contemporary possibilities and communitarian priorities as well as cognizant of the structural importance of public policy to our daily lives. As inefficient as governance may be, technological shortcuts to speed up or redirect public service delivery tend to compound inequality. And as burdensome as traditional commerce has become, innovative platforms that broker independent contractors (and take hefty cuts) may undermine the hard-won rights and protections of employees in ways far more costly than they appear. Furthermore, one of the great promises of contemporary technologies is to make the complexity of urban dynamics — how a city *works* — more legible to citizens. This potential legibility can empower citizens to practice far more meaningful and informed kinds of democratic participation than the quantification, automation, and disruption that much techno-urbanism promises. This chapter chronicles some citymakers who are pushing back, in various ways, against the ascendant strain of technological optimism that obfuscates extremely complex processes and automates decision-making in the name of greater efficiency.

An important way to do so is through qualitative analysis and inductive reasoning. Observational modes of urban understanding provide crucial and complementary counterpoints to quantitative measurement and computational formulas. As technological readings of the city exert ever-increasing influence on urban decision-making, new digital tools have a tremendous potential for urbanism. For that potential to be beneficial, democratic, and ethical, however, we need to be a little less algorithmic and a lot more heuristic. Urban experience is imprecise and unpredictable, encompassing individuals (and markets) who do not always act rationally. Understanding and improving cities requires human perception, not just computation.

Many of the tools described in this chapter have been conceived and implemented to bring local government, always a slow adopter of new technologies, into the smartphone age. Before we consider these, however, we must also question the entire infrastructure of the internet in the US, on which both basic usage (email, web-forms) and more specialized functions (smartphone apps) rely. This infrastructure is owned by a handful of media companies who can set high, mostly arbitrary prices for access. In a poor community like Red Hook, Brooklyn, in 2010, internet service

---

[1] Tom Goodwin, "The Battle Is For the Customer Interface," Techcrunch.com, March 3, 2015, as quoted in Thomas Friedman, "Hillary, Jeb, Facebook and Disorder," *The New York Times,* May 20, 2015.

was only available from one provider and almost all internet connections came from mobile phones. This state of affairs presented a blatant structural barrier to accessing web-dependent tools for applying to jobs, filing public assistance claims, or even completing homework. In yet another example of the systemic reinforcement of intergenerational poverty, new opportunities are only available to those who already possess the infrastructural and technological tools to take advantage of them. At the time, these obstacles were not yet understood as an issue that a community could organize or educate its way out of, as opposed to, say, promoting health or advocating for specific public investments. In the wake of the most destructive storm ever to hit New York, in October of 2012, when all traditional lines of telecommunication went down, such obstacles became an urgent call for the community to take control of its own digital future.

DIGITAL STEWARDSHIP AND THE LEFT BEHIND

The digital divide is easy to talk about in a community like Red Hook. This coastal neighborhood's physical geography and built environment are a neighborhood-scale object lesson in how misguided urban planning can create real barriers between poor communities and economic opportunity. Once home to the busiest freight port in the world, Red Hook has historically been home to working class poverty, including an infamous "Hooverville" of self-built shacks during the Depression. Where that informal settlement once stood is now the site of Red Hook Houses, the biggest public housing complex in Brooklyn with some 2,878 apartments. The first part of this enormous development was completed in 1939, the same year that construction started on the Gowanus Parkway, overseen by Robert Moses and built on top of the pillars of the old Third Avenue elevated train line. In a 1959 issue of *The New Yorker,* Lewis Mumford noted the irony of tearing down elevated railways only to replace them with highways, which he called "the same nuisance in an even noisier and more insistent form. But what is Brooklyn to the highway engineer — except a place to go through rapidly, at whatever necessary sacrifice of peace and amenity by its inhabitants?"[2] For the residents of Red Hook, the new road represented more than a noisy nuisance. It effectively marked a hard stop to how far public transportation infrastructure would stretch towards their neighborhood. An entire network of South Brooklyn trollies and elevated trains, some of which connected the working waterfronts to upland commuter networks, was torn up, and the New York City subway stops well short of servicing Red Hook. The closest subway stop, at Smith and 9th Streets, is more than a mile from the center of the neighborhood; the single bus line that services the area often takes 45 minutes to reach the subway station. After the Gowanus Parkway's 1950s reconstruction into the Gowanus Expressway connected the Verrazano Narrows Bridge to the Brooklyn Battery Tunnel, it became part of Interstate 278, which slices through all the outer

---

[2] Lewis Mumford, "Skyline," *The New Yorker,* November 14, 1959.

Participants in the Red Hook Initiative's Digital Stewards program work to install elements of a community-run Wi-Fi network.

boroughs and cuts Red Hook off even more drastically from its now prosperous neighbors, Carroll Gardens and Cobble Hill. If you walk or take the bus into Red Hook from Smith and Ninth, the combination of so much concentrated public housing with so obvious an absence of other forms of public investment is disarming. However, as you get closer to the water, past the clutch of squat, red brick buildings, signs begin to emerge of a small, affluent community who appreciate the neighborhood's isolation and small town feel: wine shops, hip restaurants, art venues, real estate brokerages with million dollar loft listings. An IKEA and a Fairway supermarket attract shoppers from around the region, many of whom take advantage of the resurgent waterborne transit network and are thus never confronted with the landscape of entrenched poverty that encircles this small pocket of privilege with waterfront views. Over 75 percent of the community's residents live in the Red Hook Houses complex. Its statistics do not compare favorably with other New York neighborhoods with high concentrations of public housing. Data from the US Census and American Community Survey in 2010 shows that almost half of all households earn less than $15,000 and more than a quarter earn less that $10,000. Fifty-nine percent of households with children receive food stamps. Seventy-nine percent of families with children are below the poverty line. Fifty percent of residents twenty-five or older have not received a high school degree. All of this was before Superstorm Sandy, which ravaged Red Hook and laid bare the consequences and complexity of the neighborhood's poverty.

To combat the combined effects of these challenging circumstances, a local hospital launched the Red Hook Health Initiative in 2002. In 2006, an independent nonprofit called the Red Hook Initiative (RHI) spun itself off from these health-focused efforts to meet a wider range of community needs. The majority of RHI's programs are oriented toward youth and workforce development, including after school and tutoring programs for middle school students, peer counseling for high school students, and leadership training for local residents of all ages. Some of these program offerings have included media production classes for local youth as a workforce training and empowerment strategy. The media programs are run by a man named Tony Schloss, a former recording engineer and music producer who turned his attention to developing community radio as a youth empowerment opportunity in the neighborhood where he lives. RHI's offices operate as a highly valued community center, where kids can drop in for mentoring sessions or to take specific classes. But not as many teens take advantage of these offerings as might benefit from them. Schloss wanted his community to have more options to connect to the internet, but his vision went further. He started imagining a digital community bulletin board that listed RHI program offerings and other local news. For Schloss, the initiative's "overarching goal is to use technology for community development, and a Wi-Fi network can be an incredible tool with which to do that. We are creating a community-owned network to provide internet resources and, more importantly, a platform for local communication." Given Red Hook's isolation, "It's really hard to get information to people who might need it, and there's been no central place for local communication. There are neighborhood services available to residents that not everybody takes advantage of, and people need help with things like finding jobs, getting their benefits, or responding to court orders."[3]

In early 2011, Schloss started working with Alyx Baldwin,[4] a creative technologist who had been researching the social incentives behind wireless mesh networks. They tested hardware that would offer an alternative for getting online, setting up an ad hoc system of cheap, waterproof routers on rooftops and at street level, some but not all of which connected to the internet via Brooklyn Fiber, a local Internet Service Provider. For Red Hook residents who were suddenly able to connect to the internet in a faster and more reliable way, the simple ability to log on without burning through cellular data was the immediate benefit. But for Schloss and Baldwin, an important goal was the community bulletin board. Anyone connecting to the community Wi-Fi signal would see a neighborhood map portal — a bespoke interface called Tidepools — that combined local news and announcements with some apps specifically designed to meet community needs. One app allowed users to report where and when a stop-and-frisk occurred.[5] Another tracked the B61 bus in real time.

Beyond the obvious benefits of expanded internet access and a platform for local communication, the beauty of this kind of network in infrastructural terms is its built-in redundancy: more than one path travels between any two points; if one link in the chain fails, the others pick up the slack. Significantly, analogous redundancies in other infrastructural systems are exactly what many corporate visions of the smart city seek to eliminate. The efficiency dividend — the expectation of fewer resources expended for the same yield of services — is often what data-driven governance promises. Delivering it often requires cutting out the repetitive feedback loops and fail-safes that slow things down. But ask any engineer: resilience requires redundancy. The resilience of a mesh network (what technologists call "fault tolerance," a key benefit of "multipath routing") offers lessons for other kinds of services that we risk making brittle and vulnerable in the name of cost-cutting attempts at efficiency. Furthermore, the local network still functions even when the

---

[3] "Local Connections: The Red Hook WiFi Project," *Urban Omnibus,* September 25, 2013.

[4] Baldwin began this collaboration while studying for a master's degree in design technology and continued it under the auspices of the Open Technology Institute, a program of the New America Foundation that works to improve digital access in low-income communities.

[5] Stop-and-frisk is a controversial policing tactic officially adopted by the New York City Police Department in the 1990s that endorsed police officers stopping, questioning, and frisking a pedestrian exhibiting "suspicious behavior." The vast majority of people stopped were African-American and Latino men, and about ninety percent were innocent of any crime. Despite significant protests and a breakdown in trust between the police and communities of color — particularly in areas with high concentrations of public housing, such as Red Hook — the mayoral administrations of Giuliani and Bloomberg both vigorously defended the practice, claiming it made the city's streets safer. Independent research has not confirmed this claim, and a US District Court Judge ruled it unconstitutional in 2013. Stop-and-frisk became a campaign-defining issue for Mayor de Blasio, a vocal opponent of the practice.

local Internet Service Provider is interrupted. When the internet service goes down, you can't surf the web, but you can still use the platform for local communication.

Perhaps the most significant aspect of the entire project is not its digital apps or its physical infrastructure. It's the way the maintenance and expansion of the network relies on local youth, training a corps of "Digital Stewards" in a range of essential skills necessary in a job market that increasingly requires tech savvy. (Red Hook Wi-Fi modeled the curriculum on other programs run by the Open Technology Institute; in Detroit, for example, older community members and established activists learn tech tools; in Red Hook, RHI adapted it into a youth workforce development program). The Red Hook Initiative employs these young adults, ages nineteen to twenty-four, "to install, maintain, and promote the Wi-Fi network and use technology to bring about community development."[6] They spend six months learning about hardware and software. They learn how to set up, plug in, and take care of the network components. They learn how to design and build a web site, produce audio/visual material to document the process and attract new partners. Crucially, they also receive training and counseling in some essential nontechnical skills essential to a career in any field: public speaking, leadership, and community organizing. The next step is for each Digital Steward to use these skills in community development initiatives, and they finish off the program with an internship in a tech business.

Many resource-constrained neighborhoods have robust workforce development initiatives for local youth. And Red Hook is far from the only community setting up a decentralized mesh network: prominent relevant examples include projects "in Berlin, where a tech collective shares internet access to save money; in rural Spain, where one of the largest mesh networks covers areas ignored by telecoms; in Tunisia, where the State Department has spent millions establishing a mesh network to experiment with a local network impervious to government censorship."[7] To me, what distinguishes the Red Hook Wi-Fi project is the synthesis of job training, community control of internet access, and local communication.

And then came Superstorm Sandy, the largest hurricane and second most devastating weather event in recorded US history. When the storm swept across the New York region in late October 2012, Red Hook was one of the most severely affected neighborhoods. The storm surge was fourteen feet high, inundating well up to the second floor of some buildings. Across the city, the storm's impacts revealed, once again, the alarming correlation between the city's low-lying flood zones and low-income communities, especially in neighborhoods where twentieth-century policies saw fit to site public housing such as the Lower East Side, Coney Island, Far Rockaway, and Red Hook. After the storm, more than 6,000 Red Hook Houses tenants lived without water, heat, and power for more than two weeks. As in other neighborhoods, elderly residents were stranded on high floors with elevators. Food stores lost their inventory. Homes were destroyed.

With cell phone towers and electricity down, Red Hook Wi-Fi proved essential to keeping people informed during the chaotic recovery. Mercifully, the power and the Verizon connection at the RHI's offices stayed functional, so the network continued to be a communication lifeline. According to Schloss, "RHI became the recovery hub in the neighborhood. People came to charge their phones, stay warm, and use the network to let people know that they were OK." About a week and a half later, FEMA heard about RHI's work and wanted to support it. Schloss reports that FEMA "provided a satellite uplink so we were no longer using RHI's Verizon connection, and we were able to expand the internet connection."

Red Hook became a model of neighborhood solidarity across traditional social fault lines. A report generated within the Governor's Office of Storm Recovery heralds the community's "capacity for unprecedented cooperation and action. Red Hook residents, community-based organizations, businesses, and regional partners rallied in response, piecing together an essential system of distribution and support with limited resources." The report characterizes this mobilization as "a regional precedent for grassroots organizing and response."[8]

Initiatives like Red Hook Wi-Fi work at the local scale not only to expand internet access, but also to demystify the often opaque ways that the internet works as a physical infrastructure, to distribute the tools to *build* internet access while increasing literacy in a wide range of digital skills. Distributing access to a shared resource is one thing; distributing the ability to produce the online platforms that enable sharing is another. Citymakers have a responsibility to call out this distinction and push for technologies that increase the legibility of urban systems.

That urban development has always been a technological phenomenon is axiomatic: just as irrigation begat agricultural civilization, elevators enabled skyscrapers, and the telegraph and telephone hastened intercontinental communication and commerce. Cities have fostered revolutionary inventions, from the battery to the bar code. The technological developments being applied and refined today are certainly not the first time in which rapid change is poised to transform radically the experience and management of cities. Yet, our cultural memory is short. We are now at risk of ignoring lessons learned from the cyclical history of technology's millennia-long encounter with the city. To understand and shape the major technological shifts of our time — especially the ubiquity of computing, increasingly embedded in our phones, homes, and infrastructure — we need citymakers as well as technologists.

THE OUTLOOK TOWER IN THE SMART CITY

Anthony M. Townsend, an expert on the impact of new technology on cities and public institutions, makes exactly this point in the conclusion to his 2013 book *Smart*

---

[6] Red Hook Initiative "Red Hook Wi-Fi About Page." Accessed November 20, 2015. www.redhookwifi.org/about/

[7] Noam Cohen, "Red Hook's Cutting Edge Wireless Network," *The New York Times,* August 22, 2014.

[8] "Red Hook: NY Rising Community Reconstruction Plan," New York Rising Community Reconstruction Program, March 2014. Accessed May 10, 2015. stormrecovery.ny.gov/sites/default/files/crp/community/documents/redhook_nyrcr_plan_20mb_0.pdf.

Cities, which astutely cautions against the limitations and shortsightedness of certain corporate visions — he calls out IBM, Siemens, and Cisco, among others — to lace the urban fabric with an ever-growing number of sensors and computing instruments. While much of the rhetoric surrounding contemporary information technology describes it as enabling collaboration and efficiency, Townsend's book shows how "Until now, smart-city visions have been about controlling us." Such visions actively seek to reduce the sum of human choices about how to live into streams of data in order to build shallow, brittle models of human behavior and urban dynamics. These models tend to solidify extant social inequality and exclusion and to reinforce entrenched power dynamics such that "poor communities will be at the mercy of those who can measure and control them from a distance."[9] The worrisome specter of mass surveillance, malfunctioning soft- and hardware, and malign social engineering threatens not only the most vulnerable among us, but also citizens of means.

To identify possibilities that resist such tendencies, Townsend chronicles some of the "civic hackers" who are charting a new way forward through tech projects that are open, participatory, and inclusive. He calls for "a new civics for the smart city that takes what we know about making good places as well as good technology." Answering his call requires that the "Architects and engineers of smart cities will need to draw on both informatics and urbanism simultaneously." Yet he laments that there are only "about a dozen" people who are currently equipped to do so.[10]

Townsend is undoubtedly one of them. He name-checks Adam Greenfield as another such techno-urbanist and approvingly quotes Greenfield's claim that "future designers of smart cities, 'will have to be at least as familiar with the work of Jane Jacobs . . . as they are with that of Vinton Cerf,'" an early pioneer of the internet.[11] For such a synthesis of distinct perspectives to work, however, we'll need a shared vocabulary. The ways Townsend and Greenfield critique the contested meanings and claims of "the smart city" productively reveal the extent to which contemporary digital discourse can be dangerously agnostic to the values and ethical debates embedded in other strands of urbanism. In order to move beyond the value-neutral logic of unbridled technological optimism, we need citymakers who fuse technological possibilities with strong ethical positions on social equity and a deep commitment to the kind of close analysis that enables reframing the problem. In other words, these citymakers are interested in moving beyond marveling at what is technologically possible and instead using new kinds of tools to question what kind of city is desirable. In order to do so, citymakers of all stripes must embrace and scale up the observational methodologies and inductive reasoning inherent in the advocacy planning tradition and resist the brute quantification of daily life. We want cities that are not just numerable, but legible.

Townsend's *Smart Cities* distinguishes itself from the crowded field of peer publications because of its author's mastery of the canons of information technology as well as city design and planning. In the former, Townsend reaches further back than Vint Cerf or the founding of the internet to probe the twentieth-century revolutions in the provision of electricity and telecommunications and the processing of data.

Within this history he finds the roots of the corporate philosophies of command and control that increasingly constrict the possibilities of urban life by speeding us toward a future in which cities will have transitioned from "rich, living organisms to dull, mechanical automatons."[12] In the latter, Townsend goes beyond familiar, mid-twentieth-century figures like Jane Jacobs and Robert Moses[13] to draw from the theories of great urbanists like Patrick Geddes. Contemporary urban studies often over-associates him with his disciple, Lewis Mumford, whose ideological clashes with Jane Jacobs have unfairly and inaccurately consigned Geddes to outdated urban thinking about utopian garden cities, planned and built out of whole cloth and based on a static set of idealized principles and unrealistic expectations of human settlement. On the contrary, Geddes, a Scottish polymath who lived from 1854 to 1932, trained as an evolutionary biologist before turning his attention to the practical application of sociology to urban development, believed deeply in examining and understanding the existing city and its constant growth and transformation. His preferred mode of urban intervention was "conservative surgery," and more than fifty years before Jane Jacobs' famous resistance to the policies of urban renewal and the "meat-ax" approach of Robert Moses, Geddes was decrying slum clearance policies as "disastrous and pernicious blunders."[14] He didn't just talk the talk: he and his wife spent the first few years of their marriage — a true partnership, in the modern sense — acquiring tenement properties in run-down parts of 1880s Edinburgh, living in and renovating them one by one, installing bathrooms, clearing courtyards, and taking down only the most damaged rowhouses to introduce light and air to the cramped neighborhood. According to one biography, "Patrick and Anna did not want to carry on this work from socially aloof and more comfortable

---

[9] In this instance, Townsend is citing the particularly poignant example of a World Bank-funded e-government initiative to root out village-level corruption in India by digitizing land ownership documents. In practice, the initiative removed any village-level oversight of land tenure changes, concentrating corruption at higher levels and benefitting wealthy land developers who were able to bribe a centralized land authority to dispossess villagers and consolidate land holdings. He quotes development scholar Kevin Donovan: "While in theory, the initiative was intended to democratize access to information, in practice the result was to empower the empowered."

[10] Anthony Townsend, *Smart Cities* (New York: W.W. Norton & Company, 2013).

[11] Townsend, *Smart Cities,* 2013 quoting Adam Greenfield, "Beyond the 'smart city,'" Urban Scale blog, last modified February 17, 2011. urbanscale.org/news/2011/02/17/beyond-the-smart-city.

[12] Townsend, *Smart Cities,* 2013, 15.

[13] In his definitive biography of Robert Moses, author Robert Caro quotes the master builder as saying: "You can draw any kind of picture you want on a clean slate and indulge your every whim in the wilderness in laying out a New Delhi, Canberra, or Brasilia, but when you operate in an overbuilt metropolis, you have to hack your way with a meat ax." *The Power Broker* (New York: Alfred A. Knopf, 1974), 849.

[14] Patrick Geddes, "Report on the Towns in the Madras Presidency, 1915: Ballary," in Jacqueline Tyrwhitt, ed., *Patrick Geddes in India* (London: Lund, Humphries and Co., 1947), 23.

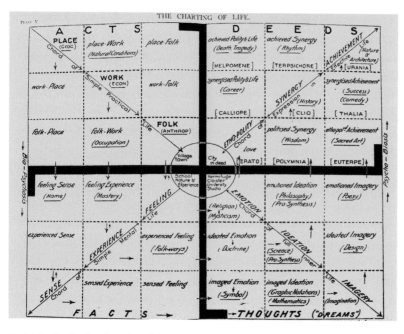

Patrick Geddes developed a variety of diagrammatic "thinking machines," including the widely examined "The Notation of Life" (pictured), which advances a model of how individuals, societies, and environments interact organized into four broad social categories — town, school, cloister, and city — and four broad affective categories — acts, facts, thoughts (dreams), and deeds.

quarters" and living among the poor provided "a point of vantage for their designs; it enabled them to acquire intimate knowledge, obtainable in no other way, of how the slum dwellers were actually affected by their surroundings and of what could be most readily done to improve them."[15] The couple's earnest, gracious, and passionate enthusiasm charmed their new neighbors and soon many were volunteering time to work alongside them on house painting, gardening, and carpentry projects to beautify and stabilize Edinburgh's squalid and dangerous neighborhood of James Court.

Even when his career advanced to the point where he and his wife were traveling throughout the British Empire to work on town planning projects of increasing scale, Geddes never abandoned his commitment to an observational, sociologically informed, and contextual approach. Nor did he relax his firm belief in the necessity and power of the participation of the citizens affected by the decisions of external advisers like him. "Diagnosis before treatment" was among his favorite maxims, a tenet that guided his work in Cyprus on one of the first known refugee integration plans (for Armenians fleeing pogroms in the Ottoman empire in the mid 1890s), his detailed town planning reports on almost twenty Indian cities between 1915 and 1924, and his authorship of the ambitious 1925 plan for Tel Aviv.[16]

This inductive approach to urban planning, greatly informed by the scientific method he'd learned and practiced as a biologist, sets Geddes apart from many of his peers and successors in the incipient town planning movement, which was primarily populated by engineers and architects with little love for existing urban conditions, let alone citizen involvement. While his peers respected classical formalism in architecture, they were more inclined to advance wholly new models for urban fabric than to improve upon extant ones. Beyond reminding us of Geddes' historic distinctiveness as a thinker, I hope that Townsend's book will also help to recuperate the urgent relevance of his pioneering theories of urbanism to contemporary challenges: Geddes' work anticipates and offers lessons to current quandaries about regionalism, systemic thinking, and civic participation.

Of particular interest both to Townsend and to me is Geddes' concept of the Outlook Tower, a kind of civic education organization that he hoped every city would institute. Greater popular understanding of the processes of urban development, Geddes believed, would lead to greater participation. Today, the touted potential of information technology to transform our understanding and planning of cities relies largely on the notion that informatics enables everyone to *be* an input. You can be an active input, like the occasional cyclist who votes online for where to place a bikeshare station, or a passive input, like the driver whose smartphone operates as one of a horde of traffic congestion monitors. Yet, just like the algorithms Google Maps and other digital platforms use to measure and deliver real-time traffic data, these technological possibilities most often obscure rather than illuminate urban decision-making. The idea of crowdsourcing may sound democratic, but its technological infrastructure is opaque. We need fewer black boxes and more Outlook Towers.

In the 1890s, Geddes created a prototype Outlook Tower in Edinburgh, taking over a property with a singular panoramic view of the city in which a local optician had installed a camera obscura in a purpose-built turret. In this place, Geddes created a permanent exhibition, "arranged as an 'index-museum' to the universe,"[17] that explained the various factors — geographic, cultural, historical, political, astrophysical — affecting the physical form and social experience of Edinburgh. Visitors would proceed from a display of astronomical charts that pinpointed Edinburgh's place in the cosmos and then enter into a hollow globe through which they could see and come to understand the orbit of Earth and the stars beyond. From there, they could step out onto the parapet and look through a field telescope at curated features of the urban and natural landscape. The displays continue to shift in scale: a room with pair of globes, one in topographical relief, the other of vegetation and climate regions; a room on the British Empire; the Scotland room highlighted how the nation's physical geography influenced its social development; an extensive room on Edinburgh demonstrated Geddes' methodology for the "regional

[15] Philip Mairet, *Pioneer of Sociology: The Life and Letters of Patrick Geddes* (London: Lund, Humphries and Co., 1957), 51.

[16] Tyrwhitt, *Patrick Geddes in India,* 1947 and Patrick Geddes, *Cities in Evolution,* (London: Williams and Norgate, 1915).

[17] Mairet, *Pioneer of Sociology,* 1957, 71.

survey" (of which he would become a well known practitioner). Throughout, the exhibits showcased "typical samples of social and civic maldevelopments side by side with curative plans of redevelopment, actual and possible."[18] For this reason, Charles Zueblin, a prominent sociologist visiting from the University of Chicago in 1895, marveled that the Outlook Tower was "the world's first sociological laboratory."[19]

Geddes was, in many ways, a thinker who embodied the synthesis of top-down and bottom-up approaches to urban change that I hope this book will promulgate. He believed the professional had an obligation to demystify complex processes as much as suggesting new ways forward, and he believed the citizen had a right to offer feedback on the personal impact of new plans. Geddes referred to his form of practical sociology as *civics,* and he hoped the Outlook Tower would prepare citizens as well as professionals like himself to practice it. This example powerfully asserts the need to study, recognize, and present how people actually live amongst one another — what kind of city we want — rather than relying exclusively on mechanized measurements.

Public participation is a vexing challenge for urban development. Many of the more civic-minded technological fixes, hacks, and apps for contemporary urban life have to do with broadening participation in decision-making. Later on in this chapter, we will see how the noble spirit behind many of these enterprises often masks a tacit undermining of democratic governance. This critique, however, is not to suggest that experiments should not be tried. On the contrary, as Townsend's book makes clear, many "civic hackers" are currently working hard to improve urban life without relying on a vision of lean government supplanted by democratically unaccountable and demographically inequitable tech-based solutions.

Furthermore, Geddes' work is relevant to Townsend's discussion of smart cities because of the way it advances a particular vision of comprehensive urban understanding, one that resists the quantitative turn of technological determinism. Whereas the corporate visions of Siemens, IBM, or Cisco would have us rush towards a completely "knowable" and predictable model of the city, Geddes' belief in the observational might forestall the excesses of an exclusively algorithmic understanding of people's behavior.

Townsend writes, "Geddes recognized that a thorough knowledge of culture — the creative social expression of humanity in a particular local setting — was necessary to understand what science could not explain." He knew that an artist's imagination and a social scientist's insight were as crucial to making good cities as an architect's designs and an engineer's calculations. Yet today, we are increasingly relying on computers to do "the work of observing cities for us," which is why "we must redouble our efforts to see those intangible aspects of urban life they may never be capable of measuring. Without this more holistic lens on the city, it will be impossible to recognize problems, design appropriate solutions, and engage citizens to participate in their implementation."[20]

Adam Greenfield shares Townsend's concern and signals that his critique of the dominant paradigm is even more pointed with the title of his own treatise on the subject, "Against the Smart City."[21] Greenfield, who served on the original advisory committee for *Urban Omnibus* and has continued to be a contributor, published an excerpt on *Urban Omnibus* in which he closely reads the marketing language used to promote blank-slate "smart cities" like New Songdo City, South Korea; Masdar City, United Arab Emirates; and PlanIT Valley, Portugal to challenge some of the claims of networked information technology. The potential of the devices and information now available is rich, but our awareness of the powerful ways in which these systems and their use will alter our world — our policies, economies, built environment, and, in Greenfield's words, "the structure and content of our own psyches" — is limited. He argues that the existing definition of the "smart city" is not only too narrow, but also that it promotes an undesirable vision of a future city with centralized surveillance and computational control, driven by those in power. However, Greenfield maintains that we are capable of imagining and supporting an alternative vision of the smart city, one that responds to the needs, demands, and desires of all of its citizens and recognizes the messy and complex realities of urban daily life.[22]

Greenfield has dedicated much of his career to exploring the rich potential of ubiquitous computing in order to make a case for his alternative vision of networked urbanism as something more informed, more sophisticated, more responsive, and more empowering to its citizens than what is currently on offer. His first book was a vanguard study: *Everyware: The Dawning Age of Ubiquitous Computing* (2006). Two of the pieces he published on *Urban Omnibus* demonstrate the reach of his technological imagination as well as the depth of his observational and analytical skill. In one of these, an article entitled "Frameworks for Citizen Responsiveness: Towards a Read/Write Urbanism," he outlines how the city might come to be seen as a kind of software, in which citizens are encouraged to identify trouble spots in the landscape, such as a pothole or a broken streetlight, and report them quickly and easily to the relevant municipal authorities and track the progress of the response online. Like Greenfield himself, this article combines exuberance for the possibilities of informatics with deep respect for the social possibilities that cities and engaged citizens present; he wants both phenomena to become as transparent as possible to the people who stand to benefit. In another article, he applies his considerable powers of observational analysis — which were honed as a sergeant

---

[18] Ibid, 72.

[19] As quoted in Mairet, *Pioneer of Sociology,* 1957, 72.

[20] Townsend, *Smart Cities,* 2013.

[21] Adam Greenfield, "Against the Smart City," (Book 1 of *The City is Here for You to Use*) Kindle Edition (London: Do projects, 2013). See also Greenfield's new release *Radical Technologies: the Design of Everyday Life* (New York: Verso, 2017).

[22] Adam Greenfield, "Against the Smart City," *Urban Omnibus,* October 23, 2013.

Above: St. Jacobi Evangelical Lutheran Church in Brooklyn served as one of Occupy Sandy's two primary distribution sites for New Yorkers to collect clothes, blankets and food.

Left: In the Queens neighborhoods of the Rockaways — among the most devastated in the storm — the community center YANA (You Are Never Alone) housed a clinic in which Occupy Sandy volunteers could offer medical care and distribute supplies.

in the psychological operations (PSYOP) division of the US Army, as well as an information architect, an interface designer, and a consultant on "the design of products, services, and spatial interventions wherever networked information technology intersects the urban condition"[23] — to a decidedly noncomputerized command center, the Brooklyn headquarters of Occupy Sandy.[24] His close reading of why the bustling hub of volunteer coordination and donation collection and distribution works quite so well reveals his constant awe at urban systems of all kinds.

Occupy Sandy was a spontaneous, self-organized relief effort that sprang up in response to the devastation of Superstorm Sandy in 2012. Its organizers drew from the ranks of Occupy Wall Street and other chapters of the Occupy movement, but it also attracted scores of volunteers who were not involved with the protests in Zuccotti Park the previous year. Presumably, for these new volunteers, the immediate and urgent work of feeding, clothing, and housing people whose homes were destroyed in the storm exerted a different kind of motivating force than the nebulous goals of protesting income inequality and corporate sway over government. Greenfield and his wife joined in and were immediately impressed with the command center's operational flow. He writes, "Occupy Sandy's effectiveness constitutes both powerfully impressive testimony as to what ordinary people can achieve when organized in a horizontal, leaderless, distributed, and consciously egalitarian network, and a rebuke to the seeming inability of the centralized, hier-archical, and bureaucratic organizations to which our society has hitherto entrusted mission-critical disaster recovery functions to cope with what this responsibility demands of them."

This kind of close reading of local, site-specific systems, however, is undervalued in the current vogue of data-driven urbanism. Just as participant-observation, contextual awareness, and qualitative analysis are required skills for social analysis of all kinds, so too are they essential to responsible citymaking. Certain strands of urbanism — particularly local economic development, advocacy planning, migration studies, and informal settlement studies — have embraced these ethnographic methodologies that have powerfully influenced the social sciences (and the arts[25]) since the 1980s. Other strands of urbanism — especially those concerning formal real estate markets, public policy and administration, and environmental impact analysis — have remained faithful to a positivist epistemology that prioritizes studying only those phenomena that can be objectively measured and classified. As urbanists, I sometimes feel as if we use qualitative methods to study the poor

---

23 UrbanScale "About Page." Accessed August 25, 2015. urbanscale.org/about/.

24 Adam Greenfield, "A Diagram of Occupy Sandy," *Urban Omnibus,* February 6, 2013.

25 See Alex Coles, ed., "Site-Specificity: The Ethnographic Turn;" *de-, dis- ex- Volume* 4, (London: Black Dog Publishing, 2000).

and quantitative methods to study everyone else. Across the board, we need to learn through *looking,* not only through counting.

The legacy of positivism stretches back to Auguste Comte who founded the discipline of sociology in the 1830s and '40s, arguing for the application of the scientific method to the investigation of social relations. Born and raised in the immediate wake of the French Revolution and the fractious, violent uncertainty that ensued, Comte intended his "science of society" to "guide the world on the certain path to social progress."[26] To this day, the social reform tradition within policy analysis and urban planning maintains aspects of its Comtian legacy. In fact, the technological optimism of our current urban moment recoups and recasts the positivist preference for data and metrics to guide us on the path to progress, which is, as ever, paved with good intentions.

The "ethnographic turn" represents one aspect of a broader "cultural turn" in scholarship of all kinds that, starting in the 1970s, moved away from strict empiricism towards the belief that culture and meaning were paramount to the study and understanding of social relations. The shift drew on emerging intellectual trends that sought to destabilize philosophical binaries and the absolute truth of scientific laws, to question the histories written by oppressors, to empower marginalized voices, and to resist the notion of humanity's linear progress. In a word, it was postmodernism. Within the distinct disciplines that comprise citymaking, these trends reflected and coincided with the rise of advocacy planning, which sought to resist, from below, the often brutal moves of modernist masterplanning.[27] The big visions of macroscale citymaking — the highways rammed through certain neighborhoods, the wholesale demolition of others — gave way to localized interventions that sought to identify existing strengths within communities and build upon them.

In this country, the observational urbanism of Jane Jacobs is often invoked as prototypical of this transition. But I think those who credit her with turning the tide against top-down physical planning often miss other key values of her contribution to urban thought. It's easy to remember her classic book, *The Death and Life of Great American Cities,* as celebrating the low-rise, mixed-use, mixed-income blocks of her beloved Greenwich Village. However, the subtler and more significant point she makes in that text has nothing to do with any particular neighborhood or her thoughts on optimum densities or the benefits of mixed-use zoning. Jacobs' great move was to show, by example, the power of place-based, inductive reasoning. She cited "eyes on the street" as a communitarian security feature, but her eyes were trained on her own block of Hudson Street not only because she saw a neighborhood that worked, but also because it was a site from which she could advance her embedded, observational methodology. Just as Geddes believed in diagnosis before treatment, Jacobs believed in the power of personal observation, in learning through looking. For her, the complexity of urban dynamics could not be reduced to diagrams, and she was deeply suspicious of quantitative metrics. Architecture scholar Nicholas de Monchaux has uncovered an interesting intellectual connection between Jacobs' views on irreducible urban complexity and research undertaken in the same period at the Rockefeller Foundation, which gave Jacobs a grant to support the writing of what would become her most famous book in the 1950s. Warren Weaver, a vice president of the foundation during that period, "was a seminal founding figure of complexity science, and was, in fact, the first to coin the phrase 'the science of organized complexity' — this notion that our attempts at measurement both freeze and oversimplify something fundamental to natural systems at every scale, from our own body to the city, upward to the ecology of the planet as a whole."[28] This field of scientific, mathematical, and increasingly ecological inquiry defines a complex system as one with multiple interacting components, like a rainforest, a city, an economy, a multicellular organism, or the internet. In each of these examples, the integrated action of the whole is more than the sum of the action of the parts. More precisely, "the aggregate exhibits properties *not* attained by summation" which means such systems are nonlinear and feature a "combination of "top-down" effects (as when the daily market average affects actions of the buyers and sellers in an equities market) and "bottom-up" effects (the interactions of the buyers and sellers determine the market average)."[29]

To see the complexity of the city, to resist the urge to simplify, Jane Jacobs advises her readers "to think about processes" and "to think inductively, reasoning from the particulars to the general, rather than the reverse."[30] The scientific method so revered by Comte and his intellectual descendants relied more heavily on deductive reasoning: starting with a hypothesis or theory and proceeding to prove it with evidence obtained through controlled experimentation. Grand theories about spatially reordering urban life fell out of favor during the final decades of the twentieth century as contextually informed urban interventions and community advocacy efforts became ascendant, helped along by growing environmental awareness, the social movements of the 1960s, and the urban crises of the 1970s. The entire field of urban planning came to be seen as a policy instrument to segregate cities by race and class.

The eventual return of the top-down big vision was inevitable. Future historians of the early twenty-first century may cite a range of impetuses: the impatience of capital in a global economy geared towards short-term profits, the reduction in crime and (visible) social conflict that allowed cities once again to be seen as

---

[26] John Friedmann, *Planning in the Public Domain* (Princeton: Princeton University Press, 1987). See also Robert A. Nisbet "The French Revolution and the Rise of Sociology in France," *American Journal of Sociology* 49, no. 2 (September 1943): 156–164.

[27] Paul Davidoff coined the term advocacy planning in his famous 1965 article that critiques mainstream physical planning for its neglect of minorities and the poor. The article is often required reading in introductory urban planning courses in the United States. See Paul Davidoff, "Advocacy and Pluralism in Planning" in *Journal Of The American Institute Of Planners* Vol. 31, Issue 4, 1965.

[28] Geoff Manaugh, "Spacesuit: An Interview with Nicholas de Monchaux," *BLDGBLOG,* April 27, 2011. Accessed November 26, 2015. www.bldblog.blogspot.com/2011/04/spacesuit-interview-with-nicholas-de.html.

[29] John Holland, *Complexity* (Oxford: Oxford University Press, 2014), 4.

[30] Jane Jacobs, *The Death and Life of Great American Cities,* 2002, 440.

convivial and as the preferred location of the young and the rich. Large-scale physical planning and design — real estate macroprojects, major rezonings, etc. — is regaining authority. As the pendulum swings back, we must take care not to allow the availability of big data to seduce us into fetishizing quantitative metrics at the expense of looking closely at what surrounds us. The dogma of data has penetrated city governments around the world. The data evangelism of Mayor Bloomberg, a man who built his multibillion dollar fortune on the notion that information was a valuable commodity, accelerated the use of all kinds of data in managing New York City. Some of the resulting policies are undeniably helpful "as a triage tool for stretching scarce city resources;" others, according to Anthony Townsend, "create perverse incentives . . . when data drives decisions, decisions about how to record the data will be distorted."[31]

Townsend's reference point for this claim is the New York City Police Department's CompStat program, which allocates policing resources based on geographic patterns in digitally mapped crime reports. But the statement could refer to any number of "smart city" initiatives, corporate as well as governmental. In Adam Greenfield's words, even the most thoroughly deployed sensors in the world will "only ever capture the qualities about the world that are amenable to capture, measure only those quantities that can be measured . . . What if information crucial to the formulation of sound civic policy is somehow absent from their soundings, resides in the space between them, or is derived from the interaction between whatever quality of the world we set out to measure and our corporeal experience of it?"

Later in this chapter, I show how critical cartography can be an essential, productively subversive tool in questioning the authority of these kinds of data sets and can therefore support the case for inductive reasoning in progressive citymaking. And I also reflect on *Urban Omnibus* interviews with public servants who marshal huge amounts of data in fire prevention and emergency management. Both stories could become exhibits in a modern-day Outlook Tower, examples of the kind of civics Patrick Geddes practiced and preached. Again, he believed that models and maps can help us to manage and understand the complexity of urban life, but their claims must be balanced by the subjective lens of cultural context, inductively observed and creatively interrogated through design. To this end, the creative faculties of the designer can show us paths forward that fuse the insights and possibilities of technology, social science, and art. Close analysis of existing systems and considerate design interventions on how to optimize them is the opposite of the brute disruption that the contemporary technology sector holds up as a positive attribute.

The target of that disruption is most often a traditional conception of employer-employee relationships. The contemporary economy is not only globalized, it also increasingly comprises independent, contract, and part-time workers. According the Freelancers Union, a labor union and insurance company for independent workers, almost 53 million Americans, about one in three of our national workforce, are now self-employed. This significant shift offers many potential benefits to the freelancer, like schedule flexibility and autonomy, but also comes with costs. That other kind of benefit — the one that's buttoned into employment contracts and policy debates about health care and retirement in this country — is at stake. Employer-provided health insurance is somewhat of an historical accident borne of a diverse range of precedents and countervailing political narratives. In the late nineteenth century, workers in the most hazardous jobs such as mining, steelwork, railroads, and lumber had access to company doctors and labor union members increasingly could find treatment at union-run infirmaries. Progressive-era reformers[32] began advocating for legislation that would require employers to insure workers against industrial accidents and would bind state governments to provide medical insurance. They were successful in the former — by 1915, thirty states had passed workmen's compensation laws[33] — and failed in the latter. In an era when capital and firms increasingly crossed state borders, state governments, which had long been the primary public providers of social welfare, became wary of laws that might put them at a competitive disadvantage to states that required less of large employers. So advocates set their sights on federal policy, only to have the World War I and the subsequent decade of peace and prosperity dislodge the Progressive-era agenda from popular attention. Not until wage controls during the World War II created an incentive for employers to offer "fringe benefits" beyond salary to attract workers did the notion of employer-provided care catch on. And when post-war paranoia about state control being tantamount to communism reached a fever pitch, employers, rather than the government, became the de facto provider of health insurance. Labor unions, of course, fought for the growth of employer-provided plans through collective bargaining agreements. Their postwar success in getting so many Americans insured (100,000 people were covered by 1951, 32 million by 1960, and 156 million by 1986) echoed earlier triumphs like the weekend, the eight-hour workday, the end of child labor, and more. During the 1940s and '50s, when most people in the American workforce belonged to a union, income inequality was at its lowest point in American history.[34] Organized labor, of course, was only one of many factors in this period of relative equality and prosperity (for white people); it was a time when government, finance, large employers, and unions respected a social contract with the American people.[35] That said, unions can and do claim credit for transforming dirty, dangerous, and insecure jobs into safe, stable, middle-class livelihoods.

---

[31] Townsend, *Smart Cities,* 2013, 210–11.

[32] Particularly the American Association for Labor Legislation, which was founded in 1906 by a group of economists at the University of Wisconsin and whose membership did not come from any one particular sector or trade.

[33] Peter A. Corning, "The Evolution of Medicare: from idea to law," 1969, republished on the official website of the Social Security Administration. Accessed October 26, 2015. www.ssa.gov/history/corning.html.

[34] Thomas Piketty and Emmanuel Saez, "Income Inequality in the United States, 1913–1998," *The Quarterly Journal of Economics,* CXVIII, issue 1, February 2003.

[35] Harold Meyerson, "The 40-year Slump," *American Prospect,* October 2013.

They also contributed to the rise of a tangled regulatory framework that slows things down, creating the culture of inefficiency that so many of the tech start-ups of the sharing economy seek to disrupt. Technology, of course, is rarely doing the disrupting all by itself; it's the business model that is disruptive. Such is the view of Clayton Christensen, a professor at Harvard Business School who preaches the gospel of disruptive innovation, a theory of change with sweeping influence over business practices of all kinds: disruption conferences praising ambitious start-ups; chief innovation officers in older, bigger companies whose job it is to bring some of the buzz of start-up culture to more established board rooms; innovation agendas in school districts and government agencies. Christensen based a lot of his original research on the disk drive industry in the 1980s, arguing that smaller, newer companies are operationally better suited to take advantage of new technologies to offer cheaper and lower-quality alternatives to the products offered by established companies. The theory has since blossomed to encompass major shifts in the production, distribution, and consumption of music, news, taxis, temporary accommodation, and much more.

Within the world of information technology that powers these shifts, disruptive innovation has become dogma. It has surprisingly few critics; those who have questioned the applicability and the evidence for Christensen's thesis include the tech consultant Ben Thompson and the historian Jill Lepore. Thompson self-identifies as a fan and adherent of much of Christensen's work but argues that his findings only hold for products purchased by businesses — like aircraft, software, and medical devices — and not for those purchased by consumers — like cars or clothes.[36] Individual consumers, unlike businesses, don't act rationally. Lepore's critique is far more damning. She excoriates Christensen's evidence as shaky and reasoning as circular before asserting the categorical difference between the logic of industries, "which turn things into commodities and sell them for gain," and "public schools, colleges and universities, churches, museums, and many hospitals, all of which have been subjected to disruptive innovation." These institutions have duties and obligations to their constituents "that lie outside the realm of earnings, and are fundamentally different from the obligations that a business executive has to employees, partners, and investors." Another way to phrase this distinction is that they provide public goods. The social contract of post-WWII America has eroded, which severely threatens the equitable provision of public goods of all kinds. Today, going to college and sometimes even going to the doctor often means going into debt; the graphs of economic productivity and median wages have been systematically uncoupled since 1974.[37] In order for civic-minded technologists to become responsible citymakers, they must find ways to apply their talents to supporting, rather than disrupting, democratic governance and hard-won social protections.

Uber, Facebook, Airbnb and the like have huge implications for urbanism, but the nature of their disruption is just as often predicated on circumventing regulation as it is on delivering convenience to customers without having to invest capital in a fleet of cars, a catalogue of media producers, or the real estate and staffing of traditional hospitality. For these companies, regulation may be inconvenient. It often serves the needs of professional lobbies in ways that increase costs for consumers or obstruct opportunities for the underemployed to enter heavily regulated parts of the job market. But regulation also "expresses a long-established rough consensus about a social contract;" ignoring or brute-forcing your way through it makes you look like a major asshole.[38]

Case in point: in 2015 in the California courts, Uber claimed that its 160,000 drivers are self-employed contractors rather than employees. That means that they are not entitled to the protections of basic labor standards like minimum wage, worker's compensation, unemployment insurance, or protection against discrimination; without the millions of dollars Uber saves by avoiding payroll taxes or reimbursing drivers for gas or vehicle maintenance, the company's ability to make a profit would be questionable. In response to the class action lawsuit, a 2015 report published by the National Employment Law Project details the ways that the sharing economy is built upon "independent contractor misclassification [that] imposes huge costs on workers and federal and state treasuries."[39] Advocates behind that report likened the current state of affairs to "turn of the century sweatshops."[40] The same socially networked technologies that have the potential to reduce consumption and increase participation may turn out to be the handmaiden of inequality.

THE WORLD IS LUMPY: TECHNOLOGIES OF GOVERNANCE AND PARTICIPATION

Remember when the internet was going to make the world flat and render cities obsolete? Digital technology was supposed to kill the commute and redistribute professionals evenly throughout the land. The traffic of bits — real-time updates on financial markets, deals closed by videoconference — would eliminate the need to be in any particular place. Frictionless flows of information would obviate the need for spatial concentration. Of course, the future didn't turn out quite as envisioned.

The transformations underway during the 1980s that falsely foretold of a placeless future were not exclusively technological. The primary force attempting to flatten the world was financial. Globalization, after all, is a term initially devised to describe the increase in international trade and investment enabled by the

---

[36] Ben Thompson, "What Clayton Christensen Got Wrong," Stratechery.com, September 22, 2013. Accessed November 26, 2015. stratechery.com/2013/clayton-christensen-got-wrong/.

[37] Meyerson, "The 40-Year-Slump," 2013.

[38] Russell Davies, "41 Lessons from Uber's Success," *Wired UK,* June 2015.

[39] National Employment Law Project, "Independent Contractor Misclassification Imposes Huge Costs on Workers and Federal and State Treasuries" July 2015, retrieved from http://www.nelp.org/content/uploads/Independent-Contractor-Costs.pdf.

[40] Stephen Gandel, "Uber-nomics: Here's what it would cost Uber to pay its drivers as employees," the website of *Fortune* magazine, September 17, 2015.

reduced relevance of national borders as an obstacle to economic transactions. Technological advances certainly eased the way to greater capital mobility, but not without the stimulus of regulatory change inspired, of course, by a neoliberal vision of economic growth. For example, since the US deregulated its airline industry in 1978, airline travel has grown, year on year, at about twice the rate of annual GDP growth.[41] The incremental removal of banking sector prohibitions adopted after the Great Depression (starting in 1978, increasing throughout the 1980s, and culminating most famously in the repeal of the Glass Steagall Act in 1999) accelerated the development of banking products like credit default swaps and collateralized debt obligations. Such forms of credit derivatives have effectively globalized risk in financial markets and remote-controlled the purchasing power of money within "national" economies around the world.[42] In 1970, the derivatives market was a few million dollars; ten years later it was 100 million. The yearly valuation was almost one hundred billion dollars in 1990, one hundred trillion in 2000, and by 2010 it was worth 1.2 quadrillion. How many zeros is that? It's a number I can't possibly begin to fathom.

The financialization of our economy may have distributed the risk of decisions made in front a few computer screens in Europe and America to farmers in Indonesia, commodities traders in India, or potential homebuyers in Peru, but it certainly didn't diminish the importance of London, Frankfurt, and New York, much less Jakarta, Mumbai, and Lima. On the contrary, the relative importance of global financial centers to the economies of the nations in which they are located has only grown, and with it the concentration of advanced producer services (lawyers, accountants, investment bankers) in these urban centers and their metropolitan regions.[43] Meanwhile, the income differential between cities and hinterlands in the Global South has fueled a rural-urban migration staggering in its pace and scope. Wander through any of the fast growing favelas, *gecekondu*, or informal settlements lining the outskirts of most large cities outside of Europe and North America and you will see first-hand the deprivations and insecurity millions upon millions of people are willing to endure in order to have access to urban labor markets and the opportunities they present. (Of course, millions are also fleeing climate chaos, agrarian feudalism, or war; yet for these migrants, too, cities remain a destination of choice). Cities matter now, perhaps, more than ever. And large technology companies have wisely adjusted their strategy accordingly.

---

[41] Global Airline Industry Program of MIT, research project information website. Accessed October 7th, 2015. web.mit.edu/airlines/analysis/analysis_airline_industry.html.

[42] See, for example, *Financial Derivatives and the Globalization of Risk,* by Edward LiPuma and Benjamin Lee (Durham, North Carolina: Duke University Press, 2004).

[43] Saskia Sassen, *The Global City: New York, London, Tokyo* (Princeton: Princeton University Press, 1991) (revised and reissued 2001).

Hudson Yards, once a large rail yard on Manhattan's west side, is now among the largest private real estate developments in American history, including 18 million square feet of commercial and residential space, 4,000 residences, a new cultural institution, 14 acres of public open space, and a 750-seat public school. **Top:** One of the Hudson Yards towers under construction. **Above:** various Hudson Yards buildings under construction as viewed from the completed northern section of the High Line.

The dean of scholars investigating the mutual influence of economic globalization and urbanization is Saskia Sassen. Her 1991 book *The Global City* has set a high bar for academic investigation into this phenomenon, articulating research questions for a veritable forest of subsequent literature in sociology, geography, economics, and political science on the political economy of contemporary cities and nations. At a conference in London in 2005, I was in the audience when Sassen referred to the globalized world not as flat, as we are led to believe, but as "lumpy, and the lumps are the cities."[44] (Sassen's characterization differs in important ways from a similar comment advanced by Richard Florida and other popular urban analysts that the world is "spiky."[45] Florida's descriptor works for his purposes given the histogram-influenced visualizations he uses to describe the economic output of cities in terms of geographically adjusted GDP data. Sassen's focus is less exclusively focused on cash or capital generated than on how that output fits into a more complex set of orders, including transnational flows of state power, migration, energy production and consumption, etc. The topology of these "assemblages" is messier than thin vertical spikes on an elegant graph; it's lumpy.)

A few decades into this shift, the agenda of the corporate giants of information technology is no longer to flatten the world but to pack those lumps with sensors. The real estate industry has taken note. A significant local example is massive real estate development called Hudson Yards, on the far west side of midtown

Since a rezoning in 2001, more than 10,000 apartments have been added to the formerly industrial neighborhood of Long Island City in Queens.

Manhattan. The developers, Related Companies and Oxford Properties, have partnered with New York University's Center for Urban Science and Progress (CUSP) to create a "quantified community," a "fully-instrumented urban neighborhood that will measure and analyze key physical and environmental attributes" in order to provide "an interactive, data-driven experience for tenants and owners of the 28-acre, mixed-use development."[46] Sensors will measure and computers will model pedestrian flows, air quality, health and activity levels of residents and workers, solid waste production, and energy production and usage. Reporting on the planned development for *Urban Omnibus,* Jonathan Tarleton concedes the beneficial efficiencies before raising the privacy concerns. "Information on energy consumption can help decrease that intake or shift energy loads across different times of day to relieve stress on the overall system . . . Air quality checks can spur interventions to keep you breathing the good stuff. But how other data would actually improve the quality of life of residents . . . is less clear."[47] He quotes Jay Cross, who is leading the development effort for Related Companies, who told *The New York Times,* "I don't know what the applications might be, but I do know that you can't do it without the data." CUSP plans to use the data "to help New York City — and, ultimately, cities across the world — become more productive, livable, equitable, and resilient."

The specific applications may be open-ended, but that doesn't mean they'll provide a transparently objective account of how people live, work, and move within the corporate architecture of the twenty-first-century global city. Models based on metrics often influence the dynamics they intend to describe. As demonstrated by the astronomical growth of the derivatives market, according to the sociologist Donald MacKenzie in his 2006 book *An Engine, Not a Camera,*[48] we'd do better to think of computational models as driving choices (an engine) rather than reproducing empirical facts (a camera), precisely because "financial equations produced to model markets also produce markets in the equations' very circulation."[49] In different ways, this

---

[44] Saskia Sassen, remarks, Urban Age Conference, London, October 10, 2005.

[45] Richard Florida, "The World is Spiky," *The Atlantic,* October, 2005. Published as a self-described riposte to Thomas Friedman's bestselling book *The World is Flat* (New York: Farrar, Strauss and Giroux, 2005).

[46] Center for Urban Science and Progress, NYU CUSP, "Related Companies, And Oxford Properties Group Team Up To Create 'First Quantified Community' In The United States At Hudson Yards," press release, April 14, 2014. www.cusp.nyu.edu/press-release/nyu-cusp-related-companies-oxford-properties-group-team-create-first-quantified-community-united-states-hudson-yards/.

[47] Jonathan Tarleton, "Quantifying Community: Hudson Yards to Partner with NYU's CUSP," *Urban Omnibus* April 23, 2014.

[48] The title of MacKenzie's book paraphrases a point Milton Friedman makes in his 1953 essay "The Methodology of Positive Economics." Positive economics, by the way, is the dominant strain in economic theory that aspires to objective analysis, as opposed to normative economics, which incorporates subjectivity and value judgments. Donald Mackenzie, *An Engine, Not a Camera* (Cambridge, Mass.: MIT Press, 2006).

feature of predictive models is just as pertinent to finance, to design, and to governance.

Technology companies have worked towards the digital instrumentation of supply chains for decades, but only recently applied this same logic to city governments. The potential here, for profit and progress alike, is increased efficiency. According to Anthony Townsend, "For a world facing rapid urban growth, economic collapse, and environmental destruction, IBM and others saw low-hanging fruit in the wasteful ways of government. Technology could fix all that, they argued, by stretching existing resources to deal with the first two problems, and ratcheting down the excesses of industrial growth to deal with the third."[50] Greater efficiency is certainly a goal to which many government services should aspire. But technology for urban innovation also promises another principle, one that has historically hindered efficiency: expanded participation in urban decision-making. Just as ubiquitous computing hardwired into the built environment can streamline urban management — for example, more than half of the 12,400 traffic lights in New York City can now be controlled remotely from a single office in Long Island City, Queens[51] — the abundance of little computers in our pockets can enable new kinds of feedback loops between citizens and government services. And, as we saw with the Forest Service research in chapter two, an untapped public desire to participate more in the management of, or at least the big decisions about, our shared landscape is emerging after decades of urban decline. Just as global climate change instills a sense of powerlessness that may inspire small-scale action such as voluntary environmental stewardship activities, the growing realization that elite interests control our political system — whether it's the financiers of global capitalism or the clientelist politicians and their benefactors closer to home — has motivated calls for more transparent and participatory governance at the local scale.

Yet, while power and money seem to be increasingly concentrated in the hands of a few, new technologies are seemingly distributing agency and decision-making far and wide. Widespread internet usage has enabled the engagement of large groups of people, especially online communities, to obtain ideas, services, content, or funding that traditional employees, vendors, or donors would formerly have supplied. The term "crowdsourcing" was coined in 2005 in the offices of *Wired* magazine. William Safire, a self-described libertarian conservative cultural critic, offers this account of the term's provenance: a reporter was pitching an article to his editor, "about how the internet was helping businesses use amateurs to replace professionals. The editor responded, 'Hmmm . . . it's like they're outsourcing to the crowd.'"[52]

The components of this portmanteau are telling. "Crowd" bears lightly its connotations of density and collectivity with faint strains of benign anarchy creeping in at the edges of signification. "Outsourcing" has become a more loaded term: it's an easy way to trigger the ire of the anti-globalization Left, immediately conjuring images of mass layoffs as everything from manufacturing to customer service is "offshored" — another neologism of the globalization era — to cheaper labor markets overseas. The conversation in the editorial offices of *Wired* was about strategic business practices ranging from competitive open calls for new product ideas to populating large data sets with fine-grained local experience. These kinds of tools have been employed for centuries, such as the reliance on volunteers to compile the entries that comprised the original edition of the Oxford English Dictionary in the 1860s and '70s.[53] But the way most people use the internet relies on a less voluntary sort of labor (though to call it "labor" is to take a particular stand). Your Google searches and Facebook likes create value for advertisers and cumulatively serve to "optimize" your results, which is effective in pushing search results or newsfeed items you're statistically most likely to click on while also narrowing the field of results overall. Jaron Lanier, a pioneering computer scientist in the field of virtual reality and an outspoken critic of Web 2.0, refers scathingly to the wisdom of the crowd — the guiding logic of open-source projects like Wikipedia or the Linux operating system — as "digital Maoism" wherein the promises of the new online collectivism quickly turn from a bright hive mind to a dark mob rule that erodes the authority of individual voices, from a scholar bullied out of correcting a Wikipedia entry within her expertise to a Facebook user reducing his self-perception to one of a rigid set of "multiple-choice identities."[54] Furthermore, Lanier argues that online economies cheat users by trading free services (like Google's translation algorithm, for example, which amalgamates user-uploaded translations and calculates its best guess) for users' valuable information and labor, profiting from ad sales without compensating users for their data or work.[55]

Beyond the ways people use their computers or phones, another kind of involuntary labor comes from passive interaction with an increasingly networked set of physical objects embedded with software, sensors, and network connectivity (often referred to as the internet of things) that triggers the collection and exchange of data. As the web gets bigger, Google tells us, it gets better.[56] It also, according to geographer Laura Y. Liu, "allows for the patterns of our behavior to become data commodities. It is as though the hyper-Fordist control over repetitive work in the factory has bled over into the expectation of our hyper-regularized mobility and activity throughout the city and other spaces."[57] When technology helps to erase the barriers to

---

[49] Orit Halpern, Jesse LeCavalier, Nerea Calvillo, Wolfgang Pietsch "Test-Bed Urbanism," *Public Culture* 25, no. 2, Spring 2013, Craig Calhoun, Richard Sennett, Harel Shapira, editors.

[50] Townsend, *Smart Cities,* 2013, 32.

[51] "City of Systems: Traffic Signal," *Urban Omnibus,* May 4, 2011.

[52] William Safire, "Fat Tail," The *New York Times Magazine,* February 5, 2011.

[53] See Simon Winchester, *The Professor and the Madman: A Tale of Murder, Madness and the Love of Words* (New York: HarperCollins, 2003).

[54] Jaron Lanier, *You Are Not a Gadget: A Manifesto* (New York: Alfred A. Knopf, 2010).

[55] Jaron Lanier, *Who Owns the Future?* (New York: Simon & Schuster, 2013).

[56] Google, "Company Philosophy" retrieved from www.google.com/about/company/philosophy/ [accessed 10/20/15].

[57] Trebor Scholz and Laura Y Liu, "From Mobile Playgrounds to Sweatshop City," *The Architectural League of New York Situated Technologies Pamphlets,* The Architectural League of New York, 2010.

participation and collaboration — compressing geographic distance or obviating professional know-how — capital can move about more freely and in a more targeted manner. This is not necessarily a bad thing. But when the ease of conscripting an unseen labor force for calling out trouble spots in urban life starts to compete with established democratic practice for identifying community priorities of investment or legislation, then we have a problem. Townsend makes the point cogently:

> In smart cities, there will be many new crowdsourcing tools that . . . create opportunities for people to pool efforts and resources outside of government. In rich countries, governments facing tough spending choices may simply withdraw services as citizen-driven alternatives expand, creating huge gaps in support for the poor . . . Crowdsourcing is highly regressive. It presumes a surplus of volunteer time and energy. For the working poor, every second of every day is devoted to basic survival. The withdrawal of any government services would remove a critical base of support for these extremely vulnerable communities.[58]

Increased citizen involvement in urban governance is not the same as more democratic government. Using Cleveland as a case study, the sociologist Michael McQuarrie has shown that many of the techniques of participation used by community-based organizations, community development corporations, and other agents of civil society are not always, as we assume, "a source of democratic renewal, social solidarity, and better decisions." On the contrary, many forms of participation "simply reinforce hierarchies, discipline public behavior into noncontroversial dialogue, and undermine social solidarity." He tells this story in the context of Cleveland's decades-long response to urban decline. The failure of a pro-growth agenda in the wake of deindustrialization forced historically pro-growth elites (particularly within the real estate industry) to change the tactics through which they grounded their authority. Whereas the voices and opinions of neighborhood residents were once seen as "a threat to elites," in the neoliberal era it has become "a resource."[59]

The participatory tools that McQuarrie is discussing — distinct strategies of community organizing[60] and distinct techniques of citizen consultation on neighborhood improvement and stabilization projects — are not ones we would broadly recognize as technologies, but that is exactly what he calls them. He uses the word precisely to question the assumed essential characteristics of participation as an unqualified good. He defines technology as "A bundle of practices, metrics, discourses, and actors" and he defines "technologies of participation" as the "arrangements of practices, metrics, discourses, and actors that perform community self-determination in ways that are designed to realize specific goals." The choice to distinguish between distinct philosophies and methodologies of citizen engagement reminds me of the assumptions embedded in all sorts of practices that aim to shore up deficits or shortcut backlogs in contemporary democracy. Beyond the specific context McQuarrie describes this line of thinking is useful to apply to more overtly technological strategies of increasing public participation. While the intentions are no doubt noble, many such participatory technologies at least mask, if not deepen, a number of troubling inequalities.

The first order of inequality is obvious: the digital divide is not only widening but also undergoing a multi-dimensional metamorphosis. It's no longer only about access to the internet, the availability of which is more evenly distributed across the socio-economic spectrum in the US and around the world than we might think (leaving aside, for a moment important, questions about broadband, bandwidth, and other variables). It's also about the uneven distribution of the capacity to create new technological tools or to harness the potential of existing ones for pressing needs. For Townsend, whose work displays a sincere concern about the failure of much of contemporary information technology to address the needs of severely resource-constrained communities, the term *digital divide* is outdated. "Thinking simply of a digital divide," he writes, "tricks us into believing this is a simple binary problem of haves and have-nots, when in fact it is a set of interlocking dilemmas that defy easy solution."[61] Access to technology alone doesn't create opportunity; the ability and willingness to exploit technological resources does. He cites 311, a widely used telephone hotline system for government services that does not require a computer, internet access, English language skills, or tech savvy to use. But even though 311 service is available to New Yorkers in 170 languages, it is underutilized in communities with large concentrations of poor or immigrant populations, such that native speakers of English (who statistically tend to have enjoyed more educational opportunities and higher incomes) "are complaining more, and the complaints are being used to disproportionately dispatch resources to address their problems."[62] And the differences in how various communities make use of digital resources does not always map neatly onto socio-economic, racial, or ethnic categories. Cell phones and smartphones have penetrated poorer communities in the US and around the world more than desktops and laptops ever did.

While Americans are more likely to connect to the internet if they are whiter and richer and have more degrees, the differential in this country is not as stark as we might think. Eighty-seven percent of white households connected to the internet in 2015, according to the Pew Research Center for Internet, Science, and Technology

---

[58] Townsend, Smart Cities, 2013, 192.

[59] *Democratizing Inequalities, Dilemma of the New Public Participation,* Michael McQuarrie, Caroline Lee, and Edward Walker, eds. (New York: NYU Press, 2014).

[60] Particular to the Cleveland case, McQuarrie distinguishes between the school of community organizing developed by Saul Alinksy and "consensus organizing" developed by Michael Eichler and adopted by a great number of mainstream CDCs, which maintains that the earlier model has limited relevance to contemporary reality because it is structured around conflict with the power structures with whom Eichler sought to find common ground.

[61] Townsend, *Smart Cities,* 2013, 189.

[62] Ibid, 191.

whereas 84 percent of black and Hispanic households did. Internet use by urban and suburban populations were identical; both came in at 89 percent (this figure was 75 percent for the rural population). Accessing the internet to check your Gmail account does create value for advertisers; the keywords in emails received are used "to deliver you the most useful and relevant ads"[63] and thus your personal correspondence becomes part of a data commodity. So, while this type of internet usage is a form of digital labor, it is not the same as using a smartphone app to interact with the built environment or participate in explicitly crowdsourced decision-making about, say, your preferred location for a bikeshare station or to push real-time transit schedule updates to your handheld device to modify your commute. When I spoke with Tom Wright and Rob Lane of the Regional Plan Association in 2010, the latter, an urban designer who heads up RPA's regional design program, reminded me of "another kind of digital divide that exists within the region: between the city and the suburbs. Even though we're an incredibly rich and sophisticated region, the world of iPhone apps and see-click-fix and design-your-own bike paths is a New York City–specific phenomenon."[64]

The second order of inequality is less about access or utilization than about authorship. What has driven the development of much recent civic software — intended to facilitate interactions between citizens and government services — has been the recent availability of municipal data and the interests of a small group of programmers who have submitted ideas to city government-sponsored apps contests or have decided to make an app with the self-selective discretion of an artist, entrepreneur, or inventor. There has been considerably less investment in consulting everyday citizens about what kinds of problems need to be solved, what kinds of interactions between citizens and government need to be improved.[65] Again, qualitative research methods and robust community engagement must inform technological solutions to urban challenges.

Municipal data wasn't always so readily available, however. In the summer of 2009, I attended a meet-up of coders who were up in arms about Metropolitan Transit Authority (MTA) data policy. There was pizza, beer, and a palpable, almost heartwarming wealth of enthusiasm for using technological skill to serve civic ends. One among them had recently taken the initiative to enter manually the published train timetables for the Metro-North commuter line in order to develop an app for riders. The MTA responded by insisting he pay the same kind of licensing fee and royalties that are required of merchandise that makes use of its intellectual property like the subway map or its logo: boxer shorts, shower curtains, etc. The programmer refused, citing the fact that data is not subject to copyright protection. MTA lawyers claimed it was wary of being held responsible for the accuracy of information delivered to its ridership by third parties. Others at the meet-up had tried something similar with the MTA bus schedule. They had to submit a Freedom of Information Law request. Then they would wait a month for a mailed CD that contained already obsolete bus route and schedule information in an unformatted document. Finally, they would go through the laborious process of parsing the data to make it conform to the General Transit Feed Specification, a common format developed by Google and the transit agency of Portland, Oregon that makes trip-planning apps possible.[66]

The tide quickly turned. In December of 2009, the Obama administration made good on the president's campaign promise to make government-collected data open by default, making the US the first nation in the world to do so. Almost seventy other national governments have followed suit.[67] The MTA's swift change of course the following month was more surprising: the agency announced it would open up its data and eliminate the burdensome procedures obstructing its usage. It put up a "Developer Resources" page on its website that proudly states, Uncle Sam style, that "The MTA wants you to build great tools for our riders" and clearly distinguishes between data, use of which is free of charge, and logos, maps, and symbols, which require a license. It even dedicated some of the lucrative advertising space inside subway cars to promote the new policy. That summer, a bill was introduced to the New York City Council that would set standards for making available all "'public data sets' with the goal of increasing transparency, facilitating connections between the public and government and assisting small business and technology startups."[68] Mayor Bloomberg signed it into law in 2012.

The deluge of government data has resulted in software that has met private as well as public needs: the homebuyer searching through online real estate databases, the aspiring small business owner comparing pedestrian traffic in different retail zones, the mysteriously sick person entering symptoms into an app to self-diagnose. I cribbed these three examples from an article in *The Economist* that sketches what the "open-data revolution" has achieved only to question why it hasn't achieved more. Apparently, the short answer to this complex question is that most of the data released "are not particularly useful."[69] I found this particular article because Adam Greenfield posted it on Facebook with the following rejoinder: "I remain optimistic about some facets of the movement toward open data, but note how very often it's used to support the 'lean government' narrative. Data is great, but it

---

[63] Google's support page explains in more detail: "For example, we may use your Google search queries on the Web, the sites you visit, Google Profile, +1's and other Google Account information to show you more relevant ads in Gmail." Accessed October 20, 2015. support.google.com/mail/answer/6603?hl=en.

[64] "Innovation and the American Metropolis," *Urban Omnibus,* March 31, 2010.

[65] Townsend, *Smart Cities,* 2013, 202.

[66] Open Plans, "New York Public Transit Data Summit With Beer." Accessed November 29, 2015. blog.openplans.org/2009/08/new-york-public-transit-data-summit-with-beer-2/.

[67] Peter Orszag, "Memorandum for heads of executive departments and agencies," Office of Management and Budget, December 8, 2009, Accessed November 29, 2015. www.whitehouse.gov/sites/default/files/omb/assets/memoranda_2010/m10-06.pdf.

[68] Jane Kelly, "Open Data Standards for City Agencies," *Urban Omnibus,* June 23, 2010.

[69] "Out of the Box," *The Economist,* November 21, 2015.

can never replace a motivated, dedicated civil service."[70] Promises about the benefits of harnessing government data regularly support another version of the efficiency dividend — the planned reduction in resources spent by an institution or government agency for the same level of output achieved through a mix of budgeting, waste reduction, and technological streamlining — wherein the "waste" in question includes the livelihoods of municipal employees.

Without the skills to participate in an economy that expects digital competence, the chasm between rich and poor will only widen further. But poor citizens aren't the only actors at risk of being left out. City Halls, which deliver far more direct services with far fewer resources than State Houses or Washington, are slow to adopt new technologies, thus compounding the inconvenience and alienation felt by citizens interacting with government services. One of the original inspirations for IBM's Smarter Cities initiative, formally launched in 2009, was the observation that local governments and the health care industry were severely lagging behind in digital instrumentation. To its credit, IBM has been explicit about the recognition of this growing market for its products as a driver. Colin Harrison, the IBM engineer credited with devising the "technical architecture" of Smarter Cities, has made this clear in public appearances and writing.[71] In the fall of 2009, the Smarter Cities team invited me (as a member of the press) to attend a convening of business and civic leaders where it fleshed out its vision of what might make cities smarter. The

In addition to the thousands of new apartments that have transformed Long Island City in recent years, over 1.5 million square feet of office space has led the Queens neighborhood to position itself as New York City's fourth Central Business District.

room was filled with governors, mayors, school district superintendents, hospital presidents, and CEOs. IBM's chief executive at the time, Sam Palmisano, hosted the event, and opened the proceedings by asking, "With four billion cell phones, 30 billion RFID tags and two billion internet users constantly providing and collecting data, what happens when we apply analytics to guide more strategic resource allocation as our digital and physical infrastructures converge?" The panel discussions that followed touched on everything from culture to transportation, but government services seemed to have the most to gain. To ensure smarter government services, the conference promised, we need an "approach that shares and conserves resources among agencies, so that they can anticipate and provide for the economic health, safety, and quality of life for all citizens."[72] Analyzing the data collected across the balkanized agencies of city government in order to coordinate service delivery is a good idea. The need for it is too great, in fact, to leave entirely to the largest corporations in the world whose responsibility to shareholders outweighs their responsibilities to consumers or citizens. Certainly, centralized digital tools to identify patterns in all that data cannot substitute for informed observation of the messy and immeasurable conditions on the ground, much less healthy skepticism about the assumptions embedded in data collection methods. All the more reason to applaud — and scrutinize — localized efforts to support municipal governments' fitful adaptation to the digital transformation.

CROSS-PLATFORM GOVERNANCE

Code for America is a service-year program that matches tech talent with city governments in need. Modeled loosely on Teach for America, which places elite college graduates in public high schools with high needs, Code for America is premised on the notion that web-based technologies can make government services more efficient and effective. Around the same time that *Urban Omnibus* was getting off the ground — that heady period that combined the optimism of a new Obama presidency with the sobering recognition of the damage wrought by the financial crisis — Jennifer Pahlka was thinking about various ways "to bring the principles and values of the web to government." I interviewed her the following year, eager to introduce *Urban Omnibus* readers — many of whom volunteer their time and design talent in the spirit of community service — to projects that foster that same burgeoning civic spirit in the tech sector. Given the priorities of the new presidential

[70] Adam Greenfield's Facebook page, accessed November 20, 2015, www.facebook.com/hiadamgreenfield/posts/10153843265311995.

[71] Colin Harrison, Ideas Economy: Intelligent Infrastructure, *The Economist* panel discussion, remarks, New York City, February 16, 2011.

[72] IBM "What makes government services smarter?" The Smarter Cities Leadership Series. Accessed December 27, 2015. www.ibm.com/smarterplanet/global/files/us__en_us__government__wide_final.pdf.

administration, Pahlka told me, her initial interest was in the White House and federal agencies, on "leveraging some of the dynamics we see on the consumer web to make government more efficient and effective." Chief among these dynamics was the notion of the web as a platform. According to Pahlka, "The technologies that have changed our lives most dramatically in the last decade have been platforms: think Facebook or the iPhone. Neither tried to provide everything a consumer would need, but rather made it possible for developers to create applications and for the market to determine what was most valuable."[73]

An old friend of hers, who had previously been a Teach for America corps member, was chief of staff to the mayor of Tucson at the time. In conversation with him, she realized that city governments needed tech help most of all. In response to shrinking municipal budgets, many cities are "cutting back services, but if you look under the hood, there are inefficiencies, clunky bureaucracies, and decades-old ways of doing things that should be re-worked before services are cut." Her friend had some ideas for web applications that could help Tucson to work better; he just needed Pahlka's help to source talented developers to help build them. The first obstacle was the technology procurement systems used by local governments, in which a complex set of rules designed to level the playing field for private sector bids often ends up privileging status quo solutions from firms with proven track records of working with government. One solution might be to create a way for City Halls to bring talented technologists in-house for a period of time, just like the high-need public schools that welcome high-performing college graduates as teachers through Teach for America.

That spark of inspiration led to the creation of a robust nonprofit that, several years in, has produced more than sixty-five software applications with thirty-eight municipal governments and 126 fellows.[74] First, Code for America issues a call for city governments to "suggest a web app that would make their city more transparent, efficient, and responsive to citizens, and one that could be reused by other cities afterwards." After working with the selected governments to refine the need, the group begins a competitive application process for fellows. Once admitted, fellows are placed in the selected city governments and begin working to deliver technical solutions. In 2014 alone, the apps and web sites developed by Code for America fellows drastically reduced demand on emergency services in Long Beach, California; streamlined the registration process for pre-kindergarten to save parents' and school administrators hundreds of hours of data entry in Rhode Island; and simplified the public assistance application in San Francisco to lower the barriers for the millions of Californians eligible for food stamps but who do not access the benefit.

The list of impacts is impressive. Like many nonprofits that depend on donations and grants, the organization tends to measure these successes quantitatively: in the number of public dollars and the amount of time saved, in the number of civic tech start-ups formed and apps and web sites built. I think one of its most significant impacts is *qualitative:* its contribution to changing cultural perceptions of public service. Young technologists' typical predilection for innovation and efficiency tends to be at odds with bureaucracy. By tapping into a latent desire on the part of many young people to "make a difference," Code for America has helped to make working for government cool. Pahlka cites one study from the Center for American Progress that shows millennials to have a more positive view of government than previous generations and another by the Pew Research Center that shows the generation to be the most open to helping others as well.[75] Furthermore, because the program brings the talent in-house, it can also change attitudes within the ranks of municipal employees about how new technologies can help them to do their jobs more effectively.

The need to change cultural perceptions is about more than marketing public service to a generation reared on smartphone convenience. In our conversation, Pahlka pointed out an alarming demographic challenge facing municipal workforces nationwide:

> In the seventies, over 70% of the local government workers were under 40. Today, less than 13% are. In many municipalities, 60% of the people who work in your city hall will retire in the next five years. Who replaces those workers (and many will not be replaced due to budget cuts) will determine whether cities use this fiscal crisis to reinvent themselves, or whether they pursue one of the other perceived options before them, including privatization, Chapter 9 [municipal bankruptcy], or simply continuing to reduce services to the point where the city government is irrelevant. We have the opportunity right now to drive talented young people into public service . . . But we have to make it culturally okay for smart, ambitious, tech-savvy people to take government jobs so they can drive change from the inside.[76]

This quote is revealing. It raises a number of questions and speaks to a broader challenge that citymakers of all kinds must address: resetting the relationship between citizens and government. This urgent task has not traditionally been a topic for professionals who deal primarily with the built environment. Even when design or planning projects do incorporate bespoke community engagement processes, enabling participation in decision-making is not the same as fostering democratic governance. The coming generation of citymakers must resist the urge to continue

73 "Code for America," *Urban Omnibus,* August 11, 2010.

74 Code for America "2016 Announcement." Accessed December 25, 2015 www.codeforamerica.org/governments/2016-announcement/.

75 David Madland and Amanda Logan, "The Progressive Generation: How Young Adults Think About the Economy," Center for American Progress, May 2008. Accessed December 27, 2015. cdn.americanprogress.org/wp-content/uploads/issues/2008/05/pdf/progressive_generation.pdf; and "Millennials: A Portrait of Generation Next," Pew Research Center, October, 2010, www.pewsocialtrends.org/files/2010/10/millennials-confident-connected-open-to-change.pdf.

76 "Code for America," *Urban Omnibus,* August 11, 2010.

to design workarounds and shortcuts. Code for America shows us a particular and laudable mechanism for bringing talent and creativity into the system. But the assumptions that lay at the root of its methodology are not innocent of the cultural devaluation of government over the past thirty-five years. The age shift in municipal workforces is not passively indicative of changing attitudes towards working in government; it's a reflection of a conscious political agenda, set into motion during the Reagan years, to starve local governments of the resources that had previously allowed them to innovate in ways responsive to evolving behavior, demographics, and technologies. The ossification of public service into inefficient bureaucracies was not a naturally occurring phenomenon. By the end of two terms of the Reagan administration, federal assistance to local governments was reduced by 60 percent. General revenue sharing, a program adopted by the Nixon administration in which federal funds are disbursed to local governments for unrestricted use, was eliminated. President Reagan "slashed funding for public service jobs and job training, almost dismantled federally funded legal services for the poor, cut the anti-poverty Community Development Block Grant program and reduced funds for public transit. The only "urban" program that survived the cuts was federal aid for highways — which primarily benefited suburbs, not cities."[77]

I'm not speculating that Reagan-era cuts are the only reason local governments have been slow to embrace new technological tools to improve service delivery. But one of the costs of the 1980s cutbacks has been the erosion of a culture of innovation that was present in many local governments in previous decades and attracted talented and motivated young people to work in the public sector. We can attribute this earlier, more empowered culture, in part, to the Great Society programs begun during the Johnson administration. Of course, the increase in federally funded programs in the 1960s that spurred a wide range of local public investments also coincided with intensifying suburbanization and white flight, weakening the tax base of and further concentrating poverty in cities, often along racial lines. Scholars will continue to debate the successes and failures of this ambitious legislative program (more than 100 major proposals enacted by the 89th and 90th Congresses).[78] Nonetheless, the basis for Johnson's ambitious experiment in reducing poverty and inequality — enacted in a moment of national prosperity — was the belief that government, especially the federal government, was an instrument to help the most vulnerable in society. An organization like Code for America is certainly based on the desire to support government efforts to serve their

---

[77] Peter Dreier, "Reagan's Legacy: Homelessness in America," *Shelterforce Online,* Issue 135, (May / June 2004). Accessed December 27, 2015. nhi.org/online/issues/135/reagan.html.

[78] Joseph Califano, "What Was Really Great About the Great Society," *The Washington Monthly,* October 1999. Accessed December 29, 2015. www.colorado.edu/AmStudies/lewis/1025/greatgreatsociety.pdf.

[79] Gerald Frug, "Democracy's Future: What's Left?" *Public Culture* 25, no. 2 (Spring 2013): 311–314.

constituents; but it does not necessarily share the vision that government should always be a service provider. Like Facebook or the iPhone, Pahlka believes government should act more like a platform:

> We've come to think of government as a vending machine, into which we put our taxes and out of which we get services . . . and we've developed monumentally large bureaucracies in order to provide these services, causing huge inefficiencies. If we start to see government instead as a vehicle for collective action, a platform for society to do collectively what citizens can't do individually, its role shifts from service provider to enabler. There will still be many services government must perform. But it should start looking at how it can do things like publish public data that allow the private sector to create applications that make citizens lives easier and connect citizens with common goals to each other to solve their own problems . . . Platform thinking is one critical skill for government to borrow from the consumer web; agility, citizen-centered design, and transparency are others.

The notion of government as an enabler of private sector innovation in the public interest is troublingly consistent with the swing towards the privatization of government services more broadly. Once again I turn to Gerald Frug, the legal scholar, who warns against the decline of liberal democracy hastened by arguments from both the Right and the Left. While conservative attempts to weaken government in favor of market logic are well known, the ways that progressives undermine government are seldom acknowledged. The progressive version "begins with a reference to local organizing, social movements, or organized resistance to government policy or, more generally, to the word *community*. Whether this action takes the form of protest, fighting crime through a neighborhood watch, organizing local housing initiatives, or planting an urban garden, the basic appeal is to 'agency' — to the actions of individuals and groups." This narrative is less explicit in its antigovernment rhetoric, yet consistently treats government as a problem rather than a solution. While it may refer "to the idea of politics as 'bottom up' . . . the 'up' actually gets no attention at all. The focus is solely on the celebration of the 'bottom.' Nor is there any attention to the mechanisms by which the 'bottom' might influence the decision making by the 'up.'"[79] The appeal to community disregards and eventually erodes the role government decision-making plays in contributing to social welfare.

At a conference on civic tech in Washington in the fall of 2010, I heard Pahlka vibrantly extol the virtues not of the Great Society, but the Big Society, a conservative philosophy of government espoused by British Prime Minister David Cameron. Cameron's brand of conservatism is softer than his Tory predecessors Margaret Thatcher and John Major. In her panel discussion, Pahlka explicitly and approvingly referenced a *New Yorker* article that describes Cameron's vision of "a garden-fence government, in which little platoons of concerned citizens, unhindered by senseless regulations and sclerotic bureaucracies, band together to conceive and execute the governance of their own communities." A more academic (and left-wing) reading characterizes the Big Society's "mix of conservative communitarianism and libertarian paternalism. Together, they constitute a long-term vision of integrating the free market with a theory of social solidarity based on hierarchy and voluntarism." It shares key tenets with President George H. W. Bush's famous reference, in his 1989 inauguration speech, to the "thousand points of light," outlining his view that volunteer-led community organizations should act as frontline service providers in American's communities. In an interesting twist to the more recent dogma of innovation, Bush said "The old ideas are new again because they are not old, they are timeless: duty, sacrifice, commitment, and a patriotism that finds its expression in taking part and pitching in."

Voluntary community service is an important part of any functioning democracy, and has been a subject of scholarly inquiry into the political culture of the United States from Alexis de Tocqueville's *Democracy in America* (1835, 1840) to Robert D. Putnam's *Bowling Alone* (2000) and beyond. It is inherently related to the ethic of stewardship described earlier in this book that I believe to be a central component to an emergent culture of citymaking. But the voluntary activities of certain citizens can never replace the efforts of a dedicated municipal workforce, at least not if we expect the services so provided to approach even distribution across socioeconomic lines. I think the idea of government-as-platform, or Gov 2.0, has some important advantages — particularly with examples like the opening up of transit data to app developers — that citymakers coming from the worlds of government, technology, and design should take seriously. That said, the government-as-platform vision also serves to obscure the tacit slide towards an austerity regime that sounds compassionate yet is often complicit in compounding inequality. Just like crowdsourcing complaints to gauge public priorities, the suggestion that volunteers can pick up the slack of under-resourced local governments is regressive: only those communities with citizens who have time to complain and are aware of the appropriate channels to do so will be doing the complaining. As the old adage goes, the squeaky wheel gets the grease. The promise of civic tech should be to spread the grease more evenly, not to give more grease to those wheels that have found new apps through which to amplify their squeaks' volume.

In other words, instead of using technology-enabled efficiencies to mask public service cutbacks, to expect citizens to do the work governments used to do, or to match public investment to the priorities of the already privileged, we should be creating platforms *for* government, tools that enable public servants to approach problems in a networked way. In our interview, Pahlka offered the example of reporting a broken streetlight to illustrate how a network model for government-citizen interactions might work. Calls to report such an issue enter a queue of requests, and after it works its way through the system, the agency responsible will send out an employee to inspect the damage. "If another call comes in about the same streetlight, it simply goes into the queue as well; we don't know that it's the same issue, reported twice." The corrective she offers involves citizens with cameras in their smart phones, meaning "we can make it easy for them to take picture of service requests, and upload them with geo-tagging. There's far more information in even one of those reports than in a phone call, but the real help is when you look at the data in aggregate and you realize that you have a) all the information that the city needs to fix the streetlight without sending out an inspector and b) the beginnings of a way of prioritizing these requests, because some issues will have more requests than others." Reading the "collective intelligence" of citizen-generated data is more powerful than treating each service request as unique.

Pahlka is cognizant of the problematics, noting the "issues to be grappled with" in the examples of networked government service that she offers. "We have to think deeply about citizen privacy and digital divide issues if these are going to work and reflect our values. But that's a challenge we have to rise to." We also have to think about how to use these tools to empower existing government departments, not only to outsource public service delivery to the crowd or recruit talent for consultant-style, short-term stints. Two public servants who have been doing just that are Jeffrey Roth of the Fire Department of New York (FDNY) and James McConnell of NYC Emergency Management (formerly the Office of Emergency Management). Their ambitions for local government to improve decision-making and service delivery in light of big data shed light on — and raise questions about — the kinds of technological change emerging from within city government.

Urban Omnibus published interviews with both men for our series "Profiles in Public Service." While my colleagues and I had been sharing the work of dedicated city government workers with our readers since the beginning, we conceived of this special series of weekly features as a way to highlight those public servants whose jobs had important but non-obvious implications for the built environment of New York. Work done in agencies like the Departments of City Planning, Parks and Recreation, or Housing Preservation and Development is clearly relevant to design-based urbanism and the physical city. Work done in the Department of Health and Mental Hygiene, for instance, or the New York Public Library is not typically considered as part of the same conversation.[82] So, given our editorial intention to broaden the public conception of who is making cities today while illuminating how the city works, we sought out individuals whose jobs — and whose passions for public service — put them in the vanguard of contemporary citymaking. Perhaps unsurprisingly, two of the examples we uncovered had to do with figuring out how to manage public data to meet operational needs in the context of emergency preparedness and response.

---

[80] Lauren Collins, "All Together Now!" *The New Yorker,* October 25, 2010.

[81] Allen Walker and Steve Corbett, "The 'Big Society', neoliberalism and the rediscovery of the 'social' in Britain," Sheffield Political Economy Research Institute, March 8, 2013. Accessed Janurary 2, 2016. speri.dept.shef.ac.uk/2013/03/08/big-society-neoliberalism-rediscovery-social-britain/.

[82] The articles published as part of this *Urban Omnibus* series include interviews with Marlon Williams, director of cross-agency partnerships at the Department of Health and Mental Hygiene and Matt Knutzen, geospatial librarian and curator of the map collection at the New York Public Library, among others. The complete series can be found at urbanomnibus.net/tag/profiles-in-public-service/.

When asked what led him to public service, Jeffrey Roth, Assistant Commissioner for Management Initiatives at the FDNY and a battalion executive officer in the National Guard, mentioned growing up in a family with a history of civic engagement and military service, including a brother who died while serving in the US Army. He described how his experience as a high school student in Michigan tutoring kids in inner city Detroit taught him "how the built environment can contribute to segregation" and how his experience spending multiple summers working with orphans in post-Ceaușescu Romania taught him "to make the link between macro policy and its effect on real people . . . how to measure those impacts, and how to make policy that actually makes people's lives better rather than worse." Graduate training in public policy and work experience in a small Massachusetts city shifted his ambitions from working in federal government towards developing and implementing local policies, especially those that "bring multiple stakeholders and multiple government entities to the table." Roth's first job in New York City, at the Mayor's Office of Operations, involved coordinating across different agencies. One project came about in response to a deadly 2007 fire in a condemned Lower Manhattan office building undergoing a complex demolition process. The failure to share crucial information about the demolition between different responsible parties — particularly the fact that stairwells had been sealed to prevent the spread of toxic residue left over from the Twin Towers — contributed to the deaths of two firefighters. The tragedy prompted reforms: City Hall "created a data bridge between City agencies and a central repository for all agency data," a shared repository into which all participating agencies dump their data. Soon Roth was working to help FDNY become one of the first City agencies "to consume these data in an operational way . . . sending field units out to actually do work based on the data we're sourcing" from the repository.[83]

One of the applications FDNY has developed is called FireCast, which sifts data from across different agencies through an algorithm that assigns and rank buildings' fire risk. This tool allows FDNY to prioritize among the 330,000 buildings it is responsible for inspecting, which are all of the buildings in New York that are not a single or two-family home. Resources only allow staff to inspect about 10% of these buildings each year. Roth is clear about the objectives: "We want to optimize resource allocation and target areas where we can have the greatest impact by creating greater efficiencies. That's a basic tenet of good stewardship of municipal resources regardless of budgets and funding." The fire risk algorithm includes almost 1,000 factors, selected by Roth and his colleagues out of an original 7,500 factors, each of which has multiple variables. Some of the variables that correlate strongly with the likelihood of a fire event "are usually proxies for negligence" like sidewalk cleanliness infractions, illegal alterations to the building, rodent problems, or 311 noise complaints.

Roth was quick to point out that the specific objectives that drive distinct agencies to collect data are not always commensurable. Even a seemingly simple piece of information like an address, for example, means something different to the Department of Finance than it does to the FDNY; the former is concerned with where to mail a tax bill, the latter with how to enter a building to fight a fire. For this reason, the algorithm doesn't obviate the need for human observation. Rather, it redirects and focuses that need in a more targeted way. Especially with cross-agency data sets, "you have to create feedback mechanisms," Roth said, "eyes and ears on the ground that can observe... [and] update the record." Importantly, the feedback refines the data for all users, not just those trying to fight fires. In this way, the data repository on which FireCast is built is a platform *for* government, a system developed within the public sector that enables specific agencies with distinct missions to create their own applications that can create unforeseen down-stream benefits for other agencies and the public at-large. The FDNY's inspection mandate means its standard deployment of inspectors is not only more directed to at-risk buildings but also might just verify or update data collected by, say, the Department of City Planning that will improve the accuracy of the data set overall. Algorithms to guide resource allocation mix with human observation to create a risk assessment system stronger than either component on its own.

Roth didn't mention it, but FDNY has a notorious history with data-driven decision-making, one that might have been far less destructive if human observation and common sense were applied to a crude computerized model. In response to increased fire rates in 1969, the City turned to analysts from the RAND Corporation (the think tank was involved in a fledgling partnership with the Lindsay mayoral administration) for advice. Despite misgivings, RAND analysts acceded to a disastrous decision to use the single factor of emergency response time to model the health of the firefighting system. In a messy and congested city with unevenly distributed resources, this factor was the easiest to quantify. Two years later, RAND's model supported closing many of the firehouses that were fighting the greatest number of fires in poorer, predominantly black and Latino parts of the city. The closures were based solely on response time calculations that failed to account for common sense considerations like traffic or whether or not a fire company was too busy fighting one fire to be able to clock a rapid response time to a second fire,[84] further distorted by political manipulation to prevent closing firehouses located near the homes of well-connected bigwigs.[85] Many people think the Bronx burned in the 1970s because of arson; shortsighted policy, enabled by data fetishism and inflected with racism, is arguably more to blame. Both Anthony Townsend and Adam Greenfield cite this example in their critiques of the founding logic of the smart city. Greenfield sees the RAND fire stations study as a canonical example of how political priorities can skew policies derived from computational models: "Inconvenient results may be suppressed, arbitrarily overridden by more heavily-weighted decision

[83] "The Analytics of Fire," *Urban Omnibus,* June 25, 2014.

[84] See Joe Flood, *The Fires* (New York: Riverhead Books, 2011) and Deborah Wallace and Rodrick Wallace *A Plague on Your Houses* (Chicago: Haymarket, 2001).

[85] Joe Flood, "Why the Bronx Burned," *New York Post,* May 16, 2010.

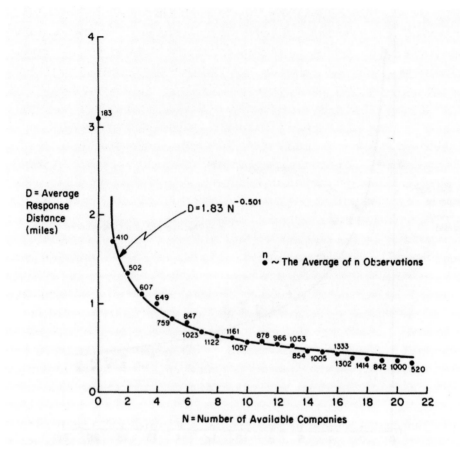

D = Average Response Distance (miles)

$D = 1.83 \, N^{-0.501}$

$\overset{n}{\bullet} \sim$ The Average of n Observations

N = Number of Available Companies

In 1969, officials from the Lindsay mayoral administration sought advice from the RAND Corporation about increased fire rates. The think tank provided a model of the health of the firefighting system based exclusively on emergency response time, failing to account for other factors that were harder to quantify. The resulting decisions about which fire stations to close were disastrous.

factors, or simply ignored." And even before the political manipulation distorts the model, the case reveals the seductive ease of "some easily-measured value used as a proxy for a reality that is much harder to quantify, and again we see the distortion of ostensibly neutral results by the choices made by an algorithm's designers."[86]

Trained urbanists are by no means immune to the appeal of data-driven decision-making. Greenfield's call for a generation of techonologist-urbanist hybrids, equally familiar with the work of Vint Cerf and Jane Jacobs, speaks not only to the need for data scientists and computer engineers to learn their urban history, or for planners and designers to keep abreast of technological tools. It's also a call for an inductive, observational approach to policy formulation, informed rather than ruled by data. Remember the warning of Warren Weaver, promulgator of the field of complexity science in the 1940s and '50s, that attempts at measurement can often suspend the variables of dynamic systems in misleading ways. He was a great advocate for science as one means to social progress yet fervently believed in the "rich and essential parts of human life which are alogical, which are immaterial and nonquantitative in character, and which cannot be seen under the microscope, weighed with the balance, nor caught by the most sensitive microphone."[87] Inductive, observational methods of analysis are important correctives to the tendency to discount the immeasurable. Consider again Greenfield's ethnographic system analysis of the Occupy Sandy headquarters, where he applied clear-eyed participant-observation (one of the primary data-collection methodologies in qualitative research, especially cultural anthropology) to ask the following questions: "Can the flow of human knowledge that drives this site meaningfully be *abstracted from place?* And, can mission-critical roles and responsibilities be decoupled from individual personalities?"

Such questions must be asked if meaningful lessons are to be learned about how to respond to disasters, whether a self-organized mutual aid society like Occupy Sandy or a coordinated government response. Emergency response is one public service that most people agree is a proper office of government. And certainly, even as we accept voluntary activities like neighborhood watch as a helpful support to crime prevention, no one is advocating that we completely crowdsource disaster relief and recovery. New York, in fact, is one of the few cities with a dedicated agency: NYC Emergency Management. This agency itself operates as a kind of platform: it's not an operating agency like the FDNY that deploys first responders; its job is to coordinate the efforts of other government departments. According to James McConnell, Assistant Commissioner for Strategic Data at NYC Emergency Management, "The goal is to think through a problem ahead of time and then work with other city agencies to develop plans that outline which agency will provide what expertise, equipment, and staff in the case of an incident . . . During an event, we monitor whether people are fulfilling their roles or if they need more resources, and throughout we keep City Hall involved and up to date."[88]

Much of the strategic data that McConnell and his team manage is spatial; he also directs the Geographic Information Systems (GIS) Division. GIS was what initially brought McConnell, trained as an urban planner, to NYC Emergency Management. He describes GIS as "just a series of data sets that have at least one way of relating information to a location on Earth — that's usually an address, but it could be an x, y coordinate or a polygon that describes a park." His staff maintains a catalog of around 1,000 layers of geo-referenced data about the city's demographics, infrastructure, geology, and more. To be ready for an emergency, they need an up-to-date picture of where non-English speaking New Yorkers are concentrated, where public facilities like schools are located, where repairs to water mains are taking place, where the soil is soft or the bedrock firm. For data to be actionable says McConnell,

[86] Adam Greenfield, "Against the Smart City," *Urban Omnibus,* October 23, 2013 (emphasis in text).

[87] Warren Weaver, "Science and Complexity," *American Scientist* 36, no. 536 (1948) Accessed January 3, 2016. people.physics.anu.edu.au/~tas110/Teaching/Lectures/L1/Material/ WEAVER1947.pdf.

[88] "The Anatomy of Emergency," *Urban Omnibus,* December 10, 2014.

it needs to associate with a particular location: "It happens somewhere." The actions that concern him are how to react in extraordinary circumstances, from transit strikes to terrorist attacks to extreme weather events, but the work helps day-to-day operations of City government as well. NYC Emergency Management staff has "the luxury of sitting down and spending time with new data sets" which firefighters, police officers, or sanitation inspectors don't have the time to do. Because it draws from so many different sources and is constantly updated, its data catalog is the most robust of any agency. Most of it is not necessarily useful in an emergency, but might be; McConnell explains, "We don't have to know exactly how we are going to use it; we just know that it's always better to have more." And the team shares its expertise in selecting which of multiple, overlapping data sets is most useful for a particular purpose with its partners in the first responder agencies, helping them "figure out what's most useful and most up-to-date." Because its primary mission is to coordinate across a vast network of bureaucracies, it has a particularly clear picture of how New York City works. According to McConnell, "Disaster response demonstrates a strong sense of what each agency does and what its strengths are, which is useful for normal operations as well." Especially in a city as large and administratively complex as New York, coordinating among and between different fields of urban management is imperative. And it requires the iterative thinking, inductive reasoning, historical awareness, and qualitative observation that I believe to be essential traits of responsible citymaking.

McConnell's work brings up another topic of immense importance to the convergence of data and urbanism: what happens when you put the data on a map? The implications of spatial information for citymaking are obviously huge. Maps have always been fundamental tools in urban planning and design, essential to understanding key urban characteristics like density, mobility, open space, and so on. As increasingly robust technological tools like GIS allow us to spatialize the data sets we are generating at exponentially higher rates, the importance of remaining focused on what kinds of questions we should be asking of all this data cannot be underestimated. One of the truths that data-driven urban analysis and management must reinforce is every map is a diagram, that is, an abstract, pictorial, and necessarily reductive representation of information. As the examples I've related in this chapter make clear, algorithmic understandings of urban dynamics are subject to hidden distortions that result from the rush to mistake "some easily-measured value used as a proxy for a reality that is much harder to quantify." In the same way, the illustrative power of the cartographic representation of urban life risks allowing us to ignore that the map is not the territory.[89]

---

[89] Alfred Korzybski, who founded the field of general semantics, coined the famous expression "the map is not the territory" in "A Non-Aristotelian System and its Necessity for Rigour in Mathematics and Physics," a paper presented before the American Mathematical Society at the New Orleans, Louisiana, meeting of the American Association for the Advancement of Science, December 28, 1931. Reprinted in his 1933 book *Science and Sanity* (New York: Institute of General Semantics,1995).

In the winter of 2010, I joined a group of urbanists, technologists, designers, and urban planners at the offices of the Rockefeller Foundation to discuss the future of "the crowdsourced city." Four presentations focused on forecasting the benefits, tensions, and pitfalls of mining the data that humans generate as they go about their daily lives.

Before the presentations began, Benjamin de la Peña, an avowed technophile trained as an urban planner and was serving as associate director for urban development at the Rockefeller Foundation at the time, set the context by referencing the Foundation's long history with funding new ways of responding to urban change, from supporting the work of an unknown Jane Jacobs to investing in innovative economic development programs in the Global South. He referenced UN Habitat's ubiquitous urbanization statistic — that over half of the world's population lives in urban areas — and then quickly recontextualized this over-cited figure by juxtaposing it with a sobering fact from the world of information technology: Between the dawn of humanity and 2003, roughly five exabytes (an exabyte is one billion gigabytes) of "information" were created. Now, we generate that amount every two days. He had convened the assembled to ponder how that amount of information produced by an incalculable number of sensors embedded in the material of everyday life, from toll booths to cash registers to cell phones, will affect how we perceive and manage cities.

The first presentation was a summary of a report, "The Future of Cities, Information and Inclusion," authored by the social sector office of the global management consultancy McKinsey & Company with examples ranging from mobile electronic systems integration in Istanbul that speed police response to electronic handsets used by New York City's Department of Homeless Services. The report focuses on benefits. Citizens can profit from direct economic and social benefits as well as tools to empower fuller participation in public life. Policymakers and administrators can rely on good data for better operational decisions and increased transparency. In another presentation, Clay Johnson, a prominent digital strategist for Democratic Party candidates, raised some of the political and managerial challenges to realizing the potential of technological advances to deliver more efficient and effective governance. His talk was notable for calling out who was not in the room, who was missing from the entire conversation about our digital future. Organized labor, he stated strongly and clearly, is a big problem for the crowdsourced city. The rhetoric of efficiency and of do-it-yourself public services often flies in the face of those things labor unions are sworn to protect: jobs. Another conspicuous absence from similar discussions is Republicans and the South. The failure to engage these constituencies runs the risk of equating, in the popular imagination, technologically enabled municipal renewal with the progressive political agenda. In other words, the failure of the community of people who care about this topic to talk to people unlike themselves means that any attempts to create political, legislative change will be blocked from both the Left and the Right.

A presentation about the work of the Spatial Information Design Lab sounded a different note, showing a particular body of work from one research organization, rather than attempting to characterize broad trends and sampling from diverse case studies. Laura Kurgan, who leads the lab, has spent the past twenty years researching new technologies of location, remote sensing, and mapping. Trained as an architect, Kurgan's work connects geographic information, social justice, and public investment through projects that have addressed challenges in public education, post-disaster rebuilding, and geographies of incarceration. She was on the original advisory board of Urban Omnibus and has been a regular contributor. Like many of our original team of advisors, she has had a long relationship with The Architectural League: she participated in a League exhibition on emerging technologies of display in 1995, and exhibited some of her groundbreaking maps on incarceration in the League exhibition "Architecture and Justice" in 2006. Her practice asserts the power of spatial representations of data while simultaneously questioning the truth-claims of such representations. For Kurgan, "there is no such thing as neutral data. Data are always collected for a specific purpose, by a combination of people, technology, money, commerce, and government."[90] At the 2010 convening at the Rockefeller Foundation, she shared projects that use various kinds of data to reveal those invisible geographies that link the social city to the physical city. The most famous and influential is the Million Dollar Blocks project, a collaboration with the Justice Mapping Center, which has contributed significantly to the increasingly urgent calls for criminal justice reform that ends mass incarceration or, at least, demonstrates its true costs, social and financial. Five percent of the world's population lives in the United States, yet we hold 25 percent of the world's inmates in state and federal prisons and local jails. About 13 percent of the US population is African-American, yet African-American men comprise 60 percent of the more than 2 million male inmates in jail and prison. According to civil rights expert Michelle Alexander in her hugely influential book The New Jim Crow: Mass Incarceration in the Age of Colorblindness, "Like Jim Crow (and slavery), mass incarceration operates as a tightly networked system of laws, policies, customs, and institutions that operate collectively to ensure the subordinate status of a group largely by race."[91]

Even as the compounding social injustices of this system come to be more widely recognized, the primary spatial questions asked in policy discussions about criminal justice have traditionally been about the locations where crimes occur, thus communicating to the public a particular geography of urban safety and security: this neighborhood is safe, that one's dangerous. Data-driven policing instruments like CompStat, which organizes policing activity based on maps of where crimes take place, maintain this approach to operationalizing the data the NYPD collects. Such maps are, Kurgan writes, "one of the most prominent instruments through which we understand and interpret our cities."[92] The resurgence of cities like New

[90] Laura Kurgan, *Close Up at a Distance: Mapping Technology and Politics* (New York: Zone Books, 2013), 35.

[91] Michelle Alexander, *The New Jim Crow: Mass Incarceration in the Age of Colorblindness* (New York: The New Press, 2012), 13.

The Million Dollar Blocks project demonstrated how a disproportionate number of the nation's two million prisoners come from a very few neighborhoods in the country's biggest cities.

Top: Prisoner migration patterns, Brooklyn, New York, 2003. This diagram shows the displacement of the incarcerated from a handful of neighborhoods to jails and prisons upstate.

Bottom: Prisoner expenditures by block, 2003. 17 million dollars were spent to incarcerate 109 people from these 7 blocks of Brownsville, Brooklyn in 2003.

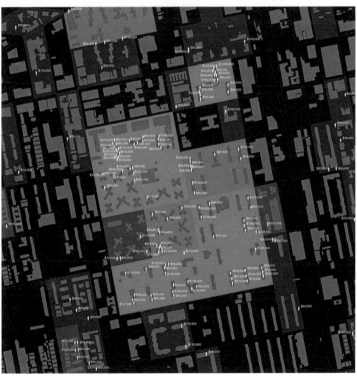

York as the preferred locations for the young and rich over the last twenty years has a lot to do with the perception of an increased security that has many more contributing factors than just increased policing (experts variously attribute it to ATMs and the decline of carrying cash, the legalization of abortion twenty years prior, the end of the crack epidemic, and more).

The profound move that Kurgan and her Justice Mapping collaborators made in their Million Dollar Blocks maps was to ask a different question of the same data set. When they shifted the research question from where crime events take place to where incarcerated people live, "strikingly different patterns become visible." They were able to corroborate and build upon what a former inmate had first uncovered years before: that 75 percent of New York State's prison population came from just seven neighborhoods in New York City. Similar concentrations of the home addresses of the incarcerated are observable in big cities across the country. "In many places, the concentration is so dense that states are spending in excess of a million dollars per year to incarcerate the residents of single city blocks" in some of the poorest neighborhoods of their cities. The Million Dollar Block maps "suggest that the criminal justice system has become the predominant government institution in these communities and that public investment in this system has resulted in significant costs to other elements of our civic infrastructure: education, housing, health, and family." The costs to society, of course, are much greater than public expenditure. Most inmates return to those same home addresses upon release, where they are legally unable to vote and are "subject to legalized discrimination in employment, housing, education, public benefits, and jury service."[93] This legal disenfranchisement and foreclosure of opportunity helps to explain why so many former prisoners in the US — up to 68 percent — return to prison within three years of release.[94]

The Spatial Information Design Lab's work is a powerful testament to how carefully and strategically choosing which data to analyze and spatialize is just as important as the technological ability to collect that data in the first place. As we move toward a future of infinitely more data, fostering a sophisticated conversation about how best to promote tough analytical choices between distinct data sets is crucial to excavating the benefits from a world awash, if not submerged, in automatically generated information. Kurgan does not consider her practice as exclusively reframing analyses of existing conditions, however. It is generative, with the power to stimulate and contextualize design interventions. She sees one potential of this project as suggesting "new strategies for approaching urban design and criminal justice reform together." As Patrick Geddes would say, "diagnosis before treatment." But don't stop at the diagnosis. Once diagnosed, perform Geddes' brand of "conservative surgery" by inserting proactive spaces of opportunity into stressed, complex contexts.

One of the reform-minded policy formulations that can activate these urban design possibilities is called Justice Reinvestment, a process used by a growing number of states to cut the costs of incarceration and redirect those savings towards community programs — like education or workforce development — that help to keep people out of the criminal justice system, reduce recidivism, and maintain public safety. But just as our policies must be redesigned, so must the spaces that administer them, especially in neighborhoods where the criminal justice system is the predominant interface between citizens and government. Like all of the policies discussed in this chapter, Justice Reinvestment defines itself as "data-driven" and emphasizes the savings in public dollars. But it can also take the form of a keenly observed, contextually informed design intervention that responds to conditions that are hard to measure yet easy to see, if you know where to look. Such is the case with the transformation of the waiting rooms of the NYC Department of Probation (DOP), which runs the second-largest alternative-to-incarceration program in the country. Based in part on her work with the Justice Mapping Center on the Million Dollar Blocks, DOP asked Kurgan to participate in a task force charged with rethinking the entire process of probation. The task force included probation officers and individuals sentenced to probation as well as a consultant team of policy analysts and designers. When I interviewed her about the project for an *Urban Omnibus* article in 2012, our conversation made clear to me that this story's importance emerges from the expanded conception of design that undergirds this comprehensive effort.[95] In order to deepen the impact of the physical redesign of underperforming local government spaces like DOP waiting rooms, the first step must be to rethink an entire system, especially the touch points between the public servants who provide critical city services and the citizens who stand to benefit from them.

DOP provides services and investigations for more than 30,000 adults and 15,000 juveniles per year, and supervises approximately 24,000 adults and 2,000 juveniles on any given day. Until recently, this large population of New Yorkers — who might be turnstile jumpers, first-time offenders, or otherwise considered to be good candidates for non-incarcerated supervision — faced long commutes to DOP waiting rooms in central courthouses, where they would sit and wait, often for hours, in uninviting spaces. In many cases, the system was doing more harm than good. People were having to take a day off work to make their way into central Manhattan to wait for a meeting with their probation officer, often risking losing the jobs their sentences demanded they keep. An evocative epigraph for the task force's report sums up the condition cogently: the hip-hop mogul Jay-Z, who grew up in the Marcy Houses public housing complex in Brooklyn, writes in his memoir "In places like Marcy there are people who know the ins and outs of government bureaucracies, police procedures, and sentencing guidelines, who spend half of

[92] Kurgan, *Close Up at a Distance*, 2013, 192.

[93] Alexander, *The New Jim Crow*, 2013, 1.

[94] National Institute of Justice, "Recidivism." Accessed June 19, 2016. www.nij.gov/topics/corrections/recidivism/pages/welcome.aspx.

[95] "From Waiting Rooms to Resource Hubs," *Urban Omnibus*, October 10, 2012.

New York City's Department of Probation (DOP) is one of the largest alternative-to-incarceration programs in the country. Starting in 2010, DOP has transitioned from traditional waiting rooms to Neighborhood Opportunity Networks, or NeONS, which help connect individuals sentenced to probation to local opportunities.

their lives in dirty waiting rooms on plastic chairs waiting for someone to call their name. But for all of this involvement, the government might as well be the weather because a lot of us don't think we have anything to do with it."[96] That's a problem that apps and algorithms can't solve. It's symptomatic of the same inefficiencies that much civic tech aims to ameliorate yet it also demands a broader arsenal of design strategies. Not just the design of environments such as waiting rooms, but also the design of *policy,* the physical expression of power dynamics in the relationship between public service providers and the public, and the ways public policy connects to citizens in specific institutional settings.

For people sentenced to probation, things started to change when Vincent Schiraldi became the DOP commissioner in 2010. Growing up in Greenpoint, Brooklyn in the 1970s, many of his friends got into trouble and spent time in local jails or juvenile detention centers. And "when they came back, two things were almost always true. They were almost always worse − more violent, more unruly. And . . . we always looked up to them more. We didn't have this phrase for it back then, but they had more 'street cred.' Even as a kid, I knew this was wrong."[97] This observation has motivated a career spent honing his expertise in alternatives to incarceration, particularly among youth.

Upon arrival, Schiraldi instituted a sweeping strategic plan, setting the course for DOP to "do less harm, do more good, and do it in the community," according to Susan Tucker, who directs Justice Reinvestment Initiatives for the agency.[98] Justice Reinvestment is more commonly associated with departments of corrections rather than of probation and with states rather than cities. But since 2010, New York City's model of probation has followed a justice reinvestment model, re-oriented towards those communities with the highest concentrations of residents sentenced to probation.

By 2012, DOP had opened five Neighborhood Opportunity Networks (NeONs) in Brownsville, Jamaica, South Bronx, Staten Island, and Harlem; and by 2016 it had opened two more in East New York and Bedford-Stuyvesant. These centers help connect individuals sentenced to probation to local opportunities, by co-locating a staffed DOP presence with community-based organizations that provide a range of social services, from housing and education support to job training, and have deep roots and knowledge in the neighborhoods they serve. Many individuals sentenced to probation are cut off from what makes their neighborhoods dynamic, Tucker told me, and if DOP is going to reduce the likelihood that the citizens it supervises will be re-arrested, it needs to reconnect them with that dynamism, to "become

---

[96] Jay-Z, *Decoded* (New York: Random House / Spiegel & Grau, 2010), 152.

[97] Jeff Storey, "Q&A: Vincent Schiraldi," *New York Law Journal,* May 25, 2012. Accessed June 19, 2016. www.newyorklawjournal.com/PubArticleNY.jsp?id=1202555952494&QA_Vincent_Schiraldi&slreturn= 20120909172952.

[98] Susan Tucker, phone interview for "From Waiting Rooms to Resource Hubs," *Urban Omnibus,* October 10, 2012.

more asset-based and less deficit-based." The agency has also worked with partners in the Department of Design and Construction to transform DOP's waiting rooms into "Resource Hubs," with brightly colored and welcoming interiors.[99] Other changes involve new technologies that improve efficiencies in the mechanics of supervision and enable differentiation between the different types of probation sentences, such as ATM-like kiosks where certain individuals can check in with their probation officer remotely, and computer programs to help find relevant information.

These changes required a profound culture shift throughout the agency. And not all these changes had to do with the quality, location, or orientation of its physical facilities. One of the simplest and yet most profound changes is a shift away from calling people in the system "probationers" or "offenders" and instead referring to them and treating them as "clients." This shift towards treating citizens as customers of City services is not unique to the DOP. In our conversation in 2013, Kurgan explained that "the introduction of 'service design' concepts throughout City agencies really comes right from the top," a reference to the Bloomberg administration.

Service design is a relatively new specialization within the design fields. While it is not explicitly technological in nature, it would not have emerged without the growth of interaction design alongside the explosion in information technology. Nor would it have matured as quickly without the internet-enabled decoupling of goods and services (think Zipcar, Uber, and Airbnb) described earlier in this chapter. Unlike traditional design disciplines such as architecture, service design has roots in the business disciplines of marketing and management and capitalizes on these fields' focus on user experience and customer satisfaction. In a 2010 *Urban Omnibus* article introducing the discipline — aptly titled "What is Service Design?" — Laura Forlano quotes a definition from Birgit Mager, who runs the Service Design Network in Cologne, Germany: "Service design addresses the functionality and form of services from the perspective of clients. It aims to ensure that service interfaces are useful, usable, and desirable from the client's point of view and effective, efficient, and distinctive from the supplier's point of view."[100] As such, it is most often applied in retail contexts, redesigning the interfaces of renting a car at the airport, say, or buying a new computer. The Apple Store, for example, is frequently cited as an example of a retail environment that reinvented the touch points between customers and salespeople, with the latter approaching prospective buyers on the shop floor and processing transactions on mobile devices rather than from behind the till.

Kurgan cites the Apple Store as one of the precedents floated during the DOP waiting room task force's research process. Following such examples, she and her collaborators took approached DOP's spaces and procedures by launching a "set of exercises with a committee of probation officers and clients, people from all over the city. We asked them to describe every step of the process: the 'offender' goes to a courthouse, passes through a security barrier, takes off his belt, takes an elevator . . . Then we asked them to describe the blockages in the process. Creating diagrams to investigate those blockages led to specific design ideas, and from there we kept on finding ways to integrate the spatial — the rooms themselves —

and the procedural — what you do in them." She applied her mapmaking expertise to demonstrate where the majority of people sentenced to probation live and also the concentration of nonprofits and community groups active in these areas, many of which would benefit from sharing space: "co-locating the resources of these community-based organizations with specially-trained probation officers and staff is the basis for what DOP is calling Neighborhood Opportunity Networks, or NeONs."

The NEoNs are designed to be architecturally inviting and procedurally efficient with technologies to connect probation clients to useful opportunities. They present an elegantly simple example of how an expanded notion of design — combining a nuanced reading of spatial information in terms of both the waiting room environments, activities, locations, and co-locations with community-based organizations — can be applied in concert with policy changes to address complex questions of poverty, crime, and public service. This approach does not evince a methodological hierarchy among design, policy, and data. It is a successful and exemplary exercise in citymaking because of the interaction between these otherwise distinct approaches of reducing incarceration on the one hand and, on the other, building platforms for vulnerable citizens.

REDESIGNING CIVIC TECH FOR THE CULTURE OF CITYMAKING

The examples I have related in this chapter, from Red Hook Wi-Fi to Code for America to FireCast to the DOP NeONs, are perhaps not the expected examples of the prospective meanings of the convergence of digital technology and the design and management of urban environments. Hugely important technological tools in how we design and manage cities are outside this chapter's scope, particularly in architectural software and modeling (and its potential interfaces with geographic information systems), 3-D printing, advances in engineering and building science, the "internet of things," and more.

To some readers, the stories I've told here may seem tangential to charting a course for urban practice in the public interest. I believe deeply, however, that citymakers of the future should heed these lessons. The promises of automatic data capture, algorithmic modeling of urban dynamics, and other forms of quantification and measurement promise real and important advantages. However, part of the mission of the comprehensive citymaker should be to meet that promise with sustained attention to the qualitative methodologies that have historically supported architecture and academic urbanism: close observation, aesthetic judgment, inductive reasoning. Serious social thought in the second half of the twentieth century

---

[99] The Department of Design and Construction (DDC) aided this effort through its See ChangeNYC initiative, which seeks to improve the spaces in which city services take place. The interiors were designed by Biber Architects with graphics by James Victore.

[100] Laura Forlano, "What is Service Design?" *Urban Omnibus,* October 27, 2010.

productively questioned the objectivity promised by the positivist tradition in the social sciences; yet the possibilities of big data risk seducing us back into a blind faith in the truth of what we can "objectively" count, which then justifies creating efficiencies that too often undermine democratic governance and reproduce new forms of inequality.

The intellectual trajectory of David Harvey, one the preeminent urbanists of the past fifty years, is emblematic. He is known now as a Marxist geographer, famous for such works as *Social Justice and the City* (1973), *The Condition of Postmodernity* (1989), *A Brief History of Neoliberalism* (2005), and many more. Like many social scientists of his generation, Harvey's doctoral training and early work in the 1960s tracked with the trend towards quantitative methods and positivist theory. The racial and socio-economic stratification he witnessed when he moved from Bristol, UK to Baltimore, USA in the early 1970s inspired him to shift the focus of his work, indeed to distance himself from the positivist orientation of academic geography and urban studies as much as possible. People don't act rationally; information asymmetries and prejudices make markets imperfect; and the structure of our political economy cannot be abstracted from lived experience. Harvey went so far as to write, in 1973, "The quantitative revolution has run its course, and diminishing marginal returns are apparently setting in." When applied to what he sees as "an ecological problem, an urban problem, an international trade problem" unfolding around us, quantitative methodologies "seem incapable of saying anything of depth or profundity about any of them."[101] Forty-five years later, those problems have become existential threats. The ecological problem is now anthropogenic global warming. The urban problem (in the US) is now unprecedented levels of inequality, deepening and multiplying the negative effects of concentrated poverty and undermining the principles of democracy. And the international trade problem is now economic globalization, which is not so much an existential threat as it is an extremely dense transnational network of intricate transactions and specialized knowledge that conceal the causes of and responsibility for the brutal conse-quences of the first two problems.

Saskia Sassen makes this argument in her recent book *Expulsions: Brutality and Complexity in the Global Economy*. She explains how the sheer complexity of the global economy masks the ways that current mechanisms for capitalist growth liter-ally expel people en masse from their livelihoods and homes while eradicating all forms of life from vast stretches of land and water. Her hypothesis is that "the move from Keynesianism to the global era of privatizations, deregulation, and open borders for some, entailed a switch from dynamics that brought people in to dynamics that push people out." The period between the end of World War II and the 1980s "was driven by a logic of inclusion, by concerted efforts to bring the poor and marginalized into the political and economic mainstream." The logic that has replaced it is "a dangerously narrow conception of economic growth . . . [that] our institutions and assumptions are increasingly geared to serve" thus enabling financial firms to cast aside any "constraints, including those of local public interest, that interfere with the pursuit of profit."Mass production and mass consumption are no longer the cornerstones of the economy they once were. More workers and more consumers won't create the kind of growth and hyperprofits that the new, financialized economic order demands, such that we see "the enclosure by financial firms of a country's resources and citizens' taxes, the repositioning of expanding stretches of the world as sites for extraction of resources, and the regearing of government budgets in liberal democracies away from social and workers' needs."[102]

Sassen's book focuses on three specific types of expulsion. First, the rise of financial securitization and the derivatives market created the subprime mortgage crisis, which reverberated around the world and forced millions from their homes. Second, rich countries buy up millions of acres of land in poor countries for agricultural or biofuel production purposes and mass evictions ensue (a modern form, particularly in Africa, of Enclosure). Third, advanced mining techniques like hydraulic fracturing (fracking) allow us to extract fossil fuels from beneath the earth while creating dead zones on its surface, inhibiting ecosystem function to the point that certain areas of land and water cannot recover without human intervention. This is "the expulsion of biospheric elements from their life space." The nature of these violent expulsions, in fact, asserts the irreversible entanglement of environmental and economic injustice. That entanglement, that inextricability, is perhaps the greatest challenge, the greatest responsibility, and the greatest opportunity before the citymakers of the future.

While the sites of such brutality are not only in cities, cities are where their causes and effects are most acute. Global cities concentrate the agents of finance, energy, industry, and even food prices that set them in motion. The greater the population density, the greater the damage will be when disaster strikes, whether it's a surging storm, poisoned drinking water, or mass foreclosure. Yet, also concentrated in cities are the small-scale innovations that just may have the capacity to influence national and international priorities.

In an opinion piece on *Urban Omnibus,* Shin-pei Tsay, a transportation and climate change policy researcher, writes, "The nimbleness demonstrated by urban innovations allude to an armory of ingenuity that would serve us well when the climate becomes more unpredictable and volatile. Whether it is top-down government-led bike share or bottom-up do-it-yourself urban reforestation, these projects are rays of hope and possibility that cut through a seemingly impenetrable rock wall of climate inaction by larger entities."[103] City governments are not empowered to enter into the kind of international agreements about carbon emissions or the systemic

---

[101] David Harvey, *Social Justice and the City* (Athens: University of Georgia Press, 2009; first published in 1973, 121–2.

[102] Saskia Sassen, *Expulsions: Complexity and Brutality in the Global Economy* (Cambridge, Mass.: Harvard University Press, 2014), 211.

[103] Shin-pei Tsay, "Cities and Climate Change: Small Enough to Act, Big Enough to Matter" *Urban Omnibus,* September 26, 2012.

reconceptualization of economic growth that are necessary to redress the crises we face. Design-led urban interventions will never scale up to remove carbon from the atmosphere on their own. Nor will they reverse the financialization of all economic activity, wherein any work product (including entire categories of livelihood) is reduced to its exchange value as a financial instrument like currency, stock, loans, debt, or derivatives.

However, on the environmental crisis, information technology's greatest potential may be to enable us to consume less by informing us where the stuff we use comes from, how much we use, and where it goes when we throw it away. I'm sure if I lived in the quantified community of Hudson Yards — as creepy as that might be — I'd be more conscious of my household energy usage and solid waste, and wasteful inefficiencies outside of any one household's control would be minimized as well. On the inequality crisis, information technology's greatest potential may be in opening up the black box of global economic operations and shedding light on the expulsions it produces. Such a project will require a lot of data and sophisticated analysts willing to learn which questions to ask. It will also require qualitative analysis, and it will require storytelling.

The citymaking projects I have discussed in this chapter do not deal with either of these potentials explicitly. They were not conceived to reduce consumption or illuminate the shadier dealings and ramifications of global finance. Yet each of these stories offers important insights into a third challenge that I believe is central to addressing the first two, which is the crisis of trust between citizens and government. Here, too, what we need is greater legibility, tools to foster awareness of the complexity of governance. Information technology can help us to design tools to make cities legible and thereby fields for action.

This kind of legibility is what Patrick Geddes was pursuing with his Victorian era Outlook Tower, a model of urban development, design, and management that was neither a static snapshot of history nor a predictive model of the future. It was a carefully considered fusion of scientific explanation and humanist principles, an active encouragement to citizens to learn about urban processes, to identify places and procedures where they might intervene. Presciently foreshadowing complexity science — the study of those systems whose properties cannot be described by summing or averaging — a half century before its invention, Geddes writes:

> All our activities — industrial and commercial, hygienic and educational, legal and political, cultural, and what not — become seen in relation to one another, as so many aspects and analyses of the city's life. To make this life more healthy and more effective,

---

[104] Geddes, *Cities in Evolution,* 1950 (1915), 268

[105] Patrick Geddes, "Civics: as Applied Sociology," Presentation to the Sociological Society at a Meeting in the School of Economics and Political Science (University of London), July 18th, 1904. Accessed July 17, 2016. www.gutenberg.org/files/13205/13205-h/13205-h.htm.

the unrelated individual activities with which we have been too long content are found insufficient; we need fuller coordination and harmony of them, like that of the instruments of the orchestra, of the actors in the drama. We expect this of soldiers in the field, of workers and organisers in the factory, of assistants and partners in the business. Is it not for lack of this orchestration, of this harmonious organization, upon the larger civic stage which our town-plans so clearly reveal, that our cities, full of detailed efficiencies of many kinds, are still so far from satisfying us as collectively efficient?[104]

Efficiency is the most touted benefit of the data revolution. To me, collective efficiency is something different altogether. It is more than the sum of all the "detailed efficiencies" that exist within cities. It is an aspirational quality of cities that will require a combination of participation from below, orchestration from above, and legibility — dare I say solidarity? — throughout.

Increased legibility should not be an excuse to forgive government for bureaucratic inefficiency. On the contrary, greater understanding of how government works — from procurement to public safety and beyond — just might enable citizens to demand it work better, to coordinate across siloes and jurisdictions. The citymaker drawn to civic tech should not aim to disrupt democratic governance. She should find ways to use the extreme technological capabilities at our disposal to reimagine government not as a vending machine of public services, nor as a platform to crowdsource DIY citizenship as a smokescreen for austerity or privatization, nor as a tacit enabler of innovative ways to sequester profit away from the 99 percent. Instead, civic tech as an element of citymaking should contribute to maintaining public goods and public services as truly public.

To help accomplish this ambitious set of goals, I believe the new practitioners of civic tech should recuperate Geddes' definition of civics. Civics, for Geddes, was applied sociology, "the application of Social Survey to Social Service." He was constant in his belief that "it is important that the methods advocated for the systematic study of cities, and as underlying fruitful action, be not merely the product of the study, but rather be those which may be acquired in course of local observation and practical effort."[105] For Geddes, this practical effort ranged from small-scale interventions in his neighborhood to urban-scale masterplans around the world. He learned through looking, but also by doing, by immersing himself in a particular community, developing platforms for the active participation of others, studying his mistakes, questioning assumptions and received wisdom, and creating genuine feedback loops between planner-designers and those affected by plans and designs. To help us realize information technology's potential for cities, the next generation of citymakers must focus on new ways and new tools to practice this type of civics.

CHAPTER 5

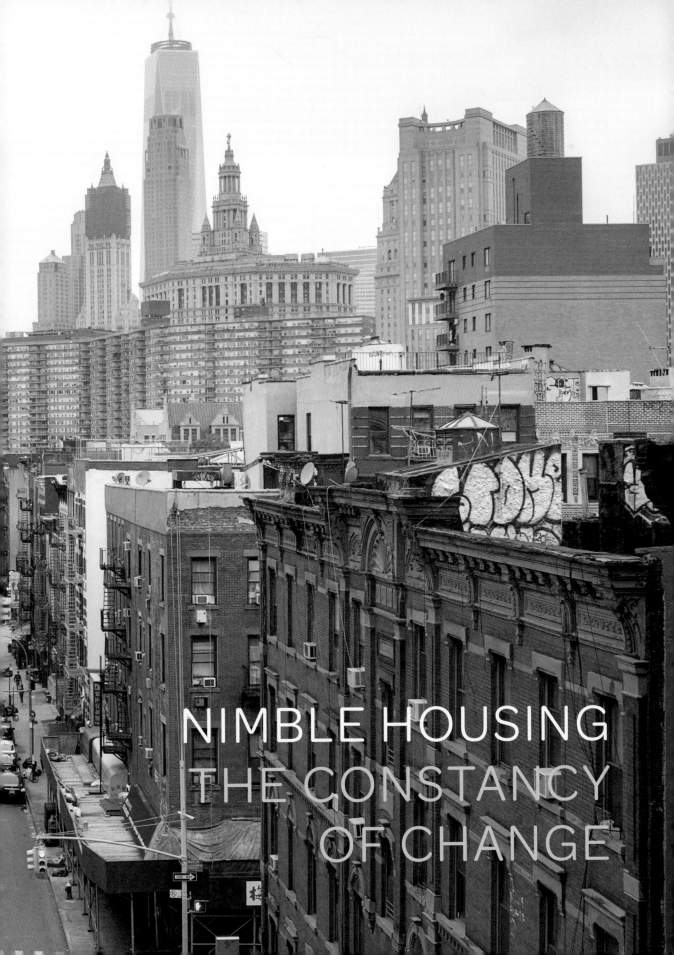

NIMBLE HOUSING
THE CONSTANCY
OF CHANGE

On a sunny day early in the summer of 2012, I took a subway ride to the Bronx to attend a press tour of a new building that was already generating a lot of buzz in the architectural and urban affairs press. The building, called Via Verde, contains 222 housing units for mixed-income tenants. It was designed by Grimshaw Architects and Dattner Architects and developed by Phipps Houses and Jonathan Rose Companies. I exited the subway at Third Avenue and 149th Street — a busy Bronx intersection known as The Hub, once called "the Broadway of the Bronx," where several neighborhoods converge — and immediately ran into Susanne Schindler, a housing-focused architect and researcher, who was headed to the same place.

In the years since, Schindler has authored several articles for *Urban Omnibus* as a regular columnist, reporting on new and historical affordable housing developments throughout the New York metro region. She eschews words like "affordable" and "subsidized" however, rightly pointing out the subjectivity of the former (affordable to whom?) and the inaccuracy of the latter (market rate and even luxury housing are government-subsidized in self-concealing ways through tax abatements and incentives, zoning bonuses, gas and highway subsidies and more). Her keen analytical ability to probe the slippage and inconsistencies in how professionals talk about the architecture and financing of housing enables her to tease out hidden connections between design and policymaking that are essential to continued efforts to provide shelter and to foster economic opportunity (for individuals and families as well as neighborhoods) through housing.

As Schindler and I walked together north along Third Avenue through the neighborhood of Melrose, we discussed how the built environment surrounding us physically manifests distinct philosophies and eras of how society should address urban poverty, from the offices of faith-based social service organizations to public housing projects to the recently constructed two- and three-family rowhouses that replaced tenements demolished since the 1970s. The walk made visible how profoundly ideas can change over time: the shift from top-down, utopian belief in the trans-formational benefits of government-built towers replacing overcrowded tenements to bottom-up community organizing and advocacy tactics to bring power to or build equity among the traditionally powerless. Understanding this history — actively doing the work to unpack the assumptions embedded within different periods of architecture, public policy, and community development — could not be more important when evaluating new design interventions intended to address the manifold needs of poor communities.

Our shared destination could be considered a promising marriage of current priorities: high design architecture; vanguard thinking on energy efficiency, sustain-ability and public health; a mix of ownership and rental units targeted to a mix of incomes; and a creative use of "grants, loans, tax credits, and other funding mechanisms from a total of 19 public, private, and nonprofit funding sources."[1] Via Verde is a beautiful building, intended to set a new bar for "affordable, green, and healthy urban living."[2] With its mix of rental and homeownership opportunities, low-rise townhouses that connect elegantly to high-rise units with spectacular views, stepped series of green roofs, solar powered lighting, and onsite medical center, it has won plaudits from the worlds of architecture, public health, real estate development, and community development. It cost just shy of 100 million dollars to build.

The following year, a leading advocate for high-quality, affordable housing design took Schindler aside at a conference and asked if she could help identify "good examples of affordable housing / public housing from the past that have been a huge success . . . because of the architecture."

Schindler responded with a question. "Successful in which respect?"

"Like Via Verde," the advocate responded.

She recounts this exchange in an *Urban Omnibus* article, coauthored with Juliette Spertus, that opens by questioning the possibility of determining Via Verde a success after less than two years of existence. Despite its impressive accolades, "We know nothing about what it will be like in ten, twenty, or forty years. Whether the single entry point across a shared courtyard will be loved, as now, or feared. Whether the roof gardens will be kept up. Whether the building will still be home to households of varying income levels. By which criteria, and in terms of which timeframe do you judge the 'success' of architecture in housing? How can we advocate for better design if we can't relate it to non-design issues such as management, maintenance, and use, in both the short and long term?"[3]

This line of questioning is provocative and critically important. Evaluating success is crucial to any meaningful disciplinary evolution, yet architecture remains stuck in a paradox: buildings are meant to last, but we tend to assess their quality only on opening day. Much of New York City's incredibly diverse housing stock is used in ways it was not intended — single-family brownstones accommodating four families, former factories converted into lofts, and so on — yet we lack criteria for long-term judgment.

This chapter cites a diverse range of projects that point out some ways that we can productively expand our notion of what one of those criteria might look like: the capacity to adapt, both in how we expect and plan for housing to evolve over time and in how we evaluate and understand the architectural, financial, and legal components of making a home in the city. I'm talking about a building's adaptability

---

[1] Urban Land Institute, "Case Studies: Via Verde" retrieved from http://casestudies.uli.org/via-verde/ [accessed July 15, 2016].

[2] Via Verde "About Page" retrieved from http://viaverdenyc.com/ [accessed July 15, 2016].

[3] Susanne Schindler and Juliette Spertus, "The Landscape of Housing: Twin Parks Northwest 40 Years On" in *Urban Omnibus,* November 6, 2013.

to new uses over time, but that's not all. I believe we must also demand housing policies to be flexible enough to adapt to the demographic, technological, and sociocultural changes that are a hallmark of the life of any city. A third kind of adaptive capacity has to do with how history figures into contemporary conversations about the components of generative urban development; the past forty years in New York have demonstrated how urban change can be so rapid and radical that we are at risk of thinking the lessons that practical urbanism has absorbed no longer apply, or that certain urban strategies designed for one era's challenges are obsolete once priorities change. In order to realize this capacity for adaptation within our housing stock, we must apply some of the same principles I've explored throughout this book: close observation of existing conditions and patterns of use, thoughtful reconsideration and reconfiguration of the existing built environment to meet multiple ends, and the stewardship of the assets we share as common resources.

Change may be the only constant: residents come and go and neighborhood demographics and the structure of urban economies shift. But most of a city's housing stock — the basic building block of urban communities — is built, in theory, to last. The expected permanence of residential real estate is part of why home ownership is still considered, despite painful historical episodes that attest to the contrary, an appreciating asset. This simple belief is embedded deep within American culture and serves to distinguish home ownership from virtually every other category of household investment like cars, appliances, most types of furniture. In fact, the way we understand the value of property likens it more to a trademark or a patent than to other forms of tangible assets like machinery or inventory, which depreciate over time. When you own a home you possess an expectation of eventual profit as much as, even more than, you possess a place to live. If you can't afford to own a home or choose not to, you pay for access to shelter through rent.

The past century of urbanization has made clear that the fortunes of urban neighborhoods reflect the upswings, downturns, and structural changes in the broader economy. Several times in the past hundred years the value of real estate has fallen sharply amid depressions, recessions, and other economic shocks and stresses. Yet both the national mythos and public policy maintain the notion that homeownership confers a privileged mode of citizenship. As recently as 2004, President George W. Bush described a key reason he was actively promoting the concept of an "ownership society" with the claim that "if you own something, you have a vital stake in the future of our country. The more ownership there is in America, the more vitality there is in America."[4] Certainly the psychic rewards of owning your own home (assuming your debt is serviceable) can have a salutary effect on community participation, and the economic security of investment with an expected return increases the amount of capital and debt cycling through banks and of cash being spent by consumers. However, almost lost in this calculative logic is the notion that housing has a use-value, a specific *utility,* as well as an expected exchange-value. It is shelter.

Via Verde is a mixed-income residential development, designed by Dattner Architects and Grimshaw, lauded in the architecture and real estate press for its commitment to sustainable design features and health-focused amenities. Located on a brownfield site in the South Bronx, the project includes 222 residential units, 7,500 square feet of retail space, and 40,000 square feet of green roofs and other open space for residents.

The challenges of providing safe and affordable shelter change along with cities themselves, in ways that are difficult to anticipate for government and advocacy organizations alike. Our understanding of bricks-and-mortar housing assumes it to be fixed and permanent yet the populations that inhabit it are by no means static. What constitutes poverty and housing affordability are moving targets, defined by means and averages and costs rather than absolutes. The demographics of the populations that fall under such shifting categories — by which I mean age, race, ethnicity, and, crucially, family size — are also manifestly dynamic. So too are the prevailing economic conditions that constrict the supply of and augment

[4] George Bush, President's Remarks at the National Federation of Independent Businesses, June 17, 2004.

[5] Shlomo Angel and Patrick Lamson-Hall make a persuasive case for a "nimble housing supply" in their thorough and novel research into the history of Manhattan's density for their working paper, "The Rise and Fall of Manhattan's Densities, 1800-2010" (New York: Marron Institute of Urban Management, 2014). Their argument — that "a more nimble housing supply not bound by restrictive regulations that limit its response to real housing demand can go a long way towards making housing in the New York metropolitan area, in New York City, and even in Manhattan, more affordable" — echoes that of advocates who appear throughout this chapter.

the demand for safe and affordable housing. Responsible and future-forward city-making requires a deep capacity for adaptation in the physical forms, definitions, policies, and advocacy efforts related to housing.

The stories of citymaking I share in this chapter offer some lessons in introducing this type of adaptive capacity, this type of nimbleness,[5] into how we understand, advocate for, design, and deliver urban housing. For advocates, it can mean adjusting skill sets and services provided to respond to new priorities while maintaining values and core missions; and it can mean critiquing and actively reformulating how we define what it means to be a homeowner or a tenant, what it means for housing to be "multi-family," or what happens when we decouple owner-ship of land from the tenure of the buildings on top of it. For designers and real estate developers, it can mean reconfiguring existing building stock to address shifts in what we expect from our homes and with whom we want to share them, to question traditional thinking about the basic components of a discrete housing unit. And for analysts, policymakers, and residents themselves, it can mean recon-ceptualizing such basic economic concepts as land, property, and capital. For all of the above, it means seeing and understanding existing housing with new eyes.

Many Queens neighborhoods have large proportions of single family homes that are, in fact, housing multiple families in illegal subdivisions. Pictured in a residential street in Elmhurst Queens. Facing page shows an informal Salvadoran restaurant in Elmhurst.

BRINGING BASEMENTS TO CODE

Urban population density is woefully misunderstood. Density is a measure of how many people inhabit a particular area, not necessarily a description of the size or shape of the buildings that accommodate those inhabitants. Yet, popular discourse consistently conflates high density with high-rise buildings. Certainly, one way to measure and to regulate urban density is via the ratio of a building's footprint to the area of all of its floors, known as floor area ratio or FAR, and limiting allowable FAR is often the primary mechanism that city planning departments use to influence where future development will or will not take place. That said, one twenty-story building with twenty luxury floor-through flats on a one-acre lot will not add more inhabitants to a neighborhood than seventeen three-story brownstones with three or four apartments in each taking up the same amount of land. In *A Country of Cities,* Vishaan Chakrabarti uses the standard measure of thirty housing units per acre, just a little higher than the minimum estimates for making public transit economically viable, as his definition of the kind of urban density he would like to promulgate. In practice, his standard looks more or less like brownstone Brooklyn (or Boston's South End, or Menlo Park, California, or most of St. Paul, Minnesota). Contrary to popular belief, the majority of buildings in New York City are single and two-family households, in neighborhoods that resemble the vast suburban stretches of much of the rest of the country. Yet for many of these technically low-density neighborhoods, official statistics and legal limits are also misleading. Particularly in neighborhoods with high proportions of lower-income immigrants from Asia, Africa, the Caribbean, and Latin America, single- and two-family homes are routinely being illegally subdivided to house more people than they were designed to accommodate.

According to Seema Agnani, the former executive director of Chhaya Community Development Corporation, "nearly 40% of the new housing [units] created from 1990 to 2005 in New York City were illegal apartments," many of which are in basements or cellars.[6] Fewer and fewer people can afford to live within the existing legal housing standard, so more and more live outside of it. In addition to increased vulnerability to fire and safety hazards, tenants in illegal units have few enforceable rights. The recent immigrants who comprise a large percentage of tenants in illegal units, some of whom are undocumented, are often unwilling to seek official help. Some of them end up seeking help from community-based organizations like Chhaya, a community development corporation in Jackson Heights that works to address the unique housing needs of New York's South Asian community, immigrants from India, Bangladesh, Pakistan, Nepal, Bhutan, Sri Lanka, and Caribbean nations such as Guyana and Trinidad. As one of Chhaya's founders and its head for seven years, Agnani has seen firsthand the challenges that illegal dwelling units, especially basement apartments, pose to immigrant tenants. And she's also seen the opportunity that legalizing some of these units presents.

I went to see her as the snows were melting in late February of 2010. When I got off the subway in Jackson Heights on my way to her office, I felt a familiar rush of cultural recognition. I grew up in a Pakistani-American household in an over-whelmingly white suburb of Boston, so Jackson Heights became a site of semiannual pilgrimage for my family to procure Indian tea and spices impossible to find in early '90s New England. Jackson Heights was by then already a recognizable South Asian enclave. More than twenty-five years had passed since the 1965 Immigration Act abolished the National Origins Formula that had actively excluded immigrants from Asia in order to prevent immigration from changing the ethnic and racial distribution of the population. The first post-1965 wave of immigration primarily included professionals such as engineers and doctors. In the decades since, the Family Reunification Clause of US immigration policy as well as the Immigration Act of 1990 further diversified the pool of immigrants, both in terms of occupation and country of origin, spurring an influx of small business owners and, more recently, taxi drivers, garment factory workers, and other laborers. The South Asian enclave in Jackson Heights did not come about because of the kind of race-based restrictions that concentrated East Asian communities in Chinatowns earlier in the century, but multiple generations of foreign influence are just as apparent in its commercial streets: foreign language books and magazines, shops offering wire services to remit money to family in the home country, the specificity of the regional cuisines available in restaurants. The congressional district comprised of Jackson Heights and the adjacent community of Elmhurst has one of the highest proportions of foreign-born residents anywhere in the US.

Once you wander into the more residential stretches of the neighborhood, however, the presence of so many people with roots in so many places around the world becomes less visible. Many of the residential buildings in central Jackson Heights are stately brick courtyard apartments. Surrounding this historic district are stretches of single and two-family homes. Picture the opening credits of the iconic 1970s TV show *All in the Family,* where aerial footage moves east from the skyscrapers of Manhattan across the East River to the pitched roofs of Astoria, Queens while reactionary conservative Archie Bunker and his wife Edith reminisce in song, hilariously off-key, about a bygone past before the welfare state and the dissolution of clear gender roles.[7] Bunker was a "lovable bigot" whose antipathy to immigrants (along with black and Latino Americans and those he perceived to be "commies," "hippies," or "women's libbers") created much of the show's humor: he was out of step with the major political, economic, and demographic shifts underway. Much of today's Queens would be even less recognizable to Bunker, not least because of its diversity. Since 1965, the foreign-born population of New York City has doubled, from 1.5 million to over 3 million. Since 1990, the percentage of the city's population born abroad has grown from 28 percent to 37 percent.[8] Queens alone is home to more than 1 million immigrants.

These figures come from *The Newest New Yorkers,* a statistical report by the Population Division of the Department of City Planning. In 2013, this extraordinary group of researchers with deep, nuanced understanding of the hidden dynamics of demographic change in New York published the fifth in a series of reports that analyze immigration statistics. It is a rich resource, tracking changes in the neighborhoods to which immigrants move, their countries of origin, average age and household size, incomes, proficiency in English and educational attainment. Of course, socioeconomic indicators are not necessarily correlated with nativity, but one correlation that does appear to be statistically significant has to do with household size and housing unit size. According to the report, immigrant households are three times more likely than nonimmigrant households to be "overcrowded" (defined by federal standards as housing units accommodating more than one person per room). "Citywide, 9 percent of all households were overcrowded . . . The share of foreign-born households there were overcrowded (14 percent) was nearly three times that of native-born households (5 percent). This is, at least in part, a function of larger households among the foreign-born, as well as a reflection of the housing available to newcomers."[9]

Immigrant families are statistically more likely to have more children, and non-family households also play a part in overcrowding (particularly among men

6 Seema Agnani, "Bringing Basements to Code" in U*rban Omnibus*, March 10, 2010.

7 "Boy, the way Glenn Miller played! / Songs that made the Hit Parade. / Guys like us, we had it made. / Those were the days! / And you knew where you were then. / Girls were girls and men were men. / Mister, we could use a man like Herbert Hoover again. / Didn't need no welfare state. / Everybody pulled his weight. / Gee, our old LaSalle ran great. / Those were the days!"

8 *The Newest New Yorkers: Characteristics of the City's Foreign-born Population,* 2013 edition, New York City Department of City Planning, retrieved from https://www1.nyc.gov/html/dcp/pdf/census/nny2013/nny_2013.pdf.

9 *The Newest New Yorkers* Report 2013.

from Latin America; for example, there are 173 Mexican-born adult men in New York for every 100 Mexican-born adult women, and groups of countrymen tend to live together in overpacked apartments to save money). Extended families and multigenerational households are also more common among immigrant groups. And for these households, according to Seema Agnani, "the rental market has nothing for them."[10] Meanwhile, overall, individuals are staying single longer and having fewer children, meaning the same number of apartments from 1950 today houses fewer people on average, putting further pressure on the housing supply. Concurrent increases in immigration and the illegal subdivision of lower-density housing is an example of correlation not of causation. Recent immigrants on the lower end of the income scale are not more likely to live in outer-borough cellars and attics simply because they have roots in other countries and cultures. Nonetheless, for many of these recent immigrants and other low-income New Yorkers priced out of the legal housing market, illegal subdivisions provide an undeniable source of affordable housing. Furthermore, the majority of illegally subdivided units are found in the outer boroughs, according to Agnani, "in immigrant communities that have established hubs. Their temples are here; their mosques are here; their community is here. People are willing to live in overcrowded conditions in order to be in these communities."

Many of these units are unfit for habitation or otherwise unsafe. But not all of them. In some cases, legalizing a unit would simply require the filing of architectural plans with the Department of Buildings. In others, a major impediment to legalization is not the Building Code but the zoning map — the unit might meet legal requirements for safe habitation but the property cannot legally accommodate multiple families. Still others are very close to meeting legal requirements but fall short in a minor way.

For these reasons, when I interviewed Agnani, Chhaya Community Development Corporation was in the midst of an advocacy campaign to create an Accessory Dwelling Unit (ADU) code for New York City, essentially creating a pathway for basement, garage, or attic apartments to become safe and legal dwellings. Bringing illegal units into the scope of regulation could have a number of positive impacts: tenants' living conditions would improve; forced displacement would decrease; rental income might lessen the burden on overleveraged homeowners at risk of mortgage default; landlords would be more likely to report rental income on their tax returns, increasing City revenues and potentially lessening the burden on social services in neighborhoods with large populations of undocumented residents.

Agnani explained to me that in 2000, as she and others were establishing Chhaya, she worked on a needs assessment of the South Asian immigrant community and learned that 50 percent of survey respondents didn't have a lease. In the years since then, both owners and renters have sought counsel from Chhaya about concerns related to this large amount of housing without any legal documentation: tenants worried about unsafe conditions and owners complained about unpaid rents. Therefore, for Chhaya, "education, advocacy, and organizing around the issues of illegal dwelling units have become a priority area."

Despite the benefits of bringing illegal subdivisions up to code, the issue has not found favor with elected officials, many of whom "see it as an issue of neighborhood preservation, with a lot of the more established residents feeling that new immigrants are coming in and ruining their communities." Undeniably, rapid population increases in low-density communities put a burden on infrastructure, congesting buses and classrooms. Community complaints are not exclusively about overstretched public resources, however. They also attest to a whiff of an Archie Bunker-style resistance to the changing complexion of their new neighbors.[11]

Even as politicians and policymakers work hard to appease constituents who don't want added density in housing, City officials have been slow to recognize the costs of inaction. "Judges in the court system are frustrated with the number of complaints, but there is nothing they can do to tackle the issue. The Department of Buildings is tired of having to issue these fines, despite the revenue. It's also a huge drain on public resources, resulting in overcrowded schools and overstretched social service provision. But if these units and the population that resides in them could be planned for, it could really be a resource for the city."

The first step to exposing the multiple benefits of an Accessory Dwelling Unit code is investigating the facts on the ground. In partnership with the Citizens Housing and Planning Council, Chhaya surveyed two Queens census tracts to document illegal subdivisions and to assess the feasibility of legalization. Out of 446 homes registered as single-family, the survey found that 80 percent showed "signs of basement use" and estimated that about 35 percent of these basements could be adapted into safe, habitable, and legal secondary housing units.

One of the reasons that an ADU code would be an effective mechanism to remove some of the impediments to legalizing illegal basement apartments is that such a legal provision would not have to change neighborhood zoning. The fact that most of the neighborhoods where this issue is prevalent are zoned for single-family homes makes "converting a property into a two-family home much more complicated. An ADU code is a way of getting around all of that — it remains a single-family home with an accessory unit."

Municipalities around the country have embraced this strategy. Agnani cites examples in Washington State, Santa Cruz, Yonkers, and other parts of Westchester County. "But in New York City, the current building code is so strict that it makes

[10] Seema Agnani, author interview, available in the video "Making Room" on *Urban Omnibus,* October 5, 2011.

[11] Benjamin Ryan, "What 311 Calls Can Tell Us About Gentrification" a "Science of Us" blogpost on the Web site of *New York* magazine, retrieved from http://nymag.com/scienceofus/2015/08/what-311-calls-can-tell-us-about-gentrification.html.

[12] Eric Klinenberg, *Going Solo: The Extraordinary Rise and Surprising Appeal of Living Alone* (New York: Penguin Books, 2013).

legalization very difficult. For example, there is a legal difference between a cellar and a basement. A cellar is more the 50 percent below ground; a basement is more than 50 percent above. We've seen apartments that are more that 50 percent above ground at the front of the unit and less in the back. Our argument is that these are decisions that should be based on health and safety, not necessarily on inches. If there is enough air and light and if it is safe, then the codes should be more flexible."

Besides elected officials, another group that needs to get on board is architects. Agnani elaborates:

> We need more architects involved in this work. There's a real need for spatial, design, and construction expertise, as well as help getting into the specifics of building codes. I think that is the actual missing piece for us right now. We have advocates, we have legal experts but we don't have enough of the design community involved in the process . . . to help individual homeowners through the process of legalization.
>
> The design community could help us think through energy conservation approaches and ways to improve energy efficiency as well . . . We could think of an ADU plan as an opportunity to green these neighborhoods.

Agnani's call to architects speaks to a need that goes beyond accessory units. The specific expertise of designers and spatial thinkers must be applied to the broader challenge of reconfiguring existing building stock to meet changing demographic needs. It's about much more than basement apartments.

MAKING ROOM: NEW HOUSING MODELS FOR A CHANGING CITY

As the work of Chayya makes vivid, our urban housing stock, as it is currently configured, is ill-suited to meet the needs of a changing America. Just as many immigrant and low-income New Yorkers are not able to find dwellings to accommodate their families, another type of apartment-seeker — singles who want to live alone — finds that the market does not serve her needs either. Sociologist Eric Klinenberg's book *Going Solo* characterizes the rise of staying single longer into adulthood and living alone — 31 million Americans are single adults — as "the most significant demographic shift since the baby boom."[12] Older adults also constitute a growing proportion of the population that wants to live alone. Single-person households live in thirty-three percent of New York City units. Yet the vast majority of those housing units were designed with nuclear families in mind. A New York City occupancy law from 1954 reifies this bias, making it illegal for more than three unrelated adults to share a living unit in New York City. Of course, and unfairly, four recent college grads sharing an apartment as roommates in a Manhattan elevator building are less likely to arouse enforcement than four Ecuadorean or Bangladeshi

---

[12] Eric Klinenberg, *Going Solo: The Extraordinary Rise and Surprising Appeal of Living Alone* (New York: Penguin Books, 2013).

laborers hot-bunking in a basement in suburban Queens. We're living longer too, and for seniors of means, New York City is a great place to retire, with its comprehensive public transit and wealth of cultural offerings. But the living arrangement underlying the comedy of a TV series like Golden Girls (1985–1992), four retired women sharing a home in Miami, would technically be illegal in New York. Options for both singles and shared households are limited.

The restrictions on unrelated adults' cohabitating and the absence of an Accessory Dwelling Unit clause are just two of the many ways in which New York City's housing regulations no longer fit our demographic reality. No one can explain the mismatch between outdated housing regulations and contemporary populations better than Jerilyn Perine, executive director of the Citizens Housing and Planning Council (CHPC), a research and advocacy nonprofit, and a former commissioner of the City's Department of Housing Preservation and Development (HPD). A major research and advocacy project she initiated along with her long-time collaborator Sarah Watson, entitled "Making Room," explores the complexity of the regulatory landscape and how it does not serve the needs of three rapidly growing household types in particular: single adults who want to live alone, joint and multigenerational families who want to live together, and groups of unrelated single adults who want to live alongside each other, sharing resources and maintaining privacy where possible. In 2011, The Architectural League partnered with CHPC to develop a design study that would suggest new prototypes of housing design unhindered by outdated regulatory roadblocks. Critical reflection on this project reveals some of the enduring tensions and creative possibilities that emerge from the strategic alliance of architectural innovation and housing policy reform.

Trained as a planner, Jerilyn Perine began working in city government at the start of the Koch mayoral administration's ten-year plan for housing in 1985. She was housing commissioner under both mayors Giuliani and Bloomberg, directing efforts to preserve or develop affordable housing during a time of rising prices and a diminishing supply of City-owned properties. She dispenses her opinions in straightforward bursts of candor, alternately acerbic or exasperated at the inertia of the policy discussion surrounding housing. Let me give you an example. I remember once visiting Perine at CHPC's offices at 42 Broadway, a 1903 building with a handsome ornamental façade and, at twenty stories, one of the tallest skyscrapers in New York when it was built. Late-twentieth-century attempts at modernization replaced the original portico with ugly slabs of shiny black granite, and inside, the building's carpeted corridors, overhead fluorescent lights in hung ceilings, and small offices make it less in demand than its sleeker, taller, newer, open-plan neighbors in the Financial District. Perine met me at the door and gestured down the drab hallway, "You think we would all *die* if that was an occupied apartment instead of an empty office?"

Current zoning does not allow that. In 1998, the Department of City Planning approved a special district for parts of Lower Manhattan that allowed certain office buildings to be converted to residential use, but residential and commercial uses still cannot be mixed on the same floor. In many cases, you can't mix uses in the same building. The spatial segregation of different building uses is the entire premise of what planners refer to as Euclidean Zoning. I remember being surprised and nerdily amused to learn in graduate school that the practice did not derive its name, as I'd assumed, from the mathematician of Ancient Greece who formalized geometry into an axiomatic system. It's named after the Cleveland suburb of Euclid, Ohio. In 1926, the town enacted an ordinance to limit the encroachment of Cleveland's growing industrial sector. A real estate company that owned sixty-eight acres in Euclid sued the town, citing an unconstitutional "taking" that would decrease the financial value of its real estate holdings. The case went all the way to the Supreme Court, which ruled in the municipality's favor that the zoning ordinance did not exceed its police powers.

Zoning is the primary land-use tool available to departments of city planning. It can be powerful, directing urban development in ways that both respond to market forces and create them. Just as determining where industrial uses can agglomerate or the bulk and height of residential buildings, zoning can also create incentives for the private sector to provide for community needs such as affordable housing. "Inclusionary" zoning allows developers to build more housing units than regulations would otherwise allow if a certain number of them are made "affordable" to households with incomes below the median for the area. (Needless to say, these designations have fueled a cottage industry in legal interpretation and manipulation). The term *inclusionary* is a direct rebuke to *exclusionary* zoning, which predates Euclidean zoning as a mechanism to keep particular populations away — an especially popular tactic throughout the twentieth century to prevent poor people of color from moving into affluent, white suburbs. In other words, while zoning is a municipal mechanism to guide the private sector towards equitable development (or at least development that conforms to a community's vision for its future growth), it is just as often used as legal means to enforce a status quo.

The kind of zoning rules that impede the owner of a single-family home from converting its basement into a rental apartment are not explicitly about maintaining socioeconomic homogeneity. They are often about maintaining the character of a residential neighborhood, avoiding excessive burden on infrastructure and public services, even ensuring available street parking. Upzonings raise the number of allowable units in a given area; downzonings do the opposite. The Bloomberg administration presided over a comparatively large number of 120 rezonings over its twelve years in office. Visible and prominent changes to the skyline, notably the new towers lining the Williamsburg waterfront in Brooklyn, suggest that City Hall helped to increase the supply of housing overall in an era of population growth in New York. Yet the city saw an almost equal number of downzonings. Unfortunately, the Department of City Planning doesn't track how much potential developable space is gained or lost in the rezoning process. So researchers are on their own to assess the net effect on the supply and demand of housing. As one small but indicative sample, NYU's Furman Center for Real Estate and Urban Policy found that "of the 188,000 lots that had been rezoned between 2003 and 2007, 14% had been upzoned, 23% downzoned, and 63% had not had their development capacity changed by more than 10% — only the type of building allowed on the lot changed. All those ups and downs didn't change the city's 'on paper' capacity for residential housing all that much — the net effect, the Furman Center found, was to increase capacity by just 1.7%."[13] The upzonings tended to take place in areas with strong transit connections at the edges of neighborhoods, places with larger proportions of immigrants and people of color, and greater numbers of renter-occupied units. The downzonings and "contextual" rezonings (designed to maintain existing character) tended to take place within the cores of traditional neighborhoods, places with higher property values and, correlatively, higher proportions of white people and owner-occupied units. Residents of these statistically wealthier neighborhoods enjoy greater amounts of political clout to influence the policies directing where growth and added density will go. Broadly speaking, incumbents — homeowners, real estate investors, developers with capital — benefit disproportionately from maintaining the status quo, precisely because the inflated costs of producing new housing raise the value of existing housing.

The zoning code is not the only set of regulations that keep the supply of housing units within existing building stock static. Building code regulations devised to ensure health and safety sometimes have an unintended consequence: they impede innovation in reconfiguring available housing to conform to the emerging needs and shifting demographics of contemporary New Yorkers.

The importance of the health and safety measures at root of building regulations cannot be underestimated. Can you escape in a fire? Is there adequate ventilation? Yet, as Perine and the sustained research of her organization remind us, we must account for the historical context in which such measures arose. The regulations that maintain minimum standards and minimum sizes of habitable dwelling — such as the requirement for every bedroom to have a window, every apartment to have a bathroom and kitchen for the exclusive use of the tenant, or for no apartment built after 1955 to be smaller than 400 square feet[14] — sprung up in response to the squalid conditions of late eighteenth- and early nineteenth-century tenements. Re-illuminating this context is an important first step to identifying how we might introduce a capacity to adapt into a deeply distorted and inflated market.

The regulatory framework of housing emerged from a culture of social reform in the Progressive Era. According to Perine, "At the turn of the early twentieth century, we transformed the ways that housing policies were used to really eradicate

---

[13] Sarah Laskow, "The quiet, massive rezoning of New York" in *Politico,* February 24, 2014, retrieved from http://www.capitalnewyork.com/article/city-hall/2014/02/8540743/ quiet-massive-rezoning-new-york?page=all.

[14] A close look at the code reveals that there have been legal ways to produce apartments smaller than 400 square feet in certain cases, but that doing so was rare. Many studio apartments fall under a different category since many of them are zoned as workspaces or "live/work" spaces, which has been studied extensively by, among others, Sharon Zukin, *Loft Living: Culture and Capital in Urban Change* (New Brunswick, N.J.: Rutgers University Press, 1989).

Jacob Riis pioneered the use of photojournalism as a tool in the pursuit of social reform. His influential book *How the Other Half Lives* included photographs, such as this one, that chronicled the overcrowded and unsanitary conditions of tenements in the Lower East Side of Manhattan.

terrible overcrowding; the conditions were incredibly unsanitary and bad for people's health."[15] New York City's population nearly doubled between 1890 and 1920, from 2.5 million inhabitants to almost five. The rapidly expanding economy continued to draw striving immigrants to the city. Another 1890 milestone in the history of housing reform was the publication of Jacob Riis' influential book, *How the Other Half Lives: Studies among the Tenements of New York,* which exposed, through extensive reporting and original photography, the extreme living and working conditions of the Lower East Side of Manhattan. Riis was a devout Christian immigrant from Denmark who had himself lived in these tenements when he first arrived twenty years prior. He initially worked as a carpenter and eventually found his calling as a police reporter, documenting the city's growing poverty. His book, which grew out of a series of slide lectures he would deliver at churches and clubs throughout Manhattan, was a success, inspiring an acceleration of charity, activism, and legislation. Riis' prose mixes hard statistics, vivid reportage, poignant photography, specific recommendations about housing quality, and lachrymose indignation at the current state of affairs. (He ends the book with some prescriptions about housing policy, yet writes despairingly in its introduction, "We know now that there is no way out; that the 'system' that was the evil offspring of public neglect and private greed has come to stay, a storm-centre forever of our civilization.")[16] He went on to publish a series of popular books on related topics and campaigned tirelessly for reform. Riis is more remembered today for the accompanying photography,[17] still-iconic images of families of six or ten living in a single room, children toiling in sweat shops or playing in fetid, trash-strewn alleyways. *How the Other Half Lives* launched the tradition of "muckraking" journalism — what we would now call "investigative reporting" — that became a powerful advocacy tool in support of Progressive Era reforms.[18]

Tenements are buildings specifically built to house multiple poor families. The original legal definition refers to any building that houses "three families or more living independently of each other and doing their cooking upon the premises."[19] These were the first multi-family buildings in American cities, appearing on the urban landscape in the 1830s and '40s, a full half century before the middle and upper classes began living in apartments. In the beginning, tenements were four- to six-story buildings with as many as four dwelling units per floor erected on a typical Manhattan gridiron lot of 25×100 feet, lots that were originally intended for single-family homes.[20] Policymakers attempted to regulate their construction to ensure some basic sanitation in 1867 and 1879, but these laws basically resulted in larger buildings covering even more of the lot area. These buildings warehoused larger numbers of poor families in equally unsanitary units that shared kitchens and toilets (a requirement for one water closet per twenty inhabitants was difficult to enforce and largely ignored). They continued to lack light and air, despite required "ventilation shafts" that became inaccessible trash shoots and, tragically, flues that fed the inevitable fires.

Ten years after Riis' book, the New York state legislature appointed its fourth Tenement House Commission. For the most part, according to Richard Plunz in his definitive *A History of Housing In New York,* the increasingly professionalized field of architecture had not paid much attention to the problems of tenement design in the previous decades. In a decisive shift, the commission published an

---

15 Jerilyn Perine, author interview, available in the video "Making Room" on *Urban Omnibus,* October 5, 2011.

16 Jacob Riis, *How the Other Half Lives: Studies among the Tenements of New York,* (New York: Charles Scribner's Sons, 1914) (originally published 1890), p. 2.

17 In photography, too, Riis was an innovator, pioneering the use of flash photography. An editor at *Harpers Magazine* wanted to use his photographs nut hired another writer, prompting an offended Riis to begin his public lectures.

18 These reforms were by no means limited to housing. Exposing political corruption, advancing education and health, expanding suffrage, and promoting temperance were all goals of the various movements that characterized the period. Across the spectrum of Progressive Era projects, improving the lot of the poor was a common theme. The sense of urgency was coupled with a sense of newfound possibility: the application of scientific and engineering methods to industry, management, and eventually governance would serve to weaken the power of clientelist political machines, increase workplace efficiency, and substantially improve the living conditions of workers' lives.

19 The full text of Clause 11 of Chapter 713 of the New York State Multiple Dwelling Law can be found archived at http://www.tenant.net/Other_Laws/MDL/mdl01.html.

20 In 1894, the architect and reformer Ernest Flagg wrote, "The greatest evil which ever befell New York City was the division of the blocks into lots of 25×100 feet. So true is this, that no other disaster can for a moment be compared with it. Fires, pestilence, and financial troubles are as nothing in comparison; for from this division has arisen the New York system of tenement-houses, the worst curse which ever afflicted any great community."

extensive survey of the evolution and shortcomings of previous attempts to legislate the tenement, also providing complementary "studies by architects on the design ramifications of alternative tenement controls." Every architect consulted agreed that the only way to improve the quality of housing was to build on multiple contiguous lots.

The New York State Tenement House Act of 1901, referred to as the "New Law," remains to this day as "the basis for the regulation of low-rise housing design in New York City." It drastically improved living conditions in the tenements by expanding futile ventilation shafts into interior courtyard proportions, requiring running water and exterior windows in every apartment. The requirements and their strict enforcement made building tenements on single lots financially unfeasible, such that "the small developer who built on a lot-by-lot basis could no longer control housing production." Thus, "Large capital began to monopolize the tenement market."[21] And whereas the requirements of the Old Law could be interpreted by any builder on his own, "The spatial complexities of the New Law, together with its mandate for larger-scale projects, assured architects a share of this market." As has often been the case in New York City, regulatory change comes most easily when it aligns with the interests of large capital.

Future reforms that built on this landmark legislation — especially the Multiple Dwelling Law of 1929 that established minimum room sizes or the subsequent prohibition of three or more unrelated adults cohabitating[22] — continued to maintain health and safety as the top priorities. Additionally, according to Perine, "there was also this real sense that good housing would transform people into good people, into good Americans." While much of the reformers' zeal had been inspired by the specific conditions of the tenement, many additional housing types also came under fire. Sitting in her office's impressive library, flanked by a century of leather-bound housing codes and zoning documents, Perine told me how New York used to have "a whole range of housing types, from lodging houses and SROs to boarding houses and even buildings that had certificates of occupancy as bachelor apartments. And all these different kinds of flexible units began to get swept away in this desire to transform both the housing stock — and the people who lived in it — to be good Americans, to form a nuclear family and to enter this new middle class life."[23]

SROs refer to single room occupancy buildings, in which each unit was a single room, and multiple units shared bathrooms and kitchens. SROs provided a source of affordable housing of last resort, particularly for single men unable to afford or maintain a traditional apartment, some of whom undoubtedly struggled with substance abuse or mental illness.[24] As a result, the housing type came to be associated with the image of the public drunkard or vagrant. The thinking went something like this: if we got rid of the kinds of housing that accommodate single men and the insalubrious and unsavory behavior that single men get up to when they are allowed to congregate, then those behaviors would magically disappear. What happened instead? Extreme increases in homelessness correlate directly to decreases in the supply of SRO units.[25] Less visibly, the kind of choice, flexibility, and affordability that once existed in the marketplace has gone underground. Perine finds "the expression of that underground black market in everything from Craigslist ads for apartment shares to the problems of fires in buildings with illegal occupancy; people are dying and our firemen are putting themselves at risk going into buildings where they don't know what kind of partition walls they're going to be facing."

Again, housing policy over the past century has, without question, drastically transformed bad housing into good housing and demonstrated a clear government commitment to enforcing a high baseline of health and safety in our city's homes. In the process, however, the regulatory framework has created an inflexible standard for what a New York apartment is allowed to be. As we have seen, the city's demographics have changed, with more single-person households, an elder boom, more extended families, and new cooperative modes of sharing living space among non-relatives. But New York's housing stock hasn't kept pace with these changes. According to Perine, "Essentially we're still asking the development community to produce the same exact housing type that we asked them to produce after WWII, which is on average a two-bedroom apartment . . . suitable for the nuclear family, the mom the dad and two kids." Technology has also advanced considerably. The decades since the Tenement House Act and the Multiple Dwelling Law have seen the proliferation of forms of electric light that emit more light than heat, air conditioning, fire extinguishers, advances in glazing and other building technologies whose applications to housing are not considered by old codes intended to eliminate squalor. Today's unsafe and unsanitary living conditions come about because of the lack of affordable alternatives rather than a lack of regulations.

Demographics and technology aren't all that has changed. These days, "We have a different view of consuming environmental resources. The greenest thing any person can do is to live in a small space, or live in a shared space, and use mass transit to get to work. That really should be where New York City is setting the bar

---

[21] Richard Plunz, *A History of Housing in New York City: Dwelling Type and Social Change in the American Metropolis* (New York: Columbia University Press, 1990) p. 46–49.

[22] According to Perine and Watson, "During the Great Depression, New York City's vacancy rate in multiple dwellings rose to an astounding 14.5 percent in 1933 at the same time that the City's unemployed and poor pitched tents in Central Park. As illegal lodgers and boarders in certain multiple dwellings increased, the policy solution was to categorize Single Room Occupancy units (SROs) as Class A Multiple Dwellings, in turn bringing SROs and lodging houses with more than two boarders under the Multiple Dwelling Law. By 1954, the backlash against such occupancy resulted in Local Law 24, which effectively banned the new construction of private SRO units and the conversion of apartments into rooming houses." [Retrieved from http://chpcny.org/2011/02/making-room-why-should-we-care/].

[23] Jerilyn Perine, author interview, available in the video "Making Room" on *Urban Omnibus,* October 5, 2011.

[24] Since the 1970s, the policy of "deinstitutionalizing" the patients of psychiatric hospitals without a concomitant investment in community mental health services has led to greater numbers of homeless people suffering from mental illness.

[25] Brian J. Sullivan and Jonathan Burke, "Single-Room Occupancy in New York City: The Origins and Dimensions of a Crisis," in *CUNY Law Review,* vol. 17:901, May 2014.

very high and creating the most innovative housing models in the world. That's not happening right now."

In order to stimulate that innovation, Perine and her team at CHPC conceived of Making Room, a multi-year initiative to demonstrate how people are currently living, to conceptualize new housing types forged from within our existing building stock to accommodate contemporary living patterns, and to identify the regulatory impediments that would prevent developers from providing those new types. The project, Perine told me, started with a simple idea. In 2007, the Bloomberg administration launched PlaNYC, an ambitious series of 127 initiatives (updated to include more than 400 in 2013) intended to prepare the city for the expected one million more inhabitants by 2030. Perine and her colleagues at CHPC wondered, "how would one million more people actually fit into our housing stock? So that led us to ask ourselves, well, how are people fitting into the housing stock today?"

The project began with several years of research CHPC had undertaken to understand trends in New York City households, culminating in a symposium that featured architects from around the world at the vanguard of reimagining housing design, from reconceiving miniature homes as a mode of luxury in Tokyo to manipulating building code loopholes to create higher density shared housing in low-density neighborhoods in San Diego.[26] From there, CHPC initiated the Making Room Design Study, partnering with The Architectural League to commission four teams of architects[27] to work on solutions for what CHPC research had identified as the three most common challenges: "1. Small, efficient studios designed for single person households; 2. Legal shared housing options for unrelated adults; 3. Accessory units to make a single family home more flexible for extended families or additional renters."[28]

The design schemes generated by the four teams were remarkable for their ingenuity. Each team took on one or more of the three challenges and developed a startlingly original solution. For example, Stan Allen, an architect also well-known as an educator and theorist, worked with Rafi Segal to lead a team of designers that wrung housing from an unlikely yet woefully under-utilized resource: "the millions of square feet of commercial office space constructed in the 1960s and 1970s that are rapidly becoming obsolete today." Their design treats the typical Midtown Manhattan office tower "as a platform for . . . a fine-grained mixture of domestic, commercial, and public programs . . . At the upper levels of the building, the higher floor-to-floor dimensions of the existing structure allow the insertion of three residential floors within two office floors, yielding a flexible matrix of living units, from duplexes for families to micro-units for singles. The shifted section creates a new urban typology that allows both proximity and separation of activities: living and office spaces sometimes share single floors yet can function independently."

Another team was led by Jonathan Kirschenfeld. This team benefited from Kirschenfeld's extensive experience designing supportive housing in New York, a category of housing that includes support services for the mentally ill, formerly homeless, recovering addicts, and other special needs groups facing diverse challenges. In supportive housing's specific zoning rules, "certain minimum dimensions, such as those governing courtyards, are less restrictive than in conventional residential construction, allowing for the development of difficult infill sites; there is no minimum unit size; and there are no requirements for providing parking." This team prepared three schemes along the Grand Concourse in the Bronx that extended the logic and regulations of supportive housing to general population housing. The first scheme reimagines the SRO as adjoining live-work 150 square foot units. Every two units would share a bathroom accessed from a semiprivate work area screened off from the sleeping area and opening into a day-lit and naturally ventilated, multi-use corridor that includes communal eating, working, and gathering space and a kitchen that serves a set of six units. The second scheme combines densely packed, self-sufficient units of 275 square feet (each with its own kitchen) for singles or couples with an array of shared spaces. The third scheme is "a large, flexible apartment building that can be easily adapted to the changing needs of a household of friends or multiple generations of a family. Each apartment features connectable rooms of similar sizes, which are suitable for living, sleeping, or working. Spaces also can easily be separated to create an independent office, rental apartment, or accessory dwelling unit (for a nanny or in-law). Apartments range from eight to twelve rooms, or a total of 1,700 to 2,300 square feet."

The New York Times architecture critic Michael Kimmelman praised the schemes presented at the Making Room symposium. He called out a few of his favorites, including Kirschenfeld's ideas for the Grand Concourse, and proposals by a team led by Deborah Gans that "retrofitted Tudor Revival cottages in immigrant-rich areas like Astoria, Queens, so they could house an evolving assortment of singles and families who might want to live together. Her plan, with buildings cleverly massed and fitted into the existing fabric of the neighborhood, conceived of up to seven apartment "pods" ("barnacles" became another operative metaphor) clinging to a 4,000-square-foot house." Kimmelman also liked a proposal by a team led by Peter Gluck and Terri Chiao that "envisioned a five-story walkup on a town-house-size New York lot. The building would accommodate twenty micro-lofts, as the team termed them, some 150 square feet each. With mini-kitchens, fourteen-foot ceilings, and public spaces for residents to socialize and work together on each floor, the plan trades basics like an elevator for private space and lower building costs."[29]

---

[26] "One Size Fits Some" on *Urban Omnibus*, September 30, 2009.

[27] "Micro-lofts" was designed by Peter Gluck, Terri Chiao, Deborah Grossberg Katz, Joseph Vidich, and Leigha Dennis. "Urban Cabins" was designed by Stan Allen Architect, Rafi Segal Architecture Urbanism, Chris Oliver, Jessie Turnbull; with research by Alix Beranger, Whitney Brooks; models by Jesus Yepez Mendoza Project. Project "Team R8" included Jonathan Kirschenfeld, Karen Kubey, Susanne Schindler, Erin Shnier, Nancy Owens, Margaret Tobin. "Hidden Housing" design team included Deborah Gans, Isobel Herbold, Kate Moxham, and Paula Crespo.

[28] Citizens Housing and Planning Council documents the project's goals and parameters on the web site "Making Room," retrieved from http://makingroomnyc.com/the-project/.

[29] Michael Kimmelman, "Imagining Housing for Today" *The New York Times*, November 16, 2011.

The growing demographic that would most benefit from this type of housing is single-person households. And, indeed, when Kimmelman summed up the entire premise of the Making Room project, the unmet needs of this group seemed to carry more weight than the other two challenges the project was also intended to address, those that promoted new forms of shared housing and those that provided accessory dwelling units for extended families or additional renters:

> In the past New York has adapted to changing household patterns. For example, grand Upper West Side apartments from a century ago were chopped up to provide more units for smaller families that no longer employed live-in servants. The question now is can the city become nimble again? Boston has zoned for micro-units to accommodate the young population and others struggling with market rates, on whom civic competitiveness and social equity ultimately depend. Can New York also meet the social and economic needs of the twenty-first century?[30]

The Bloomberg administration was much more deeply concerned with the notion that young, single professionals were finding the costs of moving to New York City to start their careers prohibitive than it was by the prospect of fostering joint-family or co-living arrangements. And so it announced a pilot program, called adAPT NYC, to develop a building of 275 to 300 square-foot apartments on a City-owned property on 27th Street between First and Second Avenues. These "micro-apartments" are smaller than the current minimum legal size for a living unit in New York.

The Mayor, in announcing the initiative, explained that, "We want people to come here to start their careers here, to start out here, to start their families here. If they can't afford to live here, then that's a problem." Stated in this way, the Mayor was clearly aware that supply is not meeting demand for the kinds of people the City seeks to attract. The primary objective of adAPT NYC thus appears to be to increase affordable options for young professionals. But it's not just young professionals who can't afford to live in New York. Across the socioeconomic and demographic spectrum, the housing options available to New Yorkers are nowhere near as diverse as the households and real estate preferences of New Yorkers themselves.

Fulfilling part of CHPC's goals for the Making Room project, the adAPT NYC experiment prompted hope that, if successful, it might lead to the easing of some of the zoning regulations and housing codes and standards that constrict the amount (and inflate the cost) of New York City housing units. That hasn't happened yet. For obvious and non-obvious reasons, policymakers find it far easier to create a new, circumscribed zone where the outdated regulations don't apply than to roll back the regulations themselves.

In theory, the enforcement of government regulation maintains a measure of flexibility: agencies administer laws, interpreting and enforcing a law's intent with respect to facts on the ground that can shift more quickly than traditional legislative processes. In practice, regulations that increase costs create counterintuitive incentives to maintain the status quo, especially in the context of urban housing markets where the financial interests of mortgage holders (banks) diverge from

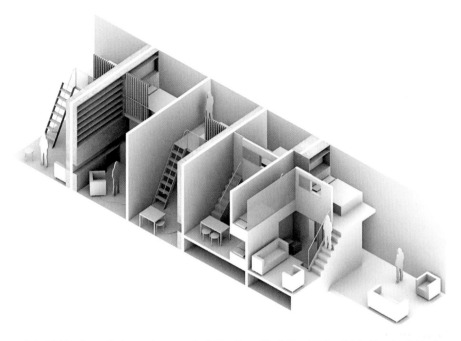

As part of the Making Room design study, a team including Peter Gluck, Terri Chiao, Leigha Dennis, Deborah Grossberg Katz, and Joseph Vidich developed the idea of "micro-lofts," which offer flexible and private spaces for inhabitants while doubling the density of the typical residential townhouse lot. The 232 square-foot "micro-loft" unit typology has a smaller footprint than a typical studio but is much taller, with a 15-foot floor-to-ceiling height and a large mezzanine.

those of residents (especially renters).[31] As we have seen, the regulations and codes that govern housing in New York were enacted to ensure a principle of public health in the first few decades of the twentieth century. For example, the preamble of the Multiple Dwelling Law of 1929 states that "the establishment and maintenance of proper housing standards requiring sufficient light, air, sanitation and protection from fire hazards are essential to the public welfare."[32] As Jerilyn Perine reminds us, there were other priorities at play: overcrowding was seen as "a menace" not only to "health," "safety," and "reasonable comfort," but also to the "morals . . . of the citizens of the state."

Today, I would argue the most urgent principles of public welfare that forward-thinking housing policy can meaningfully confront are sustainability and affordability, rather than public health. Don't get me wrong: ensuring public health is still a proper office and responsibility of government, but housing regulation is

---

[30] Ibid.

[31] The more expensive it is to create new housing supply, the greater the value of existing housing, thus property owners and banks stand to profit from maintaining the status quo.

[32] The full text of Clause 11 of Chapter 713 of the New York State Multiple Dwelling Law can be found archived at http://www.tenant.net/Other_Laws/MDL/mdl01.html.

no longer the primary or exclusive way to address it. A wide range of contemporary laws now govern health and environmental factors, including the Clean Air Act (1963), the Safe Drinking Water Act (1974), and many more. A range of technological advances, from energy-efficient lighting to air-conditioning to modern plumbing and glazing, have ameliorated the conditions that were once prima facie unsanitary such as windowless bedrooms or shared bathrooms and kitchens. In order to move us toward a more sustainable and affordable urban future, housing policy must be geared toward enabling responsible density in housing.

The new housing prototype proposals produced for Making Room would add density in ways that would yield more use out of our housing stock, utilizing a combination of new construction and adaptive reuse of existing buildings of various types (including office buildings). Of course, doing so in a way that wouldn't lead to overbuilding or overburdening existing systems would require long-range planning to guide these new types of development into neighborhoods with the appropriate carrying capacity in transit, schools, and other necessary facilities. With some sensible planning in place, they would move us in the direction of accommodating the needs of diverse household types, including new kinds of sharing, joint families, and singles. They would lower costs. Intelligent densification also has the potential to lower urban dwellers' carbon footprints.

We have to create the capacity for more adaptation in our housing stock through design, but we also have to make our regulatory framework nimble as well, including but not limited to zoning, that allows for urban housing markets to be more nimble and therefore more sustainable and affordable. One real estate analysis of the Bloomberg era rezonings uses a strikingly appropriate sartorial analogy: "The legacy 1961 zoning created an invisible city with a loose shape, like a dress bought a few sizes too big, that the physical city had plenty of room to grow into. The Bloomberg administration has left behind a building envelope that's more like a corset, pulled tight to the city's body, cinching around places that were already small and boosting its curves."[33]

At the scale of the building, New York City is home to virtually every housing typology found throughout the country, from skyscrapers to single-family homes. At the scale of the living unit, there is much less diversity. Our accretive regulatory framework has created a structural disinclination toward designing innovation, effectively homogenizing what's available to middle- and lower-income individuals and families to two- or three-bedroom apartments with proprietary kitchens, bathrooms, and windows of a certain size. New kinds of coalitions between policy and design will be necessary to jumpstart innovation, meet dynamic needs, and maintain a dense, sustainable, and affordable supply of housing.

At the same time, fetishizing innovation for its own sake has serious drawbacks. There is a limit to how much permanent shelter can ever adapt to changing social or economic circumstances. And we must not fall into the trap of maligning older forms of existing housing as tastes change and awareness evolves about how the physical environment enables or constrains different kinds of social experience. The capacity to adapt, broadly considered, also means remaining analytically agile enough not to let philosophical shifts blind us to the nuances of place that offer up surprising benefits in forms of housing otherwise considered outmoded, if not obsolete. One such shift is the gradual move away from publicly funded high-rise housing for the poor and towards a system of vouchers and subsidies to incent the private development of below-market housing.

Unfortunately, meeting the needs of the day — whether urban poverty is facing a crisis of abandonment, of foreclosure, or of unaffordability — has often led policymakers to devise short-term solutions. Specializations within urban planning education specify particular types of spatial scale but not particular ranges of time; you can concentrate on neighborhood planning or regional planning but you can't focus on, say, long-term planning. Citymakers should neither be slavishly devoted to precedent, tradition, and the built environment status quo, nor should we be in the business of predicting the future; we are still doing damage control for the faulty mid-twentieth-century belief that retrofitting our cities for unimpeded car traffic was a forward-looking, progressive strategy. Learning from recent history, even if the conditions seem totally distinct to those of the current day, offers an important corrective to our structural inclination towards short-term urban solutions. The ethic of adaptive capacity, especially with regard to the durable bricks and mortar that house us, will help citymakers foster generative and equitable urban development for conditions we can neither anticipate nor wholly control. In order to step confidently into this uncertain urban future, we must remember to look into the past. We must also train ourselves to look anew at existing built forms.

TYPECAST: UNCOVERING ASSETS HIDDEN IN PLAIN SIGHT

By the early 1970s, the apparent deficits and failures of government-supported housing for the poor were much discussed, and the architecture was often unfairly blamed for poor maintenance, crime, and massive economic shifts taking place at the time. Most notably, the demolition of the notoriously unsafe Pruitt-Igoe housing project — a complex of thirty-three buildings of eleven stories each arranged uniformly across fifty-seven acres of north St. Louis — signaled, to some, the dramatic demise of architectural modernism as a cause, if not a style.[34] The commentariat agreed that "with brute finality, the Pruitt-Igoe demolition seemed to mark both the bankruptcy of an important program of social transformation through modernist design, and, by implication, the return to traditional patterns of urbanism. Charles

---

[33] Laskow, "The quiet, massive rezoning of New York," *Politico*, 2014.

[34] According to Katherine Bristol, "Anyone remotely familiar with the recent history of American architecture automatically associates Pruitt-Igoe with the failure of High Modernism, and with the inadequacy of efforts to provide livable environments for the poor." In an influential 1991 paper, she debunks the notion that architecture was to blame for the projects' failure, citing a complex wave of factors including deindustrialization, pre-existing territorial conflicts between rival neighborhoods flanking Pruitt-Igoe and poor maintenance. Katharine G. Bristol, "The Pruitt-Igoe Myth" in *Journal Of Architectural Education,* vol. 44, Issue #3, 1991. See also the film *The Pruitt-Igoe Myth* by Chad Freidrichs, 2011.

Jencks used the precise hour of the first explosion to announce that 'modern architecture died in St. Louis, Missouri, on July 15, 1972, at 9:32 p.m.'"[35] Architecture was blamed, but the true causes of Pruitt-Igoe's failure were infinitely more complex.

That same year, architect and city planner Oscar Newman published *Defensible Space,* in which he made the case for his problematic yet influential theory that high-rise apartment buildings were more susceptible to high crime rates than low-rise buildings.[36] The theory goes something like this: the greater the shared spaces over which no individual resident feels proprietary control, the more likely those spaces are to fall into disrepair and to breed antisocial behavior. Newman's theories influenced multiple generations of low-income housing design but did not move the needle on the policies and economics of building maintenance, which many scholars have argued is a much more conclusive factor.[37]

The demolition of Pruitt-Igoe, the rise of deterministic theories like defensible space, and architects' gradual, though by no means total, disengagement from issues of social justice and inequality during the 1970s[38] were not isolated events. They were all a part of a larger philosophical shift away from modernism. One of the distinguishing features of modernism, especially in architecture but also in other forms of cultural expression, was a teleological belief in progress, and the necessity of casting aside traditional or contextual approaches to form-making. Famous edicts like architect Louis Sullivan's pronouncement that "form follows function" (1896), or architect Adolf Loos' provocative assertion that excessive architectural ornamentation was a crime (1908), or poet Ezra Pound's injunction

After years of neglect and increasing crime and vandalism in St Louis' Pruitt-Igoe housing complex, many commentators claimed that the architecture was to blame for the deteriorating conditions. The complex was demolished in July 1972.

to "make it new" (1928) were emblematic of the modernist approach.[39] Such proclamations are primarily associated with aesthetics, a call for formal innovation and a stripping away of superfluous ornament. Yet, many modernist projects had a progressive social agenda that the period's starkly uncompromising forms hide from view. It's easy to consider the harsh lines, concrete colorscape, and inoperable windows of modernist architecture as indicative of a purist aesthete's disregard for ease of use, much less social solidarity. Yet embedded within the formal choices is a political agenda that aspired to social reform through a radical newness that would cast off the social and economic hierarchies of the old order as readily as it would repudiate traditional architectural forms.

In the field of city planning, modernist thinking found its most explicit articulation in the work of Le Corbusier, who famously decried urban road systems based on the legacy of horse-drawn carriage routes and derided urban housing that similarly reflected obsolete technologies. One of his most renowned quotes, alongside "A house is a machine for living" is the almost wistful sentiment that "Modern life demands, and is waiting for, a new kind of plan, both for the house and the city."

The 1925 plan for the city Le Corbusier advanced for central Paris, Le Plan Voisin, was never realized. It consisted of demolishing the third and fourth arrondissements and replacing the then-squalid neighborhoods of Marais and Beaubourg with cruciform towers, superhighways, and subterranean high-speed trains. In describing the plan, he invited his readers to imagine walking into this manicured, light-filled network of manicured lawns and elegant skyscrapers:

> You are under the shade of trees, vast lawns spread all round you. The air is clear and pure; there is hardly any noise. What, you cannot see where the buildings are? Look through the charmingly diapered arabesques of branches out into the sky towards those widely-spaced crystal towers which soar higher than any pinnacle on Earth.[40]

---

[35] Robert Fishman, "Rethinking Public Housing" in Places, 16(2); 2004. See also Charles Jencks, *The Language of Post-modern Architecture* (New York: Rizzoli, 1977) p. 9.

[36] Oscar Newman, *Defensible Space: Crime Prevention Through Urban Design,* (New York: Macmillan 1973).

[37] See Nicholas Dagen Bloom, *Public Housing That Worked: New York in the 20th Century* (Philadelphia: University of Pennsylvania Press, 2009) and *Public Housing Myths,* Nicholas Dagen Bloom, Fritz Umbach, and Lawrence Vale, eds., (Ithaca, N.Y.: Cornell University Press, 2015).

[38] President Richard Nixon's moratorium on federal funding for public housing projects in 1973 is often cited as concomitant with a turning point that pushed many socially minded architects away from low-income housing and towards educational and cultural institutions. See David Morton, "Competition for Longevity: Architects Housing, Trenton, NJ," *Progressive Architecture,* August 1981: 69–71.

[39] Louis Sullivan designed some of our most beautifully ornamented buildings, yet his quote that "it could only benefit us if we were to abandon ornament and concentrate entirely on the erection of buildings that were finely shaped and charming in their sobriety" reportedly influenced Adolf Loos. See *Ornament and Crime: Selected Essays* by Adolf Loos, edited by Adolf Opel (Riverside, Calif.: Ariadne Press, 1997).

[40] Le Corbusier, "Plan Voisin, Paris, France, 1925" archived at www.fondationlecorbusier.fr.

Left: A model of Le Corbusier's Plan Voisin, an unrealized 1925 proposal for central Paris. **Right:** Pruitt-Igoe complex in St Louis, designed by Minoru Yamasaki, completed in 1956 and demolished in 1972, a prototypical tower-in-the-park development.

If the demolition of Pruitt-Igoe sounded the death knell of the optimism of modernist architecture as social reform, then Le Corbusier's Plan Voisin heralded its opening gambit fifty years prior. To the enduring relief of anyone who visits the chic districts of Marais or Beaubourg today, Le Corbusier never got his hands on central Paris, but a diluted version of some his architectural ideas about how to maximize light and air through "towers-in-the-park" did come to pass, and is visible in the layout of many different types of mass housing schemes across New York and other North American cities.

In 1928, Le Corbusier was one of the founders of the Congres Internationaux d'Architecture Moderne, or CIAM, a network of avant-garde architects for whom modernist architecture and city planning had the potential to be, literally, revolutionary. Its members eventually included architects who would go on to be among the most famous of the twentieth century, such as Walter Gropius, Richard Neutra, Alvar Aalto, and Josep Lluís Sert. At the time, Gropius, a German architect who founded the Bauhaus school, was actively promoting the idea that "taller, more widely spaced slab buildings can house more people per hectare" than traditional buildings that respected the block layout of nineteenth-century cities.[41] Sert, a Spanish architect and city planner who moved to the United States in 1939 and became an influential dean of Harvard's Graduate School of Design between 1953 and 1969, is responsible for the first specific effort to promote CIAM's urbanistic agenda in the United States with a book he authored, infelicitously entitled *Can Our Cities Survive? An ABC of Urban Problems, Their Analyses, Their Solutions: Based on Proposals Formulated by CIAM.*[42] The book grouped together a wide range of CIAM-inspired projects, many of which were slab buildings with clean lines on superblock sites, and presented these precedents as proof of the CIAM polemic's "scientific" response to slum conditions. Lewis Mumford, while respectful of some of the impulses behind CIAM's thinking, refused to endorse Sert's book specifically because of its limited view of "the functional city" as reducible to dwelling, work, recreation, and transportation. "But what of the political, educational, and cultural functions of the city?" he wrote in a letter to Sert. "The organs of political and cultural association are, from my standpoint, the distinguishing marks of the city; without them, there is only an urban mass...I regard their omission as the chief defect of routine city planning; and their absence from the program of the CIAM I find almost inexplicable."[43]

Nonetheless, new ideas about planned housing developments did gain traction, and not only due to the influence of elite European modernist architects; a diverse group of American urbanists, including Mumford as well as Catherine Bauer Wurster, Clarence Stein, and Henry Wright, among others, also argued for new typologies of urban form that utilized superblocks and reconsidered the relationship between shared open spaces and higher density housing.[44] While the efforts of this international vanguard of modernists did not create the widespread architectural revolution in cities that many of them hoped for, a rough distillation of these ideas — towers or slabs surrounded by fields of open space — did manage to influence powerful low-income housing reformers, certain labor unions, and other groups of city builders eager to assert a new building typology to house increasingly large groups of laborers. Violating the city's grid to develop housing towers set apart from the street and surrounded by open space found a political and an architectural agenda: replace tenements and slums with modern developments that prioritized light and air over any sense of fidelity to the existing urban fabric. Between 1941 and 1975 superblock schemes were built across New York City, most of them executed by government agencies or legislative programs charged with housing the poor or by politically connected labor unions intent on providing low-cost housing options for their members.

Destroying urban fabric to erect large-scale housing projects did not turn out to be the silver bullet to solve some of the challenges of concentrated urban poverty that some expected. As the violent displacements of urban renewal schemes fell out of favor in the 1960s and 1970s, the belief that primarily architectural solutions could solve social challenges dissolved. During the rise of citizen protest and advocacy planning in this period — typified by figures such as Jane Jacobs, who famously protested, in word and deed, the Corbusier-inspired urban renewal schemes of Robert Moses — a consensus emerged fitfully that served to throw the baby out with the bathwater, so to speak. The top-down thinking and disregard for the depth of neighborhood networks, for the benefit of mixing residential and commercial uses,

---

[41] Eric Paul Mumford, *The CIAM Discourse on Urbanism, 1928–1960* (Cambridge: MIT Press, 2002) p. 51.

[42] Josep Lluís Sert and CIAM, *Can Our Cities Survive? An ABC of Urban Problems, Their Analyses, Their Solutions: Based on Proposals Formulated by CIAM* (Cambridge, MA.: Harvard University Press, 1942).

[43] As quoted in Mumford, 2002, p. 133.

[44] Not all of these new housing typologies were high-rise towers. Stein and Wright designed Sunnyside Gardens in Queens, a low-rise, high-density development that was one of the first planned communities in the United States.

or for the importance of maintaining connections to the street system came to be seen as callously unresponsive to human behavior and healthy patterns of community life. Therefore, the buildings that were developed under the sway of this urban planning mentality came to be seen as woefully outdated and even dangerous. The planning *mentality* of towers-in-the-park came under fire, and the architectural *typology* suffered the blame. Demolitions like Pruitt-Igoe were politically and economically unfeasible in a city as densely populated as New York. But over the last few decades, a philosophical disavowal has become urbanist dogma.

In New York City, towers-in-the-park are not going anywhere. They are a part of our diverse urban fabric as much as brownstones, single family or semi-detached homes, and apartment buildings of all shapes and sizes. As distinct as these types are, what most of them share is their relationship to the street: no matter how tall or how far apart they are, the majority of our city's building stock is oriented towards our greatest public space, our streets and avenues. But towers-in-the-park diverge from this pattern. The deficits of this typology are well known, such as the perceived association with concentrated poverty or the absence of street-life integration. However, their particular benefits, which in part derive directly from their reconsidered relationship to the street, are not broadly understood or thoroughly explored.

Over the years, *Urban Omnibus* has published numerous articles about various projects related to towers-in-the-park. In the beginning, my colleagues and I did not seek these out in particular, any more than we sought out articles about Brooklyn or parks or the subway system. Yet, looking back, specific attention to the typology was bound to show up in our coverage of new ways of thinking about and acting upon New York City's built environment. For one thing, we were interested in projects that sought to contribute to a more just, inclusive, sustainable, beautiful, and emancipatory city. And the inhabitants of many towers-in-the-park developments are predominantly but not exclusively middle and working class New Yorkers who, but for the special circumstances of these buildings, likely would have migrated to the suburbs as the city has increasingly become a place that only accommodates the extremely rich and the extremely poor. Three research projects that investigate completely different contexts and were conceived for completely different reasons stand out for me, pointing out particular opportunities towers-in-the-park provide

Residents of Vladeck Houses, a New York City Housing Authority project in Manhattan's Lower East Side. NORC/Vladeck Cares, a partnership between Henry Street Settlement and the New York City Housing Authority, was the first NORC program in public housing when it was established in 1994.

for productive ecological planning, convenient elder living, minimal site coverage and the uniform access to light and air that comes with it, open space programming, and maybe, just maybe, a conception of home rooted in a sense of shared assets and social solidarity rather than private and exclusive property.

One such project is Kerri Culhane's unrealized plan, discussed in chapter three, to turn the neglected open spaces of Two Bridges into green infrastructure that would actually mitigate the effects of flooding and social infrastructure that would actually reconnect residents to the waterfront.[45]

Another project, by the innovative architecture and urban design studio Interboro Partners, explains research into the phenomenon of "naturally occurring retirement communities" (NORCs) and the phenomenon of towers-in-the-park providing some of the most seized opportunities for elder New Yorkers to remain in their homes, with their neighbors and community, able to access New York City's cultural offerings and the independence made possible by a comprehensive public transit system. Interboro partner Daniel D'Oca explains:

> Basically, a NORC is a place (a building, a development, a neighborhood) with a large senior population that wasn't purpose-built to be a senior community. NORCs are important because once a place meets the local criteria, it becomes eligible for local, state, and federal funds to retroactively provide it with the support services seniors need. Since an overwhelming majority (89%, by one measure) of seniors today would prefer to "age in place" in their neighborhood or home, and since as few as 9% of seniors say they want to live in an age-segregated community, NORCs present an attractive alternative to purpose-built retirement communities.[46]

Interboro's research uncovered that ownership structure is among the reasons why NORCs are so attractive to certain seniors: many towers-in-the-park are limited equity co-ops, often originally developed by labor unions (especially the Amalgamated Clothing Workers Union), that structurally disincline shareholders from selling their long-term apartments and moving to a purpose-built retirement community in New Jersey or Florida because the profit they stand to earn is limited by design. That's what keeps the prices and the turnover in such buildings low. Another reason is senior citizens' preference for design features that are otherwise maligned: the double-loaded corridors, ramps, and railings generously accommodate residents with limited mobility; the open spaces offer the type of onsite opportunities to congregate and socialize that many seniors prefer; the average travel time from your apartment to nearby shops and services is, on average, lower than in traditional city blocks. Interboro surveyed residents, calculated distances,

---

[45] Kerri Culhane, "Making Connections: Planning for Green Infrastructure in Two Bridges" on *Urban Omnibus* August 8, 2012.

[46] Daniel D'Oca, "Studio Report: The Good Old Days" on *Urban Omnibus,* January 23, 2013.

evaluated design choices, and analyzed land use designations and amenities near to the twenty-seven official NORCs in New York City. The fact that towers-in-the-park enable a safe and secure way for our elder citizens to age in place is indeed a hidden benefit in the face of the typology's many perceived deficits.

A third research project, by Rosalie Genevro, longtime executive director of The Architectural League and an historian of urban housing policy, focuses on Starrett City, a large tower-in-the-park development in Eastern Brooklyn that has been beloved by many of its residents. Starrett City's history is singular, formed in the urban crosscurrents of race, class, housing policy, and the ever-evolving idea of community. In the article, Genevro explains that she has long been intrigued by the development because "Starrett — renamed Spring Creek Towers in 2002 — is a community that works. It is one of the most racially integrated areas of the city; it is safe; and if the buildings themselves seem uninspired on the exterior, they nevertheless provide accommodating, affordable housing for moderate income New Yorkers in a well-tended landscape."[47] For this reason, when she was asked to speak in a series of lectures on the reverberations of the idea of "house" in American culture, she sought to reframe the assignment to reflect a New Yorker's sensibility that house and home are not the same thing. In Genevro's opinion, "American mythmaking has given far too much weight to 'house,'" a cultural weight that is reflected in the policies, subsidies, and public attitudes about single-family home-ownership that have been key drivers of environmentally disastrous low-density land-use patterns and a housing market predicated on the fallacy of limitless, perpetual growth. She is more interested in "the idea of home and the many, many different ways Americans construct that," which led her to ask how did "a group of high-rise, unlovely brick buildings designed on the much-maligned tower-in-the-park model and built on a former landfill on the very edge of Brooklyn ever manage to become 'home?'" As Genevro delved deeper into this story, speaking with long-time residents and some of the people who helped create and manage the development, she found a thought-provoking counter-example to trends in housing and urban policy that prioritize individualized kinds of built form and ownership over shared resources and collective aspiration.

Starrett City was built between 1972 and 1976 on a large, marshy, former land-fill in southeast Brooklyn, between the predominantly black and Latino neighborhood of East New York and the predominantly Italian and Jewish (at the time) neighbor-hood of Canarsie. It was one of the last major developments in New York City built on the tower-in-the-park model. The project came about after numerous attempts to develop the site; the size of the lot and the fact that it was City-owned provided a rare opportunity to develop a great number of new housing units without having to purchase land or relocate existing residents.

New York City in the late 1960s and '70s was under duress: "Crime was high and increasing; racial tensions were inflamed, the city's manufacturing job base was disappearing, and its fiscal situation was deteriorating." Mayor John Lindsay was facing an electorate increasingly skeptical of his liberal Republican policies and experimental approaches to urban planning and racial integration at the community level, including a disastrous attempt at school decentralization and the insertion of scatter-site public housing into middle class white neighborhoods that served to exacerbate racial tension.[48] As Genevro found in her research, this tension created a particular context in which white residents of the nearby neighborhoods along Jamaica Bay "equated rentals with low-income black tenants and feared that the new project would 'tip' the Brooklyn shore to all minority tenancy. To get the project approved, Starrett Housing Corporation promised the city's Board of Estimate that it would create and sustain an integrated development with a 70 percent white population, which was the figure the developers believed would prevent the project from 'tipping.'"

To deliver on this promise required keen marketing savvy that played up some of the unique architectural benefits of the development, which was designed by Herman Jessor, an architect who dedicated his entire career to mass housing developed by labor unions. He was involved in many towers-in-the-park projects and is responsible for many of the architectural amenities that have turned buildings into NORCs. (He designed Penn South, which opened in 1962 and became the country's first officially recognized NORC in 1986). According to Genevro, "Jessor designed apartment buildings from the inside out, with cross-ventilation in the bedrooms, entry foyers and windowed kitchens." Plus, they were large. All of this was emphasized in the development's marketing materials, which included "the first focus groups ever employed in multifamily rental housing, and . . . the first television ads for a rental development."

The next step was a complicated tenant selection process "to make every building and every floor integrated. In 1988, twelve years after the development opened, an article in *The New York Times* called Starrett City perhaps the most integrated area of New York City: 62 percent white, 23 percent black, 9 percent Hispanic and 6 percent Asian or people of mixed race. Twenty years later, in 2007, the Starrett City census tract was 32 percent white, 41 percent black and 19 percent Hispanic." The tactic to achieve this mix was separate waiting lists for white and minority tenants. Controversy and multiple lawsuits, involving the NAACP and the Reagan Justice Department, ensued and eventually discontinued the practice of race-based waiting lists. But in the process "something significant — a community — had been established at Starrett City." Perhaps we can attribute the formation of this community to "the aspiration to integration itself" or perhaps to some other factor. Regardless of its causes, "Starrett residents seem, from the start, to have perceived their development as something particular and appealing."

These very distinct stories all had one thing in common: a maligned and seemingly outdated building typology worthy of a fresh look. This observation led us to

---

47 Rosalie Genevro, Starrett City: A Home of One's Own — with Party Walls" on *Urban Omnibus,* November 16, 2011

48 See Jerald E. Podair *The Strike That Changed New York: Blacks, Whites, and the Ocean Hill-Brownsville Crisis* (New Haven, Conn.: Yale University Press, 2008).

Starrett City, also known as Spring Creek Towers, was one of the last major developments in New York City built on the tower- in-the-park model.

launch a special *Urban Omnibus* research project that would dig a little deeper into the typology and some of its diverse manifestations across the city. I was particularly interested in drilling down into the spatial, historical, architectural, and social specificities of particular developments. Looking back on the stories on Two Bridges, NORCs, and Starrett City revealed that many of these developments have inherent assets hidden in plain sight. If we looked a little closer, might we be able to advance a new understanding of our existing urban fabric that focused on the benefits of its diversity rather than the deficits of old models embedded within it?

For her part, Genevro was particularly interested in probing the line of discrimination between the power of architecture to respond to the needs of its users and the tendency to blame design for factors outside of its control. The notion that Pruitt-Igoe was a security failure was attributed to the architecture rather than what urban historian Robert Fishman has called "a tide of destruction [that] ripped through our inner cities, devastating good, bad, and indifferent urban design."[49] Were it possible to filter out local questions of building maintenance and societal questions of structural economic change (and turf wars between criminal gangs), then we must ask: did some of the architectural intentions behind towers-in-the-park, particularly the desire to create more light and air in dense housing, actually provide the intended benefits to residents' perceived quality of life?

To wrestle with some of these questions, we developed the first installment of a project called Typecast in early 2013, published serially on *Urban Omnibus* over the course of a year. One of the first steps to unlocking the potential of traditionally maligned building typologies, we reasoned, would be to investigate examples in a non-typological way. That is, to focus on the particular confluences of historical, economic, architectural, and social forces that have resulted in each of these building complexes becoming a singular environment. The goal was to introduce visual, ethnographic, sociological, and journalistic lines of inquiry into a conversation about the relationship of use and form, design and experience, and urban history and urban futures.

I was particularly interested to apply the documentary methods of narrative journalism and environmental portraiture photography to a series of site-specific studies. We selected five very different towers-in-the-park projects: Co-op City (Baychester and Eastchester, The Bronx); Sea Rise and Sea Park East (Coney Island, Brooklyn); Todt Hill Houses (Castleton Corners, Staten Island); Electchester (Pomonok, Queens); and Alfred E. Smith and Vladeck Houses (Two Bridges, Manhattan). Each of these sites occupies a completely distinct urban geography. They vary widely in scale, population, and demographic make-up. Co-op City and Electchester were developed by unions. Sea Rise and Sea Park East were developed by New York State's Urban Development Corporation.[50] Todt Hill and Smith Houses are New York City Housing Authority public housing projects. All of them have undergone significant changes in the decades since they were built, either in their own internal make-up or in the urban conditions surrounding them.

My colleagues and I visited each place, noted our observations, and did some preliminary research. In an attempt to reverse the typical order of operations of illustrated journalism, we commissioned five photographers first, and we specifically sought out artists who do not define themselves as architectural photographers. I asked them to make a series of images that would include portraits of residents, architectural details, environmental context shots, and other photographic evocations of how people use space. The last phrase was key: so much of the received wisdom about why these places are suboptimal environments — from Oscar Newman's defensible space theory to Jane Jacobs-inspired dogma of mixed-use, medium-density urbanism — stems from an analysis of what space does to people. We did not want to reify the notion of people as passive subjects susceptible to the harmful effects of environments considered to be determinants of social breakdown. We wanted to understand the agency of residents.

For example, when my colleagues and I visited Todt Hill Houses in Staten Island, a group of seven buildings on a hill surrounded by a middle class community of single-family ranch homes, I noticed how groups of people headed home from the nearby bus stops would take a shortcut through the complex, treading visible desire lines through the grass lawns. This simple act of taking the shortest route to your destination immediately contradicted the notion that the visual markers of separation between towers-in-the-park and the street systems that surround them create a hard boundary not to be trespassed. Another example: when I visited the swath of towers-in-the-park projects in the Lower East Side, I found active community gardens amidst the expanses of grass and asphalt. There were notable negative observations as well: Sea Rise and Sea Park East were obviously in dangerous states of disrepair, and the multiple and contradictory notices in the lobby indicated repeated transfers of ownership and maintenance contracts that certainly did not bode well for the development's upkeep or sense of security or sanitation. I asked the photographers to look out for such details that complicate or contradict the notion that architecture is somehow autonomous from lived experience.

After publishing and exhibiting the five photo-essays, we commissioned a series of writers to explore some of the specific historical and experiential conditions in each. Again, we sought writers who did not necessarily identify themselves as architecture critics or urbanists but had perspectives and expertise relevant to each place and its unique history. Electchester, for example, was developed by the Local 3 of the International Brotherhood of Electrical Workers. So we thought it would be interesting to engage someone who covers the labor movement to

---

49 Robert Fishman, "Rethinking Public Housing" in *Places,* 16(2); 2004.

50 New York State's Urban Development Corporation (UDC) was a unique "super-agency" in operation between 1968 and 1975. During this period, the UDC built 33,000 units of housing and three new communities. Many of its developments were formally innovative, taking advantage of design features like skip-stop elevators, single-loaded corridors, mews, and terraces to make apartments feel more commodious, to optimize natural light, and to facilitate true and valuable sharing of open spaces. Not all of these innovations have stood the test of time. Nonetheless, the UDC's output testifies to a singular moment of convergence between architectural ingenuity and public sector risk-taking.

Typecast is the Architectural League's long-term investigation into architectural typologies. The first phase of this project included commissioned photography of five different towers-in-the-park developments — multi-family, high-rise housing complexes located on a "superblock" of open space and disconnected from the street — in each of the five boroughs of New York.

top to bottom:
Sea Rise, Coney Island, Brooklyn
Todt Hill Houses, Staten Island
Todt Hill Houses, Staten Island

opposite page:
Co-op City, Baychester, Bronx

explore the intersecting influences of organized labor and housing design on the experience of multiple generations of people who have grown up in this corner of Queens. Smith Houses has a strong tradition of activism — several notable community leaders were raised there — and so we sought out a journalist who specializes in social innovation.

By design, the results of this special project were not scientific. We did not come up with generalizable recommendations for how to reconsider the typology in policy or architecture. That was not the point. What the body of work affirms is simple yet profound. Here are a few takeaways.

The first is the most obvious, but bears repeating: New York City's building stock is extraordinarily diverse; so, too, are the types of households that populate it. Just as architects must design for all types of individuals and households, citymakers must develop a host of strategies to analyze how a building is used ten, twenty, or fifty years after construction and be ready to produce tactical, surgical interventions to optimize for these unexpected uses. A nimble approach to housing adaptation is not only necessary to accommodate demographic change. Given the enormous carbon footprint of large construction, the environmental imperative to make do with what we already have is incumbent upon the design and real estate industries.

A second lesson, and a second order of diversity, is found within the typology itself. The quickest scan of the commissioned Typecast photos reveals that the squat six-story brick buildings of Todt Hill and the angular, terraced skyscrapers of Sea Park East have little in common architecturally. Again, what they share is a history of public institutions acting as real estate developers and a design strategy of locating multiple buildings on a superblock, disconnected from the street system and planned with dedicated open space. But the kind of nimble design sensibility we must apply to these housing developments is not only at the scale of the super-block. Renovating and reconfiguring the living units can help these buildings accommodate and attract new generations of residents whose needs are distinct from those of the original inhabitants.

The third lesson is to remember that we need responsive flexibility in policy as well as design. Policies must recognize emerging challenges and homegrown opportunities. The policy to provide funding for onsite services to NORCs, for example, sets a good precedent for strategically investing public and private money to support and enhance a naturally occurring phenomenon.[51]

Another takeaway, once again obvious yet easy to overlook, is that bold design choices are only as powerful as the quality of construction and sustained maintenance. When well maintained, the light and air that comes from onsite open space can drastically improve the perceived quality of the apartments that tower above it (as in Co-op City or Starrett City); when poorly maintained, open spaces become a nuisance (as in Sea Rise and Sea Park East).

Finally, social networks matter and evolve over time and across generations. When the policies and financing arrangements that keep a development affordable for a period of time expire, the ties that bind those networks will fray.

These five lessons about the overlooked assets of towers-in-the-park fed into a conversation that was not purely academic or hypothetical. Around the time that my colleagues and I were discussing the need to reconsider these benefits, the Bloomberg administration was thinking about ways to capitalize on the primary element that distinguishes the building type from other forms of high-rise residential architecture: the onsite open space. The New York City Housing Authority (NYCHA) is the country's largest public housing authority by several orders of magnitude, and it has developed and controls dozens of housing projects built on the tower-in-the-park model. In 2012 and 2013, NYCHA advanced a new plan to address its chronic budget shortfalls. The agency continues to suffer from the federal government's pivot away from helping local governments develop public housing projects towards systems of vouchers, tax credits, and other forms of subsidizing the private sector to develop affordable housing. With an alarming backlog of vital maintenance projects, NYCHA felt pressured to find an alternative revenue stream. Citing under-funding by Congress of $750 million annually for operating expenses and $875 million in capital improvements "to keep the buildings, elevators and heating and electrical systems in good repair," NYCHA proposed to offer 99-year leases to private developers for open space (mostly parking lots and pavement with some minimal incursions into lawns) on the grounds of eight Manhattan housing projects. According to John Rhea, the agency's chairman at the time, the so-called "land lease plan" would "generate $30-$50 million every year. Every single dollar of this money will be used for capital improvements, like fixing roofs, rehabilitating elevators and heating systems and restoring building facades at developments across the city . . . This initiative will generate approximately 800 affordable housing units for eligible New Yorkers — and the units will be required to remain permanently affordable. NYCHA residents will get a preference for these affordable units. There also will be new construction and permanent jobs for NYCHA residents."[52] Yet many of the more than half a million people who live in NYCHA projects were deeply suspicious of the proposal. Lawsuits were brought. Public opinion was not in its favor. In the final months of the Bloomberg administration, the growing national outcry over income inequality mixed with local disquiet about the outgoing mayoral administration's preference for private sector solutions to public sector challenges helped to kill the land-lease proposal.

The plan was undoubtedly a proactive strategy of adaptation: reconfiguring and capitalizing on open land owned by the public sector in order to exert local control over a revenue shortfall for a public housing agency that was no longer a top priority for federal government, which had long since shifted strategy from helping local authorities build or maintain public housing projects towards investing in vouchers and subsidies to incent private developers to create affordable housing. But a

---

[51] The original NORC to receive funding to expand services for seniors was Penn South, a tower-in-the-park development in Manhattan, in 1986, which was supported by UJA-Federation for New York, a large local philanthropy with its roots in Jewish life and public health.

[52] John Rhea, "Message from the Chairman," *New York City Housing Authority Journal* 43, no. 3 (April 2013).

capacity for adaptation in low-income housing design can be like "flexibility" in the labor market: change comes with pain and resistance, requiring great sensitivity and care. Especially when people's homes are concerned, attempts at innovation must be supported by express political will to maintain the public goods in question, and public trust in their continued good faith provision. I remember discussing the plan with Rosalie Genevro on a subway ride to a meeting, and her suggesting that the fatal flaw of the proposal's roll-out was NYCHA's foregrounding of the real estate economics as opposed to leading with a comprehensive urban design plan that would have assured residents that the buildings they called home were not going to be privatized, that no one would be displaced. The historical memory of policymakers is notoriously short, but the legacy of top-down moves by government to address social challenges through mass relocations, demolitions, and the callous disruption of place-based community continuities casts a long and painful shadow. Housing's capacity to be nimble and adaptable must be grounded in an affirmation that important values remain permanent. Elected leaders and the policymakers who work for them should be in the business of ensuring safe, habitable homes for their constituents, protecting against the exploitation and unsanitary squalor of earlier eras while enabling new design ideas to deliver housing in ways that respond to dynamic, contemporary needs. Designers should be in the business of facilitating that dynamism, creating opportunities for inclusivity, affordability, and sustainability (social as well as environmental). Citymakers must be in the business of facilitating the symbiosis between sound policymaking and high-quality design, proactively contending with the tension that arises from stewarding the built environment in ways that question received wisdom and encourage responsible manipulation of existing urban fabric, yet maintain core values.

SELF-HELP HOUSING

One of the greatest assets hidden in plain sight in any neighborhood is a core group of citizens committed to the place where they live. This commitment can take many forms, from the urban farmers of East New York discussed in Chapter Two to the teenage hackers and digital stewards of Red Hook discussed in Chapter Four. Strategies to preserve or develop rental housing in poor communities, however, often consider tenants to be passive recipients of housing provided by government or developers or landlords. Sometimes it takes a crisis — such as the crisis of abandonment that decimated large swaths of New York City in the mid-1970s — to reveal the untapped capacity of residents to exert powerful forms of agency that can stabilize neighborhoods and turn toxic liabilities into assets. Just as we must remember to unpack the assumptions that have influenced housing design in order to identify overlooked strengths, we must also pay attention to innovative strategies born of a particular set of circumstances yet manage to evolve along with a changing city. The story of the Urban Homesteading Assistance Board (UHAB) offers a pertinent example of adaptive citymaking over time. Even more significantly, this organization has upended traditional narratives about who has the agency to rebuild the city and who does not. In the process, it has reconceptualized home ownership, housing tenure, the power dynamic between owners and renters, and it has developed a durable and responsive model of advocacy and intervention.

Andrew Reicher has worked at the UHAB since 1978 and served as its executive director since 1981. Trained as an architect, Reicher has dedicated his career to creating homeownership opportunities for renters living in poverty. Over the past forty years, the unique organization he leads has evolved from addressing the mid-70s crisis of abandonment to contemporary crises of foreclosure, speculation, and affordability. In Reicher's words, "Over time, the tactics have evolved, but the mission has remained, in essence, to turn renters into homeowners and to provide permanently affordable, quality housing."[53] The tactics have changed because the circumstances have changed: UHAB has remained effective in its quest to create home ownership opportunities by adapting to the constantly shifting dynamics of New York City's economy and housing market.

Just how quickly conditions can change on the ground was poignantly apparent when I went to interview Reicher in his Lower Manhattan office. We had originally scheduled our meeting for October 29, 2012, which turned out to be the day that Superstorm Sandy made landfall in New York. We were able to reschedule six weeks later, but the devastated streets made it seem like the storm had struck just days before. UHAB's office is in the easternmost building on the easternmost block of Wall Street, steps away from the East River, whose waters swelled to break through its bulkhead, totally inundating the parts of the Lower East Side just north of Wall Street that were built on landfill. This less glamorous end of this famous street abuts the elevated FDR Drive, a hard edge to this side of Manhattan that sluices stormwater onto the ground below like a roof without a gutter or drainpipe.

The water had receded when I came to speak with Reicher about his work, but the ground-floor retail — bank branches, coffee shops — was still abandoned, a normally bustling corner of the financial district turned eerily quiet. Even though I was only a few minutes' walk from the epicenter of global finance and the American banking industry, this storm-damaged stretch called to mind the abandonment crisis that UHAB was formed to combat forty years prior.

During the urban crisis of the 1970s, much of New York City's housing stock consisted of late nineteenth- and early twentieth-century buildings in an alarming state of disrepair. Deindustrialization had left the City with one of the lowest ratios of employment to population nationwide, which exacerbated the effects of the 1972 oil crisis and the subsequent nationwide recession. The middle class fled for the suburbs and drained the city of tax revenue. Over the course of the decade, the city's population decreased from almost eight million to just above seven million inhabitants. Between 1969 and 1976, the city lost 600,000 jobs, one-sixth of its employment base.[54]

---

[53] "Self-help Housing," *Urban Omnibus,* December 19, 2012.

[54] Samuel Ehrenhalt, "Economic and demographic change: the case of New York City," *Monthly Labor Review* (February 1993). Accessed August 1, 2016. www.bls.gov/mlr/1993/02/art4full.pdf.

The intersection of Clinton and Grand Streets, in Manhattan's Lower East Side, in 1980.

As predominantly white middle-class New Yorkers decamped for the suburbs, incoming groups of African-Americans from the South, Puerto Ricans, and immigrants from Asia and Latin America arrived in deteriorating urban neighborhoods. Property owners and political leaders were unable or unwilling to invest the necessary resources to stop the steep decline or to improve conditions for these incoming groups. Landlords faced a financially untenable combination of high interest rates, stagflation, and rising fuel costs, which led many to turn to "abandonment and arson [as] common tactics for salvaging what they could from unprofitable buildings. From 1970 to 1978, the city lost an average of 3,274 units of housing per month."[55] Compounding the disastrous effects of the City's fiscal crisis during this period was the policy of *in rem* foreclosure, which put an ill-prepared city in the uncomfortable position of owning vast amounts of property. Again, *in rem* (literally, "against the thing itself") refers to the legal concept of taking action against property without regard for its owner; *in rem* foreclosure was the process by which the City took ownership of tax delinquent properties. In the chaotic economy of urban America in the 1970s, a policy originally devised as a punishment of last resort for tax avoidance became a perverse incentive for abandonment. According to a 2004 history of UHAB commissioned for its thirty-year anniversary, "In 1976, the city owned 4,611 multifamily buildings and was about to acquire 1,770 more, yet the city's foreclosure process often took five years or more — three years of arrears before the city initiated foreclosure proceedings, and two more years to complete them. In the face of rising operating costs, many landlords made calculated decisions to milk their rent rolls for five years before abandoning title to the city — at which time the buildings were often unlivable."[56] That same year, Roger Starr, the controversial outgoing housing commissioner, publicly argued for planned shrinkage: encourage residents in the most affected areas to move through subsidies and foreclosure and then cut back on City services. In an editorial in *The New York Times Magazine,* Starr writes, "Whole tax districts can be cleared by taking properties for tax delinquencies . . . Stretches of empty blocks may then be knocked down, services can be stopped, subway stations closed, and the land left to lie fallow until a change in economic and demographic assumptions makes the land useful once again."[57]

In retrospect, Starr's proposal seems unbelievably shortsighted (for New York in the 1970s, anyway; planned shrinkage has been repeatedly floated for Detroit over the past decade). Neither did it receive any shortage of scorn in its own day. Nonetheless, the proposal serves to characterize what was a semi-official mood of despair about New York City's poor neighborhoods at the time. Such was the local context in which UHAB got its start. In the face of these adverse conditions and sense of hopelessness, seasoned advocates were in search of fresh ideas to stabilize neighborhoods that were deteriorating at a rate that neither local government nor traditional charities could handle. A key player in this quest was the Cathedral of Saint John the Divine, Episcopal Diocese in New York, which named the Very Reverend James P. Morton, who had devoted his ministry to extremely poor communities, as its Dean in 1972. Prior to this appointment, Morton worked with his close friend Ivan Illich, a polymath philosopher and onetime ascetic Catholic priest dedicated to upending conventional wisdom about institutional approaches to poverty. Together, the two men convened "a group of architects, urban planners, and community activists for a session on housing for the poor. Among the most intriguing ideas that emerged from the meeting was self-help housing, the idea that abandoned properties could be turned over to poor 'urban homesteaders' who would redevelop the homes with their own hands and manage them cooperatively."[58]

Upon arrival in New York, Morton observed firsthand the effects of abandonment as he wandered the uptown Manhattan neighborhoods surrounding St John the Divine. He thought the city might be fertile ground for the novel idea of homesteading to take root. Once again, he brought together experts from the worlds of design and physical planning, alongside local activists and government officials, with an interest in this approach. Fresh though it was to America's cities at the time, the idea of housing built and rehabilitated by the people who live in it is by no means new. Before the twentieth century, most people built their own houses, especially in rural areas. Today, hundreds of millions of the world's poor, without

55 Neil F. Carlson, "UHAB Comes of Age," (2003). Accessed August 1, 2016. www.community-wealth.org/sites/clone.community-wealth.org/files/downloads/report-carlson.pdf, 2.

56 Ibid.

57 Roger Starr, "Making New York Smaller," *The New York Times Magazine,* November 14, 1976.

58 Carlson, "UHAB Comes of Age," 2003, 1.

the resources to access formal housing markets, take matters into their own hands. One of the experts at Dean Morton's urban homesteading conference was a housing expert named Ian Donald Terner, then teaching at Harvard and MIT. Terner was one of the contributors to an influential 1972 book called *Freedom to Build: Dweller Control of the Housing Process,* co-edited by his colleague John F. C. Turner. The book detailed research into various modes of "self-help housing" in urban informal settlements in what we now call the Global South, then called the Third World. It reflects on the fact that this is not exclusively a poor-world phenomenon. The conference at Saint John the Divine asked the provocative question: why couldn't that same level of owner involvement in the building process apply to multifamily apartment buildings in cities? The short answer was that residents were perfectly capable of rehabilitating and managing multifamily buildings if given some targeted help.

A few of the assembled experts, including Terner, Dean Morton, and some officials working within the housing department began "plotting a strategy for expanding urban homesteading in New York City." The group began meeting regularly at the Cathedral to figure out how its "vision of self-help housing could squeeze itself around existing laws and government programs." They contacted community groups and identified deteriorating properties that still housed residents committed to staying put in those neighborhoods. With a little technical assistance and help navigating the bureaucracy of existing government regulations, these potential urban homesteaders would be at the vanguard of reclaiming neighborhoods thought to be beyond hope. "The idea was to provide low-income people with the tools they needed — everything from seed money to legal advice, architectural plans, building permits and training in bookkeeping, contracts, and construction — to build and run limited-equity housing cooperatives."[59] By 1974, these efforts had formalized into the Urban Homesteading Assistance Board. Since then, UHAB has assisted in the preservation of over 1,700 buildings and created homeownership opportunities for over 30,000 households.

Co-ops, by definition, are stock corporations whose members receive a return on their investment proportionate to their investment and are shared among co-op members. In Reicher's view, a limited-equity co-op is a "true co-op." Co-ops that don't limit the equity of shareholders are what he considers market-rate or speculative co-ops. He explained to me, "by limiting that return for departing shareholders to the original cost of their shares plus a modest profit, we can preserve the co-op's affordability. Buyers forego possible future profits in favor of the low purchase price and monthly housing costs. The goal is to create housing that's affordable to low-income people of this generation as well as the next."[60] Limited equity co-ops had been an official approach to affordable housing for decades, from labor union developments in the 1930s to New York State housing legislation in the 1950s.[61] Today, New York City has the second largest community of limited and shared-equity housing co-ops in the country.

The simple, profound, even radical difference of the UHAB approach was to transform existing rental buildings into co-ops, capitalizing on and improving the

In the early years of the Urban Homesteading Assistance Board, residents did most of the rehabilitation work to turn dilapidated rental buildings into renovated co-ops.

city's extant fabric rather than always relying on inserting costly new buildings. "Americans have always built and renovated their own houses," Reicher told me, "but the idea of renovating apartment buildings was new in the 1970s. Before that, you would just tear a building down if it fell out of use or into disrepair. You wouldn't do these major gut renovations. That whole idea was new, especially for larger apartment buildings." Key to this transformation was the idea of "sweat equity" (a term early UHAB staffers claim to have coined), which "refers to the contribution of labor in lieu of money. In the beginning, the homesteaders did an enormous amount of the rehab work. In some of our later iterations of homesteading, we tried to limit sweat equity to an amount of work roughly equivalent to a down payment: 10, 15, 20% of the value of the property."

The first few years focused on supporting the efforts of intrepid pioneers and committed groups of residents with prior relationships, like "an extended family or a church group or just a bunch of neighbors and friends." Soon though, homesteading assistance had to scale up beyond the willingness of a self-selected few. Between 1977 and 1978, the City decreased the time it took to claim title to a building to just one year, which resulted in a huge number of foreclosures on properties

---

[59] Ibid, 2.

[60] "Self-help Housing," *Urban Omnibus,* December 19, 2012.

[61] New York State was particularly active in promoting this ownership model through the Mitchell-Lama Housing Program, established under the Limited Profit Housing Companies Act of 1955, which offered developers low-interest mortgage loans and property tax exemptions in exchange for required limitation on profits, income limits on tenants, and supervision by the New York State Division of Housing and Community Renewal.

that were largely occupied. With neighborhood fabric deteriorating at such an alarming rate, the City was shifting course away from taking over properties as punishment for tax delinquent landlords and towards an attempt to salvage abandoned buildings as housing. However, out of 11,000 buildings the City reclaimed in 1977, 4,000 were still occupied. Reicher put the figures in context : "4,000 buildings is 100,000 apartments; that's like the city of San Francisco!" For the people living in these apartments, the City was now responsible for heat, water, and general maintenance. Local government had become, in effect, an ill-equipped slumlord.

UHAB adapted what it had learned in the previous few years to this new reality in order to help residents renovate their own buildings and turn them into co-ops. UHAB programs enjoyed popularity in the press and in City Hall. Elected officials, according to Reicher, "liked these programs because they bred engaged and vocal citizens. Research has proven that folks who live in co-ops are more likely to vote and to be active in the civic realm. If you practice democracy at home, well, then you practice democracy in your community." He elaborated on the transformational effects that participating in UHAB's technical assistance could have on residents who, by virtue of their sweat equity and learned property management skills, became homeowners:

> I think UHAB has always been a "people development" program. We don't manage the buildings; we don't do the physical rehab. What we do is to facilitate groups of people to help themselves do these things. In many ways, the technical skills we brought to this were people skills. Our brand of participatory training is about learning by example how to do the kinds of things residents will have to do as leaders of a co-op board: solving bookkeeping problems, figuring out what to do with a problem resident, understanding how to go to court or deal with Con Edison, hiring a contractor . . . I think something that distinguishes UHAB's work is our firm belief that the folks out there are perfectly capable of managing their own buildings. It doesn't matter if some didn't finish high school, or if others never had a checking account. When you get a group of people together, between them they'll have — or they'll learn — the skills. And there's no better training in how to run a building than having lived through the bad days of abandonment.

During the 1990s, Mayor Giuliani made clear his belief that the City should not be a landlord, a philosophy that applied to the community gardens I discussed in Chapter Two as well as to the apartment buildings discussed here. His administration created new policies to transfer tax-delinquent properties to third-party real estate developers instead of taking them into public ownership. Thus, the source of the affordable home ownership opportunities UHAB had spent fifteen years fostering quickly evaporated. The organization had to adapt again. In order to preserve the option of residents in these properties managing them as co-ops, UHAB decided it had to become a developer.

Doing so created an inherent tension with UHAB's tenant organizing and technical assistance work. As Reicher put it, "When you're doing rehab, or helping with financing, you want the residents to be in control of the project . . . but when you're the developer, you're the landlord. And residents tend to complain about their landlords, especially since many of the buildings we took on were in extremely bad condition and renovating them was complicated and slow." The fact that the organization has learned how to accommodate these traditionally conflicting roles testifies to its nimbleness as an institution and the constancy of its mission. It also affirms UHAB's deep relationships with communities of residents.

New York City came back in ways difficult to predict in 1975. These days, "We aren't dealing with a crisis of abandonment anymore. We're dealing with a crisis of affordability," explained Reicher. In some ways, the challenge today is the converse of undesirable, dilapidated housing exerting downward pressure on value, hollowing out neighborhoods and fertilizing crime and squalor. The years of persistent economic growth between 1988 and 2008 have flipped the curves of supply and demand such that "we have price escalation because we have a housing shortage. Family and household sizes are much smaller than they used to be, so the number of housing units needed to serve eight million today is much greater than it was thirty-five years ago. Another issue is that there is value for housing in every single neighborhood, so speculators will buy up housing, including affordable housing, everywhere."

And that's not all. Since New York's economic recovery in the 1980s, we have been quick to forget lessons from the 1960s and '70s about how quickly the value of housing can decrease. Since the 1990s, the unquestioned and erroneous belief that housing would always appreciate in value led directly to the subprime mortgage crisis that was a primary trigger of the financial crash of 2008. Therefore, Reicher was quick to add, "We also have a crisis of foreclosure." This kind of foreclosure is not about government taking title of properties in tax arrears. It's about banks taking titles of properties whose owners could no longer afford mortgage payments in the wake of lost jobs and ballooning payments on adjustable mortgages; in many cases, the home's decreasing value also fell below the amount of money owed to the bank. "UHAB has been extremely active, both in the run up to the housing crash and after, with organizing in buildings that were being bought out by speculators and are now in foreclosure. We see that as an opportunity to recapture some of those units as affordable housing." Once again, UHAB has had to change its tactics while staying true to its core mission, scaling up its policy work to encourage regulatory changes that would help to keep foreclosed buildings from deteriorating.

According to Jerilyn Perine, UHAB's tactical adaptability is its key attribute, without which "it would have just been some funky group from the '70s that no one would have heard from again. There weren't that many organizations that maintained their core skill set and their core expertise and then over time, adapt it to these different circumstances. That is highly unusual. You just don't see it very often."[62]

Amid these shifts, UHAB hasn't lost sight of the conditions on the ground when they got started. While the organization continues to work building by building,

---

[62] Carlson, "UHAB Comes of Age," 2003, 12–13.

Reicher is able to take a long view. He remembers well how "at one time, the City owned 75% of the housing in the South Bronx and 70% of the housing in Harlem. This was during a time when no one cared about housing and no one thought New York would come back. But instead of giving up all that property, government might have looked at these resources as a public utility and considered retaining some interest in it, perhaps leasing it for 30 or 50 years. If we think ahead, we can preserve the ability to look at our public assets again after a generation and see how they could be used to meet future needs."

For someone whose life's work was made possible, in part, by the City's willingness to dispose of properties it was ill-equipped to manage, Reicher's interpretation of public ownership and how it might be strategically reconsidered within municipal policymaking warrants careful contemplation. For liberals and conservatives alike, the notion of government as landlord conjures images of bureaucratic dysfunction and inefficiency. Public housing in the US has seen a net decrease in federal investment since 1999,[63] with policy shifting from government-owned and operated housing developments ("the projects") towards creating incentives through tax credits or zoning bonuses for the private sector to provide affordable housing. Governments at all scales don't have a particularly good track record for property management at the local scale. Or so we're told.

The systematic reordering of American narratives to recast government as the problem rather than the solution to economic woes — uttered so clearly and with such profound reverberations at President Reagan's first inaugural in 1981[64] — belies many cases of well-managed public ownership of value-generating assets, often brought about or maintained, surprisingly, by conservative politicians. For example, the Alaska Permanent Fund Corporation distributes the income from invested oil and minerals proceeds to all state residents. The Tennessee Valley Authority is "a publicly owned company with $11 billion in sales revenue, nine million customers and 11,260 employees that produces electricity and helps manage the Tennessee River system." Publicly owned utility companies supply energy in many states. Commodity dividends flow into state-owned financial products that essentially operate as sovereign wealth funds, such as the Permanent Wyoming Mineral Trust Fund, which was instituted as an alternative to raising severance taxes and has since virtually eliminated the need for income taxes in the state.

Each of these examples is cited by Gar Alperovitz, a thought leader on post-capitalist economics, in a *New York Times* op-ed, co-authored with Thomas Hanna, called "Socialism, American-style." They contradict the popular narrative that governments can't manage profitable enterprises or distribute the gains efficaciously. They speak to the diversity of ways that government can both maintain a stake in the provision of infrastructural benefits (like electricity) and offset the costs of its own operations. At the same time, they are not necessarily arguments in favor of greater nationalization of industry. Rather, one fundamental lesson to be learned from these examples in general and from Reicher's long-range vision in particular is the benefit of having that kind of long-range vision in the first place, one that transcends electoral and economic cycles. The content of that vision recasts traditional notions about property, ownership, and the agency of residents to transform the communities where they live.

Like most economic development strategies that include housing policy, the UHAB model conceives of property ownership as a stabilizing force for neighborhoods and an asset that will benefit homeowners and communities in the long run. Unlike most such strategies, however, the UHAB model emphasizes the use-value rather than the exchange-value of housing. In other words, it starts from the idea of home as shelter rather than commodity, a home you can afford to live in and that you know you won't be priced out of. The benefits of property ownership need not be exclusively considered in terms of potential future profit for individuals and families. We need strategies to confer the security and benefits of ownership without relying on a perpetual increase in property values that makes so many people vulnerable to eviction, displacement, and poverty. Limited-equity co-ops are one model that does that. Another model that is gaining ground in urban areas is the community land trust, which has its roots in another time of extreme inequality in America's fast-growing cities: the late nineteenth century. The final story in this chapter traces some of the contours of this history in an attempt to demonstrate the kind of equitable, generative citymaking that is made possible when we question accepted categories of what it means to own, rent, subsidize, and tax land and property.

LAND HELD IN TRUST:
HENRY GEORGE AND THE URBAN COMMUNITY LAND TRUST

The real estate economics of New York City have always been extreme. The island geography of Manhattan helped to create the conditions for hyperdensity, pushing buildings up into the sky rather than spreading them out. Certain bold infrastructural investments were made in order to open up land to real estate development, such as the Commissioners' Plan of 1811 that divided Manhattan north of Houston Street into a regular grid of streets and avenues and 25 × 100 foot lots. Others were made in order to assure New York City's dominance over competitor cities like Philadelphia and Boston, such as the Erie Canal, completed in 1825, that allowed New York's port to flourish by connecting it to the country's interior. By the middle of the nineteenth century, Manhattan was the most densely populated city in the world, filled with factories, slaughterhouses, shipping companies, and a powerful banking industry to lend the capital for such industries to grow.

---

[63] Will Fischer, "House Bill's Deep Cuts in Public Policy Would Raise Future Federal Costs and Harm Vulnerable Low-Income Families," September 16, 2011, Center on Budget and Policy Priorities. Accessed August 3, 2016. www.cbpp.org/research/house-bills-deep-cuts-in-public-housing-would-raise-future-federal-costs-and-harm.

[64] In his inaugural address, President Reagan proclaimed, "In this present crisis, government is not the solution to our problem; government is the problem. From time to time we've been tempted to believe that society has become too complex to be managed by self-rule, that government by an elite group is superior to government for, by, and of the people."

These major job creators drove the city's population increase, attracting immigrants from around the world and doubling between 1890 and 1920 from 2,500,000 to 5,000,000 inhabitants. Not designed to accommodate what were then unimaginable and technologically impossible building heights, the layout of the street grid layout coupled with public transit investments, geographic advantages (like the depth of the port), and economic advantages fed the skyward trajectory of building in New York City's center of gravity. These factors also put incredible upward pressure on the price of land, which exerted a dangerous downward pressure on the living standards of the poor.

Intense overcrowding and lack of sanitation led to calls for social reform, resulting in laws and codes that drastically improved the quality of housing in New York. As Richard Plunz argues persuasively in the *History of Housing in New York,* these codes only became enforceable when they created a financial incentive for real estate developers to bundle multiple lots into a single property and thus scale up their operations. The requirements for light and air led to totally inefficient floor plans at the scale of one or two or even three contiguous lots; but assembling four units allowed developers to meet the new codes while also increasing density in housing and profiting from more units. Again, as has often been the case in New York City, change is swiftest when coupled with the promise of profit.

Today, the interests of large capital are better served by developing real estate for the wealthy or the upwardly mobile. Since the city began its rebound during the Koch administration, when the American economy was already rapidly deindustrializing, the prevailing consensus among policymakers has been that residential real estate is the surest way for the city's economic growth to continue. Despite some recent boutique attempts at the margins, the major base of manufacturing that once employed hundreds of thousands of New Yorkers is no longer expected to return, so New York must continue to attract young people with college degrees and the assets to choose where to live and what to do for work. Attempts to diversify the economy away from a top-heavy reliance on the finance industry have served to expand those sectors, like tech and biotech, that require high educational attainment. Nationwide, the costs of getting that degree are skyrocketing. According

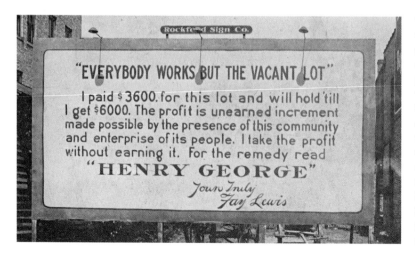

"Everybody works but the vacant lot" was a public awareness campaign initiated by a follower of Henry George. The photograph became a postcard, which was collected in a scrapbook of photographs, caricatures, and newspaper articles from the last third of the nineteenth century about the American economic reformer. Archived in the Single Tax: Scrapbook with Photographs collection of the New York Public Library, the provenance of the scrapbook content is unclear.

to the US Census, just thirty-five percent of New Yorkers over the age of twenty-five have a college degree. When New York City had a strong manufacturing sector, securing middle class comforts — job security, vacation, pension, at least a plausible chance of homeownership — with just a high school degree was within reach. Today, the only jobs available to the majority of adult New Yorkers who do not have a college degree are in shift work in the service industry, whether retail, food service, home health care, or other temporary and insecure forms of employment.

A quarter of New Yorkers live on $25,000 or less a year. Median rent between 2010 and 2014 was $1,234 per month. Two-thirds of New York City's households rent, and according to the Furman Center, a housing and urban policy think tank at NYU, about half of those, over one million households, are "rent-burdened," which means they are paying more than a third of their income in rent. Six hundred thousand are "extremely rent-burdened," spending more than 50 percent of their income on rent. The Furman Center's 2014 report puts these figures in context. In the year 2000, "a rookie firefighter married to a substitute teacher with one child could have afforded more than 70% of available housing units." Between 2007 and 2012, "that same family saw this pool shrink to less than half."[65] And, of course, it's not just modestly paid public sector employees who are feeling the squeeze. The city's chronically homeless population has almost doubled since 2006 to more than 60,000 individuals,[66] and even that high figure disguises the full scope of the problem, with tens of thousands of marginally housed individuals and families who might not yet be completely dependent on the shelter system nonetheless facing eviction and the constant threat of homelessness.

Mayor de Blasio rode to victory in the mayoral race in large part due to the centrality of housing affordability to his platform. Soon after taking office he announced a plan to build or preserve over 200,000 units of affordable housing. He has enacted measures to extract greater concessions of affordable units from real estate developers and sought to maintain tax abatement and limited-equity schemes that would otherwise have expired during his tenure. Whether or not his ambitious goals will decrease the extreme inequality that presides over New York City's housing market remains to be seen.

The media focuses on the "build" part of de Blasio's plan, but the "preserve" part bears some explanation and scrutiny. Many of the ways that governments have mandated affordability in previous eras has been through legal structures with a time limit. Part of the reason the supply of affordable units contracted so sharply since 2000 is the expiration of agreements put in place several decades prior. In our conversation, Andrew Reicher referred to the Mitchell-Lama Housing Program,

---

[65] Furman Center for Real Estate and Urban Policy, "The Cost of Renting in New York City," 2014, NYU Furman Center / Capital One Affordable Rental Housing Landscape. Accessed August 5, 2016. www.furmancenter.org/NYCRentalLandscape.

[66] The Coalition for the Homeless "Facts About Homelessness." Accessed August 5, 2016. www.coalitionforthehomeless.org/the-catastrophe-of-homelessness/facts-about-homelessness.

established in 1955 to create affordable housing for middle-income residents. In exchange for low-interest mortgage loans and property tax exemptions, the Mitchell-Lama Law limited how much profit could be earned from selling a co-op unit and required income-restrictions on incoming tenants, all to be supervised by the New York State Division of Housing and Community Renewal. A fixed number of years (usually twenty or thirty-five) after the mortgage is paid, developments have the option to withdraw from the program, at which point residents can sell their units on the open market at prices the market will bear. Withdrawal from the program is invariably contentious, pitting residents against one another. Charles Chawalko, a young urbanist who grew up in a Mitchell-Lama co-op in Lower Manhattan, reported for *Urban Omnibus* on the internal campaigns within his building in favor of and against privatizing the development. Many within the buildings' elected resident leadership believed that the removal of government oversight and the infusion of cash from a certain number of open market co-op sales per year would keep the complex affordable for existing residents while allowing them the freedom of capitalizing on their shares in a building in what had become a highly desirable neighborhood. Others felt that leaving the Mitchell-Lama program would turn long-term residents with lower incomes who wanted to stay in their homes into rent-burdened tenants or force them out. Outside of the internal politics of the debate, housing advocates worried about the net effect of losing so many affordable homes in an already stressed and unequal housing market. Over the years, 271 properties containing 139,428 apartments for middle-income families were developed in New York City through Mitchell-Lama. As of November 2013, only seventy-eight developments, containing 32,900 units, remained in the program. The rest have chosen to opt out.

When we spoke, Reicher reflected on this history with anguish: "We put an enormous amount of public money into the Mitchell-Lama Housing Program for middle-income rentals and co-operative ownership — property for which the land was already assembled, paid for, financed, tax-abated, subsidized, and re-subsidized by the taxpayers — just to watch it all walk out the door when there was a real estate boom." Strategies to foster economic diversity in cities, to ensure that the lower paid workers (including service industry workers as well as teachers, nurses, firefighters, or secretaries) are able to live within reach of the jobs on which the economy and public safety rely, cannot depend exclusively on individuals electing to forego personal profit. The mythology and economic system of the United States' rely on the notion that property entails a right to profit (perhaps even more than it enables a right to participate in collaborative, co-operative attempts at community). The political encouragement towards exploiting capital for profit often leads to the exploitation of people. Incentives, income caps, and other regulatory attempts to maintain an economically diverse community within an urban housing market do nothing to challenge the basic fact that a system of individualized private property structurally promotes speculation and exploitation.

The great social theorist and political economist Henry George pointed out this basic fact in 1879. *Progress and Poverty,* his most famous book, argues that our inherited ideas about private property always lead to the impoverishment of those who do not own any. If we continue to think of land as capital and do not distinguish between finite natural resources and the infinite combinations of labor and capital improvement (such as building, technology, and other human-made things with an exchange value), then the inequality between landlords and renters will always increase. George was not a follower of Karl Marx; he believed in the power of private capital in a competitive market to improve mankind through investments in technology that would lead to greater productivity and profits and higher wages. But to George, landlords are "parasites feeding off the productivity of others. Whenever there is economic progress . . . landowners simply raise their rents or the selling price of their real estate holdings. This constitutes, in George's words, 'an invisible tax on enterprise,' collected by those who contribute nothing themselves to increased productivity. Landlordism is a bane for capital and labor alike."[67] Classical economics has always treated efficiency and equity as incompatible goals, conceding that policies to encourage capital formation will widen inequality while asserting that policies aimed at redistribution will deter economic growth. George used the terms of classical economics — and he used them with fastidious precision — yet he believed fundamentally that "Full recognition of economic rights and responsibilities would reveal the goals of equity and efficiency to be mutually reinforcing."

George claims to have begun *Progress and Poverty* in the late 1870s with a research question but no hypothesis. The unprecedented technological progress he witnessed greatly impressed him, yet his travels presented a paradox: Why was poverty so much more abject in developed, industrialized New York than in California's frontier lands? He was baffled by what he called "the great enigma of our times." Why hadn't the enormous "increase in productivity banished want and starvation from civilized countries, and lifted the working classes from poverty to prosperity? Instead, George saw that the division of labor, the widening of markets, and rapid urbanization had increased the dependence of the working poor upon forces beyond their control."[68]

His study concludes that the path to break the pattern of "the increase of want with the increase of wealth" is to implement a single tax on land values that would assess any increased value produced by the land and apply that sum to pay for government services, thus returning the value gained from the productivity of the community back to the community. "Land-value levies should replace all other taxation," he argues, "leaving labor and capital to flourish freely, and thus ending unemployment, poverty, inflation and inequality."[69]

---

[67] John Emmeus Davis, "Origins and Evolution of the Community Land Trust in the United States," 2014, adapted from a 2010 essay published in *The Community Land Trust* Reader, published by the Lincoln Institute of Land Policy, 2010. Accessed August 7, 2016. www.berkshirecommunitylandtrust.org/wp-content/uploads/2015/02/Origins-Evolution-CLT-byJohnDavis.pdf.

[68] Kris Feder, "Progress and Poverty Today," an introduction to *Progress and Poverty,* by Henry George, Abridged edition, (New York: Robert Schalkenbach Foundation, 1998, originally published 1879).

[69] "Why Henry George had a point." *The Economist,* April 1, 2015. Accessed August 8, 2016. www.economist.com/blogs/freeexchange/2015/04/land-value-tax.

The supply and location of land are fixed yet land's exchange value is created through the labor of communities and investment in public goods, which have no natural limit. The price difference that arises is called *economic rent,* precisely defined as the difference between the actual payment made to the owner for a factor of production (such as land, labor, or capital) and the payment level expected by the owner, due to its exclusivity or scarcity. Put more simply, economic rent can be thought of as the premium paid for location, which incorporates the economic value of its access to infrastructure and the social value of its desirability based on countless intangible factors. Location, location, location.

Therefore, George's proposal was to tax only the difference in value between a developed piece of property in an open market and the value of the land it sits on were it an empty, unimproved lot. Here's a hypothetical example. Imagine a vacant lot in, say, the Bedford-Stuyvesant section of Brooklyn. A developer buys this lot for $100,000 at a time when the neighborhood is just beginning to emerge from decades of strategic neglect and chronic disinvestment. When she buys it, the nearby schools are in a state of crisis and there's no hospital nearby. Within a decade, the school improves, a hospital opens, and the nearby retail begins to gentrify in line with the demands of incoming groups of residents with more disposable income than the neighborhood's traditional inhabitants. Her lot, without any capital improvements is now worth $500,000. She decides it is time to develop the property, so she builds a building of three condominiums at a cost of another $500,000. She now markets the three properties for a combined price of $1,500,000. This price reflects its market value, or the willingness of potential homebuyers to pay. Willingness to pay comprises perceived value, which accounts for the location's public infrastructure, social infrastructure, commercial amenities etc., none of which was the result of a capital investment of the landowner and is therefore a windfall. George is not arguing that she shouldn't be able to profit from her capital investment of $600,000 (land plus development); he is arguing that the $900,000 windfall is what should be taxed, rather than the property on the whole or her income.

In the pithy prose of *The Economist,* a proud exponent of laissez-faire economic liberalism, "Land prices mainly reflect location: farmers may till the soil, or drain it, but most increases in land's value comes from the activity of other people. Nobody builds skyscrapers or shopping malls in the wilderness. Landowners, in other words, enjoy unearned income from the benefits bestowed by good transport links, and proximity to customers, suppliers and other businesses. Once they have bought their land, they keep this money." Writing for a publication that reveres the 18th century political economist Adam Smith and respects the ideas of the 20th century American economist Milton Friedman, the author justifies his admiring review of George's ideas with quotes from conservative bona fides. Of the land value tax, "Adam Smith said 'nothing could be more reasonable'; Milton Friedman termed it 'the least bad tax.' Winston Churchill said scornfully that a landlord 'contributes nothing to the process from which his own enrichment is derived.'"[70] Most taxes induce firms to move economic activity overseas or find other loop-holes. You can't offshore land. You can't increase or reduce its supply. Under

George's land-value tax system, if public and private investments improve the value of land, "the benefit comes back to the community in the form of higher tax receipts, rather than ending up as a windfall in the pockets of the owners. Taxing the unearned income that landowners enjoy should curb the boom and bust cycle in land prices." It would also create incentives that limit suburban sprawl, encouraging developers to build more densely and governments to build the kinds of infrastructure that reduce the carbon footprints of urban populations. Therefore, capturing value from economic rent is the most logical source of public revenue. Untaxed economic rent only privileges the landowner at the expense of society at-large.

Progress and Poverty sold 3,000,000 copies as Henry George traveled the world giving rousing speeches about his "single tax" plan. In the 1890s, it was the second bestselling book in the nation after the Bible. He ran two unsuccessful campaigns to be mayor of New York City. His influence as a world-famous public intellectual helped to stimulate a wide range of Progressive Era reforms worldwide, including controls on monopoly, regulation of utilities (especially railroads), and scaling back protectionist tariffs and other obstacles to free trade. George had ardent followers around the world, including Leo Tolstoy and Sun Yat-sen, who organized a wide range of efforts to promote his ideas. One of his devotees, Elizabeth Magie, invented a board game in 1903 to educate people about the benefits of the land value tax, the dangers of untaxed economic rent, and the land barons who profit unjustly from the labor and investments of the public. It was called the Landlord's Game; the board was divided into blocks representing properties' specific purchase price and rental values. New York City's Broadway, Fifth Avenue, and Wall Street were the top properties in purchase price and rent. Acquiring properties, developing them with buildings and hotels, charging rents, and forcing opponents into bankruptcy was intended to demonstrate the benefits of an economic system that rewards evenly distributed wealth creation and the social costs of an economic system in which a landed aristocracy has a monopoly on wealth. Magie's patent was acquired by Parker Brothers in 1935 and renamed Monopoly.

I find it almost impossible to imagine a public intellectual, much less a tax theorist, inspiring so much devotion today. One hundred thousand people attended George's funeral in New York in 1897. And thousands more waited in line to hear him eulogized in Chicago and elsewhere. His ideas inspired reading groups that evolved into philanthropic foundations and intentional communities that sought to put his ideas into practice at the local scale.

George was not necessarily calling for public ownership of urban land, yet attempting to realize aspects of his vision required pooling property in a shared-ownership model. Groups of admirers started "single-tax" communities including Fairhope, Alabama and Arden, Delaware, both of which still exist today with ninety-nine—year ground leases and a single-tax paid to an overseeing corporation that covers all state, county, and local taxes. In England, Ebenezer Howard used George's

---

[70] *The Economist,* April 1, 2015.

critique to structure the economic model for his garden cities movement. In Howard's utopian scheme, planned communities of 32,000 inhabitants would form a suburban ring around metropolitan regions and the land would be leased to a municipal corporation with an interest in public improvement not speculative profit. Over thirty garden cities were developed using this model, starting with Letchworth in 1903 and Welwyn in 1920.

Georgist scholar Ralph Borsodi was the first to describe leased-land communities as "land trusts." In 1936, he founded the first such community, School of Living, in Suffern, New York, which became a model for the further development of this type of intentional community. These developments included Bryn Gweled, founded by Quakers in Pennsylvania in 1940; Celo, North Carolina; and Norris, Tennessee, a planned community for workers developed by the Tennessee Valley Authority. For the most part, these were all rural or suburban communities, set apart from the urban inequality that first motivated George's research and advocacy. Nonetheless, the evolution of those intentional communities provides a prehistory to one of the few long-term solutions to the urban housing affordability crisis that have recently been gaining traction.

Community Land Trusts (CLTs) are a model of land tenure that decouples the basic components of private property. Simply stated, a CLT separates the ownership of property from the ownership of the land on which that property is built. In effect, organized citizens remove land from the private, speculative market where its value is difficult to control. The land is owned in common by the CLT, a legal entity chartered to own land in perpetuity while protecting its residents' use rights through long-term leases that can be bought and sold.

CLTs have emerged from a diversity of precedents. Henry George's ideas definitely provided inspiration, as did ancient ideas about the Commons as well as twentieth-century reform projects like the *Gramdan* movement in India[71] (which Borsodi studied in depth) or the kibbutz movement in Israel.

In 1968 Robert Swann, who cofounded the first official CLT, New Communities, traveled with a group of delegates, including some from the National Sharecroppers Fund, to visit cooperative kibbutz and moshav settlements in Israel, which were made possible by long-term leases of land owned by the Jewish National Fund (JNF), a non-profit that owns 13 percent of the total land in Israel and was directly inspired by Henry George's writing.[72] CLT advocates saw the agriculturally based *kibbutzim* and *moshavim* to be models for land reform in the rural south where black farmers faced discrimination and landlessness. (The JNF charter specifies reclamation of land for the Jewish people as its primary purpose, which has led to claims of discrimination against Palestinians as well as actively promoting Israeli settlement in occupied territories.)

New Communities managed to purchase 5,000 acres of land in Georgia in 1970, the largest single tract of land owned by African-Americans at the time. The experiment did not succeed, in part due to discriminatory lending practices that made the debt owed on the purchase price of the land financially unfeasible for the corporation.[73] But the bold vision of economically independent black farmers inspired communities of color to apply its principles in a wide variety of contexts. In 1972, Swann published a book that defined a movement, *The Community Land Trust: A Guide to the New Model for Land Tenure in America,* which surveyed the previous models of community ownership in the United States and proposed some new operational elements. The book helped to move the discussion of these projects from rural predecessors composed primarily of homogenous groups of self-selecting people (often former hippies creating a legally recognized version of a commune) towards the integrated, open models of the urban CLTs that were yet to come. Between 1968 and 1978, most of the CLTs formed "were organized on behalf of small groups of like-minded people. These homesteaders moved onto land that was leased from a nonprofit corporation in order to live in communities with others who shared their social or political values. Although they called themselves 'community land trusts,' they were closer to being intentional communities — or, as Swann later called them, 'enclaves.'"

Within a decade, however, Swann's inclusive vision of open membership in an urban context with pre-existing buildings came to pass. The first urban CLT was in a predominantly African-American neighborhood on the west side of Cincinnati, Ohio. Like its predecessors, it "served a population that had been excluded from the economic and political mainstream. It was a product of grassroots organizing and a vehicle for community empowerment." The goal was to prevent displacement in a neighborhood that had seen successive waves of disruption from urban renewal programs and the kind of negligent absentee landlordism that challenged so many urban communities of color in the 1970s.

Over the course of the 1980s, similar projects were started in Syracuse, New York and an ambitious city-scale CLT in Burlington, Vermont, set in motion by then-mayor Bernie Sanders, followed by CLTs in Durham, North Carolina; Youngstown, Ohio; Albany and Schenectady, New York; Worcester, Massachusetts; and Washington, DC. One of the most cited examples took place in a multi-racial community in Boston, Massachusetts that had suffered years of displacement and neglect. The Dudley Street Neighborhood Initiative "was typical of many of the urban CLTs founded in the 1980s and early 1990s in espousing a dual commitment to community empowerment and community development. Its service area was a single, well-defined neighborhood having an historic sociopolitical identity. Its impetus came from the neighborhood's opposition to a top-down plan for the redevelopment of Roxbury that had been put forward by the City of Boston and local foundations."[74]

---

[71] The *Gramdan* (which translates to "village-gift") movement was a program of voluntary land reform in which landowners would donate privately held lands to landless villagers. It grew out of the *Bhoodan* (or land-gift) movement, in which landowners would donate land directly to individuals, but when it was observed that these small parcels soon fell into the hands of moneylenders and speculators, the strategy was adjusted such that the land would be released to village councils who would hold it in trust and leased in plots to individual villagers.

[72] Davis, "Origins and Evolution of the Community Land Trust in the United States," 2014, 12.

[73] While many argued that New Communities failed because of the sheer amount of land it sought to bring into the CLT, the USDA admitted in 1997 that its racially discriminatory lending practices contributed to the financial unfeasibility of the entire enterprise.

[74] Davis, "Origins and Evolution of the Community Land Trust in the United States," 2014, 39.

In an article on *Urban Omnibus,* Oksana Miranova traces aspects of this history and explores its growing influence in New York City, documenting two local projects that have adapted the CLT model in Manhattan's Cooper Square and East Harlem neighborhoods. The former has its roots in "a community organizing effort against a 1959 urban renewal project initiated by Robert Moses, which would have demolished 11 blocks on the Lower East Side between the Bowery and 2nd Avenue."[75]

This effort evolved into the Cooper Square Committee, a service provider for the low-income, renter population threatened by the same kinds of fires, property neglect, and abandonment that were afflicting many other poor areas of the city at the time. The group was aware of the experimental policies (including those pioneered by UHAB discussed earlier in this chapter) that would enable tenants to convert their buildings into limited-equity cooperatives, but they also recognized that the affordability restrictions of these programs only lasted fifteen to twenty years on average. In the surrounding context of the East Village — already a choice destination for striving artists subsequently made legendary by pop cultural representations such as the musical *Rent* — the Cooper Square Committee realized that real estate speculation would continue to put pressure on affordability in ways that would make an exclusive focus on limited-equity co-ops a temporary solution.

CLTs and limited-equity co-ops are cousins. They are both examples of "the shared equity category of tenure, which operates in a zone between homeownership and renting . . . [to] ensure property affordability through sale-restriction mechanisms."[76] One key difference is that CLTs are designed to function in perpetuity, through "a dual ownership model . . . where the owner of the land is a nonprofit, community-based corporation, committed to acquiring multiple parcels of land throughout a targeted geographic area with the intention of retaining ownership of these parcels forever."[77] Miranova clarifies the diversity of types that an urban CLT can accommodate, including "single-family homes, rental buildings, condos, co-ops, and mixed-use structures with commercial or office spaces. CLTs lease land to property owners through long-term ground leases, which typically run for ninety-nine years. The sale of property on CLT land is governed by a resale formula outlined in the ground lease, which usually gives the CLT the first right of purchase. When the CLT resells the property, for a below-market price to a buyer who meets agreed-upon income-eligibility requirements, the deed to the building is conveyed to a new owner. The deed to the land remains with the CLT."[78]

In recent years, interest in community land trusts has increased significantly. These days, of course, the motivating factor is most often protecting against displacement by gentrification. According to Miranova, "The CLT model's flexibility and adaptability to local conditions make it an appealing solution to a range of problems affecting communities across the country including disinvestment, gentrification and displacement, foreclosure, loss of affordability due to expiring public subsidy, housing discrimination, and decreasing social capital." A more recent example can be found in East Harlem, a traditionally Latino neighborhood (known colloquially as El Barrio), with a high concentration of vacant lots, buildings with subsidies for affordable units about to expire, and gentrification pressure. The project concentrates on City-owned properties, which are much easier to dispose into a CLT program than private property. Land acquisition remains the greatest obstacle to scaling up this strategy of ensuring permanent affordability. Miranova ends her article with the reminder that the model becomes "more palatable when [CLTs] offer the landowners or co-op shareholders something in return for transferring control over the land to the broader community (however it may be defined), beyond the knowledge that their property will serve as a resource to future generations of low- and moderate-income New Yorkers." For properties in distress — financial or physical or both — that something in return might be a reprieve from foreclosure or unaffordable repairs. Seizing this opportunity requires political will and strong leadership. In order to take the model to scale, mayoral administrations "have to make a significant financial and political commitment to the idea. The administration's involvement is necessary for any group that may want to unravel the complex debt burdens carried by rental buildings affected by predatory equity or find a way to transfer privately held land into a CLT."

This is where ambitious citymaking comes into play. Architects and designers have not traditionally concerned themselves with the intricacies of land tenure. Policymakers have not traditionally taken stock of the local specificities of land prices and the ways that the desirability of particular neighborhoods — for which the types of units and buildings available are key factors, along with proximity to schools, transit, and commercial amenities — feeds into the crisis of affordability. Both groups of professionals must apply their skills and talent to ensuring a diverse, affordable, and sustainable housing supply. As Henry George articulated long ago, location is what leads to the distortions of economic rent. Unpacking and articulating the complex cultural values that are embedded in the locational choices to move to or to remain in a certain territory is the shared duty of a diverse host of citymakers with expertise in design, policymaking, and, crucially, the creative representation of common cause.

There are many other choices and complex dynamics that we must work hard to understand. The continuous evolution of what we expect from where we live requires vigilant study and a mix of subtle tweaks and bold new models. To be nimble requires not only flexibility but also a sure footing. Counterintuitively, the steadiest stance in urbanism is to allow for a measure of incompleteness, to plan for an uncertain future by acknowledging that change is constant and incremental. Throughout, we must be steadfast in our ethics, never losing sight of why creating responsive, generative housing environments for all citizens is our collective responsibility.

---

[75] Oksana Miranova, "How Community Land Trusts Maintain Housing Affordability," *Urban Omnibus*, April 29, 2014.

[76] Ibid.

[77] John Davis, "Shared Equity Homeownership," National Housing Institute (2006). Accessed August 9, 2016. www.nhi.org/pdf/SharedEquityHome.pdf.

[78] Miranova, "How Community Land Trusts Maintain Housing Affordability," 2014.

CONCLUSION

THE ETHIC
OF CITYMAKING

Cities are huge right now.

Since cities are so huge right now — so popular as places to live, problems to study, and backdrops to pop cultural narratives — then how can we use their energy, vitality, and appeal to realize cities' enormous potential to be the testing grounds for solutions to broad, global challenges? The stories I have related in this book are an attempt to offer a range of precedents, drawn from the intellectual history of urbanism and from the practical examples of innovative, interdisciplinary urban projects tried and tested in New York City in the years since the financial emergency of 2008.

In the United States, this period of time will be remembered first as the years of the Obama presidency, which began in the midst of the worst financial crisis since the Great Depression eighty years prior. The crash provoked and revealed a deep distrust of the institutional stewards of our economy and security at the end of a decade of profound and repeated government failures, like the Iraq War and Hurricane Katrina. Many Americans took Barack Obama's historic election to signify a "post-racial" turn in American politics. Yet what we saw instead was a sharpening of divisions between race and class, heightened awareness of multiple kinds of inequality that have intensified not only partisan discord among elected officials but also tribalism and nativism among the electorate itself. Depending on whom you talked to during this unsettling time, the focus of disquiet could variously be described as the impact of neoliberal policies on income and wealth inequality (especially trade policy and its effect on the wages and job security of the working class), systemic racism throughout the criminal justice system, the size and accountability of the federal government, or the notion that recent immigrants were somehow disproportionately to blame for the economy or crime. The reasons varied, but few would disagree that the last few years have seen a decrease in citizens' faith in government at all scales — an all-time low of 19 percent in 2015 according to one study, compared to a high of 77 percent in 1964.[1] The last few years have also been marked by an increase in the visibility of mutual mistrust between different socioeconomic, ethnic, and racial groups. The notion, propagated by the political right, that liberal "government" is geared toward economic redistribution that privileges undeserving people of color at the expense of the white working class fueled an alarming conclusion to the Obama presidency, the aftershocks of which will be felt around the world for a very long time. Many analyses agree that severe economic pain in formerly industrial inland economies found its voice in a definitive and reactionary rejection of a brand of politics largely associated with cosmopolitan, coastal elites. In this formation, *cosmopolitanism* has come to be seen as synonymous with the institutions of global finance and the service economies that surround them.

We must actively resist this conflation so that the inherent mixture that cities represent — of people, ideas, and ideals — becomes an aspirational model for social solidarity that extends well beyond the geographic limits of our urban and metropolitan areas. One of the many reasons that I love cities so passionately is because I have always believed that the politics of the city can transcend the politics of the tribe. The defining characteristic of cities, for me, is the forced proximity and interaction with people unlike oneself. Every day, I wander down any street in New York, or crowd myself into the subway, or get in an elevator in an office building, and I am confronted with a spectacular diversity of human beings with life experiences that are unknown to me yet to whom I have no choice but to relate. Even in cities that are not as multi-racial or multi-ethnic as New York — say Tokyo, or Cairo — the range of jobs, lifestyles, places of origin, dialects, and opinions can be staggeringly diverse. The culture of cities has the capacity to be a culture of tolerance and empathy. Citymaking must support the realization of that capacity by design.

I believe that the cultural diversity of the United States is its greatest asset and the true source of its exceptionalism. To realize this promise, our cities must continue to be the testing grounds for celebrating and managing diversity, creating economic opportunity, and pushing the boundaries of what citizens and governments expect from one another and ask of themselves.

Of course, cities also concentrate the extreme inequalities. New York City increasingly seems like a club for the super-rich that also happens to warehouse the extremely poor, with less and less room and less and less time for everyone in between. National policy has fed into this phenomenon, especially with regard to the globalization and financialization of our economy. Municipal policy has compounded the problem by prioritizing high-end residential and megaproject development at the expense of other land uses in pursuit of the highest short-term returns and property tax revenues. Cities, especially New York, have traditionally been the points of arrival for migrants from around the world and around the country. The urban entrepôt has more often than not acted as a salve for inter-ethnic tensions. Of course there are tragic flare-ups of violence, and New York has seen its fair share, such as in Crown Heights, Brooklyn in 1991, when racial tensions erupted between Brooklyn's Afro-Caribbean and Hasidic Jewish communities. I discussed this phenomenon with the writer Suketu Mehta as we wandered around Jackson Heights, a predominantly South Asian and increasingly Latin American neighborhood to which he moved with his family as a twelve-year-old from Mumbai:

> Here are people — Indians and Pakistanis, Bangladeshis, Russians, Greeks, Poles, Turks, Irish — many of whom were killing each other just before they got on the plane. And here they are living next to each other . . . [with] this agreement that we were in a new country, making a new life. And we could live side by side and interact in certain demarcated ways. We could exchange food; our kids could play together; they could go to school together. It's the great story of New York. It's pretty remarkable how little strife there is.[2]

[1] Pew Research Center, "Public Trust in Government: 1958-2015." Accessed November 16, 2016. www.people-press.org/2015/11/23/public-trust-in-government-1958-2015/.

[2] "A Walk Through Jackson Heights," *Urban Omnibus,* February 6, 2011.

Today, international immigrants are increasingly foregoing the city for a direct line to the suburbs, where cheaper property accelerates the creation of single-ethnicity enclaves. According to Doug Saunders in *Arrival City,* his excellent study of contemporary migration, 2005 was the first year that more immigrants lived in the suburbs than within city limits in the United States, a trend he attributes, in part, to "the gentrification of urban-core neighborhoods, which turned the inner suburbs into the last low-rent enclave."[3] This pattern coincided with suburban poverty rates overtaking urban poverty rates for the first time, in both numbers as well as percentages of the nation's poor.[4]

To be sure, New York City is not losing its status as a city of immigrants; 48 percent of Queens residents are foreign-born, with 25 percent hailing from Asia. And immigration has largely fueled the rapid population growth in the Bronx, which for the first time in 2016 surpassed its historic peak of 1.4 million inhabitants in 1970, before a decade when one in five residents moved out, primarily to escape staggering rates of crime, arson, and disinvestment.[5] Nonetheless, the middle class and working class communities that have traditionally populated most neighborhoods within city limits, regardless of nativity, are shrinking. This trend is true almost everywhere in American cities, as the gap between rich and poor grows ever wider. In New York City between 2000 and the end of 2014, the middle class decreased by 14 percent. The black middle class experienced an even more dramatic decrease at 19 percent, indicating the likelihood that in neighborhoods such as Woodlawn, Hollis, Jamaica, and East Flatbush black middle class homeowners "had largely been replaced by lower-income black families and singles who can only afford to rent their homes."[6] (The black population citywide declined by five percent during this period. Significantly, the middle class, regardless of race, did not shrink in the New York-Newark-Jersey City metropolitan area, relative to other metropolitan areas).[7] Wealthy white people are the fastest growing demographic group in New York City, though the largest single demographic group is the low-income Latino population.[8]

In the previous chapter, I wrote about how some of these demographic and socioeconomic trends, especially the widening of income and wealth inequality, affect and are reflected in the housing market. They influence much more than that. Concern about growing inequality has motivated citymaking projects within all of the broad categories discussed in this book: public space, infrastructure, information technology, and housing. Across all these areas of practical urbanism, the deterioration of social solidarity diminishes the prospects of principles like the stewardship of the commons, the appreciation of the multiple functions of infrastructural public goods, the legibility of complex urban processes, and the openness and adaptability of systems of shelter. Our cities have the potential to nurture rather than reduce that solidarity, but they have yet to deliver on that promise.

When considering the other major existential threat of our time, climate change, the legacy of bad twentieth-century planning exacerbates these inequalities even more disastrously. In the context of a warming planet with rising sea levels and stronger, more frequent storms, the concentration of low-rent and public housing within flood plains greatly distorts the impacts of storms by disproportionately affecting low-income people of color. Unequal access to infrastructure of all kinds — transit, education, information technology, affordable housing, and so on — extends the high cost of poverty across generations in many communities and intensifies the damage unevenly when disasters strike. The hard work of creating common cause across the lines that ever more starkly divide society into groups is not only worth pursuing in the name of social solidarity for its own sake. This work is also vital to our collective ability to respond to disasters and to reduce our reliance on carbon in a last-chance effort to mitigate the terrifying prospects of a world with temperatures two degrees Celsius above pre-industrial levels.[9]

In the aftermath of Superstorm Sandy, Red Hook, Brooklyn became an example for the whole region of what was possible when social solidarity in a socio-economically divided community is put into action. As I described in Chapter Four, the community demonstrated a "capacity for unprecedented cooperation and action. Red Hook residents, community-based organizations, businesses, and regional partners rallied in response, piecing together an essential system of distribution and support with limited resources." At the same time, the proximity and juxtaposition of diverse challenges and populations can foster the kind of systems-level, interdisciplinary thinking that we need to be able to link global issues like climate change to everyday struggles facing poor communities. The causes and the effects of climate change are so planetary in scope that it's easy to despair that individual action is futile, whereas activism for social justice at the local scale is more likely to see immediate results, whether those results are successes, failures, or compromises.

---

[3] Doug Saunders, *Arrival City: How the Largest Migration in History is Reshaping the World,* (New York: Vintage, 2011), 96.

[4] Confronting Suburban Poverty in America. "What is Suburban Poverty?" Accessed November 4, 2016. www.confrontingsuburbanpoverty.org/.

[5] Sam Roberts, "People Fled the Bronx in the 1970s. Now Its Population is Booming," *The New York Times,* September 10, 2016. Accessed October 15, 2016. http://nyti.ms/2cdek7q.

[6] Megan Malloy, "New York City's Middle Class Is Shrinking." WNYC, accessed December 4, 2015. http://www.wnyc.org/story/new-york-citys-middle-class-has-shrunk/.

[7] Quoctrung Bui, "Where the Middle Class Is Shrinking," *The New York Times*, May 12, 2016. Accessed November 1, 2016. www.nytimes.com/interactive/2016/05/13/upshot/falling-middle-class.html.

[8] "Making Neighborhoods: Study Summary and Highlights," Citizens' Housing and Planning Council, November 2014. Accessed October 5, 2016. www.chpcny.org/assets/MakingNeighborhoods_summary.pdf.

[9] Researchers have hypothesized that the worst effects of climate change would be prevented if we keep global temperatures from rising two degrees Celsius above pre-industrial levels. See also *Avoiding Dangerous Climate Change,* edited by Hans Joachim Schellnhuber et al. (Cambridge: Cambridge University Press, 2006).

[10] "Red Hook: NY Rising Community Reconstruction Plan," NY Rising Community Reconstruction Program (March 2014). Accessed September 19, 2016. stormrecovery.ny.gov/sites/default/files/crp/community/documents/redhook_nyrcr_plan_20mb_0.pdf.

In her persuasive polemic *This Changes Everything: Capitalism Versus the Climate,* Naomi Klein makes the case that the manifold ways in which we need to reduce consumption (including an individual's choice of lightbulb, a manufacturer's position in a global supply chain, a real estate developer's construction practices, or government policies to reduce emissions or to foster sustainability and resilience) need not be perceived as the punishing renunciation of convenient efficiencies to which we've grown accustomed. Rather, the hard choices and radical rethinking required present an opportunity to transform our economic system in ways that just might redress the structural inequity that's embedded in our history, society, politics, and environment.[11] In a distinct yet related way, Dayna Cunningham, an expert on the intersection of democratic participation, changing racial dynamics, and sustainability, makes the following argument about the need to harmonize efforts to respond to climate change and to entrenched poverty. "Increasingly," she writes, "ecological debates acknowledge that polarizing social issues are embedded in every policy choice relating to sustainability and resilience. Without significant efforts to address them, measures focused narrowly on carbon reduction or other partial measures of environmental improvement could produce great suffering among poor people and even political instability." She invokes the ideals of deliberative and empathetic democracy espoused by philosopher John Dewey when she questions how and by whom decisions should be made that might productively align environmental concerns at local *and* planetary scales. The immediacy of social justice claims around issues such as joblessness or gun violence or even toxic waste often seems disconnected from the long-range projections of mainstream environmental activism. Therefore, Cunningham calls out examples of "innovative proposals with important ecological breakthroughs for the whole community, not just their own constituents. Importantly, none of the efforts begin under an explicit environmental banner. Their starting point is often livelihoods and endemic challenges of community health. In a very straightforward way, the direct link among livelihoods, health, and ecological stewardship helps establish ownership stakes in 'green' initiatives among a broad swathe of community members."[12]

Urban density itself is associated with reduced energy consumption: when home, work, commerce, and leisure are clustered, car traffic goes down and energy use is more efficient. New Yorkers are proud of having, on average, among the smallest carbon footprints in the US, but the environmental gains of city living are offset by the consumption patterns that go beyond dwelling, whether it's the second homes and travel choices of the wealthy or the inherent carbon intensity of constructing large building projects. According to the sociologist Daniel Aldana Cohen, "including consumption's global carbon footprint and controlling for class and lifestyle make all the difference. When the people clustered are prosperous professionals, the carbon benefits of density can be cancelled out by the emissions their consumption causes."[13] The richer you are, on average, the more you consume, regardless of the neighborhood density of your primary residence: "Money gets spent, and spending in a fossil-fuel-powered economy exacerbates climate change."[14] Nonetheless, as density evangelist Vishaan Chakrabarti reminds us, "City dwellers, regardless of income level, have a lower carbon footprint than their suburban counterparts primarily because they walk and use mass transit for their daily commutes, and because they live and work in smaller quarters that heat and cool one another partly through party-wall construction."[15]

The urgency of the challenges will hopefully inspire shared solutions that cut across diverse places, incomes, points of view, approaches, disciplines, and even goals. Cities, which spatially concentrate both social inequity as well as the local institutional capacities that attempt to address it, must be the proving grounds for solutions that recognize the inextricability of economic and environmental challenges. For this to work, the diversity of urban populations must be marshaled as an opportunity, not just a challenge. All of the principled citymakers mentioned in this book — the volunteer tree planter, the civic hacker, the community activist, the affordable housing developer, the architect, and the artist — are finding small and large ways to foster empathy and deliberation among the full, spectacular diversity of city life.

There are other orders of stimulating diversity that concentrate in cities as well: professional opportunities, leisure activities, speeds and rhythms of daily life, sights, sounds, smells, and sensory inputs of all kinds. I believe responsible and forward-thinking citymaking must seek to enhance the positive experiential qualities of that mix and limit its negative qualities. Again, the task at hand is not only to make cities nice places to live in or visit; it's much more urgent. We need to operationalize cities' inherent ability to utilize diversity — to give diversity a *utility* — in order to address existential threats to our planet and our democracy, namely: climate change, widening inequality, and the crisis of trust between citizens and governments.

In 1900, the year before he was elected president, Theodore Roosevelt articulated the political importance of solidarity in diversity. He defines "fellow-feeling" as "sympathy in the broadest sense," which he considers to be "the most important factor in producing a healthy political and social life. Neither our national nor our local civic life can be what it should be unless it is marked by the fellow-feeling, the mutual kindness, the mutual respect, the sense of common duties and common interests, which arise when men take the trouble to understand one another, and to associate together for a common object." He cites public schools in areas with a

[11] Naomi Klein, *This Changes Everything: Capitalism Versus the Climate* (New York: Simon & Schuster, 2015).

[12] Dayna Cunningham, "Citizenship and Governance for a Five Thousand Pound Life," The Architectural League of New York. Accessed September 15, 2015. archleague.org/2014/01/citizenship-and-governance-for-a-five-thousand-pound-life/

[13] Daniel Aldana Cohen, "Seize the Hamptons," *Jacobin*. Accessed October 5, 2015. www.jacobinmag.com/2014/10/seize-the-hamptons/.

[14] Ibid.

[15] Chakrabarti, *A Country of Cities,* 2013: 81

religiously diverse community as one of the contexts that can create this kind of solidarity: "When in their earliest and most impressionable years Protestants, Catholics, and Jews go to the same schools, learn the same lessons, play the same games, and are forced, in the rough-and-ready democracy of boy life, to take each at his true worth, it is impossible later to make the disciples of one creed persecute those of another."[16] Public schools, however, will only ever reflect the diversity of the communities in which they are located. As ethnic and religious communities as well as communities of homogenous political beliefs continue to self-segregate, we need to continue to identify and nurture the shared values, shared experiences, and shared spaces that are common to diverse lived experiences.

Emphasizing what we have in common, however, must not slip into nostalgia for a unified public sphere of homogenous citizens that never really existed. The politics of the city must accommodate differences between people, not attempt to deliver uniformity and consensus. One of the most cogent articulations of the political possibilities of city life — of the "co-presence" with people unlike oneself that are intrinsic to cities — comes from the work of philosopher Iris Marion Young:

> As an alternative to the ideal of community, I propose an ideal of city life as a vision of social relations affirming group difference. As a normative ideal, city life instantiates social relations of difference without exclusion. Different groups dwell in the city alongside one another, of necessity interacting in city spaces. If city politics is to be democratic and not dominated by the point of view of one group, it must be a politics that takes account of and provides voice for the different groups that dwell together in the city without forming a community.[17]

The complexity of urban dynamics is not something we should attempt to simplify by building urban environments that are too rigidly fit to a singular purpose nor to impose an arbitrary order that meets the needs of the day yet may not provide the kind of flexibility that ever-evolving cities demand. Rather, this complexity is to be recognized, analyzed, interpreted, and acted upon through intentional acts of citymaking that combine deep observation and targeted intervention.

One idea that cuts across the various topics and imperatives addressed in this book is the power of long-range, sustained observation, the crucial importance of looking closely at complex urban dynamics and learning from how they work. The sheer complexity of cities is what requires that analysis, intervention, and creative interpretation to be considered as mutually supporting components of practical urbanism. Citymakers must be able to recognize that complexity — the multiple interactions between demographics, economics, politics, finance, policy, maintenance, and design — but they must not stop there. Recognizing and seeking to learn from that complexity should inspire action, not just understanding. The theorists I have cited in this book — sociologists like Richard Sennett or Saskia Sassen, environmentalists like Aldo Leopold, economists like Elinor Ostrom, legal scholars like Brett Frischmann or Gerald Frug, urban planners like Patrick Geddes, political economists like Henry George — are keen analysts of these complex dynamics.

The practitioners I have discussed, drawn from the pages of *Urban Omnibus* — urban farmers, landscape designers, civil servants, technologists, housing advocates, architects — are acting upon the urban built environment in ways that have a demonstrable and salutary effect on the experience of the city. And the interpreters I have referenced — writers, photographers, scholars, curators — support those interventions with dynamic fieldwork and representation of the textures and patterns of urban life that are often impossible to capture within the methodological rigors of social science, the means-ends rationality of public policy, or the site-specificity of professional architecture and design practice.

Many aspects of practical urbanism that have evolved significantly in recent years with important implications for city life are outside the scope of this book. The ways urbanists regard transportation, in particular, has expanded in many ways. Popular opinion about public transit and other urban alternatives to car travel, such as biking and walking, has undergone a sea change. The drivers of this shift include new urgency regarding sustainability and individual carbon footprints, new awareness of health and the drivers of obesity, and new informational technology tools (some of which I mentioned in Chapter Four) that give individuals more choice, autonomy, and information when using a shared resource. Innovations like Bus Rapid Transit, bikeshare systems, and the scaling up of water-based transit networks have real potential to add to a rich mix of transportation options that are multimodal, sustainable, convenient, and used by all classes of urban society. Certainly, the absence of political will to invest in technologies and infrastructures to make intracontinental train travel a viable competitor to air travel remains a major challenge for the United States, which continues to fall behind other wealthy countries in its development of high-speed rail networks. Nonetheless, in general, urbanists in the transit sector worldwide have made great strides in recent years, both in terms of raising awareness about the intersection between transportation issues, sustainability, and health as well as in actually diminishing the extent to which the urban road system prioritizes car travel above all other uses. The benefits of this shift are not exclusively environmental: increased usage of public systems by citizens across the socio-economic spectrum has the manifold advantage of increasing common cause among diverse citizens, expanding the political community that can agitate for improvements to the transit system, and fostering the positive aspects of the cosmopolitan "co-presence" explored by Iris Marion Young.[18]

---

[16] Theodore Roosevelt, "Fellow-feeling as a political factor," *The Century,* January 1900. 466–471.

[17] Iris Marion Young, "City Life and Difference," *The People, Place, and Space Reader,* edited by Jen Jack Gieseking et al. (New York: Routledge, 2014).

[18] In addition to Young's work, especially *Justice and the Politics of Difference* (Princeton: Princeton University Press, 1990), see also K. Anthony Appiah, *Cosmopolitanism: Ethics in a World of Strangers* (New York: W. W. Norton, 2007) and Ash Amin, *Land of Strangers* (Cambridge UK: Polity Press, 2012).

Another significant development within practical urbanism over the past few years is the new kinds of collaborations that have formed between artistic practice and community development. Projects that fuse artistic practice and urbanism take many forms. Many are rooted in various kinds of public art. Whether it's a commissioned abstract sculpture outside a large office building or a community mural painted collaboratively in a low-income neighborhood, public art has the capacity to provide momentary refuge and inspire critical reflection within the crush of urban daily life. Another mode of increasing relevance emerges when artists turn art in public spaces into potent critiques of the politics of the city and passionate insistence on the right to the city.[19] Remember the story, in Chapter 2, of Corona Plaza, an unlovely stretch of pavement that evolved, through the efforts of a broad coalition of community stakeholders, into a vibrant public space and casual venue for cultural programming. It has also become a platform for political and artistic interventions, such as Tania Bruguera's Immigrant Movement International, which serves "a community space where practical knowledge is merged with creative knowledge through *arte útil* with a holistic approach to education open to all regardless of legal status . . . [and] a lab practicing artivist tactics and new tools for communication in the public sphere to access political dialogue in an effort to transform social affect into political effectiveness."[20] Related trends are also apparent in projects that do not claim political activism as inherent. The sensibility that art projects have a material role to play in urban development has been conscripted into creative placemaking, a growing type of culture-based local economic revitalization that is rooted in the idea that arts and culture are a core component of "comprehensive community planning and development in order to help strengthen the social, physical, and economic fabric of communities."[21] We are now several decades into the awareness that artists have been unwitting catalysts of gentrification and displacement. At the same time, the promised positive effects of a wave of starchitect-designed cultural institutions intended to spur increases in property values around the world, from Bilbao to Shenzen, have been dubious. Creative placemaking seeks to instrumentalize the arts — both their creation and consumption — as a stabilizing force for neighborhoods that can simultaneously recognize and lift up existing cultural assets while spurring local economic activity.

The concrete effects of these kinds of culture-based projects will continue to be debated within both academic and practical urbanism. To me, one of the key contributions that artistic practice can make to comprehensive citymaking has little to do with explicit economic impact. Artists don't exclusively make objects; they create experiences that illuminate existing conditions. The influential modern conceptual artist Marcel Duchamp once said, "the artist of the future will simply point his finger." That future is already here, and citymakers of all stripes must incorporate that potential into urban practice. We need to invest in multiple, overlapping, and varied attempts at making the complexity of urban dynamics intelligible to citizens. An example of an innovative non-profit that puts this principle into practice is the Center for Urban Pedagogy (CUP), which uses art and design to "increase meaningful civic engagement. CUP projects demystify the urban policy and planning issues that impact our communities, so that more individuals can better participate in shaping them." *Urban Omnibus* has covered many of CUP's attempts to break down complex issues, such as the regulations that govern street vendors to perspectives on micro-apartments, into simple, accessible, visual explanations.[22] These tools, which range from pamphlets and posters to videos and other media created with public school students, "are used by organizers and educators all over New York City and beyond to help their constituents better advocate for their own community needs."[23]

Cities are mystifying, so demystification is powerful. We can't positively influence the power dynamics that hold sway over the built environment without broad understanding of how the system works. One of the defining characteristics of *Urban Omnibus* content of which I am most proud is the insistence on the notion that projects that interpret and communicate the city's inner workings are equally valid and important types of urban practice as active interventions through design and policymaking. We wanted our omnibus to present these two categories of critical and practical forms of urbanism as mutually reflective and reinforcing. In order to support attempts to make the practice of stewardship integral to how we think about, design, and invest in public space, we need data-based projects like the Forestry Service's STEW-MAP as well as local capacity-building and educational projects like East New York Farms! In order to appreciate the unseen benefits of investment in multitasking infrastructures, we need evocative imagery like the photos of Steve Duncan as well as architectural prototypes like the design by Kennedy Violich Architecture for the 34th Street Ferry Terminal. In order to realize the benefits of information technology to cities, we need service-year programs like Code for America as well as the kind of service design and cartographic approaches to the criminal justice system that guides the work of a designer like Laura Kurgan. In order to advocate for affordable housing policy and design that

---

[19] The French sociologist Henri Lefebvre is credited with coining the phrase "the right to the city," which David Harvey has summarized as "far more than the individual liberty to access urban resources: it is a right to change ourselves by changing the city. It is, moreover, a common rather than an individual right since this transformation inevitably depends upon the exercise of a collective power to reshape the processes of urbanization. The freedom to make and remake our cities and ourselves is, I want to argue, one of the most precious yet most neglected of our human rights." David Harvey, "The right to the city," *New Left Review,* no. 53, September–October 2008, 23–40.

[20] "Mission Statement," Immigrant Movement International. Accessed October 20, 2016. www.immigrant-movement.us/wordpress/mission-statement/.

[21] "Introduction," Art Place America. Accessed October 10, 2016. www.artplaceamerica.org/about/introduction.

[22] See "What is Zoning?" *Urban Omnibus,* February 19, 2014; Candy Chang, "Making Policy Public: Vendor Power!" *Urban Omnibus,* May 6, 2009; and Chat Travieso, "The Big Squeeze: Illustrating Micro-Unit Housing," *Urban Omnibus,* June 26, 2013.

[23] "Welcome to CUP," Center for Urban Pedagogy. Accessed October 12, 2016. www.welcometocup.org.

recognizes the dynamic nature of demographic change over time, we need the kind of typological analysis that challenges received wisdom practiced by a design firm like Interboro Partners as well as support for generating new architectural paradigms exemplified by non-profits like the Citizens Housing and Planning Council and The Architectural League of New York.

When I started working with Rosalie Genevro and Varick Shute on the idea that would become *Urban Omnibus* in 2008, the goal was to develop a new kind of showcase for innovative ideas for the future of cities. None of us knew the shape this project would take. Indeed, none of us could have predicted what New York City (or the United States) would look like in 2017. What we did know was that sophisticated discussion of urban issues suffered from a series of gaps. The diversity and quantity of creative approaches to the urban landscape — how to shape it and how to interpret it — was only growing. But media coverage of these projects and perspectives didn't manage to bust out from silos of professional expertise or even to communicate across neighborhoods. News was becoming hyperlocal while professional trends were increasingly discussed in international, disciplinary echo chambers. Place-based, metropolitan-scale independent media about applied, interdisciplinary urbanism was nowhere to be found. Urbanists in the South Bronx weren't reading about fresh community development ideas generated in East New York; architectural proposals generated in graduate schools in Clinton Hill, Brooklyn or Greenwich Village, Manhattan weren't accessible to a public eager for new ideas; important resonances between ecological initiatives, neighborhood-based advocacy, and novel technological possibilities risked going unnoticed. So we endeavored to bring the full range of this urban thinking and practice under one big tent: an omnibus of urban projects and perspectives conceived in the public interest and executed across disciplines.

By the time we launched *Urban Omnibus* in January of 2009, we had just inaugurated a new president, and real hope existed that urban issues — including infrastructure investment, stable and affordable housing, and disaster preparedness — would become priorities of federal policy making. We wanted to connect some dots and to hear directly from practitioners. Most of all, we wanted to demonstrate that interpreting the existing city goes hand in hand with showcasing exemplary real-world projects that seek to improve it.

For cities and all complex environments, interpretation cannot be divorced from intervention. For practical urbanism to contribute meaningfully toward creating a more sustainable, equitable, and emancipatory urban experience, we must recognize the complexity of urban dynamics but not allow ourselves to become paralyzed by that complexity. As the stories related in this book have I hope made clear, the most valuable ways to practice responsible citymaking are not to resort to imposing order on the cacophony of urban life as planners, designers, and policymakers have tried, in a variety of ways, for much of the past century. Nor is the best way forward to critique and decry all forms of institutionalized power and technocratic expertise. The power of synthesizing interpretation and intervention is to balance the strengths of top-down design, planning, and policy with bottom-up advocacy and resistance rooted in understanding, in *experiencing,* the facts on the ground. We must conceptualize practical urbanism to include the kind of long-range deep observation that can empower citymakers to recognize assets embedded within the complexity of contemporary cities. And we must utilize the appreciation of that complexity as a point of departure for informed interventions. The single most important lesson that I have personally learned from six years of editing *Urban Omnibus* and sharing stories of citymaking is that the greatest undervalued asset in any city is the diverse cohort of individuals acting on the city in an intentional way, concentrating creative efforts to make urban life just a little bit better. Another, complementary way to affirm the social and political potential of city life is to lift up and shine a light on the spaces and experiences that city-dwellers have in common: sidewalks and subways, schools and emergency services, leisure opportunities and spontaneous encounters that encourage connection with each other and the city we share.

Nurturing a *culture* of practical urbanism is as important as honing the *craft.* The craft of citymaking is not limited to traditional design and planning. Spatial and visual thinking and creative problem-solving — hallmarks of what we think of as design — must be integrated with the mastery of the details of everything from community organizing and activist tactics to real estate economics and public policy-making. The culture of citymaking is not limited to analytical or evocative projects of observation, interpretation, and representation. It also includes the wealth of intellectual history that helps us to name — or at least point our Duchampian fingers at — what we're talking about when we talk about cities. A city is more than the territory governed by a particular local government; it is more than a dense built environment; more than people living in close proximity; more than the concentration of organizations and institutions and businesses. It is the interactions between different individuals and different institutions that make a city, the commercial transactions on the street, exchanges between strangers on the bus or in the temple.

Practical urbanism cannot determine these interactions, nor can it force them to produce greater fellow-feeling. But it can, and it must, enhance the possibility for common ground. The ethic of citymaking is an ethic of solidarity, of co-presence, of coalition building, of mutual tolerance. Establishing this ethic as a constituent element of what we expect from the design, delivery, and maintenance of the built environment will not be easy. It will take a lot of experimentation and many failures, deep observation as well as bold innovation, historically informed interpretation as well as future-forward interventions.

This work has to start in the city. It must not end there.

ACKNOWLEDGMENTS

All books are collaborative, and this one more than most. I thank all of the contributors to *Urban Omnibus* for collaborating with my colleagues and me to share their work with our readers.

From my first day on the job, I worked alongside Varick Shute, whose tireless devotion to detail and unparalleled editorial instincts shaped every piece we published. None of the insights that have sprung from this sample of stories would be possible without her passion, camaraderie, and hard work.

Long before, Rosalie Genevro conceived and incubated the idea. Over thirty years at the helm of The Architectural League, she has presided over a sea change in how cultural institutions can marshal the power of architecture and design towards the greater good. *Urban Omnibus* is only one among her many innovations in pushing forward the interface between design and society. Rosalie is responsible for many of the ideas in this book, especially the relationship between stewardship and public goods.

The pilot phase of *Urban Omnibus* was made possible by a grant from the Rockefeller Foundation. Joan Shigekawa saw the potential of Rosalie's bold vision for an online showcase of design innovation and supported it from the outset. Years later, the writing of this book was made possible by a grant from the National Endowment for the Arts, a stalwart champion for the civic value of creative work that our nation so desperately needs.

Over the years, Varick and I were supported by an incredible group of colleagues. Some of the many who contributed immeasurably include those who were there at the beginning — Meg Kelly, John Donalds, Nick Buccelli, Shumi Bose, and the brilliant designers James Reeves and Steven Baker — as well as those who helped *Urban Omnibus* begin its transition to what it will one day become — Daniel Rojo, Gabriel Silberblatt, Jonathan Tarleton. Jonathan in particular went beyond the call of duty to chart a path forward as Varick and I prepared to move on. Also invaluable along the way were Jessica Cronstein, Jane Kelly, Will Martin, Purva Jain, Sam Silver, Katie Stapleton, and especially Caitlin Blanchfield and Alicia Rouault, among others too numerous to name. Nothing the League has done in recent years would be possible without the work of Nick Anderson, Anne Rieselbach, and Greg Wessner.

I have been extraordinarily fortunate to learn from many mentors, some of whom, like Jerry Frug, Rosalie Genevro, Richard Sennett, and Larry Vale, influenced the insights in these pages directly. Others, especially Mani Kaul, Robb Moss, and Susan Meiselas, have had a less discernible but no less powerful impact on how I think about ideas such as juxtaposition, montage, narrative, and the interplay between creative, intellectual, and political work.

I began writing this book while traveling abroad, immersing myself in some of the world's great cities in search of insights on my own. A research fellowship at the University of Western Sydney offered a jumpstart, made possible by my first urbanist mentor, the geographer Donald McNeill. Old and new friends who hospitably nurtured my writing include Sarah Ichioka and Jack Stiller in Singapore, Emre Eren, Miräy Ozkan, and Ozhan Önder in Istanbul, Fran Tonkiss and Shumi Bose in London, and Taiye Selasi and the tribe of Berliners to whom she introduced me — especially Alex Albrecht, Annabelle Assaf, Ida-Marie Corell, Leo Grünbaum, and Nana Oforiatta-Ayim — whose companionship and creativity spurred me on in the most intensive phase of writing. In Berlin, Agora Collective in Neukölln proved the perfect place and community in which to write.

Once I returned home to New York, several close friends read and gave valuable feedback on parts of this manuscript, especially David Giles, Alex de Lucena, and Tim Sohn. The friendship of Jim Meeks and Alex Marson is a constant source of support. The first public airing of some of these ideas took place in the Culture / Politics reading group at New York University's Institute of Public Knowledge; thanks to Becky Amato and the participants who make such a forum possible.

I am especially indebted to Alan Rapp of The Monacelli Press for believing in this project from the beginning and shepherding it so elegantly into being. Eric Schwartau provided invaluable assistance and offered insightful edits along the way. Copy editing and proofreading by Laurie Manfra and Janet Adams Strong significantly improved the finished product. Jena Sher's design beautifully enhances the messages of this book. Alex Fradkin's seemingly boundless enthusiasm for representing the people and places that make this city what it is have greatly heightened the crucial connection between a city's physical form and its social experience.

My parents, Richard Shepard and Samina Quraeshi, did not live to see this book published, but their influence is on every page. My father was an architect with a deep, infectious commitment to the social and communitarian responsibilities of design. My mother was an artist, designer, and author who made it her life's work to advocate for art and design as a catalyst for intercultural communication. I would not be the urbanist that I am today without the luxury of spending time in her native Pakistan throughout my life. And I reflect on her service to and faith in this country's ideals when I start to lose heart. I grew up in my parents' architecture and graphic design studio, playing after school with X-ACTO blades on discarded foam-core models, and although I did not fully understand it until recently, their shared passion for the ethics implicit in the designed environment informs everything I do. I am so grateful to my sister Sadia Shepard and my brother-in-law Andreas Burgess (and their two children Noor Jehan and Idrees) for their unwavering support and belief, and for working hard to keep our family's traditions alive, especially in striking a perfect balance between the pursuit of artistic excellence and the nurturing of community.

My greatest debt is to my best critic, my wife Heather McGhee, who teaches me in new ways every day what it means and what it takes to be a citizen, and to do it with love.

BIBLIOGRAPHY

This bibliography lists all the print sources cited in this book (including printed reports that are currently available online).

For a complete list of resources that appear online only, including *Urban Omnibus* articles, please visit urbanomnibus.net/citymakers-online-resources

Ahmed, Heba Farouk and Basil Kamel. "Cairo: Three Cities, Three Periods, Three Maidans" *Built Environment* (1978–) 22, no. 2 (1996), 104–123.

Alexander, Michelle. *The New Jim Crow: Mass Incarceration in the Era of Colorblindness.* New York: The New Press, 2012.

AlSayyad, Nezar, Irene A. Bierman, and Nasser Rabbat. *Making Cairo Medieval.* Lanham, Mass.: Lexington Books, 2005.

American Society of Civil Engineers. "2013 Report Card for America's Infrastructure," accessed April 15, 2015. www.infrastructurereportcard.org.

Amin, Ash. *Land of Strangers.* Cambridge: Polity, 2012.

Angel, Shlomo and Patrick Lamson-Hall "The Rise and Fall of Manhattan's Densities, 1800-2010" (New York: Marron Institute of Urban Management, 2014).

Appiah, K. Anthony. *Cosmopolitanism: Ethics in a World of Strangers.* New York: W. W. Norton, 2007.

Arendt, Hannah. *The Human Condition.* Chicago: University of Chicago Press, 1958.

Baird, Gregory M. "Defining Public Asset Management for Municipal Water Utilities." *Journal of the American Water Works Association,* May 2011.

Barber, Benjamin R. *If Mayors Ruled the World: Dysfunctional Nations, Rising Cities.* New Haven: Yale University Press, 2013.

Bell, Bryan and Katie Wakeford, eds., *Expanding Architecture, Design as Activism.* New York: Metropolis Books, 2009.

Bell, Bryan ed., *Good Deeds Good Design, Community Service through Architecture.* New York: Princeton Architectural Press, 2003.

Bergson, Henri. *Creative Evolution.* New York: Cosimo Classics, 2005 (1907).

Blackmar, Elizabeth and Roy Rosenzweig, "Central Park" in *The Encyclopedia of New York City,* edited by Kenneth T. Jackson. New Haven: Yale University Press, 1995.

Bloom, Nicholas Dagen. *Public Housing That Worked: New York in the 20th Century.* Philadelphia: University of Pennsylvania Press, 2009.

Bloom, Nicholas Dagen, Fritz Umbach, and Lawrence Vale, eds. *Public Housing Myths.* Ithaca, N.Y: Cornell University Press, 2015.

Brauman, Robert, Dana Gumb, and Chris Duerkes. "Designing for Wildlife in the Bluebelt" *Clear Waters* 39, no. 4 (Winter 2009): 41-43.

Brenner, Neil and Nik Theodore, "Cities and the Geographies of 'Actually Existing Neoliberalism'" in *Antipode* 34, no. 3, July 2002: 349–379.

Bristol, Katharine G. "The Pruitt-Igoe Myth" *Journal of Architectural Education* 44, Issue 3 (1991).

Bui, Quoctrung. "Where the Middle Class Is Shrinking." *New York Times,* May 12, 2016. Accessed November 1, 2016. www.nytimes.com/interactive/2016/05/13/upshot/falling-middle-class.html.

Bush, George. President's Remarks at the National Federation of Independent Businesses, June 17, 2004.

Califano, Joseph. "What Was Really Great About the Great Society" *The Washington Monthly* (October 1999). Accessed December 29, 2015. www.colorado.edu/AmStudies/lewis/1025/greatgreatsociety.pdf.

Cannato, Vincent J. *The Ungovernable City: John Lindsay and His Struggle to Save New York.* New York: Basic Books, 2001.

Carlson, Neil F. "UHAB Comes of Age" (2003). Accessed August 1, 2016. www.community-wealth.org/sites/clone.community-wealth.org/files/downloads/report-carlson.pdf

Caro, Robert. *The Power Broker.* New York: Alfred A. Knopf, 1974.

Chakrabarti, Vishaan. *A Country of Cities.* New York: Metropolis Books, 2013.

Coase, R.H. "The Lighthouse in Economics" in *Journal of Law and Economics* 17, no. 2 (October, 1974): 357–376.

Cohen, Daniel Aldana. "Seize the Hamptons." *Jacobin.* Accessed October 5, 2015. www.jacobinmag.com/2014/10/seize-the-hamptons

Cohen, Noam. "Red Hook's Cutting Edge Wireless Network" *New York Times,* August 22, 2014.

Coles, Alex, ed. "Site-Specificity: The Ethnographic Turn;" *de-, dis- ex-* 4, Black Dog Publishing, 2000.

Collins, Lauren. "All Together Now!" *The New Yorker,* October 25, 2010.

Corner, James. "Terra Fluxus." In *The Landscape Urbanism Reader,* edited by Charles Waldheim. Princeton: Princeton University Press, 2006, 23.

Corning, Peter A. "The Evolution of Medicare: from idea to law," 1969. Republished on the official website of the Social Security Administration. Accessed October 26, 2015. www.ssa.gov/history/corning.html.

Cranz, Galen. *The Politics of Park Design: A History of Urban Parks in America.* Cambridge, Mass.: MIT Press, 1982.

Crean, Sarah. "Did City's Industrial Policy Manufacture Defeat?" *City Limits,* January 3, 2011.

Davidoff, Paul. "Advocacy and Pluralism in Planning" *Journal Of The American Institute Of Planners* Vol. 31, Issue 4 (1965).

Davies, Russell. "41 Lessons from Uber's Success" *Wired UK,* June 2015.

Davis, John Emmeus. "Origins and Evolution of the Community Land Trust in the United States" 2014. Adapted from a 2010 essay published in *The Community Land Trust Reader.* Cambridge, Mass.: Lincoln Institute of Land Policy, 2010. Accessed August 7, 2016. www.berkshirecommunitylandtrust. org/wp-content/uploads/2015/02/Origins-Evolution-CLT-byJohnDavis.pdf.

Davis, John. "Shared Equity Homeownership" National Housing Institute (2006). Accessed August 9, 2016. www.nhi.org/pdf/SharedEquityHome.pdf.

Demsetz, Harold "Toward a Theory of Property Rights" in *The American Economic Review* 57, no. 2, Papers and Proceedings of the Seventy-ninth Annual Meeting of the American Economic Association (May 1967): 347-359.

Dwyer, Jim. "De Blasio Postpones Work on Crucial Water Tunnel." *New York Times,* April 5, 2016.

Easterling, Keller. *Extrastatecraft: The Power of Infrastructure Space.* New York: Verso, 2014.

Economist, The. "The Shaming of America." *The Economist,* September 8, 2005.

— "Out of the Box" *The Economist,* November 21, 2015.

Ehrenhalt, Samuel. "Economic and demographic change: the case of New York City" *Monthly Labor Review* (February 1993). Accessed August 1, 2016. www.bls.gov/mlr/1993/02/art4full.pdf.

Environmental Protection Agency. "Green Infrastructure." Accessed May 7, 2015. water.epa.gov/infrastructure/greeninfrastructure/gi_policy.cfm.

Fairlie, Simon. "A Short History of Enclosure in Britain," *The Land* 7 (Summer 2009).

Feder, Kris. "Progress and Poverty Today" an introduction to Progress and Poverty, by Henry George, Abridged edition. New York: Robert Schalkenbach Foundation, 1998. Originally published 1879.

Federal Writers' Project. The WPA Guide to New York City: The Federal Writers' Project Guide to 1930s New York. New York: Pantheon Books, 1939.

Fisher, Dana R., James J. Connolly, Erika S. Svendsen, and Lindsay K. Campbell, "Digging Together: Why people volunteer to help plant one million trees in New York City," Environmental Stewardship Project at the Center for Society and Environment of the University of Maryland White Paper #1. Accessed April 1, 2015. www.nrs.fs.fed.us/nyc/local-resources/downloads/digging_together_white_paper.pdf.

Fishman, Robert. "Rethinking Public Housing," *Places,* 16, no. 2 (2004).

Flood, Joe. "Why the Bronx Burned" *New York Post,* May 16, 2010.

— *The Fires.* New York: Riverhead Books, 2011.

Florida, Richard. "The World is Spiky." *The Atlantic,* October, 2005.

Forman, Adam. "Caution Ahead: Overdue Investments for New York's Aging Infrastructure" Center for an Urban Future (March 2014). https://nycfuture.org/pdf/Caution-Ahead.pdf

Friedman, Rachel S. "The Construction Boom and Bust in New York City" *Monthly Labor Review* (October 2011). Retrieved from www.bls.gov/opub/mlr/2011/10/art2full.pdf.

Friedman, Thomas. *The World is Flat.* New York: Farrar, Strauss and Giroux, 2005.

Friedmann, John. *Planning in the Public Domain.* Princeton: Princeton University Press, 1987.

Frischmann, Brett M. "An Economic Theory of Infrastructure and Commons Management" *Minnesota Law Review* 89 (April 2005): 917–1030.

— *Infrastructure: The Social Value of Shared Resources.* Oxford: Oxford University Press, 2012.

Frug, Gerald E. "Democracy's Future: What's Left?" *Public Culture* 25, no. 2 (Spring 2013): 311-314.

— *City Making: Building Communities without Building Walls.* Princeton: Princeton University Press, 1999.

Frug, Gerald E., and David J. Barron. *City Bound: How States Stifle Urban Innovation.* Ithaca: Cornell University Press, 2008.

Furman Center for Real Estate and Urban Policy. "Housing Policy in New York City: A Brief History," April 2006.

Furman Center for Real Estate and Urban Policy.

"The Cost of Renting in New York City." 2014 NYU Furman Center / Capital One Affordable Rental Housing Landscape. Accessed August 5, 2016. www.furmancenter.org/NYCRentalLandscape.

Gandel, Stephen. "Uber-nomics: Here's what it would cost Uber to pay its drivers as employees." *Fortune,* September 17, 2015. fortune.com/2015/09/17/ubernomics.

Gannon, Michael "Assemblymen Call for New Rail Service," *Queens Chronicle,* February 16, 2012.

Garin, James and Dana Gumb et al. "Bluebelt Beginnings" *Clear Waters* 39, no. 4 (Winter 2009): 10-21.

Geddes, Patrick. "Report on the Towns in the Madras Presidency, 1915: Ballary." In *Patrick Geddes in India,* edited by Jacqueline Tyrwhitt. London: Lund, Humphries and Co., 1947.

— "Civics: as Applied Sociology." Presentation to the Sociological Society at a Meeting in the School of Economics and Political Science (University of London), July 18th, 1904. Accessed July 17th, 2016. www.gutenberg.org/files/13205/13205-h/13205-h.htm

— *Cities in Evolution.* London: Williams and Norgate, 1915.

Goodwin, Tom "The Battle Is For the Customer Interface" Techcrunch.com, March 3, 2015, as quoted in Thomas Friedman, "Hillary, Jeb, Facebook and Disorder" *New York Times,* May 20, 2015.

Gopnik, Adam. "The Plot Against Trains." *The New Yorker,* May 15, 2015. Accessed May 2, 2015. www.newyorker.com/news/daily-comment/the-plot-against-trains.

Greenfield, Adam. *Radical Technologies: the Design of Everyday Life.* New York: Verso, 2017.

Greenwood, Daphne T. and Richard P. F. Holt, "Growth, Inequality and Negative Trickle Down" in *Journal of Economic Issues* 44, no. 2, (June 2010): 403–410.

Grunwald, Michael. *The New New Deal: The Hidden Story of Change in the Obama Era.* New York: Simon & Schuster, 2012.

Gumb, Dana. "Staten Island History and Bluebelt Land Acquisitions" *Clear Waters* 39, no. 4 (Winter 2009): 22-26.

Halpern, Orit and Jesse LeCavalier, Nerea Calvillo, Wolfgang Pietsch "Test-Bed Urbanism." *Public Culture* 25, no. 2 (Spring 2013)

Hardin, Garrett. "The Feast of Malthus," *Social Contract Journal* 8, no. 3, (Spring 1998).

— "The Tragedy of the Commons," *Science* 162, no. 3859 (December 1968): 1243-1248.

— "The Tragedy of the Unmanaged Commons," in *Commons Without Tragedy,* edited by R.V. Andelson. London: Shepheard-Walwyn, 1991.

Hardoon, Deborah, Sophia Ayele, and Ricardo Fuentes-Nieva. "An Economy for the 1%" *Oxfam Briefing Paper,* January 18, 2016.

Harrison, Colin. Ideas Economy: Intelligent Infrastructure, *The Economist* panel discussion, remarks, New York City, February 16, 2011.

Harvey, David. "The Right to the City." *New Left Review* II, no. 53 (September–October 2008): 23–40.

— *Social Justice and the City.* Athens, GA: University of Georgia Press, 2009.

Holland, John. *Complexity.* Oxford: Oxford University Press, 2014.

Hsu, David. "Sustainable New York City." Project of the Design Trust for Public Space and the New York City Office of Environmental Coordination, 2006.

Jacobs, Jane. *The Death and Life of Great American Cities.* New York: Random House, 2002.

Jay-Z, *Decoded.* New York: Random House / Spiegel & Grau, 2010.

Jencks, Charles. *The Language of Post-Modern Architecture.* New York: Rizzoli, 1977.

Katz, Bruce, and Jennifer Bradley. *The Metropolitan Revolution: How Cities and Metros Are Fixing Our Broken Politics and Fragile Economy.* Washington D.C.: Brookings Institution Press, 2014.

Kimmelman, Michael. "Imagining Housing for Today," *New York Times,* November 16, 2011.

Klein, Naomi. *This Changes Everything.* New York: Simon & Schuster, 2015.

Klinenberg, Eric. "Adaptation: How can cities be climate-proofed?" *The New Yorker,* January 7, 2013.

— *Going Solo: The Extraordinary Rise and Surprising Appeal of Living Alone.* New York: Penguin Books, 2013.

— *Heat Wave: A Social Autopsy of Disaster in Chicago.* Chicago: University of Chicago Press, 2002.

Koehler, David H. and Margaret T. Wrightson, "Inequality in the Delivery of Urban Services: A Reconsideration of the Chicago Parks" *The Journal of Politics* 49, no. 1 (February 1987): 80–99.

Korzybski, Alfred. *Science and Sanity.* New York: Institute of General Semantics, 1995.

Kurgan, Laura. *Close Up at a Distance.* New York: Zone Books, 2013.

Lanier, Jaron. *Who Owns the Future?* New York: Simon & Schuster, 2013.

— *You Are Not a Gadget.* New York: Knopf, 2010.

Leopold, Aldo. *Sand County Almanac.* Oxford: Oxford University Press, 1949.

Linebaugh, Peter. *Stop, Thief! The Commons, Enclosures and Resistance.* Oakland: PM Press, 2014.

LiPuma, Edward and Benjamin Lee. *Financial Derivatives and the Globalization of Risk.* Durham, NC: Duke University Press, 2004.

Loos, Adolf. *Ornament and Crime: Selected Essays,* edited by Adolf Opel. Riverside, Calif.: Ariadne Press, 1997.

Mackenzie, Donald. *An Engine, Not a Camera.* Cambridge, Mass.: MIT Press, 2006.

Mairet, Philip. *Pioneer of Sociology: The Life and Letters of Patrick Geddes.* London: Lund, Humphries and Co., 1957.

Marshall, Alfred. *Principles of Economics.* London: MacMillan, 1890.

Martinez, Miranda J. *Power at the Roots: Gentrification, Community Gardens, and the Puerto Ricans of the Lower East Side.* Lanham, MA: Lexington Books, 2010.

Mayne, Thom, and Stan Allen. *Combinatory Urbanism: The Complex Behavior of Collective Form.* Culver City, CA: Stray Dog Cafe, 2011.

McEvoy, Arthur. "Towards and Interactive Theory of Nature and Culture: Ecology, Production, and Cognition in the California Fishing Industry" in *Environmental Review* 11, no. 4 (1987): 289–305.

McQuarrie, Michael, Caroline Lee, and Edward Walker, eds. *Democratizing Inequalities, Dilemma of the New Public Participation.* New York: NYU Press, 2014.

Melcher, Henry. "Bottom-up Urbanism," *The Architects' Newspaper,* July 29, 2014.

Meyerson, Harold. "The 40-year Slump," *American Prospect,* October 2013.

Mill, John Stuart. "Principles of Political Economy" in *Collected Works of John Stuart Mill,* edited by V. W. Bladen and John M. Robson. Toronto: University of Toronto Press, 1965.

Miller, Jonathan. "Change is the Constant in a Century of New York City Real Estate." Miller Samuels, October 2012. Accessed March 2, 2015. www.miller-samuel.com/files/2012/10/DE100yearsNYC.pdf.

Morton, David. "Competition for Longevity: Architects Housing, Trenton, NJ," *Progressive Architecture* (August 1981): 69–71.

Mumford, Eric Paul. *The CIAM Discourse on Urbanism, 1928–1960.* Cambridge, Mass.: MIT Press, 2002.

Mumford, Lewis. "Skyline" *The New Yorker,* November 14, 1959.

National Employment Law Project, "Independent Contractor Misclassification Imposes Huge Costs on Workers and Federal and State Treasuries" July 2015. Accessed June 15, 2015. www.nelp.org/content/uploads/Independent-Contractor-Costs.pdf.

National Research Council, *Measuring and Improving Infrastructure Performance.* Washington D.C.: The National Academies Press, 1996.

Nisbet, Robert A. "The French Revolution and the Rise of Sociology in France" *American Journal of Sociology* 49, no. 2 (September 1943): 156–164.

Ostrom, Elinor. *Governing the Commons.* Cambridge: Cambridge University Press, 1990.

Ouroussoff, Nicolai. "The Greening of the Waterfront," *New York Times,* April 1, 2010.

Parkinson, John. *Democracy and Public Space: The Physical Sites of Democratic Performance.* Oxford: Oxford University Press, 2012.

Pigou, A. C. *Economics of Welfare.* London: MacMillan and Co., 1932.

Piketty, Thomas and Emmanuel Saez, "Income Inequality in the United States, 1913–1998." *The Quarterly Journal of Economics,* CXVIII, issue 1, February 2003.

Plunz, Richard. *A History of Housing in New York City.* New York: Columbia University Press, 1990.

Podair, Jerald E. *The Strike That Changed New York: Blacks, Whites, and the Ocean Hill-Brownsville Crisis.* New Haven, CT: Yale University Press, 2008.

Pressler, Jessica. "Times City Section to Close" *New York Magazine,* March 30, 2009. Accessed March 26, 2015. nymag.com/daily/intelligencer/2009/03/times_city_section_to_close.html.

Reed, Chris and Nina Lister, eds. *Projective Ecologies.* Barcelona: ACTAR and Harvard Graduate School of Design, 2014.

Rhea, John. "Message from the Chairman," New York *City Housing Authority Journal* 43, no. 3 (April 2013).

Riis, Jacob. *How the Other Half Lives.* New York: Charles Scribner's Sons, 1914.

Roberts, Sam. "People Fled the Bronx in the 1970s. Now Its Population is Booming," *New York Times,* September 10, 2016. Accessed October 15. 2016. nyti.ms/2cdek7q.

Roosevelt, Theodore. "Fellow-feeling as a political factor," *The Century,* January 1900. 466–471.

Rousseau, Peter L. "Jacksonian Monetary Policy, Specie Flows, and The Panic of 1837," *The Journal of Economic History,* 62, no. 02, (June 2002): 457–488.

Ryan, Benjamin. "What 311 Calls Can Tell Us About Gentrification," *New York Magazine.* Accessed July 21, 2016. nymag.com/scienceofus/2015/08/what-311-calls-can-tell-us-about-gentrification.html.

Safire, William. "Fat Tail," *New York Times Magazine,* February 5, 2011.

Samuelson, Paul A. *Economics: An Introductory Analysis.* New York: McGraw-Hill, 1955.

Sassen, Saskia. *The Global City: New York, London, Tokyo.* Princeton: Princeton University Press, 1991.

— *Expulsions: Complexity and Brutality in the Global Economy.* Cambridge, Mass: Harvard University Press, 2014.

— Remarks, Urban Age Conference, London, October 10, 2005.

— Territory, Authority, Rights: From Medieval to Global Assemblages. Princeton: Princeton University Press, 2006.

Saunders, Doug. Arrival City. New York: Vintage, 2011.

Schellnhuber, Hans Joachim et al., eds. Avoiding Dangerous Climate Change. Cambridge: Cambridge University Press, 2006.

Scholz, Trebor and Laura Y. Liu. "From Mobile Playgrounds to Sweatshop City" The Architectural League of New York Situated Technologies Pamphlets, The Architectural League of New York, 2010.

Selasi, Taiye and Cassim Shepard, "The Gwangju River Reading Room" in Gwangju Folly II, edited by David Adjaye, Rem Koolhaas, and Do Ho Suh. Berlin: Hatje Cantz, 2015.

Sennett, Richard, and Jonathan Cobb. The Hidden Injuries of Class. New York: Knopf, 1972.

Sennett, Richard. Authority. New York: Knopf, 1980.

— Families against the City; Middle Class Homes of Industrial Chicago, 1872–1890. Cambridge, Mass.: Harvard University Press, 1970.

— Flesh and Stone: The Body and the City in Western Civilization. New York: W.W. Norton, 1994.

— Respect in a World of Inequality. New York: W.W. Norton, 2003.

— The Conscience of the Eye: The Design and Social Life of Cities. New York: Knopf, 1990.

— The Corrosion of Character: The Personal Consequences of Work in the New Capitalism. New York: Norton, 1998.

— The Culture of the New Capitalism. New Haven: Yale University Press, 2006.

— The Fall of Public Man. New York: Knopf, 1977.

— The Uses of Disorder: Personal Identity and City Life. New York: W.W. Norton, 1992.

— Together: The Rituals, Pleasures, and Politics of Cooperation. New Haven: Yale University Press, 2012.

Sert, Josep Lluís and CIAM, Can Our Cities Survive? An ABC of Urban Problems, Their Analyses, Their Solutions: Based on Proposals Formulated by CIAM. Cambridge, Mass.: Harvard University Press, 1942.

Sidgwick, Henry The Principles of Political Economy, London: MacMillan and Co., 1887.

Slater, G. "Historical Outline of Land Ownership in England," in The Land, The Report of the Land Enquiry Committee. London: Hodder and Stoughton, 1913.

Smith, Neil. The New Urban Frontier: Gentrification and the Revanchist City. London: Routledge, 1996.

Solnit, Rebecca. A Paradise Built in Hell: The Extraordinary Communities That Arise in Disaster, Penguin, 2009.

— "5KL: Land," remarks, The Architectural League of New York, September 26, 2014, www.archleagueorg/2014/10/5kl-land/.

Starr, Roger. "Making New York Smaller," New York Times Magazine, November 14, 1976.

Steinhauer, Jennifer. "Ending a Long Battle, New York Lets Housing and Gardens Grow." The New York Times, September 19, 2002.

Storey, Jeff. "Q&A: Vincent Schiraldi." New York Law Journal, May 25, 2012. Accessed June 19, 2016. www.newyorklawjournal.com/PubArticleNY. jsp?id=1202555952494&QA_Vincent_ Schiraldi&slreturn=20120909172952.

Sullivan, Brian J. and Jonathan Burke, "Single-Room Occupancy in New York City: The Origins and Dimensions of a Crisis," CUNY Law Review, 17, no. 901 (May 2014).

Thabit, Walter. How East New York Became a Ghetto. New York: New York University Press, 2003.

Thompson, E.P. Customs in Common. New York: The New Press, 1993.

— Moral Economy of the English Crow. Oxford: Oxford University Press, 1971.

Townsend, Anthony. Smart Cities. New York: W.W. Norton & Company, 2013.

Tyrwhitt, Jacqueline. Patrick Geddes in India, 1947.

Walker, Allen and Steve Corbett, "The 'Big Society', Neoliberalism and the Rediscovery of the 'Social' in Britain," Sheffield Political Economy Research Institute, March 8, 2013. Accessed January 2, 2016. speri.dept.shef.ac.uk/2013/03/08/big-society-neoliberalism-rediscovery-social-britain.

Wallace, Deborah and Rodrick Wallace. A Plague on Your Houses. Chicago: Haymarket, 2001.

Weaver, Warren. "Science and Complexity," American Scientist 36, no. 536 (1948) Accessed January 3, 2016. people.physics.anu.edu.au/~tas110/Teaching/ Lectures/L1/Material/WEAVER1947.pdf.

White, Norval, Elliot Wilensky, and Fran Leadon. AIA Guide to New York City, 5th ed. Oxford: Oxford University Press, 2010.

Winchester, Simon. The Professor and the Madman. New York: Harper Perennial, 2005.

Wright, Tom. "Update on the Fourth Regional Plan," remarks delivered at the 2015 Regional Assembly of the Regional Plan Association, April 24, 2015.

Young, Iris Marion. Justice and the Politics of Difference. Princeton: Princeton University Press, 1990.

— "City Life and Difference." (1990) In The People, Place, and Space Reader, edited by Jen Jack Gieseking et al. New York: Routledge 2014.

Zipp, Samuel. Manhattan Projects: Rise & Fall of Urban Renewal in Cold War New York. Oxford: Oxford University Press, 2010.

Zukin, Sharon. Loft Living: Culture and Capital in Urban Change. New Brunswick, N.J.: Rutgers University Press, 1989.

IMAGE CREDITS

© Alex Fradkin *Cover, 2–6, 8, 16–19, 33–35, 38–41, 45, 48 (above), 81, 85 (below), 86, 94–97, 116, 119, 138–141, 156, 165, 166, 174, 200–203, 207–209, 264–267, 280–282, 286–287, 295*

© Cameron Blaylock *23*

© Bettmann/Getty Images *27*

© Al Jazeera English/Flickr *48 (below)*

© Rob Stephenson for the Design Trust for Public Space *51*

Courtesy MillionTreesNYC *67 (above)*

© Gowanus Canal Conservancy *67 (center)*

© Anna Beeke *67 (below), 232*

Diagram from William R. Shepherd, *Historical Atlas,* New York, Henry Holt and Company, 1923 *73*

© Andrew Nicholas *85 (above)*

© Michael Van Valkenburgh Associates, Inc. *90*

© Alex MacLean *92 (above)*

© Elizabeth Felicella/Esto *92 (below)*

© V. Elias, USACE *99*

Map from William Bishop, *Manual of the Common Council of the City of Brooklyn, 1871. 102 (above)* Courtesy of Ephemeral New York *102 (below)*

© Steve Duncan/Undercity.org *112*

© New York City Department of Environmental Protection *123 (above)*

© Nathan Kensinger *123 (center and below)*

Image from "The Gateway to a Continent; Grand Central Zone," New York Central Railroad, 1939 *125*

Courtesy of Kennedy Violich Architecture *129 (above)*

© John Horner *129 (below)*

© Regional Plan Association *132*

© Red Hook Initiative/Stefanie Deji *145*

Patrick Geddes Diagram republished in Amanda Defries, *The Interpreter Geddes,* G. Routledge & Sons, 1927 *152*

Diagram from RAND Corporation, *Using Simulation to Develop and Validate Analytical Emergency Service Deployment Models,* August 1975.13. *184*

© Laura Kurgan, David Reinfurt, Eric Cadora, Sarah Williams. *Million Dollar Blocks.* 2006 *189*

© David Sundberg/Esto *192*

© Jessie Tarbox Beals for Jacob A. (Jacob August) Riis (1849–1914)/ Museum of the City of New York. *218*

A Home Of One's Own – Micro-Lofts For Single Adults and Small Families Project team: Peter Gluck, Terri Chiao, Deborah Grossberg Katz, Joseph Vidich, Leigha Dennis *225*

Courtesy of U.S. Department of Housing and Urban Development *228*

© FLC/ADAGP *230 (left)*

Courtesy of United States Geological Survey *230 (right)*

© Jason Bergman *236–237*

© Amani Willett *240*

© David Lang *241 (above and center)*

© Ben Stechschulte *241 (below)*

Courtesy of Urban Homesteading Assistance Board *236, 239*

Archived in *The Single Tax: Scrapbook with Photographs,* collection of the New York Public Library *254*

IMAGE LOCATIONS

INDEX

This book has been supported in part by the
National Endowment for the Arts. To find
out more about how National Endowment for
the Arts grants impact individuals and
communities, visit www.arts.gov.

ART WORKS. **National Endowment for the Arts** arts.gov

Additional support has been provided by the
J. Clawson Mills Fund of The Architectural
League of New York.

THE ARCHI
TECTURAL
LEAGUE NY

Library of Congress
Cataloging-in-Publication Data

Names: Shepard, Cassim, author. |
    Genevro, Rosalie, writer of foreword.
Title: Citymakers : the culture and craft
    of practical urbanism / Cassim Shepard ;
    foreword by Rosalie Genevro ; principal
    photography by Alex Fradkin.
Description: New York : The Monacelli Press,
    2017. | Includes bibliographical references.
Identifiers: LCCN 2017016142 |
    ISBN 9781580934855 (paperback)
Subjects: LCSH: City planning — New York
    (State) — New York. | Land use — New
    York (State) — New York. | BISAC:
    ARCHITECTURE / Urban & Land Use
    Planning. | ARCHITECTURE /
    Sustainability & Green Design. | SOCIAL
    SCIENCE / Sociology / Urban.
Classification: LCC HT168.N5 S55 2017 |
    DDC 307.1/21609747 — dc23
LC record available at https://lccn.loc.
gov/2017016142

ISBN 978-1-58093-485-5

10 9 8 7 6 5 4 3 2 1

Printed in Singapore

The Monacelli Press
6 West 18th Street
New York, NY 10011

www.monacellipress.com